Working with Mr. Wright is a personal recollection by one of Frank Lloyd Wright's former apprentices of his years in the Taliesin Fellowship. Based on letters written by the author during his two stints at the Fellowship, from 1939 to 1955, Curtis Besinger provides a lively account of daily life in the community of architects established by Wright at its two locations, in Wisconsin and Arizona. Unlike standard architectural training, an apprenticeship with the Fellowship entailed architectural tasks, such as drafting, designing, and overseeing projects, including the actual building of Taliesin West; as well as humbler assignments – from milking the cows to harvesting grain – related to maintaining the farm that surrounds the Fellowship in Wisconsin. The social life of the Fellowship, which was filled with music and film, and planned in detail by Wright himself, is also recounted with wit and humor. Through these engaging recollections, illustrated with photographs, plans, and drawings made during Besinger's years at the Fellowship, the eccentric personality of Wright, his working practices, and his unique creative vision emerge, along with a host of personalities who were key to creating the unique character of the Taliesin experience.

Working with Mr. Wright

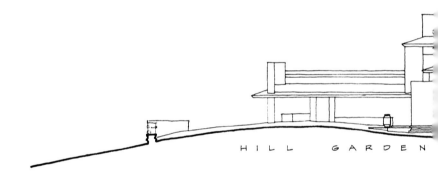

HILL GARDEN

C R

CAMBRIDGE
UNIVERSITY PRESS

Working with Mr. Wright

What It Was Like

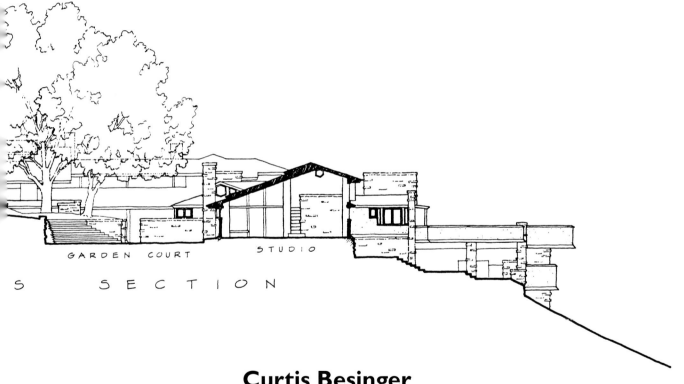

GARDEN COURT · STUDIO

S SECTION

Curtis Besinger
University of Kansas, Emeritus

This book originated with The Architectural History Foundation.

Published by the Press Syndicate of the University of Cambridge
The Pitt Building, Trumpington Street, Cambridge CB2 1RP
40 West 20th Street, New York, NY 10011-4211, USA
10 Stamford Road, Oakleigh, Melbourne 3166, Australia

First published 1995

Printed in the United States of America

Library of Congress Cataloging–in–Publication Data

Besinger, Curtis.
    Working with Mr. Wright : what it was like / Curtis Besinger.
        p. cm.
    Includes index.
    ISBN 0-521-48122-8 (hardback)
1. Besinger, Curtis. 2. Architects—Education—United States.
3. Wright, Frank Lloyd, 1867–1959—Contributions in architectural design. 4. Taliesin (Spring Green, Wis.) 5. Taliesin (Scottsdale, Ariz.) I. Title. II. Title: Working with Mister Wright.
NA737.B48A2 1995
720'.92—dc20
[B]   95-25
                                                     CIP

A catalog record for this book is available from the British Library

ISBN 0-521-48122-8 Hardback

Contents

List of Illustrations

Preface and Acknowledgments

The writing of this account could be said to have begun in the fall of 1955 when I left Taliesin and assumed the role of an instructor of architectural students at the University of Kansas. In this new role I was frequently confronted with students who wanted to know what it was like to work for – or with – Frank Lloyd Wright. It was difficult to give a brief answer to their question. The effort to answer this question began to take a more definite form in the summer of 1970 when Fred Koeper, then a professor of architectural history at the Chicago Circle campus of the University of Illinois, wrote and asked if I was willing to participate in a "Taliesin record" which he was putting together. I was agreeable.

He came to Lawrence on July 25th and tape recorded an interview. This was later transcribed into 19 double-spaced pages of text. To my knowledge Koeper's project progressed no further than interviews with several former apprentices. He was hoping to interview Wes Peters and Jack Howe, but I don't believe he did.

The transcription of my interview, which I had revised, was read about a year later by William P. Thompson, a friend who had taught at K.U. for several years but who was then teaching at the University of Manitoba. Bill's comments and questions suggested further development of this transcription, but at that time I did no more work on it.

In 1956 I began making summer trips to Aspen, Colorado, to work with Fritz Benedict in his architectural practice. While there in the summer of 1974, I read Robert Twombley's "interpretive biography" of Mr. Wright. His "interpretation" of the Fellowship and its activities irritated me; I felt that a more objective account needed to be written. Encouraged by some of my friends I began to record my memories on paper, whenever they surfaced in my mind. When Edgar Tafel's *Apprentice to Genius* appeared in 1979 the purpose of my writing became somewhat clearer to me. I felt that Edgar's book, which might have concentrated on his experiences in the first nine years of the Fellowship, had been diluted by being combined with one more biography of Mr. Wright. I decided that I would do a book based only on my experiences.

However, between full-time teaching and my own limited practice of architecture, I did not find much time for writing until 1986, two years after my mandatory retirement from teaching. (I was sidetracked for about two years while I served as the representative of the Department of Architecture and Architectural Engineering on a School of Engineering committee, formed to write a history of the School. This was published shortly before the celebration of the School's 100th anniversary in 1991.)

Work on this account would not be complete without some recognition of those who have contributed to it. They include the following:

• Mr. and Mrs. Frank Lloyd Wright, who in the depth of the Great Depression ventured to start an "experiment in education," the Taliesin Fellowship. Without this "experiment" this account could not have been written.

• All those former apprentices who, during their years in the Fellowship, shared in and shaped my experiences.

• All those students of architecture who, at the University of Kansas and elsewhere, asked, "What was it like to work with Wright?"

• All of those friends who felt that an account of an apprentice's experiences needed to be written and who insisted that I was the one to write it.

• Professor George M. Beal and his wife, Helen, who initiated and fostered my interest in Mr. Wright and his work.

During my early years in the Fellowship I wrote only to my parents and the Beals. I wrote my parents each week. My mother saved those letters, but whenever I visited home I insisted that the growing collection be thrown away. Unfortunately, when I started writing this account, after her death, the letters were nowhere to be found. It seems she had finally followed my advice! The Beals saved the letters I wrote them. These letters, and others they had received from Mr. and Mrs. Wright and from apprentices with whom they had become acquainted during their summer as apprentices at Taliesin in 1934, were deposited with the Department of Special Collections, the Kenneth Spencer Research Library, University of Kansas, before the Beals' deaths. These letters and other memorabilia, along with a collection of photos which Elizabeth Gordon gave to the university after her retirement as Editor of *House Beautiful* magazine, formed the nucleus of a growing collection of Frank Lloyd Wright material in the Research Library.

• Other former apprentices who saved letters I wrote them during my years as an apprentice, and who returned them to me when they learned that I was working on this account, include Marcus Weston, Howard TenBrink, and Roland Rebay. Robert and Ann Pond loaned me most of the letters I had written them in order that I might make copies. John Mitaraky, a friend from World War II C.O. camps, returned the few letters he could find. All of these letters were useful in refreshing my memory. They will be deposited with Special Collections. Also to join this collection is a most helpful contribution from Robert Carroll May. When Bob learned that I was working on this account, he sent me

"Thirty-One pages of Notations – extracted from the contents of letters written by him while at Taliesin." This "extraction" was helpful in placing some events in time between 1939 and 1942. Many of the photos used as illustrations came from former apprentices who either gave me photographs or loaned me their negatives from which prints were made. These are John H. Howe, John Geiger, Robert Carroll May, Howard TenBrink, Fredric "Fritz" Benedict, Lois Davidson Gottlieb, and Jan Zeeman.

Other photographs were taken by professional photographers: Ezra Stoller, Pedro E. Guerrero, and Maynard Parker. The Stoller photos were made readily available by Erica Stoller and Esto Photographics. Guerrero's photos were provided by him. Pete was a member of the Taliesin Fellowship for two years preceding World War II. As an apprentice he established a relation with Mr. Wright that enabled him to capture images of the less public Mr. Wright. The photos by Maynard Parker were copied from those in the Wright collection given to the University of Kansas by Elizabeth Gordon and made available by the estate of Maynard Parker and the staff of Special Collections, Kenneth Spencer Research Library: Alexandra Mason, James Helyar, and Ann Williams.

Photos taken by John Newhouse during construction of the Unitarian Church in Madison were made available by Iconographic Collections of the State Historical Society of Wisconsin. Some photos of the Price Tower, Bartlesville, Oklahoma, were made from slides loaned by Sherry Davis, Photo Librarian, Phillips Petroleum Company. Sidney Robinson loaned me a slide of the Grant House for this purpose. There are some photos from unidentified sources. These were acquired by me in the Fellowship when I exchanged slides or borrowed them to have prints or copies made. No record of photographers' names was kept. Jim Regan, a photographer and sometime student of architecture, made prints from most of the negatives borrowed. All other photos are by the author. Special comment must be made about the drawings of the plans and sections of Taliesin. The drawings were made by Steve Padget, Associate Professor of the School of Architecture and Urban Design, University of Kansas. They were made because I felt that the available plans of Taliesin, including the plan drawn for the January 1938 *Architectural Forum*, did not make clear the multilayered relation of Taliesin's spaces both internal and external. All other drawings and sketches are by the author. Also to be recognized are:

- Cynthia Muckey, Director of the Word Processing Center of the School of Architecture and Urban Design. She has patiently persevered and "processed" the text through its several additions, deletions, and revisions.
- Dennis Domer, Associate Dean of the School, who read and commented on the first half of the text; and Robin Molny and Fritz Benedict, former apprentices, who also read the first section.
- Fritz Benedict and his wife Fabienne, who made possible the summers in Aspen which nurtured my desire to put my experiences on paper.

- David DeLong, a former student, who remained interested in knowing "what it was like," and who has read, commented on, and made suggestions about the entire text.
- Victoria Newhouse, of the Architectural History Foundation, who early on expressed interest in knowing "what it was like."

I dedicate the book to Eugene Masselink. As Mr. Wright's secretary for many years, Gene's grace, awareness, and sense of humor served to anticipate and ameliorate many of the strains of Fellowship life. Unfortunately he didn't live to write the book which in some stress-filled situation he threatened to write: "Mr. Wright goes to New York..., to Italy..., to Paris

Foreword

Early in 1939 Curtis Besinger faced a decision which, given its position in the history of twentieth-century American architecture, loomed as large and as formative as did the choice of Hercules at the crossroads between virtue and vice, or, perhaps more appropriately since Mr. Besinger was a self-confessed Southern Baptist, of Christian's between good and evil in *Pilgrim's Progress*. What a dilemma for this modern young man! Where among three strongly opposed positions was he to place himself as he continued the education in architecture he had begun at the University of Kansas: would he go to Cranbrook Academy to study with the Finnish romantic, Eliel Saarinen, to Harvard University's Graduate School of Design, then under the direction of the German International-Style master Walter Gropius, or to Taliesin, where seventy-two-year-old Frank Lloyd Wright, with the help of his apprentices, was in the process of reviving his long career in American organic architecture? Oh, brave new world! These institutions represented powerful leadership in divergent, indeed mutually and vehemently exclusive, ideas about what architecture ought to be in the twentieth century.

Mr. Besinger chose Taliesin in the Lloyd-Jones Valley of Wisconsin, "the place at which [Wright]...established...a Jeffersonian life on the land surrounded by younger people wanting to share in and to learn from him and his works." The Taliesin Fellowship turned out a modern architecture rooted in – among other sources – Emerson, the land, and history; its constitution reflected as much. Compared to Cranbrook or Harvard, Wright's was an unorthodox educational environment, but it was not without precedent. At the beginning of his career there had been Wright's own studio in Oak Park, Illinois, but, more cogently, the Fellowship's roots reached into the communities based upon idealized medieval models of the master craftsman surrounded by apprentices that had sprung up in this country and abroad around the turn of the century, all more or less inspired by the ideals of the Englishmen William Morris and John Ruskin. These rural arts-and-crafts communities – C. R. Ashbee's at Chipping Camden in the Cotswolds (1902–7), Ralph Radcliffe Whitehead's Byrdcliffe Colony at Woodstock, New York (1902–4), Will Price's at Rose Valley in Pennsylvania (1901–6), among others – embraced a dedication to the handicraft qualities of preindustrial production, a fellowship of cooperation and, ideally, collaboration between the master and his assistants, and the bucolic life eulogized in Morris's *News from Nowhere* (1891). Wright, an early member of the Chicago Arts and Crafts Society, had, in his pivotal Hull House speech of 1901, married the medievalized arts-and-crafts ideal to modern industrial production, and his 1932 statement of purpose in founding the Taliesin Fellowship reads like a blueprint for an updated arts-and-crafts community. He envisioned his rural association of Fellows as dedicated, under the watchful eye of the master architect and his associates, to the interchanging production of sculpture, painting, music, and, eventually, biology (!), typography, ceramics, woodcraft, and textiles. Although his dedication to "machine-craft art in this machine age" rings the modernist note, in statements such as "the principles underlying life and the arts are the same," and in his emphasis on the "simple" life of the Fellowship, he echoes early twentieth-century ideals like those of Philadelphia's Will Price, who subtitled his short-lived arts-and-crafts publication, "The Art That Is Life," and of California's Charles Keeler, whose *The Simple Home* (1904) espoused the kind of unaffected domesticity Wright sought at Taliesin. Price and Keeler reflected the thinking of many others of the time. In one aspect, however, Wright's Taliesin Fellowship differs from the arts-and-crafts communities that were its predecessors: they all vanished after a brief moment in the sun, while Wright's Fellowship has long outlived him and the deflections of his widow, Olgivanna. Chipping Camden, Byrdcliffe, and Rose Valley had moth-length lives in part because they preached fellowship while run by an autocrat who shared little of the decisions of governance or design. This was largely true of the Fellowship as well, and why it has nevertheless survived is a question to be answered by some future student of creative collectives.

The Taliesin Fellowship was to be an association of apprentices, not scholars. In his 1943 *Autobiography* Wright describes the kind of college-bred young man that Mr. Besinger was in 1939, with his academic degree from the School of Architecture at Kansas, as "impotent," less than half a man because he was narrowly trained in art but not in the life that supports art. At Taliesin, on the contrary, the Fellows were to share in the life of the community as a whole. This is spelled out, in Wright's 1932 statement, as work not only in the crafts, and – perhaps eventually – in the drafting room, but in and on the buildings, and on the land. The Fellowship espoused agriculture as well as culture. Each member would be engaged in all the daily work necessary for the maintenance of the establishment. This contribution in kind was added to the Fellow's tuition; "wage slavery" was to be eliminated.

As we learn from this memoir, the Fellowship did and did not work the way Wright envisioned it in 1932, and the clarity of its purpose blurred over time. In 1939 the center of authority was Wright, or rather, the partnership of Mr. and Mrs. Wright, he in charge of the professional life of the drafting rooms, she in charge of day-to-day living. Wright is here variously characterized as a "Bedouin chieftain," a "Czar," and "distant" except when Mrs. Wright was absent; she exists in the early sections of this chronicle as an *eminence grise*. The Fellows apparently lived in fear that she would materialize with a "reprimand" or to point out an "impropriety." Around the Wrights were the widening rings of senior Fellows, junior Fellows, and recent arrivals. Maintaining the community meant a wide variety of individual chores largely performed by "us lesser creatures," chores which for the summer of 1947 Mr. Besinger catalogues as rehearsing the chorus, weeding the garden, cooking breakfast, drafting, and doing stonemasonry. He also at other times ran the movie projector, fed the boilers, cleaned and arranged the Wrights' private dining room, played the piano and other instruments for performances of many descriptions, and acted as bedroom orderly for Mr. Wright. "Physical labor," manual work out-of-doors in Wisconsin and Arizona that Wright seems to have thought of as "sexual sublimation," appears to have been constant, and here too there was a hierarchy: one worked on the Wrights' quarters before one worked on one's own.

Work, whether in or out of the drafting rooms, was the central feature of life at Taliesin; an apparently rigid schedule (including "spontaneous" picnics which all attended) theoretically left little time for idle hands or idle minds. Mr. Besinger reports all this with equanimity. He seems to have been a model Fellow, who here describes the process of making morning coffee with as much detail as he gives for designing and erecting a building. It was, nevertheless, Wright's architecture that drew apprentices from all over the world: without it, there would have been no Taliesin, and no memoir. We appreciate the intimate glimpse at the daily life of the Fellowship, but it is for those sections devoted to Wright as designer and builder that the architectural historian will find himself most grateful for these recollections.

Mr. Besinger joined the Fellowship as Wright's career entered its final and highly productive phase, with a variety of public work that had eluded him earlier, and a lengthy catalogue of "Usonian" houses that continued his lifelong quest for the home as a work of art. The architectural products of Wright's "restless creative mind" were developed from one of a variety of basic geometrical units, or modules, 90-degree (square or rectangle), 30–60 degree (triangle, hexagon), or arced (the circle and its segments), that governed both plan and elevation. They were first tentatively revealed on paper and further evolved at the site, often utilizing available materials in imaginative structural systems. I find the design process outlined here somewhat akin to that followed earlier in H. H. Richardson's office, in which, in the formula of Mariana Griswold Van Rensselaer, Richardson's own sketches, the "initiative impulse," were succeeded by "constant criticism, and final over-sight" of the developed drawings of his assistants. Mr. Besinger's description of the "exciting moment" when Wright put thought on paper as a completely realized project for the Watkins studio, the Burlingame house, the Crystal Heights development (all, alas, unbuilt), or other works suddenly makes clear why one would voluntarily be a Taliesin Fellow. Here was, indeed, demonstration of architectural genius. Once the concept had been given graphic form, the senior Fellows translated it into detailed presentation and working drawings which were in turn to greater or lesser degree criticized by Wright and then redrawn (for some works, over and over again). The process did not end with the production of drafting-room sheets, however, for Wright often began his home projects with oral instructions or "shingle sketches," and he as often changed the buildings of his clients during the process of their erection, again either verbally or using scantling graphics. Mr. Besinger frequently remarks on the lack of detailed drawings. If Wright, then, failed to confide all of his intentions to prescriptive graphics, it was because he thought of drawing and building as parts of a continuum. What he called the "grammar" of a building could be revealed, as at Auldbrass plantation, by a graphic process, but it had to be proven at the site. Mr. Besinger is as usual an astute guide when he equates the ruptured frames of the presentation drawings prepared in the Taliesin drafting rooms with the sense of spatial extension beyond physical borders that is an essential characteristic of Wright's buildings.

The frequently changed drawings and frequently altered buildings under construction described in this memoir suggest flexibility, a willingness to accommodate, that has not been sufficiently emphasized in discussions of Wright and his work. It is especially arresting to learn of buildings that were designed for one material or one structural system materializing without essential change in another. But Wright could also be stubborn. His experiment in "textile architecture" in the desert at Scottsdale, Arizona, was certainly predicated on a concept of the location as hot and dry when in fact it rained buckets during the winter when the Fellowship was in residence. Mr. Besinger's important descriptions of building and rebuilding the camp are filled with references to the rain and rain-dripping canvas enclosures; when I last stayed at Taliesin West in January 1991 the water still poured through the flat roof into my guest quarters. Rather than work with the character of the climate, Wright fought it. Like Canute the Great commanding the rising tide to roll back, he raged against the flood. As Mr. Besinger observes, "the elements seemed to be working against the realization of a beautiful vision." So much for the principles of regional architecture! The canvas was eventually replaced with sturdier (although as my experience shows, not necessarily waterproof) materials.

The drafting rooms at the Taliesins turned out a great many Usonian houses during Mr. Besinger's tenure, more than one man could possibly control. By the postwar years domestic design seems understandably to have taken second place in Wright's mind to larger works such as the Lacy Hotel project, the Guggenheim Museum, the Price Tower, and the Elkins Park synagogue. According to our guide there was a hierarchy of importance in the houses too, with gradations of interest and therefore of criticism from Wright himself. All of the work was, of course, in the larger sense Wright's, but with his advanced age and the increased volume of commissions it comes as no surprise that his oversight was at times perfunctory. This memoir makes explicit the contributions of individual Fellows, Wes Peters's engineering and Jack Howe's draftsmanship, for instance, and it also makes clear that some houses were in fact largely designed by the senior Fellows: Mr. Besinger himself lays specific claim to the Anthony house of 1949 and the Kalil house of 1955. Historians take note.

By 1955 Curtis Besinger was over forty and had been at Taliesin on and off since 1939. He was clearly entitled to leave. His departure was not, however, occasioned by his age, or the length of his tenure, or the opportunity to teach part-time at his alma mater. He left because the Fellowship in 1955 was not what it had been in 1939. When he arrived Wright was clearly the center and architecture clearly the focus of the community; when he left there had developed a "schism" in its creative life. The influence of Emerson was being increasingly challenged by that of Gurdjieff; Wright's aging authority by that of his younger wife.

There are two halves to this memoir, the divide characterized by the divergent personalities of Mrs. Wright's daughter, Svetlana, and Mr. and Mrs. Wright's daughter, Iovanna. "Svet" is here described as "just," possessed of "humor and grace" in tight situations, a "builder of bridges." Her tragic death in 1946 removed her from the scene near the middle of Mr. Besinger's tenure. Three years later Iovanna returned from Paris, where she had worked with the "Russian philosopher/guru" (as he is labeled elsewhere by Wesley Peters) Georgi Gurdjieff, as had her mother before her, and according to Mr. Besinger, her return "marked the beginning of a series of changes . . . that eventually led to my decision to leave." From 1949 on, Iovanna, supported by Mrs. Wright, who increasingly in these later pages emerges from the shadows, appears as a wedge splitting the Fellowship into two halves, one devoted to architecture, the other to "soul-searching" and "movements," or Gurdjieff-inspired theatrical expressions through dance of inner exploration. Our Baptist observer found the latter difficult to accept.

By 1953, with Wright reaching his upper eighties and preoccupied with great public works like the Guggenheim Museum, the division of the Fellowship's energies into architecture and dance was made manifest in the exhibition of Wright's work in New York, and of a coeval "movement demonstration" in Chicago under the direction of Mrs. Wright and Iovanna. The Fellowship's loyalties and energies were pulled in different directions. It was becoming increasingly unclear who was in charge and what was the mission. Architecture had been Wright's life. When in 1954 Mrs. Wright, in conversation with Mr. Besinger, reduced it to "how we make our living," to a financial prop for "soul-searching," our memoirist could see the writing on the wall. Reading on and between the lines we gather an inkling about the stresses caused by the transformation of the Fellowship as led by Wright, who died just short of ninety-two in 1959, to that under the direction of his widow, who died in 1985. It was a transformation perceived by Mr. Besinger and others as painful and unfortunate.

This is not the first – and will certainly not be the last – memoir to describe life in and out of the drafting rooms in Wisconsin and Arizona. Edgar Tafel, who was in residence from 1932 to 1941, led the way in his *Apprentice to Genius* (1979), and his recent *About Wright* (1993) collects some memories of some other Fellows and friends of Taliesin. The temperament of the observer colors his observations, of course, and Mr. Tafel and Mr. Besinger are very different personalities who have produced very different kinds of recollections. Each enriches the record; each offers a distinct angle of vision about nearly subsequent decades in the history of the Fellowship, but they agree in the essentials. The cumulative result provides the student of architectural history with telling details of Wright's later professional practice, and others with insights to the communal life of an important twentieth-century American social and cultural milieu. Given the variety of valuable information made available by this memoir, posterity will no doubt judge that, at his definitive career crossroads, young Curtis Besinger chose well when he directed his steps toward Taliesin rather than Cranbrook or Harvard.

James F. O'Gorman
Summer 1993

Introduction

My interest in Frank Lloyd Wright and his work began in the fall of 1932 when I enrolled as a student in the Department of Architecture and Architectural Engineering in the School of Engineering at the University of Kansas. At that time in the United States the so-called Beaux Arts system of architectural education was dominant. But the Architecture Department at the University of Kansas was pursuing a different approach, one well removed from this system. (This innovative approach was recognized by Bosworth and Jones in their book *A Study of Architectural Education,* sponsored by the Association of Collegiate Schools of Architecture and published by Scribners in 1932.)

The department's move away from the Beaux Arts system began in 1922 when Goldwin Goldsmith, the chairman of the department, appointed Joseph M. Kellogg to the faculty. Professor Kellogg had received undergraduate and graduate degrees from Cornell.[1] He had been a top student in design and had received a fellowship for graduate study in the school. He was a teaching assistant while working for his master's degree and had twice been a finalist for the Prix de Rome, the top prize awarded in the competitions of the Beaux Arts Society of Architecture. But Professor Kellogg did not believe that the grandiose "programmes" issued by the society (later to become the Beaux Arts Institute of Design) were appropriate design exercises for students who were preparing to practice architecture in Kansas.

Professor Kellogg's belief was shared by a younger member of the faculty, George M. Beal. Professor Beal had been a student at the University of Kansas and had received bachelor's degrees in both architecture and architectural engineering in the spring of 1923. That fall he was appointed an instructor and started work toward a master's degree in architecture, which he completed in 1925. He spent the summer of 1927 in France at the Fontainebleau School of Fine Arts and was awarded its *diplome.* He was, however, an avid modernist and most enthusiastic about the work of Frank Lloyd Wright. Although it was not Mr. Wright's policy to accept apprentices for a period of less than a year, Professor Beal and his wife, Helen, were at Taliesin in the summer of 1934 as apprentices. The Fellowship as an actuality had started only two years before in the fall of 1932.[2]

The idea for such an activity had, however, been present in Mr. Wright's mind for several years before this, years during which he had received few architectural commissions and had sought an income in lecturing and writing. In the Princeton Lectures, published in 1930,[3] Mr. Wright spoke of a need for "industrial style centers." These centers, as described in the second of the five lectures, were to be schools allied with and supported by industry. They were to be equipped with modern machinery donated by industry and operated by competent machinists supplied by industry. Seven industrial arts were to be represented. Forty or fewer students, apprentices and not scholars, were to be "put in contact" with industry by working with these machines under the direction of seven resident artist/workers. In doing this, the students were to achieve an understanding of the processes of machine production. With this understanding they would be capable of designing well-styled objects to be produced by machines. The machine was to become a tool in the hand of the artist.

A similar proposal is contained in Mr. Wright's book *The Disappearing City,*[4] in the section titled "The Design Center." Another is in a brochure by Mr. Wright, "The Hillside Home School of the Allied Arts," published in 1931.[5] The site for this school was the former Hillside Home School, a progressive coeducational institution started in 1887 by two of his aunts. Mr. Wright had designed several buildings for this school. Though operated successfully for many years, the school had closed several years before the aunts' deaths, Aunt Jennie in 1917, Aunt Nell in 1919. In 1931 the buildings were standing empty and much neglected.

This proposed School of the Allied Arts was not to be an art school but a "hive of industry." At its core, as inspiration, were to stand the Fine Arts, with Architecture as the leader. Grouped with and supplementing Architecture were to be divisions of Painting, Sculpture, Music, Drama, and Dance. Allied with this inspirational core were to be seven branches of the Industrial Arts.

In the summer of 1932 Mr. Wright sent a circular letter to his friends announcing "An Extension of the Work in Architecture at Taliesin to include Apprentices in Residence."[6] This more modest proposal was, in effect, a continuation of Mr. Wright's practice of the 1920s when he accepted young architects who wanted to work with him as apprentice draftsmen. They lived as well as worked at Taliesin, and included Richard Neutra, Henry Klumb, Werner Moser, and others. From those applicants who responded to this circular letter, Mr. Wright accepted 25 apprentices. They were working and living in temporary quarters at Taliesin by October 1932.[7]

In all of these proposals, and in the Fellowship that developed from them, there was one constant theme: Work. Whatever one was to learn was to be learned while working – on the daily chores of living, in the garden, on the farm, in construction, and in the studio or drafting room. And although the early proposals contained within them a visionary hope for external support, the Taliesin

Fellowship began operation with Mr. Wright's realization that, except for any tuition that apprentices might pay, the activity would be largely self-supported and self-sustaining.

On January 15, 1935, following Professor Beal's summer at Taliesin, Mr. Wright gave a lecture to an all-university convocation at the University of Kansas.[8] The lecture, entitled "Taliesin, an Experiment in American Culture," was sponsored by the convocations committee and the Department of Architecture and Architectural Engineering. Mr. Wright and his wife were guests of the Beals during this visit.

As a student in architecture my interest in Frank Lloyd Wright and his work had increased. I bought copies of his autobiography[9] and *The Disappearing City*. I spent much of my spare time browsing in the architectural library that was adjacent to the top-lighted drafting rooms in Marvin Hall. I was particularly interested in publications of Mr. Wright's work: the 1910 Wasmuth folios[10] with the reproductions of the marvelous drawings of his early work; the 1925 Wendingen book[11] with its plans and photos – including the Allen house in Wichita; and the 1926 de Fries book[12] with the reproductions of the wonderful colored pencil drawings of the California houses and the Lake Tahoe projects.

I was in the third year of the four-year architectural curriculum when Mr. Wright came to lecture. Professor Beal was the instructor of the design class in which I was enrolled. The class had just completed the last project of the fall semester, a natatorium. In the afternoon, following the lecture to the morning convocation, Professor Beal took Mr. Wright on a tour of the department – through the drafting rooms where the students, except for those who were following the tour, were working at their desks, and past the display areas where student work, including my natatorium, had been pinned up for the occasion.

I had rendered my presentation in watercolor and in what I considered a modern style. My drawing did not have the traditional border; it "bled" to the edges of the sheet of paper. I had composed the drawing somewhat in the manner of the Midway Garden murals. The title of the project was in a wide band of blue across the bottom of the sheet. From this band and along the left side of the sheet rose a column of abstract "bubbles." During the tour, Mr. Wright paused, quite briefly, in front of my drawing, made a comment to Professor Beal – which he later assured me was complimentary – and moved on. Of course I was pleased and more convinced that I should try to emulate his work.

I received my bachelor's degree from the university in 1936. This was a time when jobs, including those in architectural offices, were not plentiful. After an apprehensive summer of wondering if I was going to find work in an office, I was hired in early September by Joseph W. Radotinsky. His office was in the Commercial National Bank Building in Kansas City, Kansas. I had been recommended for the job by two friends, Bob Dunham and Ray Meyn, who had graduated from K.U. in the spring of 1935, and who were working in the office.

The majority of commissions in the office were either W.P.A. (Works Progress Administration) or P.W.A. (Public Works Administration) projects.[13] And most of these were schools – new buildings or additions to existing buildings. The office was also working on other projcets, including hospitals and swimming pools, which were federally funded. I was hired because of the pressure to get the drawings and specifications for these projects completed so that construction could begin and the unemployed building trades workers could be put to work.

Having no office experience, and as the cub draftsman, I was asked to do almost all kinds of drafting. I traced details which others had quickly roughed out. I did structural and mechanical drawings for which engineers had done the layout and detailed design. I was also frequently asked to help the secretary, to run the mimeograph machine, and to bind the copies into sets of specifications. And on one desperate day, when there had been a change of secretaries, I typed the stencils for the specifications, and mimeographed and bound them.

During that fall and into the winter we worked overtime, at nights and on weekends, until Joe decided that this work schedule was becoming unproductive. We stopped working nights on Wednesdays and weekends.

One day, in the spring of 1937, when the pressure to get the work out decreased, Joe called me into his office and told me that he was going to let me go. The blow of this bit of news was softened by his telling me that there was a job for me in A. W. Archer's office in Kansas City, Missouri. This was my introduction to the fact that architecture as a profession was something of a "feast or famine" activity, that the less experienced persons often moved from office to office, reflecting which offices were busiest at the time. It happened that Herbert Cowell, who had been in my class at K.U., was the lone draftsman in A. W. Archer's office. Under A. W.'s direction he was also doing the designing. The project on which we worked was a W.P.A. commission: a group of somewhat naturalistic appearing pits to be built around the lagoon at the zoo in Swope Park. At the end of that summer I went back to Radotinsky's office.

When work in his office slackened again, I went next door to Charles E. Keyser's office over the Home State Bank. Charlie's work was largely commercial and industrial: store buildings for the A. and P. (Atlantic and Pacific) grocery chain and warehouses in the Fairfax Industrial district of Kansas City, Kansas, then being developed by the Union Pacific Railroad. Charlie's buildings were mostly "three-stripe modern." They were built with tan brick. Above the windows was a soldier course of dark brown brick. The parapet wall above this was also tan brick capped with a cast stone coping. Below the coping was a dentil course of dark brick. And in the center, running horizontally, there were always three stripes of dark brick.

While working in these offices and gaining needed experience about how buildings were put together, how to do construction drawings, and how offices operated, I felt that there was something lacking in what I was learning.

On October 17, 1937, I wrote a letter to Mr. Wright asking for information about the Fellowship. The letter also expressed my dissatisfaction with what I had learned in four years of architectural education and a year of office work. I wanted a "grasp of real architecture." Almost as though in response to this letter, an article by Meyer Levin about Mr. Wright and the Fellowship appeared in the December 1937 issue of *Coronet* magazine.[14] In this issue there also appeared a fable written by Mr. Wright. The moral of this fable was that St. Peter, in admitting persons to heaven, favored those who had planted trees.[15] In the following month, January 1938, the special issue of *Architectural Forum* devoted to Mr. Wright's work appeared.[16] I read it avidly and wrote Mr. Wright an enthusiastic and laudatory letter on January 14. My interest in Mr. Wright and his work was further reinforced by an article by Talbot Hamlin published in the March 1938 issue of *Pencil Points*.[17]

Early in January 1939 I began to make plans to further my education. There were three places where I believed I might gain the ingredient I felt lacking in my education and experience: Taliesin, Cranbrook, and Harvard. Mr. Wright was at Taliesin. Eliel Saarinen, whose work was then being published in the magazines, was at Cranbrook. And Walter Gropius, whose work in Germany interested me, was at Harvard as the newly appointed head of the Department of Architecture in the Graduate School of Design.

I wrote to Eugene Masselink[18], Mr. Wright's secretary, saying that I had the Fellowship brochure but wanted additional information – about average expenses, in addition to those of a year's tuition, and about whether or not I would work with Mr. Wright. I also wrote to Cranbrook and Harvard asking for information about graduate study.

In the spring of 1939 Joe Radotinsky told me that there was a job available in the county engineers office in the Wyandotte County Courthouse. It was a job that would pay me more than he felt he could pay me. Joe knew of my hopes for further study and was encouraging me to go to Harvard; he knew this job would enable me to save more money. I worked with Roy Ferguson, a landscape architect, who was doing the design of the recreational areas in the park around the Wyandotte County Lake then being constructed.

I've no evidence that I received a response from Cranbrook. I did receive an informative pamphlet and an application form from Harvard. I filled out the application form, which applied to both admission and scholarships, and sent it back. I asked Joe Radotinsky and Professors Beal and Kellogg to write letters of recommendation. And after sending in requested additional information with regard to my experience in building construction I was accepted for admission to Harvard to study with Gropius,[19] but I also received a letter telling me that I would not receive financial assistance. Since I did not think that I could afford Harvard without receiving financial assistance I more seriously considered going to Taliesin. But I was hesitant to apply for admission to the Fellowship; I was shy and had doubts about how I would adjust to an environment that I, with my midwestern, Southern Baptist upbringing, thought of as unconventional and bohemian.

Professor Beal encouraged my interest in Taliesin; he proposed that I visit it some weekend with him. I suggested the weekend of the Fourth of July as this would not interfere with my work at the courthouse. Professor Beal wrote to Gene Masselink asking if Mr. Wright would be at Taliesin on that weekend and if a visit by us would be possible. He replied, "Mr. and Mrs. Wright and all of us are happy that you are coming over the week-end of the fourth. We will be happy to meet Curtis Besinger."

The Beals picked me up at the "Y," where I was living, on a Friday afternoon to begin the trip to Wisconsin. This was the beginning of the longest trip I had ever made in a car.

We left Kansas City shortly after I had gotten off work and drove about 150 miles that evening, stopping at a tourist court just after we crossed into Iowa. We drove the remaining 350 miles the next day in order to arrive just before tea.

Summer 1939 – Visit to Taliesin

We arrived at Taliesin at teatime, four o'clock, just as the Beals had carefully planned. We approached Taliesin from the southwest, along the road from Dodgeville, on Highway 23 (Fig. 1). When we topped the ridge dividing Wyoming Valley from the Lloyd-Jones Valley and began the curving descent my anticipation began to build, anticipation both of arriving and of seeing any of Mr. Wright's

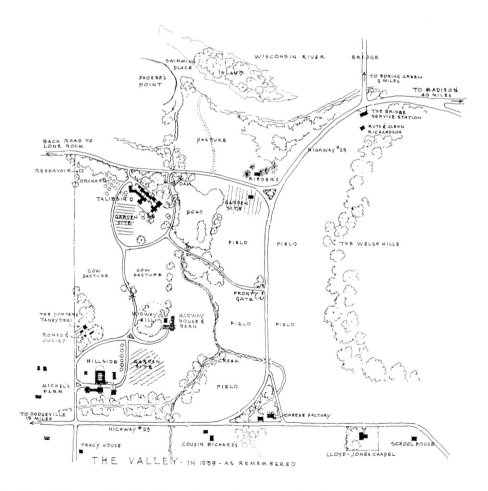

1   Plan of the Valley of the Lloyd-Joneses. Drawn from memory by author.

2A and 2B (above and opposite)   View of the valley from the north end of the Welsh Hills. Taliesin is partially visible in the trees above the lake at the right of the photo. Midway, a complex of farm buildings, is visible on the side of the hill at the left of center. The Hillside buildings are in the trees slightly above and to the left of Midway. Highway 23 extends across the fields in the foreground.

On the back of the photo is a note, "Fine. but take out road in foreground if possible. FLW." This note is an indication of Mr. Wright's ongoing effort to improve the landscape of the valley. It is one of his major – and frequently overlooked – works. Maynard Parker, photo, copyright Maynard L. Parker Estate.

work in actuality for the first time. There was the excitement of the first sighting of the landmark, the windmill Romeo and Juliet, which the Beals pointed out. And as we followed the highway through the valley there were glimpses of the red roofs of the Hillside Home School buildings through the screen of willows paralleling the road. At the turn there was Cousin Richard's house behind its fence on the right. On the left was a view of the red barns on Midway hill, and beyond that a view of the roofs of Taliesin seen through the trees and of stone chimney masses rising above the wooded slope.

From Highway 23 we turned into the farm on which Taliesin sits, through the front gate marked by stone piers and partially hidden in pine trees (Figs. 2a and 2b). We followed a gravel road across the fields, through willows near the creek, across a low stone bridge, and up the curving line that swung past the vegetable garden, the vineyard, and the farm buildings at the west end of the Taliesin complex (Fig. 3).

When we arrived near the gate to the back court the Beals were momentarily confused about where to go next. Something had been changed since their last visit; there was an unfamiliar drive and gate to the left. They chose the familiar

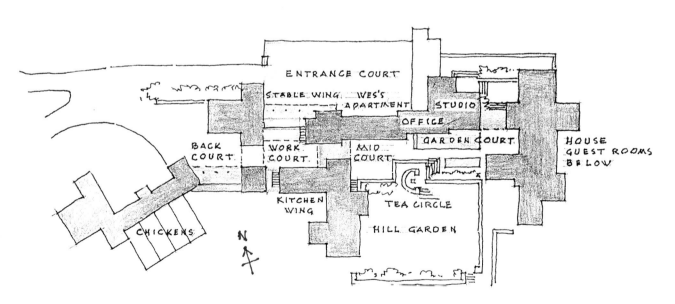

3   General Plan of Taliesin.

way into the back court where they found a spot to park the car. From there they led the way through several graveled courts toward the tea circle. They were greeted by acquaintances, apprentices who were headed the same way. I followed along, puzzling about just what I was expected to do. Tea was already being served when we reached the broad stone steps leading from the garden court up to the tea circle. It was a semisecluded place under two great oak trees in a corner of the Hill Garden but a little below its crown, defined on one side by a semicircular stone seat backed by a low stone wall. In its center was a small fountain, a pool about eighteen inches square recessed in the gravel floor. In the pool was a small bronze casting of Carl Milles's sketch for "Jonah and the Whale" with a small jet of water playing over it. A great swatch of white mosquito netting, pulled to one side, hung from the oaks. I assume that I was casually introduced to Mrs. Wright and to Mrs. Barney (Mr. Wright's sister Maginel), as well as to some guests and apprentices who were already there. If so it was not an indelible event.

Other apprentices were arriving. They were coming from different directions, from wherever they may have been working, and in the clothing in which they had been working. No one seemed dressed for the occasion. Tea was simply a break in the workday. Some may have paused somewhere to comb their hair and rinse their hands and faces. It was a warm, humid day; some were hot and sweaty from the work they had been doing.

There was a mingling of many sounds: of cars, of doors being opened and closed, of other people walking in the graveled courts, of conversation, of people being greeted and introduced, and of music coming from somewhere. Tea was being served from a large brass samovar sitting on a brightly colored tablecloth on a stone pier at one end of the seat. Scones, butter, and jam were being passed. In the midst of this, someone came running up to the tea circle from the direction of what I was later to learn was the Taliesin Studio. He asked if anyone knew where the Montgomery Ward catalogue was, and added that Mr. Wright wanted to pick out some plumbing fixtures.

After a bit Mr. Wright arrived, his coming announced by the banging of the Dutch door at the east entrance to the studio and a clearing of his throat. He came across the flagstone walk in the Garden Court and up the steps to the tea circle. He greeted the Beals and other guests and then settled back on the Indian blanket and colored canvas pillows on the stone seat beside Mrs. Wright. As he drank his tea he explained, as a beginning to the conversation, that he was looking for some economical plumbing fixtures for a house on which he was working. After about a half hour of conversation, drinking tea, and munching scones he arose, brushed the crumbs from his shirt front with a brightly colored napkin, and sauntered down the steps and back to the studio. That seemed to signal the end of tea. No one seemed in a hurry to leave. A few remained, finishing their tea and chatting.

After tea we were shown to guest rooms "below the house." "The house," as the east wing of the Taliesin complex was called, contained Mr. and Mrs. Wright's

4   The east side of the house. Family quarters, on the upper level, are, left to right, Mr. and Mrs. Wright's bedrooms, loggia, behind screened balcony, main guest room, chimney mass of guest room fireplace, and screened porch and balcony off living room. Rooms for guests are on the lower level. Photo by author.

private living quarters at the Garden Court level. Below these were the guest rooms (see Fig. 3). The room that I was to stay in was below the main guest room of "the house" (Fig. 4).

As one entered the room that I stayed in, there was a small stone fireplace in the far left corner. To the right of it a band of casement windows, painted a terracotta red, wrapped around the corner providing a view of the valley. The view included, beyond the highway and pond, the Lloyd-Jones Chapel and farmhouses. It was a cool and dimly lit room, deeply recessed beneath the projected corner of the guest room above and the balcony of the loggia. It had a red-enameled concrete floor. (I was later to learn that this particular red was called "Cherokee red.") There were a few sheepskins and small handwoven rugs in geometric patterns on the floor. (These had been brought back from a trip earlier in the summer to Europe for the "London Lectures" given for the Sulgrave Manor Board. The trip had also included a visit to Montenegro, Yugoslavia, Mrs. Wright's birthplace.) All of the furniture seemed to be built in and to be made of plywood and a few strips of cypress trim. There were a few matted Japanese prints on the wall. The casement windows had long metal hooks on them to hold them in an open position, and rather curious large brass thumb screws to pull them shut, as well as turn latches to hold them shut. There were insect screens on the windows.

My most vivid memory of that room is of lying there in the humid darkness, too warm for the wool blanket that was on the bed and too cool for only a sheet, listening to the sounds of a seemingly silent summer night. The water falling at the dam at the lower end of the pond. The rustling of leaves on the trees on the hill slope outside, the croaking of frogs down at the pond, the chirping of birds and insects. All of these were mingled with a murmur of other unrecognized voices, singing through the night.

The Playhouse

That evening we went over to the Playhouse at Hillside for dinner and to see a movie. I had studied the photos of the Playhouse, which had been published in the 1938 *Architectural Forum.* But these photos had given me no idea of what it was like to enter or to be in the room. It had a kind of magic that seemed to welcome and simultaneously defy analysis.

Originally the room had been the gymnasium of the Hillside Home School. It had been symmetrically organized around two intersecting axes. There was a fireplace in a deep bay on the west side and projected bays on the north and south sides with tall windows having sills above head height. A suspended balcony around the upper part of the room had formed what I assumed had been a sort of elongated octagonal running track.

The room was puzzling. It was different from the one I had studied in *Architectural Forum.* During a process of remodeling – or a continuous restudying – the original symmetry had been retained. But it had been overlaid with an asymmetrical rotation of about 30 degrees formed by the arrangement of the seating. Mr. Wright called it a reflex arrangement. What had been a level wood floor was now a series of stepped terraces, some of wood, some of stone and concrete. On these were low benches with thin seat and back cushions covered with a dusty rose fabric. The back of each bench had a ledge on which multicolored place mats and tableware had been set for serving the meal. The lowest floor level, the stage, was covered with a waxed and gleaming coral-red rubber sheet. When the movie was being shown this reflected the images on the screen. At either side of the stage hung curtains of monk's cloth with an intricate and boldly colored pattern of coarse yarns, velvet ribbons, and pieces of felt appliquéd to it. Over the stage was a plywood tympanum supported by wooden members that projected, seemingly unsupported, into the room. From the high darkness of the wood-beamed ceiling hung cubical stalactites of plywood and oak boards. These concealed and reflected numerous small light sources. The room seemed mysteriously dark, yet it was brilliantly accented with light. An enigmatic stone Buddhist figure stood at the left of the stage, bathed in a soft light from a hidden overhead source.

What I assumed had been a rather simple room had been made richly complex. It had strong contrasts in height; it seemed both intimate and vast.

Dinner was served by several apprentices from an area behind a low screen of oak boards and dark-stained plywood at the south side of the room, an area partially concealed by an arrangement of oak branches over the grand piano. Mr. and Mrs. Wright and some of their guests sat at small, low, hexagonal tables in an off-center "box" formed at the fulcrum of the seating arrangement.

I do not remember what the movie was. It is possible that one was not shown or that we may have seen *Czar Durandi,* an animated Russian cartoon Mr. Wright had been given and, as I later discovered, would show to guests at every opportunity. The movie shown on Saturday nights for the Fellowship was generally the same film that was shown to the public on Sunday afternoons.

The next morning I walked over to Hillside with the Beals and Mrs. Barney; I was interested in seeing the Playhouse again. With only a few people present I felt more free to explore it. In the morning light it was, of course, a different place. All of the woodwork in the room appeared to be either dark-stained rough-sawn oak or painted or stained one-quarter-inch fir plywood. The balconies and roof were framed with oak timbers. A head-height wainscot of horizontal oak boards with applied oak battens lined the lower walls to the sills of the high windows in the projected bays on the north and south. The room, although still mysteriously dark in its upper reaches, was now lighted by these tall windows. Great streaks of morning sun fell across one plastered wall, kalsomined a strong, terra-cotta red. Another wall was a brilliant, intense, pure blue. Others were white.

When coming through the doors from the vestibule one had a diagonal view of the room, over the terraced seating area and toward the fireplace deeply recessed beneath the lowest part of the balcony. One passed the tall windows on the north and beneath a segment of the balcony which was separated from the windows. From here there was a view over the screen panels of the long north–south dimension of the room. Next one moved around the stone Buddha, standing as a kind of pivot, toward the fireplace alcove under the balcony. In front of the fireplace one turned toward the opposite deep recess of the stage in which the screen stood.

I wonder now how many of the people who have entered that room by that particular path realized that it seemed to have been planned to present them with a teasingly disclosed, cumulative view of the room. I now know that as an experience it was very much like a Japanese stroll garden, the "pleasure walk," realized in terms of construction. This magical playhouse has since been replaced by another theater, built within the shell of the stone walls that remained after a fire destroyed that part of the Hillside buildings in the spring of 1952. Although the replacement had a similar seating configuration, it did not have the qualities of the first playhouse.

Sunday Picnic

We returned from the walk to Hillside by way of the Midway Barn (see Fig. 1), then across the pasture and back up to Taliesin, where people were getting ready to go to the picnic. A part of the picnic caravan, seven or eight Cherokee-red Austin Bantams, was being assembled in the back court near the stables. It included a small, panel-body truck referred to as "The Dinky Diner," which was

5 Construction of entrance court. This concrete structure, partially cantilevered from the hillside on the north side of Taliesin, was built by the apprentices early in the summer of 1939 while Mr. and Mrs. Wright were in England. The man with the shovel, at the left side of photo, is Will Weston, the master carpenter who helped with the construction of Taliesin from its beginning. Photo courtesy of Robert C. May.

equipped to carry the food and eating utensils; a small pickup truck; a small wood-paneled station wagon; and four or five small convertibles each of which would seat two people comfortably. On this occasion they carried three or four, the extras sitting in a little backseat. The convertibles belonged to some of the senior apprentices: Edgar Tafel, Bob Mosher, Jack Howe, Gene Masselink, and Burt Goodrich. Another part of the caravan was forming in the lower entrance court. This new parking terrace, partly cantilevered from the hillside on the north side of the main east–west wing of the Taliesin complex, had been built earlier in the summer while Mr. and Mrs. Wright were in Europe (Fig. 5).

Everything seemed to be in an agreeably unsettled state. Cars were being loaded with pillows and Indian blankets. People were disappearing to pickup forgotten items or to prompt stragglers. There was talk about who should ride with whom. And then, almost as though by a prearranged signal, Mr. and Mrs. Wright's car, with Herb Fritz as the driver, pulled out of the lower court and went down the back entrance road followed by the caravan. The caravan proceeded east on the county road, passing between the Rieder farmhouse and its barn on opposite sides of the road. (In the fall of that year Mr. Wright bought this farm and removed these buildings.) At the highway it turned right, moving across the Lloyd-Jones Valley, past the Hillside buildings, up over the hill, and down through Wyoming Valley. From there, still on Highway 23, it wound its way to

6   Picnic at Borglum Rock. A part of the group as it left the picnic spot. At left with camera, Professor George Beal. In line, front to back, Mrs. Wright, Mr. Wright, Jack Howe, Svetlana Peters, Wes Peters, Ellis Jacobs, unknown, Cornelia Brierly, Peter Berndtson, unknowns. Photo by author.

the top of the plateau. After going several miles more toward Dodgeville, Mr. Wright's car stopped. A farm gate to a field on the right side was opened, and the procession followed a dusty track along the side of a field to the selected picnic spot, Borglum's Rock, so christened when Gutzon Borglum, the sculptor, had been there with the Fellowship on a similar picnic a few years before. It was a rock promontory, a part of a limestone ledge with a vertical drop of about one hundred feet to the valley below. From here there were views to the north and west across the valley to other limestone walls enclosing the fields and pastures of the dairy farms below. Birches, pines, and junipers grew from fissures in the face of the limestone walls and in the moss-fringed and lichen-covered weather-eroded rock at the top edge.

I do not remember the meal itself, only its setting. In addition to the colorful blankets and pillows, there were colored cloth napkins, brightly glazed dishes, stainless-steel tumblers and tableware. The food and all of the equipment had been brought from the Taliesin kitchen and the meal was served with surprising ease by a few of the apprentices. After a couple of hours, everything was packed away for the trip back to Taliesin (Fig. 6). It was approaching the time for the opening concert of a summer series being given by the Taliesin String Quartette (Fig. 7) at the Playhouse.

7 The Taliesin String Quartette in the Playhouse, the theater at Hillside. Left to right: Mark Kondratieff, Irving Ilmer, Salvatore (Sam) Sciacchitano, Anton (Tony) Bek. Photo courtesy of Robert C. May.

Sunday Evening

Shortly before seven o'clock on Sunday evening the apprentices and guests began to gather for dinner in the Taliesin living room. It was a warm and humid evening. Some lingered in the Hill Garden, the tea circle, or in the Garden Court (see Figs. 9, 10) near the entrance to the house. The apprentices previously seen in casual or working attire were now more formally dressed, the women in long, summery dresses, the men in dark suits or formals.

It was not long before the cast-iron Chinese bell, hung by a chain from one of the oak trees in the tea circle, was sounded to announce dinner. Some people were seated at small tables, large enough for one place setting, that were placed about the perimeter of the room; some were at the long, high-backed, built-in seat near the fireplace, others were at the long, black, glass-topped dining table that was near the entrance to the room, and still others were out on the screened porch.

This too was a room that I had seen and studied in the 1938 *Architectural Forum*. There was a large, black grand piano, a Beckstein, in the northwest corner of the room. Before it was a music stand and seating for the string quartet. In the southeast corner of the room, diagonally opposite the piano, were two upholstered chairs for Mr. and Mrs. Wright – obviously the place of honor. The chairs were in front of an old, carved and painted, wooden Chinese screen. Places for guests were grouped near Mr. and Mrs. Wright within conversational distance.

The center of the room beneath the high ceiling remained open, occupied only by a square, blue-bordered, gold and white Chinese rug. The colors of the rug seemed to have established the color scheme for the upholstered chairs and ottomans in the room. Some were tan; others were a cerulean blue. There were other sources of color in the room. There was an arrangement of oak branches in a large bronze vase on a ledge behind the piano, and smaller arrangements of flowers on the built-in tables. A cast-iron bodhisattva, about three feet tall, stood on the ledge in back of the seat near the fireplace. Numerous ceramics and bronzes from Japan and China were placed about the room.

Many people have seen published photographs of this room, yet, like all great architecture, it is a room that must be experienced if one is to understand it. About forty feet square, it easily absorbed the forty or fifty people who were there for dinner that evening. Both intimate and spacious, it is visually rich, yet constructed in a somewhat ordinary way in somewhat ordinary materials: plaster walls and ceilings, flat cypress boards and strips, and an ochre-colored limestone taken from a nearby quarry. The space is both noble and, as Mr. Wright often said, "homily, in the English sense of the word." After the meal, the small tables were removed and people rearranged themselves for the music that was to follow. The evening began with a surprise for Mr. and Mrs. Wright. During their absence, Anton "Tony" Bek, the violist of the string quartet, had organized and trained a chorus of mixed voices. The chorus, which seemed to include more than half of the Fellowship, sang several numbers including a polyphonic "Ave Maria" – sometimes attributed to Mozart – and a Russian folk tune, "Kalinka." Although he often said that he didn't like surprises, Mr. Wright seemed delighted. After he had expressed his pleasure at this bit of music making by the Fellowship, the string quartet played. The Taliesin Quartette was composed of young musicians from Chicago who were spending the summer at Taliesin. Its members were Mark Kondratieff, first violin; Irving Ilmer, second violin; Tony Bek, viola; and Salvatore ("Sam") Sciacchitano, cello. During that summer the quartet also played before the Sunday movies in the Playhouse and for a weekly program broadcast from WIBA, a radio station in Madison.

The music seemed to be cut short that particular evening. Mr. Wright wanted to listen to the broadcast of a Groucho Marx radio program on which he had appeared as a guest. Most of those present moved from the living room into the loggia where the radio controls were located. I don't remember who got the best of whom in the encounter between Groucho and Mr. Wright. I remember Mr. Wright's hearty laughter but none of his comments while listening to his verbal sparring with Groucho.

Other First Impressions

One of my most vivid memories of that weekend is Fauré's *Requiem*. I remember it as a kind of theme song; it seemed to dominate the whole visit. Mr. Wright had been given a Capehart record player and radio by "Hib" Johnson of the S. C. Johnson Company, whose new administration building was then nearing completion. Mr. Wright had the controls of the radio and record player built into a nook in the loggia, but he had located speakers for it in several places about Taliesin: in the loggia and living room of the house; in the Taliesin studio; and outdoors in the Hill Garden on the tower near the main kitchen. As a result the sound from the record player filled the Hill Garden, the tea circle, the Garden Court, the studio, and the house itself. The *Requiem* must have been Mr. Wright's favorite recording at the time. One heard it early in the silver summer morning when the valley was still filled with mist, in the stillness of the quiet heat of noon, and in the evening when long shadows were being cast across the lawns, the valley, and the hills.

Fauré's *Requiem* was often heard again during my years in the Fellowship, but never with the steady continuation of that weekend. It is a sound that I associate with Taliesin; it still recalls the sounds and sensations of that first brief visit. Taliesin, as rebuilt after the tragedy of 1914, was itself an architectural requiem, not a prayer for repose, but repose itself, a quality that Mr. Wright was always striving for in his work.

I remember too the impression of a simple life being lived with a seemingly small income and yet with luxurious abundance. Fresh produce came from the vegetable garden, eggs from the henhouse, milk and butter from Midway via the cool, damp milk room beneath the kitchen. Contained within that Wisconsin Valley with the stream running through it and emptying into the sand-barred Wisconsin River nearby – to which one could walk for a swim on a summer afternoon – were the vineyard, the orchard, the pastures spotted with cows, and the various fields devoted to crops such as hay, corn, and oats.

On the morning preceding our departure, I spent some time in the Taliesin studio (Fig. 8), waiting and wandering about, with the hope that I could talk to Mr. Wright. I did not have an appointment. The room was filled with drafting tables. There was the familiar activity of a drafting room about which I was curious. Some people were sitting quietly at their boards, working on drawings. Others were gathered in twos or threes about a drafting table in discussion. Mr. Wright was in and out of the room, stopping to look briefly at a drawing or sitting down to study it and to indicate changes. Some of the time he was at his desk in his office, just around the corner, reading and responding to the mail. Sometimes he was on the phone. There were no doors between the studio, Mr. Wright's office, and his secretary's office. Taliesin was then on a country line, and when talking on the phone the caller felt compelled to talk loudly or, on long-distance calls, to shout.

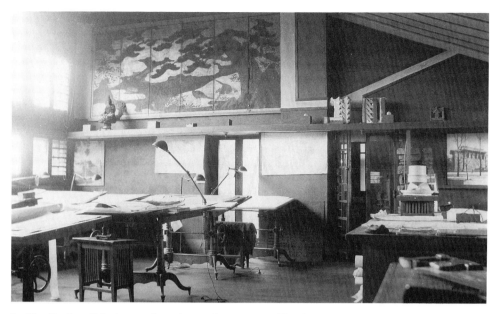

8   The Studio at Taliesin, seen from the southwest corner. The doorway at right leads to kitchen entrance to house. All drafting was done here until the fall of 1939. Photo courtesy of John H. Howe.

The studio was an active place. It seemed to be a kind of nodal point. Anyone on his way to anyplace – whether from the Taliesin kitchen to the little kitchen in the house or from Hillside to Spring Green or Madison – went through it. The apprentices' mailboxes were there and outgoing mail could be left there. And Gene Masselink, who was Mr. Wright's secretary, seemed to act as a kind of secretary to the Fellowship as a whole.

I do not know how long I waited around in the studio, but at about midmorning – I presume after the day's work had gotten under way and the things needing his more immediate attention had been tended to – Mr. Wright turned to me and asked, "Did you want to see me?" I suppose that I said yes, because we went into his office and talked briefly. I do not know what was said by either of us. I don't know whether I even sat down or remained standing. I do know that in a few brief moments it was decided that I was to join the Fellowship that fall.

The use of the terms "tea circle," "Hill Garden," and "Garden Court" suggests a familiarity with Taliesin which I did not possess. I had studied the plan and the photos of Taliesin that had appeared in the 1938 *Architectural Forum,* but that plan did little to prepare me for this first direct experience of Mr. Wright's work. I found that it had a spatial richness and complexity for which I was not prepared, and which this plan did not represent unless one already knew that the complex as a whole had four distinct levels: the main living level (Fig. 9) on which the studio, the various courts, the living room, the loggia, and Mr. and Mrs.

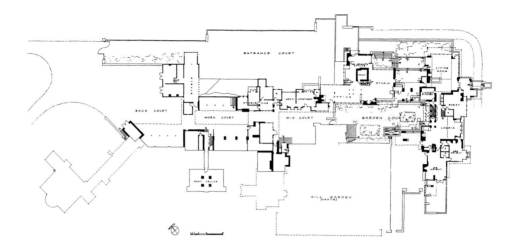

9   Plan of Taliesin at level of Garden Court, studio and house.

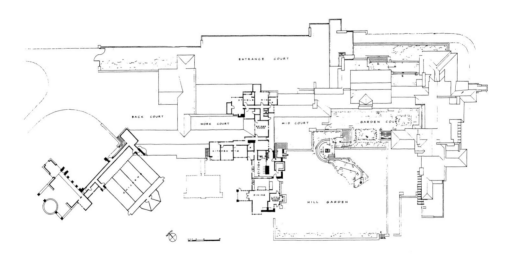

10   Plan of Taliesin at level of Hill Garden, dining rooms, kitchen, and upper level of the stable wing.

11 Longitudinal section through courts and house, facing north.

12 Cross section through Hill Garden, Garden Court, and studio, facing west.

Wright's bedrooms were located; the level below this with rooms for guests, and the entrance court with parking for guests; the level of the Hill Garden (Fig. 10) on which were the main kitchen, the dining rooms, and some apprentice rooms; and then a few rooms above this level. I began to realize that it would require multiple plans and many sections to begin to represent this and that even then the representation would fall short of the reality of the experience (Figs. 11 and 12). I have gone into a description of some of these first experiences at some length because they created impressions that, with each repetition during the years that I was at Taliesin, did not change or diminish.

Fall 1939

I arrived at Spring Green, Wisconsin, Friday morning, October 6, 1939.[20] Gene Masselink met me at the railway station and immediately drove me to Hillside. The Fellowship was having lunch there on the lawn west of the drafting room. After lunch Gene took me to Taliesin and to a room below the house in which I stayed that fall until we went to Arizona. It was a small room below the northeast corner of the living room, with a large walk-in closet at the northeast corner. Beside the closet was an alcove for a single bed. The room had a concrete floor painted a terra-cotta red with some sheepskins on it, and three narrow slit windows facing the north. On the north wall was a built-in desk. There were steam pipes on the ceiling for radiators in the living room above; these generally kept the room too warm.

I had arrived at Taliesin on a Friday in order to give myself a weekend to become oriented and acquainted. I had brought with me a small trunk and a weekend bag. In the trunk, in addition to my clothing, were my drawing equipment, a hammer and saw, a sleeping bag, blankets, and bedding. The application form suggested that all apprentices bring these things with them.

I had already met some of the senior apprentices, who were friends of the Beals, during the Fourth of July holiday. And having visited Taliesin and having talked with the Beals about their experiences I was somewhat familiar with what a newcomer might expect and with what was expected of him. I learned later that many newcomers arrived at Taliesin completely unprepared and with preconceptions that were misconceptions. When life in the Fellowship did not agree with their preconceptions, they were disillusioned and, not infrequently, bitterly disappointed. Some came expecting an academic environment, a school with required and regular hours of classwork, and with some free time during which they could do as they pleased. Some came expecting an artistic community, a sort of bohemian life of freedom in which one could do what he wanted, when and if he wanted. Some came expecting an egalitarian co-op with everyone having an equal say. Some came expecting a lesser degree of commitment and involvement than was expected of them.

Few newcomers to the Fellowship received special treatment. There was no orientation program; no one explained the daily schedule – what there was of it – to him or her. They were left pretty much on their own. Of course, there were exceptions, but "wholesome neglect" was the practice and the policy. I discovered later that there was an unstated, but structured, hierarchy among the apprentices, determined by how long one had been in the Fellowship: the "seniors" who had been there for many years, those who had been there for a few years, and those who had just arrived and who were submitted to the same neglectful treatment the others had received upon their arrival.

One of the other difficulties confronting many new arrivals was the discovery that they were expected to work not in the studio or drafting room, but at physical labor on construction or other manual work out-of-doors. Apprentices were generally not assigned to work in the drafting room until they had been in the Fellowship about six months. Mr. Wright often said that he was not interested in producing drawing board architects. And, since there were no hired servants to wait on the apprentices, they were expected to do their share of work related to the maintenance of Fellowship life. This included work in the kitchen.

The many misconceptions about Fellowship life resulted in a rather high percentage of apprentices who stayed for only a short time. Many came for a year, and then left. But others stayed for a month or less. I knew of one apprentice who arrived from Chicago one day at noon. After lunch he was assigned to a room on the west side of the drafting room, a room that had been fairly well furnished with built-ins by Cary Caraway, the first of its occupants. This newcomer immediately tore out all the furnishings and threw the debris out a window onto the lawn west of the building. I do not know precisely what happened after that, but he was on the four o'clock train heading back toward Chicago. He was there such a short time that I never learned his name.

According to a December 30 letter[21] which I wrote the Beals after being at Taliesin about three months, six new apprentices had arrived after I had, and only two of them remained at the time.

Teatime

The fellowship had two visitors that fall who were well known and warmly received. Mies van der Rohe, who, according to Mr. Wright, was "wasting his fine talent teaching at Armour,"[22] was one of these. He arrived at teatime, and in honor of his visit we had tea in the Taliesin living room instead of in the tea circle. Mies spoke no English. Walter Peterhans, who was traveling with him and was acting as his interpreter, spoke English with a heavy German accent. Conversation was limited; tea was brief. Mr. Wright, who liked to hold forth on his favorite subject, architecture, seemed thwarted by speaking through an intermediary and by Mies's one- or two-word responses. Mies: "Ja." Translator: "He says 'yes.'"

Another visitor was Buckminster Fuller, whom Mr. Wright affectionately called Bucky. Again we had tea in the living room at Taliesin. I do not know what brought up the topic – perhaps Bucky and Mr. Wright had been discussing it earlier – but after everyone was seated in a circle, Mr. Wright proposed that each person give his definition of reality. And so the question "What is reality?" went around the room, finally returning to Mr. Wright and Bucky. Unfortunately, I don't remember anyone's precise response, not even Bucky's or Mr. Wright's. I do know that "Bucky" didn't give one of his sixty-minute answers to questions, which he later gave during his visits to schools of architecture in the 1950s and 1960s. Mr. Wright's definition was one of his one-liners and something like "What is in what I am."

Teatime was when the Fellowship and Mr. and Mrs. Wright and guests gathered for a quick afternoon refreshment. It marked the end of the workday and the beginning of the free time between tea and supper. Free time was a period during which apprentices did their laundry, made trips to Spring Green or Scottsdale to shop for personal needs, or spent time in the drafting room becoming familiar with Mr. Wright's work, improving their drafting skills, or working on individual design projects.

Teatime was when Mr. Wright often commented on books or articles that he had read, events – political or otherwise – which had come to his attention, projects on which he was working, or activities being planned. If guests were present they might be the focus of attention. If there was a problem that involved the Fellowship as a whole it might be discussed at tea. Sometimes his comments provoked questions or comments of agreement – or disagreement from the more vocal members of the group.

One comment that Mr. Wright made early in my apprenticeship was indelibly inscribed in my mind: "If you are going to do something different you must do it with taste." This comment made a deep impression because it seemed in contradiction to much of his writing about the question of taste. It seemed to me that he had derided taste, particularly "good taste," in his comments on and criticism of culture in Chicago and the United States. And yet here he was saying that one must exercise taste!

Another comment that he made that fall has also remained in my mind: Never get on a first-name basis with the client's wife. He offered these words of caution to the more experienced apprentices who were being sent out to supervise the construction of the Usonian houses.

One of the topics much discussed at tea that fall was Hitler's invasion of Poland and the declaration of war against Germany by England and France. Also of much concern was the increasing possibility of United States involvement in this war. Mr. Wright was opposed to war in general and to the United States's becoming involved in this particular war.

Outside Work

On my first Monday morning in the Fellowship, not having been told what to do after breakfast, I walked over to Hillside. I knew that construction was under

13   Construction at Hillside, summer and fall of 1939. Living room in scaffolding is at left. Entrance to apprentice rooms and drafting room is at center of photo. Stone piers were built to support roof of a covered walk leading to Home Building. Photo courtesy of John H. Howe.

way there, and volunteered to work with a crew, headed up by Gordon Chadwick (Fig. 13). In preparation for replastering the exterior of some of the Hillside buildings, this group was putting metal lath on the broad exterior soffits of the roofs and the exterior walls above the sandstone base. Some of these areas had been previously plastered, but the plaster had deteriorated. Mr. and Mrs. Wright came by later that morning and seemed pleased to see me at work. I do not know how long we worked on this project, but I do remember the worn-out cotton gloves and the cut and bruised fingers acquired while working on those cold October mornings, attempting to drive nails to fasten the black expanded metal lath to the well-seasoned oak boards with which the soffits were framed. Looking upward, with grit from the previous plaster and specks of paint from the lath falling into our eyes while we attempted to drive those long, big-headed, galvanized nails into hard oak, was a test of patience and endurance.

While working on this job I began to develop an awareness of Mr. Wright's appreciation of – and seeming affection for – craftsmen. The plasterer, who was from one of the nearby towns, was an amazing craftsman. He could apply an acceptable, one-coat, integral color, plaster finish as fast as it could be mixed and carried to him by two helpers, and about as fast as we could nail on the lath and dismantle and rebuild the scaffolding. Mr. Wright enjoyed watching this man at work.

After this project was finished I was assigned to work at Taliesin with a group that was framing the new terrace outside Mr. Wright's office. This terrace was to cover the carport at the east end of the entrance court (see Fig. 9) which had been built earlier in the summer. The carport had space for two cars, Mr. and

Mrs. Wright's new Lincoln Continentals. The stone piers to support the terrace were already in place. They had been built by Phil Volk, a stonemason, and his tender, Allen Brunker. Mr. Wright enjoyed seeing this pair at work also. Although Mr. Wright had established the general character of the masonry elements, asking that the stone be laid as it came from the quarry, with little shaping or squaring-up, to reflect the stratification of the limestone out-croppings found in that area of Wisconsin, he gave the masons much leeway in how they achieved this. At one level of observation the masonry work appears to have much of the same texture and character. But close observation will reveal that each of the different masons gave his work identifiable individual characteristics. Mr. Wright did not discourage these individual variations.

While working on this project I became aware that the construction and detailing of Taliesin was both conventional and innovative. From reading Mr. Wright's autobiography I had come to expect the innovative, but I was surprised to see that some of the moldings used as trim in the construction of Taliesin had conventional stock profiles. Construction was also experimental when and if Mr. Wright wanted to try something. The finished floor of the terrace was an asphalt-impregnated, fiberboard tile, about twelve by twenty-four inches in area and about a half-inch thick. It was laid in tar over roofing felts laid on a wood sub-floor. This was replaced after a few years with a built-up membrane of tar and felt with a gravel topping.

I was also involved in one other construction project that fall, a remodeling of the Taliesin dining room (see Fig. 10), where the Fellowship had breakfast and dinner. Lunch was served at Hillside, outdoors or indoors, depending on the weather; it was carried there every noon from the Taliesin hill kitchen. One day, as we were eating lunch at Hillside in its still unfinished state, Mr. Wright remarked rather jokingly that "we should go over and tear the ceiling out of the dining room at Taliesin lest we get soft by eating in finished places."[23] Within a few days we were doing it.

One morning, having finished his breakfast in the nearby little dining room, Mr. Wright came into the Fellowship dining room and announced that he wanted to put a clerestory in the ceiling to let more light as well as the morning sun into the room. The room was a bit dark. The primary source of daylight was a bay of windows at the south end. Some light also came into the room from doors opening out to a screened porch on the west side and from small slot windows in the entrance area on the east side. He directed some people to start knocking off the plaster on the ceiling along the east side of the ridge. The interior ceiling conformed to the exterior roof shape. He made a rough drawing to indicate how he wanted the clerestory built. At this time he was putting clerestories, slots of light, between the flat roof planes of the Usonian houses.

After the carpentry work was completed and the clerestory glazed, the ceiling and some of the walls were replastered and the entire room painted. I was particularly interested in the repainting which was done by Gene Masselink, Eleanor Ullman, and me. It was a process that Mr. Wright said he had used in some of his earlier work and in the Johnson House then being completed in Racine.

The walls and ceiling were painted a strong terra cotta red, somewhat more orange than that of a red lacquer. Over this we applied a dirty gray-green "wax glaze," scrubbing it on with rather dry brushes to achieve a coat that was neither even nor spotty. Mr. Wright had demonstrated how this should be done. It resulted in a color that had depth, richness, and an aged mellowness. The Taliesin studio was later repainted in a similar manner.

Like many Taliesin projects, this one had a deadline; it was started shortly before Thanksgiving and had to be completed in time for Thanksgiving dinner. At this dinner Mr. Wright remarked "that the Fellowship was getting too large, and worst of all, on the way to becoming successful."[24] There were then forty-four people in the fellowship.

Studio Work

When I visited Taliesin during the summer, all of the architectural work was being done in the studio there. But when I arrived in the fall, the drafting room at Hillside had been completed and furnished, and the drawings for architectural projects were being done there (Figs. 14, 15, 16).

It was not the usual practice for a new apprentice to be assigned to work in the studio, but I was asked to work there several times during the fall. In a November twenty-first letter to my parents I wrote, "I've worked out-of-doors most of this week doing carpentry work of a rough sort. But today I got sent back to the studio. There is some work that Jack Howe, the head man in the studio, wants to get out in a hurry."[25]

Earlier in the fall I had volunteered to trace some drawing for Jack (John H.) Howe in my free time between tea and dinner. In preparing working drawings for houses, Jack attempted to have duplicate sets of drawings: one, a set on which

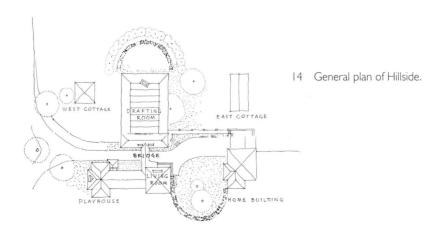

14 General plan of Hillside.

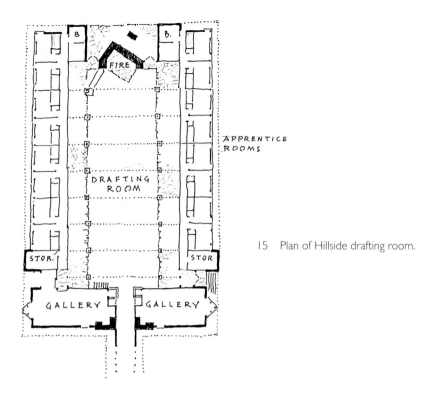

15   Plan of Hillside drafting room.

16   View of Hillside drafting room seen from the northwest corner and looking toward southeast
entrance. Peter Berndtson is at a table near center of photo. Photo courtesy of John H. Howe.

Mr. Wright worked and made changes, and the other a set that could be kept clean. When working on the drawings and making changes, Mr. Wright did not work carefully; he was not intent on keeping the drawings clean. He drew with a soft pencil, and when erasing often smeared the drawing. Changes were made on both sets, but better prints could be made from the clean one.

The paper used for the drawings was a rag paper. It was more durable but less transparent than some tracing papers that were available. The ozalid machine at Hillside, used to make prints of drawings, produced prints of very uneven quality, largely because of fluctuations in the source of power, a Kohler electric generator down in the Hillside boiler room. Inevitably when someone was attempting to run prints, someone else was using the power saw over in the shop in the East Cottage. This overloaded the generator and caused the print machine to run more slowly.

Most of the work I did in the drafting room that fall involved tracing Jack's drawings and making Mr. Wright's changes on one of the sets of drawings to keep them current with each other. I don't believe that Mr. Wright was aware of the two sets of drawings. If he was, he chose to ignore them, not to make an issue of this.

Although I was assigned to work in the studio only for brief periods of time, I did spend much of my free time there after tea and in the evenings. For the apprentices who lived at Hillside the drafting room was also a living room, particularly the area near the large fireplace at the north end. There was a radio/record player there and a fire was always burning in the fireplace. In the early fall, before the heating system was turned on, it was the one warm place at Hillside. The Hillside living room was not furnished at that time. And the Hillside dining room and kitchen were still being constructed.

The preliminary drawings for recent projects were generally hung on the east and west walls of the room, tacked to wooden strips. These provided me with a means of becoming familiar with Mr. Wright's current work, and I spent much time studying them, both as drawings and as designs for buildings. I had done a lot of freehand drawing and was interested in the use of colored pencils. This was a technique I had experimented with as a student but without much satisfaction. The composition of the drawings, their placement on the sheets of paper, also interested me, and raised the question of why there were no borders. I was accustomed to drawings with borders and title blocks.

I was particularly intrigued with the composition of the drawings. As a student I had generally followed the tradition of presentation drawings having borders. But I had also experimented with making drawings without borders. I knew that modern painters had rejected the use of the traditional frames around their drawings and had, in some instances, reduced the frame to a minimal piece of trim. I had no idea why they did this, except to appear "modern." Although I had experimented with presentation drawings without borders, I did not feel that my watercolor sketches were complete until they had been put into an appropriate mat with a border of lines and colored bands.

The preliminary drawings that Mr. Wright showed or sent to clients did not have these traditional borders. The plans and elevations were drawn on sheets of paper with titles giving the name of the client, the location of the project, and the name of the architect. These titles were generally in bands of lettering across the bottom of the sheet. This was clean and straightforward. But the perspective drawings were another matter. They did not have borders, but had a kind of reference to a border or frame. This reference was a segment of a rectangle – or rectangles – enough to imply a rectangular area of sky or background, sometimes even foreground. Portions of the drawings could be seen as having broken free or having escaped from this "frame." Other parts of the drawings receded and accepted the "frame" and even though the drawings extended outside the implied "frame" they always had the two-dimensional flatness of Japanese prints.

I knew that Mr. Wright was an admirer of Japanese prints and that he had said that his architectural work – as well as the presentation drawings – were influenced by the prints. But most of the prints in his collection were mounted in mats that conformed to the borders on the prints. In the prints there was none of this breaking out of the border, none of this engagement of the drawing with the area of the mat around it. There was a clear boundary between print and mat. But with more study of the prints I began to see something in them that I had not seen before – that they seemed to "reach out" and include more than was seen within the borders, that their organization or "composition" seemed to extend beyond their borders and to include, by implication, things that were outside the border, and not inside.

I began to form a nebulous idea that there could be a similarity in the way a drawing could extend beyond its frame and a house could, by its design, extend or be seen as extending, into the space around it, and by so doing make its site seem larger by reaching beyond the boundaries of the site. There seemed to be a relationship between the fracturing of the traditional border of the drawing to achieve a kind of freedom in space, a sense of spaciousness, and that achieved by making a building's site seem larger.

One group of drawings that I found particularly interesting were Mr. Wright's sketches of designs for the three entrances to the grounds of Taliesin: the Hillside entrance from the highway on the south; the front entrance from the highway on the east; and the back entrance from the county road on the north. Each design was based on a different geometric motif: a square, a triangle, and a circle. The gates themselves were to be metal and hung from stone piers laid similarly to the masonry of the Taliesin buildings. None of these designs was ever built. It has since puzzled me that only one of these sketches was published in Mr. Wright's lifetime, the one based on a square, or three dimensionally, a cube. Perhaps this was because although the geometry of the triangle or the circle seemed appropriate when executed in the plane of the gate and in metal, it did not seem right when translated into the rough-textured masses of Taliesin stonework as spheres or pyramids. Or perhaps these sketches were only another part of the product of a restless creative mind that entertained itself by coming up with variations on a theme – such as working on four playhouses with the same plan but different roofs, or rearranging the furniture and art objects in any room these items occupied for long.

The major activity in the studio during that fall was the production of drawings for the many and varied Usonian houses. They were in different stages of the building process from design to construction. Several of the senior apprentices were working on these. Jack Howe was working on the Lloyd Lewis house which Edgar Tafel later supervised. Burt Goodrich was working on the Rosenbaum house, which he was to supervise. Gordon Chadwick was revising the drawings for the Loren Pope house, which he was supervising. There were preliminary drawings for these houses on the walls of the drafting room. Working drawings for some of them were in progress on the boards. Supplementary drawings for cabinets and furniture were being done for some of the houses already in construction. The Jacobs house in Madison was being completed. (Mr. and Mrs. Wright and the entire Fellowship were invited there for dinner late in the fall. It was an opportunity for all of us to see the first of these houses completed, furnished, and occupied.)

I was intrigued with the concept of these houses. It seemed infinitely variable as it was adapted to the differing needs, sites, and budgets of the clients. It was completely different from that of the prairie houses both in construction and in the handling of the space. I became somewhat familiar with the construction and details of these houses while doing the tracings that Jack Howe had asked me to do. It was then that I began to wonder how these houses could be built with so few drawings. Based on my previous office experience, particularly in having helped a friend in Radotinsky's office do a set of drawings for a small, conventional house, it seemed to me that more drawings would be necessary to explain this unfamiliar and unconventional system of construction.

It was a system that eliminated most of what would have been called "rough carpentry" and consisted essentially of "finish carpentry." The details approached those that would be called "cabinet work."

As such they required careful workmanship and a different kind of participation and involvement on the part of the various building trades. Each had to understand the system as a whole. Some builders, when asked to bid on these houses and when given a set of drawings lacking the usual strings of dimensions which located walls, doors, windows, etc., and gave overall dimensions, either expressed no interest in bidding or submitted excessively high bids as protection against the unfamiliar. Others, with more inquiring minds, found the unfamiliar to be interesting and challenging.

The houses were designed on a grid, generally a rectangular unit system. In some instances the system was triangular or hexagonal. Dimensions were determined by the location of parts in relation to this grid. One had to have studied the standard detail sheet and to have understood the position of the parts in relation to the grid in order to calculate dimensions. Once a person had done this he found the system of construction logical and simple.

It was a system however that required precision in execution. The grid itself had to be laid out carefully on the site. Any sloppiness at this point in the building process resulted in problems and headaches as construction proceeded. In addition to precision in layout it also required precision in certain parts of the work that in much construction is rather roughly done because the workmen know that it will be covered up later with "finish" work. For example, the floor of the house was, in most cases, a concrete slab on grade. This concrete slab edged on the exterior with a rolock course of bricks was the base for the house. Beneath the slab, laid on top of an eight-inch bed of crushed rock, were the wrought-iron pipe coils of the hot-water heating system. The concrete slab, as the finish floor, was to be integrally colored a terra-cotta red, and the lines of the unit system were to be marked into it. Also, into this finished surface, metal splines to which the wooden interior and exterior walls were to be fastened had to be inserted. All of this had to be done while the concrete was still workable. Builders used ingenious means to pour this slab and to achieve a good finish. The detail of the spline inserted into the slab was later modified to an angle that could be fastened to the floor slab after it was poured. Some other details were changed when experience and ingenuity suggested modification.

In Mr. Wright's original concept for these houses the thin wood walls were to have been assembled in the shop and set in place at the site after the floor, roof, and masonry elements supporting it – brick walls, fireplaces, and piers – had been constructed. The wood walls, a sandwich of a three-quarter-inch plywood core (other cores were used in some houses for economy) with a layer of building paper on either side and faced on both sides with boards held in place by recessed battens fastened to the core with screws, were to have been joined at the mitered corners with a bent metal spline. The Bazett house in Hillsborough, California, supervised by Blaine Drake, was the only one in which an effort was made to assemble the house in this manner.

It is possible that Mr. Wright may have borrowed this idea from the Japanese; the roofs of their traditional houses were supported on the main columns of the structural system in order that much of the work toward completion could proceed beneath it protected from the elements. Or it is possible that since the "overhead," the "sense of shelter," was such an important element in buildings designed by Mr. Wright, he wanted to see the roof in place early in the construction process.

Kitchen Work

All apprentices, except the seniors, were expected to take their turns as kitchen helpers, and all apprentices, including the seniors, took their turns at doing the dishes after the evening meal. Everyone, except Mr. and Mrs. Wright and their guests, did their own dishes after every meal, except on Saturday and Sunday evenings when dinner was served in the theater or in the Taliesin living room. On those nights there were three dishwashers rather than two.

When I first joined the Fellowship, certain people designated as cooks took their weekly turn in cooking all three meals of the day. Their day, like that of the kitchen helper, began before breakfast and ended after the evening meal was served. A "tea cook" prepared tea and made cookies or cake to go with it. After about a year, in order to shorten the long workday of the cook, "breakfast cooks" were introduced. They cooked only breakfast and were then assigned to other work for the rest of the day.

To assist the cooks, two apprentices were named kitchen helpers. Both of the helpers cleaned or peeled vegetables, did the pots and pans and the dishes from the little dining room, and kept the kitchen clean. One of the helpers was assigned to take care of the little dining room. The other was responsible for the Fellowship dining room. These two rooms were adjacent to each other and to the main "hill" kitchen at Taliesin (see Fig. 10).

The little dining room (Figs. 17, 18) was where Mr. and Mrs. Wright and their guests had their meals. The person assigned to the little dining room was responsible for the care of the room, giving particular attention to its cleaning, to setting the table, to starting and maintaining a fire in the fireplace when it seemed desirable, and to serving the meals. There were proper ways in which the table must be set, the food served, and the plates removed from the table. Any impropriety might bring a reprimand from Mrs. Wright. Mr. Wright was more casual; he did not seem so concerned about these proprieties. But the inexperienced little-dining-room helper served with a fear that he might be caught in error.

In setting the table much thought and imagination went into selecting the color of the dishes to be used, the choice of tablecloths and napkins, and the floral arrangement for the room. The Fellowship had enough Fiesta ware, place settings, and serving dishes in various colors to serve the entire group. The arrange-

17 Plan of the little dining room at Taliesin.

18 View of the little dining room seen from the fireplace alcove. Photo courtesy of John H. Howe.

ment might consist of wildflowers or flowers from the garden; it might include oak or pine branches or whatever seemed appropriate. Sometimes there might be arrangements on both the dining and side tables. Mr. Wright seldom failed to notice and comment on the overall appearance of the room. Certain apprentices were known for their skill in setting the table and arranging the room. There was always an effort to come up with a different idea. Ben Masselink, the brother of Gene, when taking his turn as a kitchen helper in the summer of 1940, went so far as to include a small pond with a live toad in one of his arrangements!

The other kitchen helper took care of the Fellowship dining room, cleaning it, setting the tables, and hopefully finding time to arrange flowers upon the tables. During those first years this helper was also responsible for starting the Kohler in the morning. The Kohler was the generator that provided electricity for Taliesin as a supplement to the "hydro" down at the dam below the pond.

The Kohler was located beneath the far north end of the stable and two flights down from the kitchen level. At about five-fifteen Taliesin time, the kitchen helper would find his way through the dark and silent courts of Taliesin and down one or two flights of stone stairs to the Kohler and attempt to start it. One was always relieved when, after a few coughing starts, the thing would at last catch hold and the lightbulb in the Kohler room would begin to glow.

It was also the responsibility of this helper to make coffee for the Fellowship. The little-dining-room helper made Mr. and Mrs. Wright's coffee. Making coffee was something of a ritual. It was made in a large, porcelain-enamel, metal coffeepot that held several gallons of water. It was necessary to get the water on to heat early so that coffee would be ready for the first to arrive at breakfast. One carefully measured the required number of cups of water into the coffeepot and put it on a burner on the gas stove to bring it to a boil. Then one went into the storeroom where staples were kept and ground coffee beans for the required amount of water. The coffee, freshly ground, was then put into a stainless steel mixing bowl and one egg was broken into it, shell and all, and mixed up with the ground coffee. When the water came to a boil, this mixture was put into it. The water was then brought to a boil three more times, the pot removed from the flame between each boil. After this, one cup of cold water was put in to "settle the grounds."

During my first turns as kitchen helper, before a walk-in cooler was built adjacent to the kitchen, there was a large refrigerator in the back entrance vestibule. Butter and eggs and a few other items requiring cool temperatures were stored there. But before each meal one had to go down an exterior flight of stairs to the milk room and bring up a five-gallon can of milk that was kept cool in a concrete trough filled with water. After filling the pitchers for the tables one had to take the can back. There were also trips to the root cellar during the day to bring up canned or preserved items, or vegetables such as potatoes, carrots, turnips, and rutabagas.

Of the many times I took my turn as kitchen helper, several particular stints stand out. I had been at Taliesin about three weeks when I was first assigned to the kitchen during the last week in October. Kenn Lockhart was the cook that week. He was experienced but temperamental. Leonard Meyer, the other helper, was assigned to the little dining room. Just out of high school, he had joined the Fellowship the previous year. He seemed imperturbable; he was a great help to me during that strenuous week which culminated in a Halloween party on Saturday night.

The party, the Seventh Anniversary Halloween Fete, an elaborate affair with many invited guests, was held at Hillside. Planning had probably begun several weeks before since guests were invited, but preparation for the party began only in the week preceding it. Some of the apprentices gathered in the playhouse at night to rehearse their skits which were to be part of the entertainment – and a surprise for those not involved in them. There was talk of the previous years' skits, including one which it seemed had not been very well received and had brought a reprimand to those involved. Discussion of it was somewhat hush-hush but it seemed that four of the newer apprentices at the time had formed a quartet and sung a take-off of the Wisconsin "fight" song that went something like this:

> Taliesin, Taliesin
> Dear old Shining Brow
> Push the pencil 'round the paper,
> Try to please Jack Howe
> Hail the red square, and the T square
> And the long hair too.
> Fight freshmen, But the stu-de-oo
> Is not for you.

19 Party costumes. Left to right: Kenn Lockhart, Kay Schneider, and John Hill. Photo by Pedro E. Guerrero, a young photographer who joined the Fellowswhip in the spring of 1940.

The party began in the Hillside living room and ended in the playhouse where dinner was served and the program presented. Somehow the three of us managed, despite my inexperience, to get the food, the dishes, the tableware, and the placemats and napkins from the Taliesin kitchen to the Hillside playhouse. And we did it in our masquerade costumes (Fig. 19). I don't know when we found time during the week to assemble costumes. Mine began with a straw Chinese coolie hat that was hanging in my room at Taliesin and was completed with a kimono of sorts which I found in the grab bag of costumes brought out of storage for the occasion.

In retrospect this week seemed to have been a test. It began at five-thirty Taliesin time on a Monday morning, reached its peak with the Halloween party, and then tapered off with a noon picnic on Sunday and dinner in the living room of the house that evening. This party was my introduction to the first of many elaborate parties held at Taliesin. In addition to the thirty-five or so members of the Fellowship there were many guests. These included former members of the Fellowship, parents of some of the apprentices, a few clients, and friends of Mr. and Mrs. Wright.

The rooms at Hillside were decorated in cornstalks and pumpkin lanterns for the occasion. There were fortune-teller's booths, haunted rooms, and specialty acts in the rooms along the upper corridor leading from the living room to the playhouse.

20   Lunch out-of-doors at Hillside near Romeo and Juliet, the windmill designed in 1896. The metal windmill was at Tanyderi, the Porters' house. Photo by author.

Later that fall I was assigned to be in the kitchen with Rowan Maiden. I do not know whether Rowan went out of his way to make that week in the kitchen unpleasant for me or not, but it seemed that he was never in the kitchen to help prepare the vegetables or scrub the accumulating piles of burnt pots and pans. He was always in the little dining room, waxing the floor or polishing the glasses. (They were spotless.) Or he was out somewhere looking for foliage or flowers to arrange for the table. Or he was contemplating the effect of the arrangement. When he was in the kitchen, with his dour nature, he was of little help to me or to my state of mind. It was a very long week with very long days.

I remember with considerable pleasure another week in the kitchen, this one with John Hill. This may not have been one week but actually several weeks during the summer of 1940. Johnnie had been with the Fellowship about three years; he had joined during the summer of 1937, after graduation from high school. The Fellowship was having breakfast and dinner at Taliesin, but lunch was served out-of-doors at Hillside (Fig. 20). I do not remember who the cook was – probably Kenn Lockhart or Grace Sciacchiatano – but we all worked together so well that things seemed to go quite quickly and easily. For example, we got a certain satisfaction out of "packing the box" with dishes, tableware, tumblers, and napkins at about eleven-thirty, taking it and the food to Hillside, serving lunch, repacking the box, and being back at Taliesin and finished with the lunch dishes and the pots and pans by one-thirty.

Until after World War II, when the kitchen at Hillside was put to use, the "hill kitchen" at Taliesin was one of the centers of Fellowship activity (see Fig. 10). It was near the rooms where apprentices lived, and they would often stop by to see what was for lunch or dinner, to get warm on cold days, to beg a cup of coffee, to check if they were on the list of people scheduled to do dishes that evening, or, if they were on their way to Spring Green, to see what supplies might be picked up. And since it was somewhat open to nearby rooms, smells of fresh-baked bread, of soup or the stockpot boiling, or of a roast in the oven, served to attract passersby.

In the fall of 1939 Svetlana Peters, Wes Peters's wife and Mrs. Wright's daughter by a previous marriage, was responsible for making dishwashing lists and assigning kitchen helpers and cooks. She also checked each cook's proposed menu for the week, checked on the supplies of staples in the storeroom, and did most of the shopping for the kitchen. The assignment of these chores and the approval of menus was done in consultation with Mrs. Wright, who guided much of the day-to-day living of the Fellowship as well as special social events. I think that Mrs. Wright, who operated somewhat behind the scenes, also decided where apprentices were to live.

Most of the apprentices had rooms by themselves. There may have been a few who shared a room. During that first fall I had only a general idea of where people lived. Much of Taliesin and Hillside was unexplored territory.

Although my exploration of Taliesin was limited, I began to realize just how inadequate the one plan that had been published in the 1938 *Architectural Forum* was as a description of the spatial richness of the place. More plans representing the different levels – and particularly sections – were necessary if one was to begin to understand how Taliesin was "of the hill" and not "on the hill."

Winter 1939

The first touch of winter had come with a light dusting of snow on the fields and hills in the week preceding the Halloween party. October had been a month of bright, brisk days and cool nights. With the arrival of cool weather, fires had been lit in the fireplaces at Taliesin and Hillside in the morning and evening. When we had gotten up in the dark to go to breakfast in the dining room, there was something quite comforting about an oak fire crackling in the fireplace.

With the arrival of colder weather the boilers were fired up, and the Fellowship members started taking weekly turns at tending the two boilers at Hillside and the three at Taliesin. The boilers were fired with long, bark-covered slabs of oak, a waste product bought from a nearby sawmill that made railway ties. A crew of apprentices went with the dump truck to pick up more slabs whenever the wood piles began to get low. In very cold weather, the boilers required replenishing about every hour during the day.

Colder weather also brought with it an anticipation of the migration to Arizona. The Fellowship brochure I had received stated that seven months of the year were spent in Wisconsin and five in Arizona. There was no mention of the migration, except that the list of recommended equipment had included a sleeping bag. I did not know much about the "adequate camp and workshop," sometimes referred to as Taliesin West or as Taliesin in the Desert, to which we would soon be heading.

It was then something of a tradition that the Fellowship stayed in Wisconsin for Thanksgiving dinner. That fall an advance party of three left Taliesin for Arizona on November 21, "to try and finish Mr. and Mrs. Wright's quarters and to do some other work around camp."[26] The main body of the migration left Wisconsin in a caravan about two weeks later, on December 7.

I gave Gene Masselink a check for $15.00 the day before our departure. This was an incidental charge to cover my part of the cost of the trip. (My application for membership in the Fellowship had been accompanied by a check for $200, a deposit toward the $1,100 tuition cost. After arriving in Wisconsin I had given Mr. Wright a check for $450, on October 9. This was half the remaining tuition cost. I paid the balance on the first of February when Mr. Wright requested it.)

The caravan consisted of a stake-body truck, a pickup truck, a station wagon, and four cars. In the caravan were "twenty three people, two dogs, one cat, and 'Lulu', Svetlana's pet macaw."

Packing the trucks had started the day before our departure and had continued late into the evening. Everything was packed including kitchen equipment, canned goods, a large plywood box containing manila paper folders with the drawings of current architectural projects, and cabinets with the files of active office correspondence. Also included were luggage, blankets, sheets, pillows, and towels for Mr. and Mrs. Wright. (Taliesin West had not yet been equipped with kitchen equipment or with bedding.) Only the sleeping bags and personal overnight luggage of the apprentices were kept aside.

Although some people worked late into the night packing the truck in the cold and under the glare of a hissing Coleman lantern, everyone was up quite early the next morning. Breakfast was served before the five o'clock departure. The plan for the trip was to take a southern route through El Paso, Texas. The intent in leaving early on this first day was to get far enough south to get out of the cold weather and to be able to camp out overnight in our sleeping bags.

The caravan stopped after dark that night at a tourist court near Excelsior Springs, Missouri. We stayed in two rooms: the girls slept in one room, the boys in another. Some slept in the beds; others in sleeping bags on the floor. The next morning breakfast was prepared in the girls' room. There was proportionately more space in their room since there were only four of them.

Food for the trip was packed in a trailer pulled by the station wagon. This trailer, with metal sides and top, was equipped with a plywood cabinet that could be pulled out of the rear door of the trailer to serve as a kitchen. Bennie Dombar had designed it and I had helped him make it in the shop at Hillside. The cabinet, about four feet wide, was divided below into storage compartments. The counter above was divided into two work areas by narrow shelves for condiments, cooking utensils, and other supplies. When pulled out, one end of the cabinet rested on the back of the trailer. The other end was supported by a leg that dropped down.

The meals had been planned and the quantities of food needed had been determined during the week before the trip. Many of the items, such as baked ham, a roast beef, sauerbraten, and stews, had also been prepared. When we stopped for an evening meal it was largely a matter of opening canned vegetables, slicing some bread, and warming the precooked food. In the morning we made coffee and cooked either pancakes or eggs and bacon on a gas-fired camp stove in the glaring light of a Coleman lantern. We huddled in the cold around our portable kitchen waiting for breakfast and anticipating the first cup of coffee, which helped to warm our hands as well as to get the taste of the night out of our mouths.

Sandwiches of sliced meat and homemade bread were made and distributed after breakfast. This eliminated the need for a midday rendezvous for lunch.

After each stop for a meal, the dishes and pans were washed and the kitchen trailer repacked. Sometimes the caravan stopped to have supper in the evening while it was still light. We then packed up and drove for a few hours before camping for the night.

Wes Peters, who was in the lead car, decided when and where we would stop for an evening meal, for the night, or to buy gas. He would bargain for the price of gas for the entire group when the caravan pulled into a filling station. This lineup of cars, many of them painted the same Cherokee red, was an object of much curiosity wherever we stopped. When we got out of the cars we were a motley lot. Many of the fellows had long hair in emulation of Mr. Wright, or because of limited budgets. Some of the girls had scarves tied over their hair to keep it from being windblown. All of us were dressed for camping out and beginning to show the effects of it. Bystanders would often ask us if we were a traveling sideshow. Some acted as if they thought we were gypsies.

The Fellowship traveled in this manner in the spring and fall of 1940 and in the spring of 1941. At these times Mr. and Mrs. Wright did not travel with the group, as they had before the fall of 1939. Beginning in the fall of 1941, the bi-annual migrations were made in smaller groups.

I rode in the station wagon the first day and with Peter and Cornelia Berndtson on the second. I do not recall with whom I rode on the next two days. On the third day we stopped in the afternoon at the Carlsbad Caverns to take a tour. On the fourth day we stopped in El Paso to go over to Juarez, Mexico, to shop. But on the fifth and last day I rode in Wes and Svet's new Ford convertible. When we were approaching the border of Arizona and the agricultural inspection station, Svetlana was concerned that Lulu might not be permitted into the state. So we stopped to figure out what we could do as well as to stretch a bit. We then proceeded with the top of the convertible down, with Gene driving and Kay Cuneo and Jan Zeeman sitting in front beside him. Svet and I were in the backseat. We had a lap robe over our legs, ostensibly to keep us warm but actually to conceal Lulu and the leather gloves that we were wearing to keep her from biting us as we held her between our legs. Fortunately, she remained quiet. And we went through the inspection station with no questions about Lulu's right of entry.

In the late afternoon we rendezvoused in Scottsdale at Jim Frederick's gas station to assemble the caravan for the fourteen-mile drive out to camp, where we arrived just at dusk. When driving north along Scottsdale Road we could see the camp as a white fleck against the mountains in the distance. It became a bit more visible as we turned off and drove east along Shea Boulevard, a misnamed and bumpy desert road crossed by the dips of frequent washes. For me, the excitement of this first arrival began to increase as we turned off at a directional marker incorporating the Fellowship symbol, two interlocked square spirals, and onto the road heading straight north. Although I had no clear idea of what I was looking for, I was told that I should be able to see it up on the rise and a bit to the right of the road. It was about a mile and a half away. I could see a few spots of light against the darkening silhouette of the mountains. As we came closer I began to see rectangular areas of white which, apparently, were the open canvas flaps of the drafting room, lighted from within. When the road began to wind through the desert the drivers began to honk the car horns to announce our arrival.

With much eagerness and enthusiasm we pulled into the graveled area near the entrance to the camp. Blaine and Hulda Drake and Bob Mosher, who had spent the summer there as caretakers, had come out to greet us. The fellows who had preceded us as an advance party were also there waiting. While exchanging greetings we learned that Mr. and Mrs. Wright had arrived in Phoenix that afternoon by train. They were in camp, but being tired from travel, they had had their dinner and retired early.

For us newcomers to the Fellowship and the camp the place was mysterious and unknown. And in the darkness it was frustrating to explore. Having been told of the prickly nature of the cactus and the rocky roughness of the ground, we did not dare to venture out into the desert even with a flashlight. So after a short and tentative exploration of what we could see, most of us wondered where we were going to roll out our sleeping bags for the night. Some of us finally settled on the concrete-paved terrace to the east of the triangular pool south of the drafting room.

Sleep did not come quickly. And when it did, it was intermittent. The strangeness of the situation, the hardness of the concrete slab, the vast and deep brilliance of the star-filled desert sky so near and yet so far away, and the yipping and howling of a pack of coyotes somewhere nearby made it difficult to sleep.

Taliesin West

It was still dark and the coyotes were still yipping when those of us who had spent the night trying to sleep on the concrete terrace were up and about, getting dressed and crawling out of our sleeping bags. We had begun to stir when the generator was started and lights had come on in the drafting room and the kitchen area nearby. The sound of activity in the kitchen attracted us there long before the first breakfast bell sounded. Since there were no bath facilities, those of us who were new to the camp were wondering where we might get some water to at least wash our faces. We were directed to a hose spigot outside.

After we had finished breakfast, Mr. Wright led a group of us on a tour of the camp, explaining what had been done, pointing out what needed doing, and indicating what he planned to do (Fig. 21). I had previously learned that construc-

21   Mr. Wright and a group of apprentices toured the camp after breakfast. Mr. Wright pointed out what had been accomplished in the previous year and what he hoped to accomplish in this one. The group from left to right: Gordon Ingraham, Fred Benedict, Jack Howe, Mr. Wright, Victor Cusack, Gordon Chadwick, Gene Masselink. Photo by Jan Zeeman.

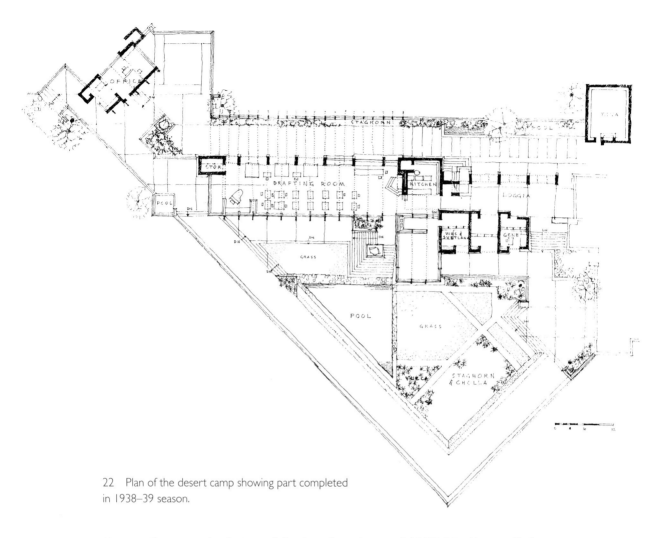

22 Plan of the desert camp showing part completed
in 1938–39 season.

tion on the camp had started during the winter of 1937–38. About all that was
accomplished that season was the clearing of a road up to the site. Actual construction on the buildings of the complex started the following winter, 1938–39.
The camp at which we arrived consisted of "the office," the drafting room (Figs.
22, 23, 24, 25, 26), the kitchen and its storeroom, rooms in which Gene and Wes
and Svetlana were to live, and the "small theater," which Mr. Wright referred to
as "the Kiva." The small theater had been one of the last construction projects in
the spring of 1939.

Taliesin West, as originally conceived, appeared to have been the ultimate realization of two seemingly opposed objectives in much of Mr. Wright's work: the
massive masonry and wood elements – which Mr. Wright often said "would make
a marvelous ruin" – sought strength, security, and permanence, shelter as something maximum and cavelike, something that would offer protection from nature.

23 Entrance to camp at end of 1938–39 season. Mr. Wright's office is at left. Drafting room is at center. Mr. Wright's Cord is at the right. Photo courtesy of John H. Howe.

24 The drafting room seen from the northwest. Photo courtesy of John H. Howe.

25   South side of the drafting room. Future dining room is at right. Photo courtesy of John H. Howe.

26   Completed portion of camp seen from the southeast. Drafting room is at left. Future dining room is at center. Upper part of kitchen and bell tower is visible over rooms of Wes and Svetlana at right. Photo courtesy of John H. Howe.

The light canvas elements, the flaps, represented the search for the ephemeral and insubstantial, shelter as minimum enclosure, being in nature, space and light shaped with a minimal membrane.

The design of the camp was based in part on Mr. Wright's previous experience of living in the desert, at the Ocatillo camp built near Chandler, Arizona. The canvas-covered flaps were conceived primarily as sunshades and as light diffusers and controllers. Mr. Wright, irritated by the weather, once commented that if he had known what winter could really be like, the design of the camp and its orientation would have been different.

But the design was also based on certain characteristics inherent in the site itself. Mr. Wright stated that "the desert line is the dotted line." He didn't trouble to explain what he meant by that statement. I assumed that he was referring to the contrast between the jagged, prickly profiles of the cactus and rocky desert landscape, and the soft, smooth profiles of the grass-covered Wisconsin hills; and that the points formed by the wood trusses in the camp's profile and the rough texture of the concrete walls and the square wooden dentils along the edges of some members were the "dotted line."

There were other ways in which the landscape was integrated into the camp. One of these I did not appreciate at first, but as I lived, worked, and moved about in the camp over the years it became a source of much pleasure. This was the way in which all paths of movement within the camp seemed to be consciously directed toward, to focus upon, and to reach out and "pull into the camp," major features of the much larger landscape. Few views, as such, were terminated within the limits of the camp walls. They terminated at mountains interrupting the horizon or lying upon it, mountains which were near, in the middle distance, and those many miles away.

There was another feature in the design of the camp which, after I had discovered it, intrigued me very much. It became a kind of game to discover other manifestations of it. It was a feature which I thought of as "the hook." Large rocks found near the camp had been brought into the camp and placed as sculptural features. On them were pictographs made by "prehistoric campers" in the area. Among these was a pictograph of an interlock of two right-angled spirals forming a square (Fig. 27). This interlock, combined with a red square, had been translated into the "mark" of the Fellowship. It appeared on the stationery and all printed matter relating to the Fellowship, as directional signposts along the road to the camp from Scottsdale, and at the entrance to the camp. It also appeared in other forms in the construction of the camp itself.

The wood "trusses" (they were not trusses although we did call them that!) supporting the canvas panels of the roof of the studio/office, drafting room, and living room, formed a "hook" at their lower end where they terminated in two right-angle turns and came back to penetrate the concrete walls on which they were supported. This suggested an interlock with the masonry. Many of the walls

27 Rock with pictograph. The interlocking, square spiral which is on a rock found near the campsite was the basis for the development of the Fellowship's mark or sign.

terminated in a "hook." Low walls were turned back at the ends to shape a space around a saguaro, a palo verde tree, or a cluster of lower plants. High walls defining a space for human presence and activity all formed an interlock with the vastness of the desert space.

The camp, as experienced that winter, was elemental, barbaric, and rude – a "rough charcoal sketch for a building" as Mr. Wright jokingly referred to it. For me, it was a completely new experience; it was like no other kind of building I had ever seen. And, as I soon learned, it was also an experiment, an experiment using a textile as a major architectural element. I wrote Professor Beal that "Life in the desert isn't an easy one. But so far the weather has been swell. I'm glad it hasn't rained because they tell me there isn't a spot in the building that doesn't leak except the kitchen. But we've done considerable work on the roof – and it really hasn't had another test since."[27]

On sunny days, when the "flaps" were opened to catch the sun and breeze, the drafting room became a very open, outdoorlike place, a splendid, radiant, light-saturated area. But on those few days when it rained, it was miserable – shut in, gray, and wet. There were pools of water all over the place. Water came through and around the sides of the flaps, dripping from pools of water within the flaps.

When first put in place the flaps consisted of a wooden frame about one-by-three inches in section, over which was slipped a canvas cover. The cover was a machine-sewn envelope, closed on three sides but open on the fourth, to slip over the wooden frame. The open end was then folded and tacked to close it. The result was, in effect, a thin, translucent, white plane. Clearly Mr. Wright had not done any camping in the rain in a tent. Nor, apparently, had it rained very much during the winter that Mr. Wright and his family and staff had lived in the Ocatillo camp. He was embarrassed, frustrated, and much annoyed by the behavior of the canvas in the rain. The elements seemed to be working against the realization of a beautiful vision. Although he accepted nature's "challenge" and continued to struggle against it, it was evident that different detailing or some material other than coarse white canvas was required to realize the concept of a textile architecture.

Over time many experiments were done to solve this problem. The flaps were covered with a single layer of canvas rather than the double layer. The canvas was wrapped around the frames to conceal the wood and tacked on the inside. The rows of tacks were covered with a 1½"-by-½" wooden strip. This eliminated the pools of water within the flaps, but water still soaked through at the edges. The flaps were painted with a clear and colorless liquid that was supposed to make them waterproof. This was not successful. The waterproofing seemed to be leached out by the brilliant sun and lose its effectiveness. Other waterproofing liquids were rejected; they would have discolored the white canvas.

Eventually, with further trials and errors, the amount of water that came through was reduced in volume and limited to a few places where we would simply put buckets when it began to rain.

When we arrived in the winter of 1939–40 plumbing facilities were minimal. There was a generator for electricity, a large butane tank out in the shop area, a deep well located on the southern slope below the camp, and an electric pump and pressure tank near the well. Hot and cold running water was available only in the kitchen. Cold water was available from several hose taps about the camp. The waste water from the kitchen drained into a draw to the southeast of the camp.

If you wanted to bathe during the week, and one did after a strenuous day of moving cactus or placing the concrete and rubble for the masonry walls of the camp, you took your turn standing beneath the end of a hose thrown over a wall. The place had some privacy, since it was not within view of the camp. We did have a few flat stones or boards to stand on so that we didn't have to stand in the mud. If you got there first, the water was still warm from standing in the hose during the afternoon; if not, you hoped that there was still enough warmth in the air to lessen the "exhilaration" of a cold shower.

Toilet facilities at the camp were canvas-enclosed privies over holes dug in the ground. There were separate privies for men and women. These were the responsibility of Bob Goss. Bob was a sailor who had arrived at Taliesin in the summer of 1938 after having read the article about the Fellowship in *Coronet* magazine.

Bob was not interested in becoming an architect. He wrote poems, took his turn as kitchen helper, and sang a resonant, full-chested bass in the chorus. He was sturdy and muscular. And he seemed, most of all, to enjoy and take great pride in his latrine responsibility. During the day you could very often hear the clink of a pickax or a shovel striking the concretelike caliche accompanied by the sound of a hearty voice singing away, and you knew it was Bob digging a hole for a new latrine. The story was that Mr. Wright, who had a real affection for Bob, liked to have him with the Fellowship because he had eyes – or was it a voice? – just like Louis Sullivan.

When we arrived in Arizona those apprentices who had occupied and worked on tent sites the previous year reoccupied them. The newcomers had to find un-occupied sites and time to do whatever construction might be necessary to put up the nine-by-nine "sheep herder" tent – Mr. Wright's concession to providing shelter for the apprentices. It was – and is – my interpretation that the provision of only a "sheep herder" was quite intentional, not only as an economy but as a fundamental architectural test to see which apprentices could get themselves in out of the weather. There were some apprentices who never managed it, some who never managed it very well, and others who with ingenuity and imagination lived with considerable style and comfort (Fig. 28). I never did manage to live in style or comfort in a sheep herder.

I had been in camp several weeks before I found a tent site and was given a tent. I shared a tent that first winter with Kenn Lockhart. We selected a site at the top of a slope near a palo verde tree and started construction with only a vague idea of what we might eventually build. We made a floor of thin flat stones in a random pattern and grouted it with cement, and put up a pyramidal frame of two-by-twos to support the tent about two feet above the ground. This would give us some head room inside. Around the frame, at the bottom edge of the tent, we put a wide redwood board to which to fasten the tent. Beneath this we started a wall of stones, standing on edge, to fill in the space between the floor and the redwood board. We were about half finished when Mr. Wright held a meeting of the Fellowship to let us know his feelings about all the energy and materials that were going into construction on tent sites while his own living quarters were moving too slowly toward completion. At that point construction on apprentice tent sites slowed or even came to a halt, particularly on those tents that were easily visible from the camp itself. Kenn and I did no more work on our tent.

I occupied our site the following winter by myself, but I did no more work on construction. It was not occupied in the following years; Mr. Wright decided that apprentice tents were not to be put on sites that were visible from the road up to the camp. He did not like to see those scattered spots of white above the profile of the camp itself.

By the end of the first week in camp there was talk about and anticipation of "Town Day" on Saturday. Town Day had been generated the previous year by the lack of bathing facilities in camp. On Town Day you could get a bath, shop, and perhaps go to a movie. (There was, as yet, no place in camp to show movies.)

I soon learned that on Town Day those who didn't own a car would make arrangements in the morning for a ride to town. We were free to leave for town after lunch. The first stop in Scottsdale was Jim Frederick's gas station, where checks could be cashed. Jim seemed to be the Fellowship's banker. Upon arriving in Phoenix after the dusty ride across the desert, the men went directly to

28   Apprentice tents. Gordon Ingraham and Bob May connected their tents with an "outdoor living space," complete with a stone fireplace. Their tents were primarily used for storage and as a place to sleep in inclement weather. Photo courtesy of Robert C. May.

the Y.M.C.A. There, for a small charge, we could enjoy the luxury of a hot shower, a brief swim in the pool, and a fresh, clean towel. I don't know how the females managed; perhaps there was a Y.W.C.A.

There were very interesting shops in Phoenix that handled Indian arts and crafts – baskets, blankets, pottery, beaded work, and silver and turquoise jewelry – and also Porter's and Goldwater's, which had western wear; they were outfitters for cowboys and ranchers. You might also go out to the Heard Museum to see its collection of Indian arts and crafts.

At that time the name of the desert complex had not been determined; sometimes we called it Taliesin West and sometimes Taliesin in the Desert; most often we simply referred to it as "the camp." When we went into Phoenix, we spoke of going "back to camp." When we were in Wisconsin, we spoke of "the desert camp" or "the camp," and not of Taliesin West. Our use of the word "camp" indicated something about Mr. Wright's concept of it and of the kind of life that was lived in it.

The Suntrap

Mr. and Mrs. Wright shared the camping experience with the Fellowship the first part of the winter. Their quarters were far from finished when they arrived in the desert. The advance party had accomplished very little of what Mr. Wright had anticipated. So Mr. and Mrs. Wright and Iovanna lived in the Suntrap, which had been built the previous year.

The Suntrap was constructed of a single-board wall of shiplap and of canvas (Figs. 29, 30, 31). It consisted of three sleeping boxes, one each for Mr. and Mrs. Wright and Iovanna, arranged on three sides of a square, concrete-paved courtyard. The open side of the courtyard faced to the south, away from the mountains and toward the desert. The sleeping boxes were long enough for a mattress (with a little space at one end to hang clothing), wide enough for a person to stand alongside the mattress and dress, and high enough, on the high side, for a person to stand. A terrace on the south side of the courtyard was enclosed with a chest-high wall and served as a kind of outdoor sitting room. The "bathroom" was also enclosed with a chest-high wall; it contained a chemical toilet, wooden shelves for a tin washbasin and an olla (a container for water), and an oleander bush. Herb Fritz was the "house boy" for the Suntrap that winter. Shortly after Mr. and Mrs. Wright's arrival in the desert, a thin, flat, stepped roof was built over the square courtyard, connecting the sleeping boxes. Still later in the winter, a small and cozy sitting room with a fireplace at its far end was built at the northeast of the courtyard. It extended diagonally from it.

Any overnight guests also camped out. They stayed in "guest tents," which were put up to the east of the camp in a shallow wash. Their sites were selected so that they were tucked in among palo verde or ironwood trees, secluded and shaded. A path, cleared of rocks and cactus and covered with coarse sand from the washes, led to the tent sites. Each tent had a small cleared and sand-covered area in front of it where one could sit outside. The guests slept on air mattresses supported on wooden platforms. These had brightly colored canvas covers. With a few brightly colored cushions here and there and a few Indian blankets spread about they had a rather sybaritic air. Perhaps they were not too comfortable physically but they had great style visually.

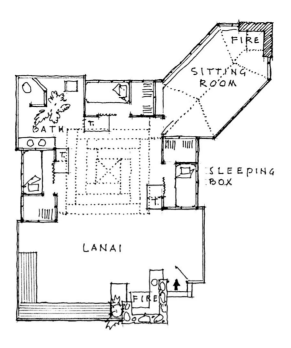

29   Plan of Suntrap, the family's living quarters during the first part of the winter. Suntrap began the previous winter as three sleeping boxes placed on three sides of a square open space.

30   Suntrap seen from the southeast after the entrance was relocated to the southwest corner of the lanai and the sitting room was enlarged and extended diagonally to a fireplace built at the northeast corner. Photo courtesy of John H. Howe.

31   View of covered outdoor space and west sleeping box. Opening at right of center is to the "bathroom." Photo courtesy of John H. Howe.

For decorating our tents (or, if we were lucky, our rooms), our favorite items were things made by the Indians of the southwest. The acquisition of these items was made easy not only by the many shops in Phoenix which sold Indian handicrafts, but by the visits to camp of Elmer Shupe, the Indian trader (Fig. 32). His visits had the festive air of a market. When he arrived at the camp he would open the rear doors of his panel-body truck and proceed to take out his wares and to spread them on the terrace and steps between Mr. Wright's office and the drafting room. It was not long before a group would gather to see his rich collection of baskets, blankets, santos, and pawn jewelry made of turquoise and silver. He had an easy familiarity with members of the group, including Mr. and Mrs. Wright, whom he knew and who had bought things from him on previous visits. His annual visits came to an end with gas rationing during World War Two.

The Fellowship had many guests that winter: friends of Mr. and Mrs. Wright and parents of some apprentices. Some came only for tea, others to visit for several days. One group that came to tea consisted of Clarence Buddington Kelland, a Mr. Hopkins, the president of Dartmouth, and Gene Buck. The Fellowship anticipated hearing "Bud" Kelland's conversation with Mr. Wright, but the entire conversation was dominated by Gene Buck with the story of his struggles with the broadcasting chains.[28] As he informed us, Buck was president of the American Society of Composers, Authors, and Publishers, and had written some thirty-two musical shows.

32   Visit to camp by Indian trader. Elmer Shupe, the trader, is standing at center, back to camera. Hulda Drake is seated before him. Svetlana Peters is at left foreground. Behind her are Gene Masselink and Kenn Lockhart. Wes Peters is standing, back to camera. Ellis Jacob is perched on top of wall. At right of trader, in white hat, is Mrs. Wright. The Pauson sisters, Gertrude and Rose, are seated at her right. I am leaning against the low wall and talking to Gordon Chadwick and Edgar Tafel at right. Photo courtesy of Robert C. May.

The guest who made the most vivid impression that winter was Marc Connelly who visited the camp for several days in mid-March in the company of Mr. and Mrs. Lloyd Lewis, friends and clients. Lloyd Lewis was a writer as well as sports and drama editor for the *Chicago Tribune.* He and his wife had come to discuss the plans for their new house.

Mr. Wright enjoyed Connelly's and Lewis's company immensely. They sat long after lunch on the terrace, deep in conversation, a colored napkin shielding Connelly's bald head from the sun. Connelly, best known as the author of the play *The Green Pastures,* was a delightful storyteller. One afternoon at tea he read a new play that he was writing to the Fellowship.

Life in camp that winter was lived almost entirely in the open by everyone. The Fellowship had its meals at long tables on the terrace south of the drafting room. It was pleasant to relax in the sun at midday. There were a few times during the winter – days when Mrs. Wright had gone to Phoenix and had not returned by lunchtime – when Mr. Wright had lunch with the Fellowship. These were times when I felt that he was closer to the members of the Fellowship, not so distant. These were times when he did not talk to the Fellowship, but relaxed and chatted with those at the table where he happened to be seated.

Supper in the evening with the sun setting behind Camelback Mountain across the desert was delightful. The early evening chill was dispelled by the accumulated warmth being radiated from the concrete and stone surfaces. But breakfast at six-thirty Taliesin time, five-thirty regular time, was grim, particularly when it was still cold and dark. It was even grimmer for the kitchen helpers and the cook who had to extract themselves from their sleeping bags and get dressed an hour or more before breakfast, find their ways to the camp on paths that led through the cactus and over the rocks which, even with a flashlight or moonlight, were barely visible and get the sometimes uncooperative generator started.

There were no electric lights on the terrace. And the harsh glare of Coleman lanterns, hissing away during breakfast, added no warmth or cheer. The apprentices arrived for breakfast, aroused out of their sleeping bags by the first breakfast bell at six-fifteen. They were bundled in jackets and sweaters which would be discarded later with the sun's first warmth. I was assigned to be a kitchen helper several times during this winter.[29] The kitchen at the camp was, like the "hill kitchen" at Taliesin, a center of Fellowship activity (Fig. 33). Planned after the Fellowship had been in operation for about six years, it seemed to have been located to further this characteristic. It was near the center of the camp rather than on the periphery where the delivery of supplies and the removal of garbage would have been easier and more convenient. It was open on one side to a frequently traveled circulation route. Mr. Wright would often pass by, stop to chat, or savor the activity. Apprentices went by to check the dishwashing list or just to see what might be cooking for lunch or dinner.

Mr. and Mrs. Wright had their breakfast at one end of a long table, near the fireplace, at the east end of the drafting room. A large fire helped dispel the gloom and cold, but they too arrived for breakfast bundled in warm clothing. When Mr. and Mrs. Wright's quarters were finished that winter, they continued – unless there were guests – to have breakfast at the long table. When there were guests they had breakfast with them later in the morning on the terrace west of the Garden Room, after the sun had begun to warm that area. They often had lunch there also. Mr. Wright had designed – and had made – moveable, folding wind screens that could be positioned to enable a person to be in the sun and out of the wind.

33　The kitchen in the camp is at its center and open to persons passing by. The cook, in this photo, is Kenn Lockhart. Photo by Pedro E. Guerrero.

The drafting room was then what would now be called a multipurpose space. It was one of the few places where one could be warm and dry. In addition to being a drafting room, it was Mr. and Mrs. Wright's dining room, a lounge for the Fellowship, a sleeping place for some apprentices who rolled out their sleeping bags on a long bench near the table, and a rehearsal place for the chorus. The only piano in the camp was a grand at the west end of the room. Lacking any other place to eat except the terrace outside, the Fellowship had some of its meals together at that table in the drafting room. Three meals in particular stand out: a Christmas dinner, an Easter breakfast, and a dinner with Lawrence Tibbett and his wife, and Maynard Hutchins, President of the University of Chicago, and his wife and daughter, as the principal guests. At Christmas the table was covered with bright red cloths and lighted with candles placed among great heaps of fruit. At Easter the table was laden with baba, paschal cheese, and heaps of brightly colored, hard-boiled eggs. Tibbett was nearing the end of his singing career. I assume that he sang following dinner, because he complained that his musical instrument was one swilled with liquor and food. These were all occasions of abundance, occasions that were heightened by contrast with the otherwise Spartan rigors of camp life, the absence of soft beds, heated rooms, hot water, and bathing facilities. They were simply an explanation of Mr. Wright's statement that given a choice between necessities and luxuries, he would choose luxuries.

I sat near the drafting room fireplace to make my drawing for the 1939 Christmas Box. Shortly before Christmas I was told that twice a year – at Christmas and on Mr. Wright's birthday – all of the apprentices made drawings which were put in a box and presented to Mr. and Mrs. Wright, and that I should "do something for the box." Bob Goss put in some of his poems. Not knowing what I might do and being intrigued with the "abstractions" I had seen, I thought I would try to make one. I chose the desert landscape as a subject and then proceeded to make a geometric representation of it in watercolor on watercolor paper. Mr. Wright did not make a "memorable" comment on the drawing at the time the box was opened on Christmas morning, when Mr. and Mrs. Wright, with all apprentices looking on, went through the box.

I spent part of that winter moving cactus with a crew headed by Fred Benedict. At that time Mr. Wright insisted on using only native growth as planting in and adjacent to the camp. We were moving prickly pear, staghorn, and cholla to heal over some areas south of the triangular garden, where construction activity had scarred the desert, and into planting areas in the triangular garden where flowering plants had been planted the previous year. Being on the cactus moving crew provided a pleasant excursion, a chance to explore the nearby desert. Handling the cactus, particularly the cholla, could be painful. At first I wore leather gloves thinking that these would protect me from the thorns. But I soon discovered that these gave a false sense of safety; they only made extracting the thorns more difficult. I soon learned why some cactus were called jumping cholla. Segments of them seemed to jump at you and imbed their thorns in you. The fishhooklike barbs went in very easily. They came out quite painfully, if they didn't break off beneath the skin.

Construction of Mr. and Mrs. Wright's Quarters

The major project of the winter was the construction of Mr. and Mrs. Wright's quarters. Mr. Wright had sent the advance party to the desert with the idea that they could complete these quarters before the Fellowship arrived in the desert. He always underestimated the time required for construction. Construction started the previous year was resumed with "pouring" the "desert concrete" walls and other masonry elements of Mr. and Mrs. Wright's wing. It began with the high walls and the fireplaces of the loggia and the cove which make up a massive pivotal element in the camp. This mass was to contain a girl's bath, a bathroom for Mr. and Mrs. Wright, and a small buffet kitchen. A guest room was built in the upper part of this element later, and the lower level was revised to include the bathroom for the women in the Fellowship as well as a bath and a more complete kitchen for Mr. and Mrs. Wright's quarters (Figs. 34, 35, 36, 37).

The "desert concrete" of which these mass elements were constructed was, strictly speaking, neither concrete nor masonry. Nor was it poured. "Desert concrete" was a way of building with the abundance of rock readily available at the site. This rock was very hard, brittle, and difficult – if not impossible – to work with the usual masonry tools. In using it we grouped it into two kinds: "face rock" and "rubble."

"Face rocks" were the stones, selected for their shape, size, and color, which were to be placed in the forms so that their "faces" would be exposed when the forms were removed. Ideally they were nearly flat and not too thick; they could vary in size and shape. The only limit on size was getting them into the forms. They were rocks that appeared to have split off from larger formations and to have acquired a patina of color ranging from black to a rust red.

The "rubble" was a similar kind of stone, but its shape and color were not important. It was used only to fill the center of the wall and to hold the face rocks in place until the relatively dry mix of coarse sand and cement could be shoveled into the forms and poked and tamped into the interstices between the stones. The walls and piers were placed directly on the ground without footings. The site on which the camp was built was a talus slope, consisting of fractured rock which, with time, had acquired enough dirt in the crevices to support some plant growth. In places it had bonded into a concretelike caliche. To start a wall, we simply

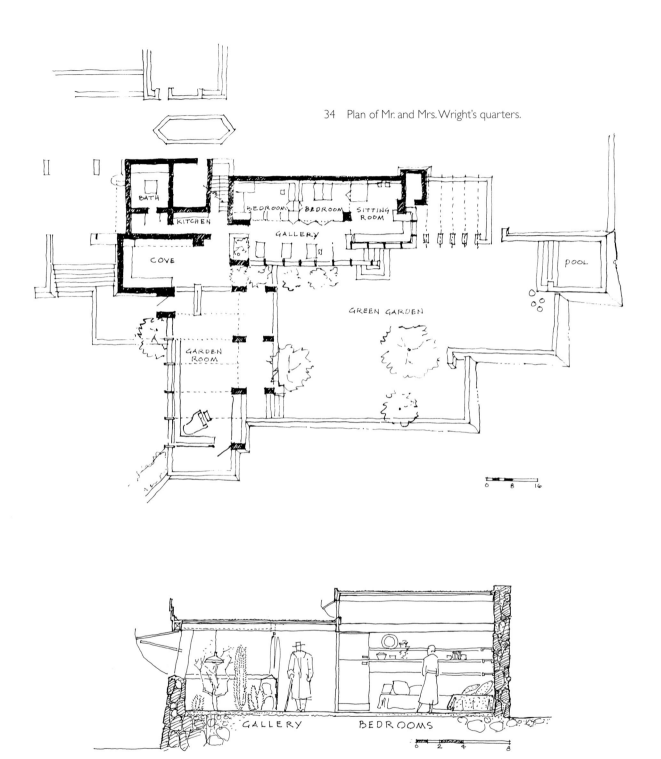

34 Plan of Mr. and Mrs. Wright's quarters.

BATH

KITCHEN

COVE

BEDROOM   BEDROOM   SITTING ROOM

GALLERY

GARDEN ROOM

GREEN GARDEN

POOL

0   8   16

35 Section through the bedroom wing.

GALLERY   BEDROOMS

0   2   4   8

36 View of gallery from west end and looking toward door open to sitting room. Photo courtesy of John H. Howe.

37 View of Green Garden from Garden Room, the living room. Mr. Wright is standing near small pool in center of photo. Photo courtesy of John H. Howe.

cleared away any growth, and brushed away the loose dirt. One side of the form for a wall would be framed and braced in place and, perhaps, sheathed with one-by-eight shiplap sheathing to its full height. The other side would be framed and braced in place but sheathed only high enough to receive the first face stones, their backing of rubble and the filling of the spaces between with concrete.

The pouring of these walls and fireplaces was organized by Wes as a race between the "form builders" and the "pourers." It was a race that involved all of the Fellowship except those assigned to the kitchen and the laundry. The objective in the race was for the pourers to fill the forms faster than the form builders could build them. Or for the form builders, given a head start, to build forms faster than the pourers could fill them. The pourers groups consisted of several subgroups: those who went with the dump truck to the washes to get the coarse sand for the concrete; those who went out with the flatbed truck to gather face rock and rubble; those who ran the wheelbarrows to haul the concrete and stone up the ramps for placing in the form; those who placed the stone and concrete in the forms; and the person running the concrete mixer.

I don't know who won this particular race. It was only one of many such races, which were won on several occasions by the pourers when the form builders had used up all of the available lumber and could not yet strip the forms from the walls in order to build more forms. It was a tradition that the losers treated the winners to a steak dinner at a restaurant in Phoenix on the next Town Day.

I often wondered – and still do – that these pouring races didn't result in serious accidents and injuries. Scaffolding or formwork could have collapsed. Wheelbarrows filled with concrete, stones, or rubble were pushed up the ramps and onto platforms supported by scaffolding. Sometimes these were fifteen feet or more above the ground. On the lower lifts of the ramp it was possible to get enough of a running head start with the wheelbarrow to push it to the top. But on the higher lifts it took a "puller" as well as a "pusher" to make it to the top. A few loads of concrete or stone were spilled when someone slipped on the ramp or lost his balance. But luck seemed to be with us.

I worked with the pourers, sometimes running a wheelbarrow, sometimes placing stones in the forms. Placing stones in the wall was accompanied with the possibility that a large rock might be dropped on one's foot or that one's leg might be caught between a large stone and the form. It did happen. But it also meant that one got a certain satisfaction out of a wall which, when stripped, revealed a pleasing pattern and texture. Placing the "face rocks" was an artless art. One tried to achieve a satisfactory proportion between concrete and stone areas, between large and small stones, in colors of stones, and in the directional characteristics of the stones. One sought to achieve a random "no-mindedness," as though it had been done without giving it any thought. Some apprentices, in placing stones, achieved a wall surface that was too self-conscious, too "arty"; others a wall that reflected little awareness of relationships in its "no-mindedness." We were critical of the results of our efforts after the walls had been stripped of forms. Sometimes, to keep the concrete off the surface of a particularly choice "face rock," we would place a kind of necklace of pebbles around it. These pebbles came from the washes. Sometimes we used crumpled-up newspapers to do this. And, after the forms were removed, we might take a hammer and knock away concrete from the face of rocks to expose more of the surface.

Work started on the canvas and wood elements of Mr. and Mrs. Wright's quarters before all of the masonry walls enclosing their private garden were completed. It was during this phase of construction that I became aware that there were no working drawings for the camp. There was a perspective drawing, a bird's-eye view from the southwest, which was on display in the drafting room. In the vault at the west end of the drafting room there was a plan drawn on brown wrapping paper. Also on wrapping paper were cross sections of the office and drafting room and some larger scale sections of the wood trusses of the office and drafting room. But there were none of the kinds of drawing on tracing paper which, based on my previous experiences in an office, I would have expected to find.

Details were worked out as construction proceeded. In some instances, such as the "trusses" for the canvas superstructure of the garden room, the details had already been established in the construction of the office and the drafting room. But in other instances the apprentices either received instructions from Mr. Wright, perhaps a quick drawing on a piece of board explaining how he wanted it done, or, if this was not satisfactory, were asked to make some drawings for him to work on. These drawings, also done on wrapping paper, generally consisted of a plan and section, setting down the construction already in place and any other givens. These would include, of course, the relation of that portion of the work being built to the unit system of the camp.

In making these drawings, an experienced apprentice might make a proposal indicating how the work could be done, based on his understanding of what had preceded it. Mr. Wright might accept this proposal, he might make a few changes, or he might reject it and use the drawing only as a basis for his own study. Some of these drawings were very much worked over, erased, and re-erased before a satisfactory solution to a particular problem was achieved.

But even when construction was in place – or being put in place – there was no guarantee that Mr. Wright would not make changes. One day, when working on the completion of the bedroom-wing ceiling, I was nailing "cheek" pieces on the beams supporting the roof deck. Mr. Wright was there directing the work and asked me not to set the finish nails that I had driven to hold the cheeks saying, "We may want to change it."

That winter the portion of the camp completed for Mr. and Mrs. Wright's use included the Garden Room (see Fig. 68), the fireplace cove, and the bedroom wing which extends east from the cove. The bedroom wing contained a row of two small bedrooms for Mr. and Mrs. Wright and Iovanna and a sitting room at the east end in which Mr. Wright slept. The bedrooms were along an enclosed gallery on the south side. They opened into this with canvas-covered doors. In section, the ceiling of the bedrooms was higher than the ceiling of the gallery. This difference in height made possible a clerestory above the wall between the bedrooms and the gallery. There were canvas-covered panels in the clerestory openings which could be opened for light and ventilation. When these panels were closed the bedrooms were rather dark and unpleasant, even on sunny days. Mrs. Wright's bedroom, at the west end, had a small fireplace.

The sitting room at the east end of the gallery had a fireplace as well as a bathroom in the masonry mass behind it which terminated the east wing. The sitting room was also used as a dressing room, as a dining room in cold weather, and as Mr. Wright's study where he could write and see to his own correspondence.

With an evolving pattern of use, much continued to be changed, and only the overall configuration remained constant. In thinking about this process of change in both Taliesin and Taliesin West – and about the few great cities of the world that are admired as positive environments in which to live – I have become convinced that satisfactory living places cannot be designed and built in one operation. They result only from incremental growth and change over time.

The Los Angeles Trip

Early in February 1940, when most of the pouring of the concrete floors and desert concrete walls for Mr. and Mrs. Wright's quarters had been completed, Mr. Wright announced at tea that the Fellowship deserved a reward for – and a respite from – its long hours of hard work. We had often not stopped work at teatime but had continued working until dinner. He told us that we were going on a trip to Los Angeles.[30]

This trip, as it turned out, was an extended overnight picnic. During the early part of the winter we had had Sunday midday picnics (Fig. 38) at scenic spots in the desert, including the site of the no-longer existent Ocatilla camp near Chandler. We had also gone farther afield on overnight picnics to Cave Creek and Superstition Mountain. For these we had also taken supplies for breakfast as well as a picnic supper. On the day of our departure for Los Angeles, we loaded our sleeping bags and overnight bags into the back of the stake truck. Food for four days was packed in a trailer behind the station wagon. A few people rode in the station wagon, but most of us rode in the back of the truck. We camped that night at Andreas Canyon near Palm Springs. It was a spectacular site with great rocks thrusting into the air at dramatic angles. After supper we built a camp fire at the base of one of these large upthrusts. It was a brilliant desert night. The firelight against the rocks made it seem like a setting for some pagan ritual. In this setting the chorus gathered around the fire and sang all of the songs that it knew.

We got up with daybreak and after breakfast drove over to Palm Canyon where we spent an hour exploring that seemingly enchanted setting, wading in the ice-cold stream until our feet were numb. We ate a picnic lunch there and then drove into Los Angeles arriving early in the afternoon. We spent the afternoon at John Lautner's new house. Later in the day we went to the Sturges house, in Brentwood Heights, and had our supper there out of the supplies in the trailer (see Fig. 38). We stayed at the Sturges house that night. This house, designed by Mr. Wright, had just been completed. Some slept on the flat roof in their sleeping bags, others on the large exterior terrace balcony.

The next morning Mr. Wright joined us. He had been driven to Los Angeles by Herb Fritz in his Cherokee-red Lincoln Continental convertible. Mr. Wright

38   Sunday overnight picnic, the portable kitchen in use. Left to right: unknown, Herbert Fritz, Fred Benedict, Grace Sciacchiatano, unknown, Wes Peters, Hulda Drake. Photo courtesy of Robert C. May.

had bought two Lincoln Continentals early in the fall of 1939, a convertible for himself, and a cabriolet for Mrs. Wright. He guided us around the city to see most of the buildings he had designed: the Storrer house and some of the cottages on Olive Hill (exterior only), and the Freeman house with its furniture designed by Rudolph Schindler. The Freemans were living there at that time. The Ennis and Barnsdahl houses were unoccupied but we somehow managed to get in and see their interiors. Mr. Wright was unhappy with the interior of the Ennis house; it had not been finished in accord with his intentions. The Ennises had put in marble floors, wood-paneled ceilings, and Mayanesque wrought-iron light fixtures and grillwork that he had not approved.

The Millard house was also unoccupied and locked, but we got inside this one also. While we were there the new owner happened to show up. She was delighted to meet Mr. Wright. She had just come back from Paris and had with her a large black poodle who understood only French. Recovering slightly from her surprise at seeing Mr. Wright, she proceeded to tell him how she was going to do the interiors. She thought that the house was rather "Renaissance" in character but she was going to do it "Baroque." Mr. Wright tried briefly to set her "Wright."

Late in the afternoon, we separated from Mr. Wright and drove south out of Los Angeles along the ocean. We were looking for a place to stop for a picnic supper on the beach and to camp for the night. As it grew darker and colder, several bottles of wine circulated in the back of the truck. It was quite dark by the time we decided upon a place to camp. The wine had taken effect, and getting supper prepared and eaten was a disorganized affair. The next morning, after breakfast and a wade in the surf, we went to see the Mission of San Juan Capistrano and took a boat ride in the Harbor at San Diego. Late the next afternoon we started the all-night ride back to camp by way of Yuma and Gila Bend, and we arrived just when light was beginning to appear in the east. Fortunately Mr. Wright was not in camp, so we had a day to recover from the ride before resuming the finishing of Mr. and Mrs. Wright's quarters.

Spring 1940

Toward the end of February Mr. Wright increased the pressure on the Fellowship to complete the family's living quarters, and announced that he intended to be in them by the weekend of March 9 and 10. This began a hectic week of work. Until Saturday we continued work each day until dinner time. On Saturday we worked until eleven at night. And on Sunday we worked until eight in the evening when we had dinner in the Garden Room.[31] The dinner was a gala affair with many invited guests. They included Lucretia Bori, a well-known opera star, Marc Connelly, Mr. and Mrs. Lloyd Lewis, a Mrs. Garrett (who was the wife of the ambassador to Italy), John Hill's parents, and Betty Cass, a columnist for the *Capital Times,* a Madison newspaper.

The just-completed living room, which was called the Garden Room, and the cove were quite handsome. We had built in seats of redwood planks along the west wall of the living room (Figs. 39, 40) and on the south and west walls of the cove. These had been covered with mattress pads over which was tacked a maroon-colored cotton fabric woven with a large-scale herringbone pattern. There were loose pillows covered with the same fabric. The concrete floor was covered with a rose-colored shag carpet. The grand piano had been moved from the drafting room and placed at the south end of the room. Near it was Iovanna's harp with its gold trim. There were small, square, wooden hassocks, which we had made, with cushions covered with the herringbone fabric. These were grouped near low, hexagonal tables. Near the built-in seats were baskets of plants hanging from the trusses. Sheepskins and other fur rugs were scattered on the seats and on the floor. What had been a busy construction site only a few hours before had been transformed into a setting rivaling that of a Bedouin chieftain.

This was my first, but not my last, experience with many such intense pushes to complete a construction or remodeling project before, and for, some social event in the life of the Fellowship. It was an experience that had its humorous aspect. Shortly before the event was to begin, the Fellowship was a scruffy collection of workers, putting the finishing touches in place under Mr. Wright's direction. Then, just before guests started to arrive, the workers would disappear only to reappear appropriately dressed as guests – the men showered and shaved and in their best attire, the women appearing as though they had spent the afternoon

39   The west side of Garden Room. Tall mass is the chimney of the cove fireplace. Photo by author.

40   Garden Room as seen from the north end. Entrance is at left. Photo courtesy of John H. Howe.

at the hairdressers. I still don't know how we managed it at that time when there were still no bathrooms or shower facilities in the camp.

With Mr. and Mrs. Wright moved from the Suntrap and into their more permanent quarters, and with the arrival of more resortlike weather, the tempo of life in camp became less arduous and more leisurely. Work in the drafting room had been largely ignored but now Mr. Wright shifted his attention in that direction and toward work on some of the projects for which clients were awaiting drawings. One of these was the Pauson house for which the preliminary design had already been done.

At night the drafting room became a study or lounge for the apprentices. There was a fire in the fireplace. The room had no general illumination; light was provided by bulbs with green, industrial-type, porcelain-enamel reflectors hanging from rubber-covered drop cords. These were suspended over the drafting tables from wires along which they could be moved, creating pools of light which gave an intimacy to the large room at night.

One evening after dinner Mr. Wright came to the drafting room, seated himself at a drafting table in a pool of light, and started to draw. Some of the apprentices, curious about what he was doing, stood behind him watching over his shoulder. Soon there was a ring of apprentices around the table. As he became aware of his growing audience, he started to talk about what he was doing. He had had an idea for the Franklin Watkins studio and wanted to get it on paper. The site of the proposed studio was on sand dunes near the ocean. For some reason, unclear to me, the studio was to be built almost completely of one by-twelve lumber. Whether this was a constraint that Mr. Wright had placed on himself or whether Watkins had a large supply of one-by-twelves was not clear. As Mr. Wright continued to draw, working on a plan, elevation, and section on one piece of paper, the studio began to appear as an abstract pattern of lapped boards. After about two hours of drawing, the studio was there in sketch form. He had done little erasing or changing, and had drawn it to scale with small accompanying sketches of details at the side to show how it was to be constructed. And he had used a few colored wax pencils to indicate materials, the sand of the dune, the wood, and the surrounding vegetation. When he seemed to feel that he had gotten the idea on paper, he put his pencil down with a gesture of completion, rose, and walked out past the kitchen on his way to the family's living quarters.

He left behind him a group of apprentices marveling that he could design something in such a short time. It was obvious, however, that he was drawing something that was already clear in his mind. It was a matter of putting what he had in mind on paper so that a senior apprentice could then take that drawing, sort out the information, and translate it into more finished drawings, complete with a perspective, to be sent to Mr. Watkins. This was my first experience seeing Mr. Wright in the process of putting his thought on paper. The interesting project never went beyond the preliminary design phase, nor did Mr. Wright ever exhibit or publish the sketches.

On a Town Day afternoon there might not be many people in camp, and the camp became pleasantly quiet and serene. One could enjoy a detachment from both "Taliesin time" and "town time." I imagine that Mr. Wright experienced these afternoons similarly. It was on these afternoons that he put some of his most innovative projects on paper. The house for Lloyd Burlingame, to be built of adobe near El Paso, Texas, was one of these. Some of us had returned from town shortly before dinner, and there were the first drawings for this new house. It was unlike any that Mr. Wright had done before in shape or construction. It was an exciting moment, one that was to be repeated often. It is difficult to say whether the designs for projects that appeared in this fashion were the product of sudden inspiration or long meditation and thought. I doubt that it was sudden inspiration. Mr. Wright's first drawings for a building had none of that tentative quality of searching for an idea or of an idea only vaguely realized. The designs for these projects were put on paper almost completely fleshed out. Very often they were accompanied by notes and sectional drawings that explained the construction system as well as the spatial configuration. These drawings were not always easy to decipher. In one drawing, but in several different-colored wax pencils, might be superimposed several layers of drawings: a roof plan, over a second-floor plan, over a first-floor plan. Sometimes one layer might be smudged with partial erasure, to make way for the next layer, depending upon which layer Mr. Wright was working on. The first sketch for the Arch Oboler residence, "Eaglefeather," which Mr. Wright put on paper in the summer of 1940, was one of these. From this first sketch Jack Howe proceeded to make separate drawings of the upper and lower floors and of the elevations and sections.

On these separate drawings Mr. Wright made changes and refinements before the presentation drawings were made to show to the client. My own theory regarding these designs is that Mr. Wright, having studied the client's requirements and site, held this information in his mind and on this basis studied the project mentally. Later, when I was more familiar with work in the studio, I observed his actions a bit more carefully. He would ask that the client's site plan, photos of the site, and the client's list of requirements be left out on one of the drafting tables where these could catch his eye. I assume that these served as a kind of reminder and as a stimulus to the inner process that eventually produced the image of the building that first appeared on paper. Of course all projects did not come into being in this way – only those that seemed to strike a new direction in his work.

The Fellowship that winter was a group varying in number between thirty-five and forty: one-quarter of it was female, three-quarters male. One of Mr. and Mrs. Wright's concerns was the relation between the sexes. Only two of the women were unattached: Mr. and Mrs. Wright's daughter, Iovanna, who was then in her teens and attending the girls' school at Jokake Inn; and Grace Sciacchiatano, Sam's sister. The others were wives of men whom they had met and married in the Fellowship. Some of these marriages, such as that of Wes and Svetlana, had not been approved by Mr. and Mrs. Wright. Except for Mr. Wright, who was then in his early seventies, the men ranged in age from late teens to thirties.

One morning, when the Fellowship was shivering at breakfast, Mr. Wright came out, seated himself at the head of one of the tables, and started to talk in a general way about this problem, about the sexual instinct and its gratification. He presented his image of the Fellowship as an ideal, as a somewhat ascetic – if not monastic – community of men and women as dedicated to architecture as he was. In it, this "problem" was solved by self-discipline and sublimation through vigorous hard work out-of-doors.

He contrasted this ideal with what he perceived to be the public image of the Fellowship – affected in part by his own marital history – as a "sex-starved community" which sought satisfaction on Saturday nights in Phoenix. It seemed that he saw Town Day not as an innocent opportunity to get a bath, shop, go to a movie, and get a haircut, but as an occasion for indulgence in the physical pleasures, after which some apprentices appeared at breakfast on Sunday mornings "looking like sucked oranges."

There was no response from the Fellowship. And Mr. Wright, having let his feelings be known, rose and left.

After Mr. and Mrs. Wright had moved into their quarters, construction was started on the apprentice wing at the northeast corner of the camp which was to be a group of fourteen rooms, three for girls and eleven for boys, wrapped around and partially enclosing what came to be called "the apprentice court" (Fig. 41). At the west side of the court was the small theater, which had been poured the previous year. It was still unfinished inside. To the north were to be a boys' shower room and toilet rooms for boys and girls. North of this group of facilities were the three girls' rooms and their toilet room, entered from the terrace on the west side. The eleven rooms for boys, on the north and east sides of the court, ended with a "hook" around a palo verde tree at the southeast corner. The court was to have two badminton courts and a large chess board of alternating squares of concrete and gravel. There was to be a terrace, raised three steps, at an opening between rooms on the north side. This opening was also an entrance to the camp from the desert.

Progress on construction of this part of the camp was slower than anticipated. Fewer people were assigned to it than to the work on Mr. and Mrs. Wright's quarters. And as the days grew warmer in April the pace of the work slowed. By the time we left Arizona at the end of April, all of the masonry walls had been

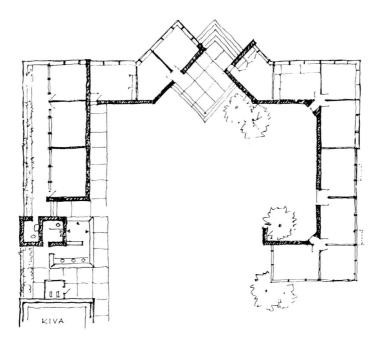

41   Plan of apprentice court.

poured. It was the intent that the apprentices remaining in Arizona during the summer would continue framing the other walls, the partitions, and the roof. All of these were to be wood.

In addition to work in the studio and on the construction of the rooms on the apprentice court, some of the work in camp was devoted to getting the camp in shape to be photographed. An issue of *Arizona Highways*[32] was to be devoted in large part to Mr. Wright, the Fellowship, and the camp. (The plan of the camp published in this issue of the magazine was drawn by Bob Mosher.) The photos published in this issue were taken at the end of the first year of construction, or during the past winter's construction of Mr. and Mrs. Wright's quarters, but Mr. Wright wanted to have more recent photos made. And he wanted them taken before we left for Wisconsin. In retrospect it appears that he was beginning to think about material that might be included in the exhibition of his work which was to be held at the Museum of Modern Art in the fall of 1940.

Early in April Gene Masselink introduced a young photographer, Pedro ("Pete") Guerrero, at tea. Pete, whose parents lived in Mesa and who had studied photography at the Art Center School in Los Angeles, had come that afternoon to talk to Mr. Wright about doing the camp's photography. During their conversation Pete became convinced that he should join the Fellowship and become its photographer. He went to Wisconsin with us that spring.

Migration to Wisconsin – 1940

During the second week in April the dump truck was packed and an advance party of three apprentices went to Wisconsin. That started speculation among the rest of us about when we might be leaving. Edgar Tafel had already gone to Chicago to start construction of the Lloyd Lewis house in Libertyville. (He was also supervising construction of a house in Racine for one of his own clients.) Blaine and Hulda had gone to San Francisco; he was supervising the Bazett house. Peter and Cornelia had gone to Pittsburgh to complete a house being built for her aunts, Hulda and Louise Notz. Gordon Chadwick was in Virginia supervising the house for Loren Pope, and Burt Goodrich had returned to Florence, Alabama. He had gone there in the fall to start construction of the Rosenbaum house and had come to the camp during the winter to resolve some questions about construction. Bob Mosher was going to stay in camp. He was supervising construction of the Pauson house which had started. Bob Goss was going to stay in Arizona to help Mosher take care of the camp and to work on the construction of the apprentice wing.

Some of us had started packing when the advance party left, but Mr. Wright insisted that we were going to stay in Arizona until he got some good photographs of the camp. Pete Guerrero was taking the photos. The packing of the stake truck, which was to travel separately from the caravan, began a couple of days before we were to leave. I gave Gene Masselink a check for $15.00, my share of the travel expenses, on April 29.

Our trip north, led by Gene and Wes, was planned to move at a leisurely pace for the first few days. "We were going to travel Conoco,"and had stickers for each of the cars and maps specially prepared for us by the Conoco travel service. The trip was planned by Wes who had a great interest in the Indians of this area, and we were going to see some of the Indian country of northeast Arizona and to go through Sante Fe and Taos. Since the intent was to go only as far as the Grand Canyon on the first day, we did not leave camp until after lunch.

I looked forward to this trip with much anticipation. The Fellowship had explored the desert near the camp on its many Sunday picnics, but this was the first time that I and many other apprentices had seen northern Arizona. It was an intoxicating, habituating experience, and developed a thirst which, after many subsequent visits to this area, still remains.

We stopped first at the tourist area on the south rim of the Grand Canyon long enough to look at the interior of the El Tovar hotel and down into the canyon. I questioned why we stopped so briefly. But when we arrived at a spot east of the village, where the canyon bends to the north, and where we were to have supper and camp for the night, my question was answered. From this spot we had a view down a great length of the canyon. The late afternoon sun was filling the depth with shadows and modeling the shapes of the formations. The sunset from there was sublime. No picture postcard of a sunset was acceptable after that. We absorbed the wonder of it all until light was gone from the sky. With the arrival of light in the morning we drank pine-crisp air with our coffee and feasted, while shivering through breakfast, on a scene that changed as the sun rose and its rays penetrated into the mist and the cloud-filled canyon. The changing light revealed shapes not previously seen. It was fascinating. We packed up and pulled away from the spot with great reluctance.

From there we drove to the Tuba City Trading Post (Fig. 42). Having been introduced to Indian rugs and silver by the shops of Phoenix and by Elmer Shupe's visit to the camp during the winter, we all hoped that we might spot

42   Tuba City Trading Post, the first stop in a tour of the Indian country and the mesa villages. Photo by Pedro E. Guerrero.

some rug or bit of silver that we could afford. After a brief stop there we left the more developed gravel highway for a day of travel across the Indian country. We followed a single-track rutted road that wound across the Hopi reservation and past the villages on the mesas. We stopped below Walpi and Oraibi and climbed up the trails to the villages. Moving slowly on those roads the cars followed close upon one another as we anticipated that one might become mired in the sand or have engine trouble. We emerged from this dusty travel – and another age – in the late afternoon when we drove back onto Highway 66 shortly before Gallup. We camped that night in the desert just to the east of Gallup.

The next day we left 66 at Albuquerque and went north through Santa Fe, Taos, and La Veta Pass, stopping only long enough to walk around the plaza in Santa Fe and the pueblo in Taos. We camped that night in a bleak and windswept field of dust near LaJunta, Colorado. From there it was a day across the high plains of Colorado and Kansas. We camped somewhere in eastern Kansas that night. We spent another day crossing the rolling hills of Missouri and southern Iowa. On our last night we camped in a triangular area within a highway intersection south of Cedar Rapids, Iowa. We arrived at Taliesin shortly before lunch.

The advance party had assisted those who had spent the winter in Wisconsin in opening up the buildings and getting the plumbing systems, which had been drained for the winter, back in operation. The "house" had been aired and its furnishings uncovered and put back in their previous arrangement. And the garden had been plowed and harrowed, and some of the planting had been done.

In all my years with the Fellowship the winter and spring migrations were annual events except for the winters of the war years. After the war we ceased traveling as a caravan, but we did not cease searching out new routes between Wisconsin and Arizona and new landscapes to experience. It was in this fashion that I saw much of the United States between Wisconsin and Arizona.

These migrations were so much a part of the Fellowship's life that I am always surprised by the first question people ask when they learn that I was a member of the Fellowship: "In Wisconsin or Arizona?" From this question it is clear that they thought of the Fellowship as two different groups, one based in Wisconsin and one in Arizona. It had not occurred to them that the Fellowship as one group would change its base of operation twice a year, that an architect's office would load up its active files of drawings and correspondence and move twice yearly.

In writing about the Fellowship I have avoided using words such as organization and institution. I have called it a group instead. Mr. Wright resisted the notion that the Fellowship was an institution or an organization or that it would become one. In *Taliesin,* the magazine intended to be a bimonthly publication, Mr. Wright stated, "Work and life here will never be 'established' in the current sense of the term nor will Taliesin ever be an institution if I can help it."[33] He even objected to calling it a school, though he was willing to do so as a concession to the immigration service. Potential apprentices from foreign countries would not be given visas for an extended stay in the United States unless they had applied for a student visa. In order to receive a student visa they had to show that they had applied for admission to a school and had been accepted.

Ideally, in Mr. Wright's mind, the Fellowship was not a school but an apprenticeship, one which was much like those of feudal times but with one important exception. His apprentices were to be his comrades, not his slaves. All of them, according to their abilities, were to have equal access to him and an equal opportunity to share in his work and to learn from it. In actual operation, however, the Fellowship tended to become institutional and to assume a hierarchical structure. Mr. and Mrs. Wright were at its peak, or its center. Below or around them were the senior apprentices. The seniors were those who had been at Taliesin longer and who, having more experience and being more useful in the activities of the Fellowship, were given limited responsibilities. Below or around these, the other apprentices were loosely ranked according to the length of time they had been at Taliesin and their experience.

As Mr. Wright objected to calling the Fellowship a school he also objected to being thought of as a teacher. He claimed that he was not trying to teach anyone anything. But he was willing to agree that people might learn something from working with him, particularly if in working with him they would ask themselves – not him – why he did what he did. Even if they were working outside on construction, they might ask themselves why Mr. Wright was making a certain change and what the result of the change would be. One did not need to be in the drafting room in order to learn. One could learn only by "getting his hands in the mud with which the bricks are made."

His objection to "school" as formal education raised unanswered questions about his own educational experiences, and it is puzzling since he came from a family that valued education. It also contained teachers and preachers whom he admired. Aunt Nell and Aunt Jane had founded a school and taught there; his mother had been a teacher. Uncle Jenkins was a well-known Unitarian preacher; and his own father was a sometime preacher and teacher who had taught him music. He objected to schools in part because they were places with schedules and routine activities. He saw routine activity as habit-forming and explained that it was for this reason that he avoided habitual action in his life. It was also for this reason that whenever he felt that the life of the Fellowship was settling into routine he would attempt to "break it up." Despite Mr. Wright's desire to avoid routine, a schedule, which was generally followed, did develop: On weekdays breakfast was served from 6:30 to 7:30 daylight saving time; lunch was at noon; tea was at four in the afternoon; dinner was at seven, and as long as we were "on the Kohler" the generator was turned off at 10:30. On Saturday nights we had dinner in the theater followed by a movie, and on Sunday evening we dined in "the house" followed by music.

Moving between Wisconsin and Arizona twice a year was a way of "breaking up" the routine, of interrupting the schedule. It originated also in a desire for a change of scenery as well as in the desire to continue work out-of-doors on construction. The change of scenery and the opportunity to explore unfamiliar landscapes was stimulating and refreshing. Change served to avoid – or cure – cabin fever, that state of mind, the factions and fixations, that can develop in a small group of people living in close association for any length of time. With these changes of scenery came other changes. You never knew from year to year – and place to place – where you might be living, who would be your neighbors. Moving discouraged us from surrounding ourselves with too many personal possessions, too many things that would have to be packed up and moved. You tried to keep only the essentials. And you found yourself associating with a different mix of people than those with whom you had previously associated.

Summer 1940

In the fall of 1939 I had lived in a room below the house. When we arrived in Wisconsin in the spring of 1940 I was told that I was to live at Hillside in the room at the south end of the corridor on the east side of the drafting room in which Kan Domoto had lived the previous summer. For the Birthday Box that June I made a drawing of a proposal for finishing the construction he had started. And I made a start at completing it. The materials for it were easily available: piles of plywood in several thicknesses were in the shop in the cottage east of the drafting room and piles of rough-sawn oak boards were at the west side of the cottage. I assume that these were left over from the construction of the drafting room and the apprentice rooms, but I didn't find the time – or perhaps take the time – that summer to complete my proposal.

The Fellowship's brochure had emphasized that work – "even while resting" – was the essence of life at Taliesin: work in the drafting room, work on construction, work in the daily upkeep, and work in the farm fields and gardens. The last of these did not play much of a part in our life in the desert, but work in the farm fields and gardens was very much a part of our life in Wisconsin. To Mr. Wright, work with growing things was fundamental to a person's development, particularly to his understanding and appreciation of an "organic architecture." It had been a part of the students' life in Hillside Home School which Aunt Jane and Aunt Nell had founded.[34] He recognized that the summers he had spent working on the farm, though resisted at the time, had been an invaluable experience. All of Mr. Wright's pre-Fellowship proposals for some sort of educational activity had included as a requirement that the school also be a working farm, that it be in the countryside and on sufficient land so that the group's work with the soil would insure its living. The plan and perspective of the buildings proposed for the Hillside Home School of the Allied Arts showed garden plots and orchards extending up to the windmill, Romeo and Juliet, on the hill slope above the buildings.

It was in Wisconsin that the Fellowship came nearest to realizing one of Mr. Wright's goals – that the Fellowship be self-sustaining. In Arizona all of our food, except for the heaps of grapefruit that friendly owners of groves allowed us to pick and the sacks of potatoes and the canned tomatoes that we brought with us

43   Apprentices helping get in the hay. Left to right: Jim Charlton, Leonard Meyer, and Fred Benedict.
Photo by Pedro E. Guerrero.

in the trucks, was bought from the local wholesalers and at the local produce markets. When the Fellowship returned to Wisconsin in the spring, all of the Fellowship was involved, with varying extent and with varying degrees of acceptance and pleasure, in work on the farm and in the garden. There, we had a large vegetable garden, a flock of chickens that provided fresh eggs and occasionally meat, and a herd of dairy cows providing fresh milk twice a day as well as cream for butter and sour milk for cottage cheese. The orchard on the hill provided apples in the fall, and the vineyard on the hill slope provided some grapes, never in great abundance. We were surrounded by farmland with pastures for beef cattle as well as for the milk cows. And there were fields producing hay, oats, and corn which, according to the season, crews were sent out to help harvest (Fig. 43).

For me such work was not an entirely new experience. I had grown up in a rural community. My parents had always planted a large vegetable garden. Its produce, canned and stored, had provided a large part of our food the year round. Several of my aunts and uncles were farmers. Through them, and thanks to weeklong visits to their farms in the summer, I had become familiar with farm life.

The farm and garden work in which the Fellowship was generally involved were about finished when I arrived at Taliesin in the fall of 1939, but with our return to Wisconsin in May 1940, I received an immersion, of a kind, in farm work. Wes Peters had recently acquired the farm just west of Taliesin. I was a member of a crew assigned to clean out the lower level of the barn in which beef cattle had been sheltered during the winter. It had not been cleaned out for some time, and was about a foot deep in fresh manure – or so it seemed. Wearing rubber boots and equipped with manure forks and with a manure spreader pulled by a tractor, we waded in to clean it out. Taking brief pauses for fresh air, while the manure was being spread on the pastures, we finished the job by the end of the day. After that experience, other farm assignments, such as bringing baled hay from the fields to the barn loft, or stacking oat sheaves, were relatively pleasant, though equally strenuous.

The Fellowship's greatest involvement was with the vegetable garden. During the summer planting and growing season the Fellowship went, as a group, to the garden after breakfast in the morning. Very often Mr. and Mrs. Wright were there too, or they would come by during the garden hour. Mr. Wright liked to demonstrate how to pull weeds.

During those cool mornings, when mist might still be lying in the valleys and the night's dew had not yet evaporated, the landscape was most beautiful. And the Fellowship working in the garden made a very picturesque scene, like those romantic movies of peasants in the fields. Various costumes were adopted for working in the garden and for protection from the mosquitoes. I always wore a long-sleeved shirt with the collar buttoned and a neckerchief to protect the back of my neck. The sleeves became wet from the dew on the plants we might be thinning or the weeds we were pulling, and my hands muddy from the damp earth.

I often wondered just how effective the work of the Fellowship was at that hour of the morning. With damp earth clinging to our shoes and hoes many weeds were probably transplanted rather than killed. My favorite time to work in the garden was midafternoon, when the topsoil had dried somewhat from the sun. One year, each member of the Fellowship was assigned responsibility for particular vegetables. I was assigned green peppers and eggplant. I would take a break from work in the studio in midafternoon to go out and cultivate my patch of garden. It was weed-free but it didn't produce any eggplant. I blamed it on the cool nights and the short growing season. But it did produce a super abundance of green peppers. Bushels of them were carried to the kitchen to be pickled, stuffed, or put into salads.

I was never in charge of the garden or, except for the daily hour in the garden, assigned to work there for long. For this reason I do not know what part Mr. and Mrs. Wright played in the planning of garden work, or in deciding what to plant and where to plant it. But I am sure that they were consulted by the person who was responsible for the garden. And I expect that a determining factor was the experience of the preceding years.

There was, however, one vegetable that was always a puzzle to me: rutabagas. Few members of the Fellowship liked to eat them. Yet they, along with turnips, were always planted after the potatoes had been harvested. Rutabagas would start appearing on the menu in late summer. They were harvested late in the fall after they had gotten large and woody, and were stored in the root cellar for winter use. Sacks of them were taken to Arizona. But most of them were carried out and dumped when the root cellar was cleaned out in the spring. Perhaps Carl Sandburg's *Rootabaga Stories,* for which Mr. Wright expressed an affection, played a part in their being planted. Perhaps they had been a staple in the diets of the Welsh aunts and uncles. I never did find out.

During the summer, as different kinds of vegetables became available from the garden, the menus for meals changed. There were times when some apprentices complained that the meals consisted of nothing but vegetables. This was one of my favorite times, particularly when sweet corn and tomatoes were at their peak. Corn on the cob, boiled fresh from the field, and ripe tomatoes, still warm from the sun, together with a slice or two of whole wheat bread with butter made one of my ideal meals. There were times when some of the surplus from the garden was trucked to neighboring towns and sold. And as the summer progressed, produce from the garden was accumulated to take with us to Arizona. Hundreds of half-gallon jars of tomatoes and tomato sauce were canned; many jars were filled with thick plum jam; and many bags of potatoes were put away in the root cellar in anticipation of the winter's needs. All of this was done to reduce as much as possible our dependence on external sources of supplies.

Although all members of the Fellowship worked in the garden during the garden hour, and although one apprentice was assigned responsibility for the garden, other apprentices were assigned to work there on a daily or weekly basis. When Fred Benedict was in charge of the garden during my first summer in Wisconsin, three people seemed to be assigned to work with him most of the time: Jim Charlton, Ben Masselink, and Chip Harkness. They complained, partly in jest and partly in earnest, that they were assigned to work in the garden all of the time. When Chip Harkness left at the end of the summer to return to Harvard, he said that he had spent the summer picking tomatoes. But they did not spend all of their time in the garden. Jim Charlton spent some of the summer in the drafting room drawing perspectives of Eaglefeather, the house Mr. Wright had designed for Arch Oboler. And Ben Masselink, Gene's brother, who was spending the summer at Taliesin, said that he had spent a part of it in the root cellar, "hiding from Mr. Wright and tasting the wine." This was the summer of Mrs. Wright's wine-making project which produced several hundred gallons of wine made from everything from tomatoes to wild cherries. It varied in quality from undrinkable vinegar to drinkable. The drinkable was served at Sunday evening dinners.

There were times during the summer when I was somewhat envious of this congenial and jovial group, particularly on those days when I was assigned to work on construction in the basement of the Hillside Home School building which Mr. Wright had designed for his aunts in 1902. Remodeling of the lower floor of the building into a new and larger kitchen and dining room for the Fellowship had been started as part of a move to concentrate the activities of the Fellowship at Hillside.

While working on this dining room project, I became aware of the fact that the school building was essentially an English half-timber building, but transformed. The floors, walls, and roofs were framed in heavy oak timbers. But in place of brick, the timber framing of this building rested on a rock-faced, sandstone base. It had the tall projecting window bays of the Tudor style. These window bays had originally been glazed with diamond-shaped leaded panes of glass. But the pointed gables and the emphasis on the vertical had been replaced with broad, hipped roofs and an emphasis on the horizontal. It was then that I began to notice that Mr. Wright had what I called a "busy eye." He was not above "borrowing," but what he "borrowed" he did not copy directly; he transformed it and in the process made it his own.

To make this larger dining room for the Fellowship, Mr. Wright had removed the existing partitions on the lower floor to make one large space. The partition which had separated the corridor from the classrooms, and which had supported the floor above, had been replaced by a system of stone piers and wooden beams. There were also beams similarly placed beneath the floor of the new dining room. A new oak floor was being laid and plumbing was being installed below the living room for the new kitchen. The crew that I was working with was nailing new joists alongside the existing ones to strengthen the floor of the new dining room.

After a warm, humid day of working in the basement, with years of accumulated dust, shaken loose by our hammering, falling on us, we needed hot showers. But there was then no hot water in the showers in the bathrooms at Hillside. So we had two options: go to the river for a swim, or try to use one of the showers that were available to apprentices in bathrooms at Taliesin.

Unless the day was too cool for a swim, the river was easily the preferred option. And so, while living at Hillside that summer, I discovered the pleasures of the Wisconsin River.

The river, a dominant feature of the landscape, formed part of the northern boundary of the valley. It was within easy walking distance of Taliesin and was a major source of summer recreation. In the months of July and August and into early September, the clean sand and the clear, tan-bark-colored water of the river were especially attractive. Just north of Taliesin (see Fig. 1), across the back road, where the creek of the Lloyd-Jones Valley emptied into the Wisconsin, the river was divided into two channels. Between these was a tree-covered sand bar, an island, that formed the division. On a summer weekend the main channel could be very active and noisy with powerboats and water skiers, but the south channel was always relatively quiet. The pasture across the road from the north side of

Taliesin sloped gently to the river's edge. One could let oneself through the pasture gate, drive in, and park near the river. There was a story that Daniel Webster had once owned this land and that there had been a sawmill at this spot. To the west of this place where access to the river was easy, a great sandstone cliff, "Phoebe's Point," rose directly out of the water. It was like a great boulder standing at the water's edge. Generally there was a pool deep enough for swimming at the base of this boulder. The river appeared calm and smoothly flowing on the surface, although it was constantly changing and hid treacherous currents and deep pools. It had to be approached with care.

Sometimes in the summer, to interrupt the routine, Mr. Wright would decide to have a picnic lunch or dinner at the river. And at any time during the summer, when a group of fellows had been working in the hay or oat field or at other dusty, sweaty work, we went to the river after tea for a quick swim and a bath before supper. If one had been working in the drafting room most of the day and felt the need for a change of activity and some exercise, again the choice after tea, for me at least, was to go to the river.

Movies

Early in the summer of 1940 Bennie Dombar asked me if I would be interested in learning to run the movie projectors and take my turn showing films for the Fellowship. I had had no experience with movie projectors, but I was a movie fan. Without much hesitancy I answered yes.

One of the decisive experiences in my first visit to Taliesin had been the Saturday night dinner in the Playhouse at Hillside. At that time I had no idea of the important role that the Playhouse, as a place to show movies, had in the life of the Fellowship. Mr. Wright was a movie fan; he enjoyed good films. But he saw the great movies of the world as something more that entertainment; he saw them as a form of education in the deepest meaning of the word. They were not only a means of acquiring information about the various cultures of the world, but of nourishing and developing one's own creative resources. They were like the works of art which he acquired and with which he surrounded himself and the Fellowship. They were, as he often said, his library. Like great literature, they were sources of nourishment and inspiration. The Playhouse was a place, a setting, in which to view these works of art and to share them with the Fellowship and its guests.

The Playhouse was the first part of the complex of buildings at Hillside to be renovated. It was put in use in 1933. Its renovation and remodeling into a place to show movies during the first year of the Fellowship set in motion a continuing process of transformation, the study and change of that space directed toward making it a more congenial environment in which to see films. Two people were assigned to clean and decorate the theater every Saturday in preparation for the movie that evening. The floors would be polished and fresh arrangements of foliage and flowers put in place. It was not unusual for Mr. Wright to drop by the theater, either before or after lunch, to see how preparations were progressing. And it often happened that if he saw a change he wanted to make he would send the cleaning crew for a wrecking bar and for a few other apprentices to help them make the change that he had in mind. There was no questioning whether or not the change could be completed and the room back in order before dinner that evening.

During my first summer with the Fellowship, movies were shown at least twice a week – on Saturday evenings for the Fellowship and on Sunday afternoons at three for the general public. Posters of coming attractions were made and displayed on a small signboard on Highway 23 near the entrance drive to Hillside. And programs of future events were printed and available. People from the nearby towns and cities came to see the movies. Sometimes tourists passing by on the highway would notice the sign and decide to stop. The admission charge of fifty cents included coffee and cakes served and prepared by an apprentice. For an added dollar one was given a tour of the Taliesin grounds. Serving as a guide for this tour was also an assigned job.

There was always the possibility that a visitor attending the movie might meet Mr. Wright. If he enjoyed the film shown on Saturday night he often went to see it again on Sunday afternoon. After the movie he frequently stayed to meet and talk with others in the audience. If he met people that he found interesting he might invite them to stay for dinner that evening at Taliesin. And the cook would get the word to prepare for additional guests. The practice of showing the movies to the public was discontinued in the summer of 1941 and was not revived following the war.

Projecting the films was another of the shared chores of the Fellowship, but it was shared by a smaller group of people. In addition to Bennie Dombar, who taught me how to use the equipment, Ellis Jacobs, Cary Caraway, and Gene Masselink were running the projectors that summer. Davy Davison also became involved in this activity.

The projectors were not the latest equipment available. They were rather antiquated, thirty-five millimeter, carbon arc machines. And many of the films that we showed were old prints with many splices of repaired breaks. One of the experienced projectionists stayed near or in the projection booth with me during my first several turns at projecting. But then I was left to solo. Being in the booth with those hissing and sputtering machines with the film speeding through them, watching for the changeover signal, or for the film to break, was to me a nightmare. I anticipated it with dread and suffered through it. If a break did occur and if the machine was not quickly shut off, it could become jammed with film. And if this happened it could be extracted only in bits and pieces.

Much to my relief these machines were replaced the following summer with newer ones that were smaller and quieter. They used high-intensity bulbs and it was easier to thread film through them. They were also machines that could be easily disassembled and reassembled and moved back and forth between Wisconsin and Arizona. Although these machines were much less terrifying I still felt that I had to be near at hand in the booth, waiting for the film to break, a bulb to burn out, the sound to go off, the image to be out of focus on the screen, or some other unknown to happen.

The terror of projecting was compounded for me by the smallness of the booths, both in the Playhouse and in the Kiva in Arizona. There was just enough room in them to get around the machines to see to their proper threading. Fortunately, the booth in the second theater, built in Arizona in 1949 and 1950, was much larger.

There were two Russian films that were kept in the booth and which could be shown at a moment's notice: a short cartoon, *The Czar Duranday,* and a feature length film, *The Czar Wants to Sleep.* Mr. Wright was the proud possessor of these films and enjoyed seeing them himself. Sometimes it seemed that he simply used the guests as an excuse for seeing them once more. The cartoon was given to him when he was in Russia in 1937. The other he had purchased from the distributor. (Both of these films were destroyed in the fire at Hillside in the spring of 1952.)

The Czar Duranday (1934) was a black-and-white animated film with music attributed by Mr. Wright to Shostakovich. The film was an allegorical fairy tale about the triumph of the oppressed workers over their oppressors. The animation was beautifully drawn and had handsome patterns reminiscent of those of Bakst and the Chauve Souri. *The Czar Wants to Sleep* (1933) was a satire on the czarist bureaucracy, with a musical score, now known as *The Lieutenant Kijé Suite,* by Prokofiev. I am sure that part of the film's appeal to Mr. Wright was its similarity to some aspects of life at Taliesin. He always left the theater after seeing this film with his eyes brimming with tears from laughter, and saying to himself the last line of the film, "It is difficult to be a czar."

In addition to these two Russian films we saw many others, including those directed by Sergei Eisenstein which were distributed in the United States by Amkino. These included: *Battleship Potemkin* (1925); *October: Ten Days That Shook the World* (1927); *Alexander Nevsky* (1939), also with music by Prokofiev; and *Ivan the Terrible, Part I* (1944) and *Part II* (1946). Mr. Wright also enjoyed the comedies directed by Rene Clarie. These were booked whenever they became available: *A Nous la Liberte* (1931); *The Last Billionaire* (1935); *The Ghost Goes West* (1935), and, of course, the *Flame of New Orleans* (1940) which starred Marlene Dietrich.

Gene Masselink, Mr. Wright's secretary, booked the films. He was on a constant search for new and interesting films. A list of the films shown would include most of the great ones.[35] His choice was wide-ranging and catholic. Many of these were booked more than once. There were several Hollywood westerns with heroes with whom Mr. Wright identified. These included *High Noon* (1952) with Gary Cooper and *The Gunfighter* (1950) with Gregory Peck. And there were two westerns which we saw at least once a year. *Stagecoach* starring John Wayne and featuring the landscape of Monument Valley was a favorite of Wes Peters. *Destry Rides Again,* with Marlene Dietrich singing "See What the Boys in the Back Room Will Have," was one of Mr. Wright's.

Summer and Fall 1940 – Work in the Drafting Room

One of the projects completed early in the summer was Community Church in Kansas City, which I was concerned about and anxious to work on, but to which I was not assigned. Early in November 1939, after I had been in the Fellowship about a month, I received a telegram from Joe Cleveland, the associate minister of Community Church in Kansas City, Missouri. Their building, on Linwood Boulevard, had burned; he was inquiring if Mr. Wright would be interested in designing a new building for them.

I gave the telegram to Mr. Wright. He was interested. He did not have any large architectural projects at that time. The many small Usonian houses were the only work in the drafting room. The Johnson Building and the residence for Herbert Johnson were essentially complete. Mr. Wright went to Kansas City on November 21 to meet with the building committee of the church and to talk to the members of the church.[36] He talked to an audience of about 800. It included, in addition to members of the church, many local architects, George Beal and a group of architectural students from K.U., and my mother.[37] Following this talk, he was selected as the architect for the new building, but an agreement for his services was not signed.

To me this seemed like a wonderful opportunity. There had been several public buildings, designed in the "moderne" style, constructed in the city. But, Kansas City was conservative and traditional architecturally as well as in other ways. I hoped that the new building for Community Church might be the kind of landmark in Mr. Wright's career that Unity Temple had been, and that it would give Kansas City an example of what a good, modern building might be.

After Mr. Wright was selected as the architect for the church I began to hear from friends in Kansas City that this had made several architects angry, particularly those who had appeared before the building committee and who expected that the job was going to be theirs.

During that winter, Mr. Wright did not do any visible work on the preliminary design of the church. Though a site had not been selected, concern was expressed about the status of the design; I received inquiries from Kansas City asking why no preliminary design had been done or presented. (Was it then a practice for architects to do preliminary design for a building before a site was

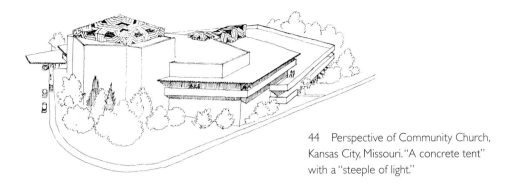

44 Perspective of Community Church, Kansas City, Missouri. "A concrete tent" with a "steeple of light."

selected, while there was still so little understanding of the essential relation of the building to its site?)

The church board approved the purchase of the proposed site on March 21. Mr. Wright went to Kansas City on April 8, 1940,[38] and signed an agreement for his services. At that time he said that he would have preliminary sketches ready in about two weeks. It was hoped that construction could be started in May and completed before winter. The cost was to be about $100,000. He did verbally describe what he thought the church should be. "I am going to start with the parking problem in this case and then build the church around it." Although he gave no idea of the building's shape he suggested that the entire site would be devoted to parking with the church supported on graceful pillars over the parked cars. I wrote Professor Beal on April 20, shortly before our migration to Wisconsin at the end of April, saying that there was "nothing on paper yet in way of pre-liminaries for Community Church."[39]

It was not until the Fellowship was settled in Wisconsin that Mr. Wright made his first sketch of the project (Fig. 44). It was a design based on the New Theater project which he had done in 1932 and which he later related to the Broadacre City project.

The preliminary design for the church was accepted and working drawings were started immediately.

With many of the seniors away supervising houses, Rowan Maiden was assigned to work with Mr. Wright on the working drawings for the church. At one point in the summer Davy Davison and I were asked to do some brown ink per-spective drawings of the church for publicity purposes. Davy did the view of the church from the northwest; I did the one from the southwest. These are the draw-ings of the church that appeared in various publications, including Hitchcock's *In the Nature of Materials*.

Although I was not assigned to work in the studio on Community Church, I was concerned about the progress of the working drawings. The drawings did not seem to be developing beyond what I regarded as a preliminary stage. The draw-ings that I had seen of the Usonian houses were much more complete in detail than these were. But the church was not similar in construction to the Usonian houses. There was no precedence in the drawings of Mr. Wright's work for this kind of construction. And yet, to me, the construction was essentially simple.

It was to be a "thin" building, to be framed with two-inch-square steel tubing. The framing of the walls was to be very much like the wood-stud framing of an ordinary house except that the sill and head plates and the studs were to be steel tubes. There were to be a few steel columns supporting floor or roof beams. The floors and roof were to be framed with steel joists in much the same manner that wood joists were used. All of this framing was to have an inner and outer skin of gunite concrete sprayed against a paper-backed steel wire mesh. The walls were to be only about four inches thick.

I did drawings for the framing of the roof, the balcony, and the structurally supported floors. Some of the concrete floors rested on the ground. I also did reflected plans of the ceilings to indicate the location of the hemispherical recesses for the lighting. Wes Peters did the structural calculations. Over the weekend the drawings were completed and signed.

A letter that I wrote to George Beal on July 22 reported that "at long last the church plans are on their way to Kansas City. Mr. Wright left this afternoon." In this letter I also wrote, "I hope that the plans are complete enough to get a decent bid – that is, if bids are taken. I can see lots of loop holes in them, but that doesn't seem to worry anyone here much. They say they will be changed anyway and cite the number of times changes were made in the Johnson Building."

In his original conception of the building all of the thin edges of the projecting roof planes were to have an edge of copper, a facia with a pattern stamped into the sheet metal. Below the exterior balcony surrounding the sanctuary there was to have been a narrow band of glazing to admit natural light. This band, somewhat like the "perforated boards" of the Usonian houses, was to have been covered with a stamped and pierced pattern of sheet copper. The elaborate pattern of ornament on the hexagonal "dome" over the chancel and the skylight above the central axis of the chapel were also to be made of stamped and folded copper. These details were eliminated as copper shortages developed and copper for building was rationed. During the summer of 1940, with the war in Europe building up, shortages of building materials were beginning to appear. The church committee was anxious to get construction started before shortages became acute. Even before the working drawings were completed Mr. Wright began to revise some of his ideas about the detailing and construction.

Following that project Jack asked me to help him with the preliminary drawings for Auldbrass, the ranch project for Leigh Stevens. Mr. Wright had already made a sketch of the general plan of the complex. It included a main house, a guest house, a caretaker's cottage, cottages for employees, kennels, stables, barns, and machine sheds. Jack had drawn this plan for Mr. Wright to work on, but his plan was based on a grammar of construction similar to that of the flat-roofed

Usonian houses. Mr. Wright did not feel that this grammar was appropriate for a flat, swampy site covered with large, moss-draped trees. So even though Mr. Stevens was saying that it was urgent to get this project started, the preliminary drawings were set aside and stood incomplete.

One morning Mr. Wright arrived at the Hillside drafting room eager to draw. Apparently that morning an appropriate grammar for Auldbrass had come to him. Mr. Wright often said that the best time of day for him was about three or four in the morning. He sat down at his drafting table and quickly drew, to scale, a typical wall section for the grammar for the house. It showed roof, wall, and floor construction. It included the battens on the sloping copper roof and the ornamental downspouts which were to occur at the corners. With this information we quickly completed the presentation drawings. I redrew the master plan making changes to suit this new grammar, and made an aerial perspective of the entire complex. Jack did the more detailed plans and perspectives of the main house and the employees' cottages. Working drawings were done later in the summer (I did not work on them) and construction was started.

Early in September, when Jack Howe was at Taliesin for the weekend, Mr. Wright asked him to work on preliminary sketches for the Crystal Heights project in Washington D.C. (Jack was in Kansas City much of this summer supervising construction of the Sondern house.) This project, as I understood it, was being promoted by a developer as an investment for money that had "fled Europe" with the outbreak of the war. This was a project for which, according to my September 5 letter to George Beal,[40] Mr. Wright was "doing something he had never done before. He is going after a job." It was a $10 million project with the prospect of a $1 million fee.

It was to be "a sort of Radio City" with apartments, a hotel, shops, theaters, an art gallery, tea rooms, cocktail bars, and other appurtenances of a social center expected to cover an area of about two city blocks in a section known as Temple Heights. The hotel rooms and apartments were to be in towers similar to those of St. Mark's in the Bouwerie "planted in an oak grove" and surrounded by terraces for parking on five different levels. Jack had started an aerial perspective of the entire complex on Sunday afternoon. When he realized that he would be unable to complete it before he had to catch the afternoon train to return to Kansas City and the Sondern house, he asked me to complete the layout of the perspective and to render it in ink. I started work on it that afternoon. Davy Davison was also working on another perspective of the complex.

On Monday morning I resumed work on this drawing. I had completed constructing the perspective in pencil and had started to render it in brown ink when Mr. Wright came into the drafting room. He came to my desk, looked over my shoulder at the timid start I had made, and asked to sit down. I gave him the stool I had been sitting on. He then asked for a small paintbrush. He dipped it in the bottle of brown ink I was using and rather quickly started painting in masses of trees where I had blocked them in lightly in pencil. I was afraid that he was going to spoil my drawing with all of these dark blobs of ink. But despite a few accidental drops of ink which were converted into trees or automobiles, the drawing quickly took shape in its overall distribution of light and dark areas. After a while he got up, stood back, and looked at the drawing. Seemingly satisfied he turned to me and said, "There, you can finish it." These drawings were published in various newspapers at that time, a part of the promotion of the project.

As the end of the summer and the beginning of the school year approached some of our summer visitors started leaving. These comings and goings started me wondering whether I should plan to leave or to stay. The end of my year was approaching. I had enough of my savings left for about a half-year of tuition. My inclination was to stay. There was no hint or suggestion that I should leave. There were things about the Fellowship that I did not like, but these seemed less important than the things which I liked and enjoyed. So for the time being, I decided to stay.

As fall moved toward winter I began to be concerned about the church project again. During the summer and fall I had heard rumblings in my mail from Kansas City. There were difficulties in getting reasonable and satisfactory bids from any of the general contractors in Kansas City. Many would not consider submitting bids. Those who did submitted proposals many times the proposed budget. After the church had burned, a money-raising drive had been started to raise $200,000 for the construction of the new building. When they were taking bids their budget was about $100,000. The story is told that the original budget was "something like a hundred thousand" and that Mr. Wright upon hearing this exclaimed, "Why, that's only enough to build a tent! That's what we'll do; we'll build a concrete tent."

There was speculation about why the bids for the "concrete tent" came in so high. Some said that the drawings were not clear or complete and that the contractors were bidding high to protect themselves from unknowns. It was an unfamiliar system of construction. There were also suspicions that someone was making things difficult since Kansas City was a "closed town" when it came to bidding on work by out-of-town architects. As a solution to the problem, Mr. Wright proposed to the building committee that Ben Wiltscheck, the contractor who had constructed the Johnson Building and the Johnson residence, "Wingspread," be asked to supervise this project. The building committee agreed to this proposal and Wiltscheck agreed to do it. With the problem of selecting a builder solved it was hoped that construction could proceed. Mr. Wiltscheck sent Victor Holmes to Kansas City as his representative to supervise construction.

Other problems arose. One of these was the difficulty that Wiltscheck encountered in getting a bid or letting a contract for the steelwork. It was normally assumed that if one was using structural steel in Kansas City, Kansas City Structural Steel would do the work; they were the steel fabricators and erectors for the city and the surrounding area. Wiltscheck was unable to get a bid from them or to sign a contract with them for this work. He was finally able to get a price for the steelwork and to sign a contract with the Darby Company in Kansas City, Kansas, just before steel rationing went into effect. The Darby Company did not usually do steelwork for buildings. Their work was largely in the realm of industrial plants such as oil refineries. They fabricated the steel and sublet the erection of the steel to the Tobin Construction Company.

Resistance also appeared when a building permit was applied for in December.[41] The building commissioner, Frank Lloyd Lang, would not issue one. He and the city engineers found the drawings to be incomplete and many of the construction details unacceptable. They required more complete drawings and changes in the construction details before they would issue a permit. In lieu of the system of crushed rock footings which Mr. Wright had proposed they insisted on a standard foundation system of reinforced concrete. Mr. Wright refused to make this change. To resolve this problem, the building committee of the church, at the city engineers' suggestion, hired Irwin Pfuhl, a structural engineer who practiced in Kansas City, to revise the footings and to do detailed drawings for them. Mr. Wright objected to this and wrote the committee a letter to the effect that he wouldn't be responsible for any cracks or the like that might develop. The city engineers also doubted that the steel tube walls were strong enough as designed. The building commissioner insisted upon tests of the wall system and a doubling of the tubes in some areas.

In a letter to my parents on December 5, 1940, I wrote that "Mr. Wright sent the Building Committee of the church a letter saying that he was going to withdraw his plans and superintendence and stop construction on the church because the building committee wasn't cooperating with him in securing the building permit." It did seem that they were working against him. Mr. Adams, the chairman of the committee, was quoted as saying that they would never get a building permit with Mr. Wright's plans. Both Burris Jenkins and Joe Cleveland seemed willing to support Mr. Wright's position. The building committee did not.

A letter written to my brother, Connie, on the following day, December 6, indicated that all of these problems were temporarily solved: "Mr. Wright talked with Jenkins on the phone this evening and they have all of the church's troubles settled. The City issued a permit. And the church bought more land. So everything will be o.k. for a while." Work on construction started soon after that.

During that season in Wisconsin Mr. Wright also designed two large and expensive houses for clients with Hollywood careers – one was in radio and the other in film. The careers of both Arch Oboler, best known for the "Lights Out" series of radio plays, and John Nesbitt, with Metro-Goldwyn-Mayer's "Passing Parade," seemed to be on the rise at the time, but their houses were never built.

Mr. Wright did a sketch for the Oboler house one morning in August. This aerie, which Mr. Wright called Eaglefeather, was to be built into a mountain peak in the coastal range west of Los Angeles. From this site there were views over the valleys on all sides and to the Pacific Ocean not too far in the distance. The design was the most spectacular of a series of houses having canted walls of horizontal lapped boards and projected balconies and terraces.

The preliminary sketches for John Nesbitt's house were done early in December, shortly before we left for Arizona. The site for the Nesbitt house was a plot of windswept, cypress-covered land on the ocean near Carmel. In addition to this marvelous site, Mr. Nesbitt had presented Mr. Wright with a grandiose "script" for how he wanted to live in the house. He had let his imagination run free in his description of his needs and desires. Mr. Wright responded in kind with a grand rambling house. A covered walkway surrounded the site and connected the house to guest and caretakers quarters. Complete working drawings for this house were done during the winter, but it was never built.

The War in Europe

After I joined the Fellowship and became involved in its activities, the war seemed remote, even though it was a frequent subject of conversation at tea. Mr. Wright was opposed to war in general as a way of settling international disputes. And he was quite specifically opposed to the United States involvement in this war. He talked about it every day at tea. It was the topic of conversation – and some violent arguments – with guests at the movie on Saturday nights and at Sunday evening dinners. He also lent his voice to those who were publicly speaking out against American involvement in the war, men such as William Allen White and Charles Lindbergh.

During the summer of 1940, after the fall of France in the spring and the beginning of the Battle of Britain, the United States appeared to be moving toward direct involvement in the war. With this Mr. Wright's opposition to the war grew stronger. That summer, my first with the Fellowship, life at Taliesin did not seem to be much affected by the war. I wondered if it was a typical Taliesin summer. In a letter to George Beal,[42] I described it as a "combination country club and summer camp for children." There were eight children Iovanna's age or less. "Three Bloodgoods from Madison; two English refugees, and their mother; Mary Myers, daughter of Howard Myers, editor of the *Architectural Forum,* and so on." There were many guests including several former apprentices.

Our "two English refugees," Adam and Jimmie, were the sons of Mr. and Mrs. Stanley Nott, guests of Mr. and Mrs. Wright. They stayed most of the summer. Mrs. Wright had become acquainted with the Notts through her work with Georgi Gurdjieff at his Institute for the Harmonious Development of Man at the Prieure, near Paris. Although the Notts were from England, they shared Mr. Wright's opposition to American participation in the war. Mr. Nott, a publisher, wrote articles for the two issues of *Taliesin* which were published: "A Way to Beat Hitler" in the October 1940 issue, and "An Englishman Looks at Taliesin" in the February 1941 issue.

The apprentices were far from unanimous in their attitude toward the war. None volunteered for service in the army during the summer as conscription was being debated. After the passage of the Selective Service Act in September, the formation of the Selective Service System, and the appointment of county draft boards, those apprentices who were eligible for the draft registered, some in their home counties, some in Iowa County where Taliesin was located. I registered in Iowa County on October 16, 1940, when the clerk of the Iowa County Board came to the drafting room at Hillside at teatime to make it convenient for those who had not registered to do so. I received my registration papers on Saturday, November 30. After we had our registration papers, those who had registered with the Iowa County Board were not much concerned about being drafted. Iowa County's draft quota was being filled by volunteers.

Of course work was proceeding as usual, especially the preparations for Mr. Wright's exhibition in New York.

The Exhibition at
the Museum of Modern Art, New York

There was much optimistic talk of the forthcoming exhibition when I arrived at Taliesin in the fall of 1939. It was going to be a major exhibition of Mr. Wright's work, occupying the entire Museum of Modern Art in New York. A house was to be built in the courtyard of the museum. Mr. Wright was looking forward to this exhibition with much enthusiasm.

Larry Cuneo was building a photography studio in one of the former classrooms at Hillside. It was to be equipped to make large prints. (After Larry left in February 1940, this activity came to a standstill until Pete Guerrero joined the Fellowship in April.)

The first involvement of Fellowship members in the preparation for this exhibit began when Bob Blandin was assigned to make a model of the Johnson house. Bob joined the Fellowship in February 1940. He was from Iowa, and although appearing healthy enough he had some physical condition that prevented his being involved in the strenuous construction activity of the Fellowship. So he was assigned to build a model of Wingspread, "the last of the prairie houses," designed for Mr. and Mrs. Herbert "Hib" Johnson. The model was to be built at the scale of three-eighths of an inch to the foot.

The base of the model was eight feet square. It consisted essentially of two four-by-eight sheets of three-quarter-inch plywood. These were backed with a system of wooden stretchers to give it stiffness. At one side the plywood was built down in layers cut to represent the contours of the ravine which the broad terrace on the east side of the house spans and overlooks. This was the ravine to which Mr. Wright referred when he commented that the design of the house made one aware of the rolling topography of its site, that it made an interesting site out of one that otherwise lacked much interest. These contours were sanded to produce a smoothly modeled surface. Bob had put together a flexible cable electric sander for this operation. The base of the model was complete when the Fellowship moved to Wisconsin.

Bob Blandin left the Fellowship during the summer, and the making of the Johnson house model was assigned to me and Burt Goodrich early in September.[43] (I don't recall that he did much work on it. He was working on other models.) At this time the making of models of other buildings was being assigned to other apprentices: the Press Building – the skyscraper for the Spreckels estate in San Francisco – to Marcus Weston; a smaller scale model of the site and the group of seven Usonian houses for Okemos, Michigan, to Aaron Green; and the Affleck house in Bloomfield Hills to Bob May. Other models were assigned during the fall as the date for the exhibition drew closer. It was a slowly accelerating process which began after the preliminary sketches and working drawings for Community Church in Kansas City were completed and grew more intense during the fall.

In beginning work on the Johnson house model and in searching for information, such as drawings that I could use, I discovered, after going through the rather full, manila file folder of drawings and prints, that there was no definitive set of working drawings for the house. It is possible that Ben Wiltscheck, who built the house as well as the office building, had more complete drawings in his files. The plan I decided to use to lay out the model was the drawing which appeared in the 1938 *Architectural Forum*. I soon realized that some of the other projects of this time did not have the kinds of drawings which, according to the practice of architecture that I was familiar with, would have been considered a complete set of working drawings. At that time I found this a bit disturbing. I had had experience in offices which followed the generally accepted practice of preparing drawings on which bids could be taken and which also served as legal, contract documents. But based on my experience of the previous winter, when I learned that there were no working drawings for Taliesin West, I should not have been surprised. This discovery started me thinking about just what it is that an architect does. I became more aware of the secondary role of drawings and of the fact that buildings can be and have been built without drawings. This was all confirmed and reconfirmed in the years that followed, when additions or changes to Taliesin or Taliesin West were made; most, if not all, of the information about what was to be done was oral. Mr. Wright told people what to do. Sometimes this was supplemented by his pointing with his cane or a quick rough sketch on a piece of board, a "drawing on a shingle." There was something else, perhaps more important, that I also began to be aware of. It is the difference between those buildings that are conceived as the process of construction, as the actual putting together of materials, and those that are designed on paper and in terms of visual appearance only.

I began work on the model by laying out the plan of the house at three-eighths-inch scale on large sheets of brown wrapping paper. Then I transferred this to sheets of one-quarter-inch plywood. This was to represent the concrete floor mat. I scribed the unit system of the house into the plywood, sawed out the overall profile of the plan, and painted it a rusty red color. On this floor mat I then proceeded to build up the walls, building the model in much the same way that I envisioned the house as having been built (Fig. 45).

Models of more recent buildings, on display in the drafting room, served as

45 Model construction. Work on construction of the model of "Wingspread," the Herbert F. Johnson residence. Marcus Weston, who worked with me some of the time, is at the left. Photo by Pedro E. Guerrero.

prototypes for model-making techniques. Other techniques evolved as work on the models went forward. These resulted from experimentation on the part of apprentices and from suggestions by Mr. Wright. I was particularly intrigued with a device that someone had developed for the previously made model of the Jacobs house. It consisted of two steel rollers about ten inches long, between which one could push a one-quarter-inch-thick board that emerged on the opposite side with grooves on both sides representing the horizontal joints in brick work. One could build replicas of brick walls rather quickly with this device. Some details could be replicated at small scale on equipment in the model shop which had been set up in the east gallery at Hillside. For other details of the Johnson house, such as the roof facia, I made drawings of the desired profile; these were taken to a millwork shop in Madison and small molding strips were milled which I could then use to replicate certain details of the house.

One morning in late summer Mr. Wright arrived at the drafting room at Hillside at about his usual time. But when he walked in it was clear that he was furious about something. He announced to the room in general and to the few of us who were working there that "there is not going to be a catalogue." He did not say what had disturbed him or why there was not going to be a catalogue, nor did we dare to ask "why not" at that point. I assumed that something in the morning mail, which he usually read and took care of before coming over to the drafting room, had caused him to reach this decision. The question about what this something was remained unanswered. (It still remained unanswered following the publication of Hitchcock's *In the Nature of Materials*[44] which was, in a sense, a substitute for the noticeably absent catalogue, and which, incidentally, Mr. Wright had asked Hitchcock to write.)[45]

Many models of projects were made that fall. Others, such as the large model of Broadacre City and many of the smaller models that accompanied it, made by the Fellowship for the 1935 exhibition in New York, were completely refurbished for this exhibition.

Mr. Wright's written efforts to explain Broadacre City are, on the surface, a critical enumeration of the ills of the city, problems created by the industrial revolution. But between the lines is a glimpse of a philosophy of culture, a holistic vision of a way of life founded in a harmonious and integral relation to Nature, spelled with a capital N. It is a philosophy that shares much with – and borrows much from – the progressive and liberal thought of its time.[46] I also find it interesting that it shares much with more recent writing concerned about man's destructive relation to nature.[47]

In the early fall, many of us worked alone on our assigned models in our spare time or on rainy days when we couldn't work outside on some other project. But as the date for the exhibition drew nearer (at one time it was supposed to start during the second week in October) much more of everyone's time was required, and the pressure and tempo of work increased. Toward the end of October the opening was postponed. Mr. Wright was still thinking of other projects that he wanted to include, but most questions about such things as model-making techniques and colors had been answered and these models could be produced more quickly.

Finally, at the end of the first week in November, all of the material for the exhibition – drawings, photographs, models, and model bases – were packed and sent off to New York in a large moving van. It had been determined that this would be simpler and safer than crating the models individually for shipping. Five apprentices – Gene Masselink, John Hill, Davy Davison, Marcus Weston, and Victor Cusack – were sent to New York a day or so later to help with the installation of the exhibit.[48]

A letter of November 19 to my parents said that Mr. and Mrs. Wright and Gene Masselink had returned on the 18th from New York and that the opening of the exhibition had been a great success. It also said that they had "had quite a time getting it set up," and that Mrs. Wright "had called in all of her friends in New York and got them to come in and help."

Winter in Arizona, 1940–1941

Before leaving for Arizona that fall the Fellowship experienced a month of Wisconsin's winter weather (Fig. 46). It was a month during which much of our energy went into keeping warm, with lots of hauling of wood to feed the fireplaces and boilers. It was also a month in which there were rumors that Mr. Wright was "hard up for money" and that "some of the boys who are not paying anything are going to have to leave." On December 5 I wrote my parents, "We are all packed and just waiting to go to Arizona. Mr. Wright is in New York City and Washington, D.C., trying to get enough money together to take us to Arizona. We will probably leave pretty quick after he gets back." The next day I gave Gene Masselink a check for $20, my share of the cost of the trip. The day after that I gave Mr. Wright a check for $150, toward tuition, a large chunk of my remaining back account. Early the next morning we headed south through St. Louis, stopping there late in the afternoon to see the Carl Milles fountain, which had been com-

46   Taliesin in the snow. Seen from below on the road over Midway Hill to Hillside. Photo by author.

pleted that summer. Mr. Wright seemed to like Milles's sculpture. From St. Louis we headed southwest on Highway 66 to Albuquerque, down to Socorro, and across through Springerville and Globe. We arrived at the camp in Arizona before the end of the week.

During my year in the Fellowship I had not known nor had I been much concerned about who the paying or nonpaying apprentices were. There didn't seem to be much distinction made between them. The differences between the paying and nonpaying apprentices that I did see had to do with the amounts of money available to various people for the purchase of items such as clothing, movies, laundry, dry cleaning, and the like. Those who had money to spend on clothing were evident for they were the ones who wore Russell boots and Pendleton shirts. Except for this there seemed to be no difference in one's participation in the life of the Fellowship nor in one's relation to Mr. and Mrs. Wright. At that time I still had some money in my bank account and could write checks when I needed money. After I had been in the Fellowship for several years and had little or no money, I did begin to experience subtle differences resulting from the amount of money available to be spent on one's own wants.

During the early part of the winter I spent some of my time weeding the beds of cactus that Fred and I had moved into the triangular sunken garden the previous winter. Summer watering of the grass and the winter's rain had encouraged the grass to grow into these beds. Mr. Wright wanted the grass cleaned out.

Weeding these areas of cactus, reaching beneath the prickly pear and the cholla to get at the grass, was as hazardous as the moving and planting had been the previous winter. But while working on my hands and knees around the cactus I discovered an interesting phenomenon.

This garden was separated from the desert on two sides by a low, desert-concrete wall. On its side toward the desert, this wall varied in height from eighteen inches to three feet. The top of the wall was about sixteen inches wide. It provided a low curb to the red gravel walk that defined the boundary of the garden on two sides. From this walk a band of grass sloped gently down, about twenty inches, to the level of the garden.

When standing in the garden or sitting on the terrace or on the steps on the south side of the drafting room one saw the desert in the foreground coming up to the base of this wall. But when sitting or kneeling in the grass area, and if one's eye level was at or below that of the top of the low wall, the view of the desert in the foreground was cut off. And, if one's attention were shifted away from the desert view for a few moments and then returned to it, one had the sense of being quite high above the desert floor which could be seen only in the distance.

There was a change in elevation of several hundred feet between that of the desert floor and that of the camp, but when approaching the camp along the two miles of road leading up to the camp from Shea Boulevard you became aware that you were going uphill only when the road became curved and the grade a bit steeper.

After I discovered this phenomenon, I played with it whenever I was in the garden, whether working there or simply relaxing in the sun. And I wondered if this experience was intentional on Mr. Wright's part. (I knew, for example, that Mr. Wright's awareness of lines of sight, demonstrated in the design of the balcony on the south side of the living room of the Robie house, had provided its occupants with a sense of both privacy and openness.) Here, in the desert camp, there was a sense of exhilaration, a feeling of being in this high place and from this vantage point looking out over the desert's infinite extension to the horizon. Mr. Wright often described the desert camp as a "look over the rim of the world."

The Arizona winter of 1940–41 is vivid in my mind for several reasons. It was the winter that it rained. It was the winter that I twisted an ankle skiing. And it was the winter that the Fellowship issued a statement in reaction to the war and conscription.

It started to rain soon after we arrived in the desert.[49] All of the washes in the valley into which the roads dipped were running with water. Five cars from the camp were stuck in the desert Christmas Eve, and lost in the darkness. Some of them were abandoned in washes in which the water was several feet deep. Eugene Masselink's parents were coming for Christmas and Rowan Maiden had gone to meet them with the station wagon. They were marooned in a wash on the way back to camp. Rowan came to camp and got another car, but they did not reach camp until noon on Christmas Day when the water began to recede.

We were marooned again on New Year's Eve when newspaper reporters were trying to contact Mr. Wright. Mr. Wright had been sent a cablegram announcing that he was to receive the Royal Gold Medal for Architecture of the Royal Institute of British Architects.

> "Windsor Castle, 29th Dec. 1940. The King has been pleased to approve that Mr. Frank Lloyd Wright should be His Majesty's Gold Medalist of the Royal Institute of British Architects, for the year 1941. The Medal will be presented after the war. Keeper of the Privy Purse."

There was no telephone in the camp. The reporters were trying to contact Mr. Wright for a statement.

This winter's rain seemed to be a particular affront to Mr. Wright. The canvas roof flaps of the drafting room had leaked some the previous winter but we had taken measures that seemed to put a stop to this. But this winter one could hardly describe the condition of the drafting room as one caused by a leaky roof. It was almost as though there were no roof. It was as wet inside as outside. This was due in part to Mr. Wright's effort to fix the roof while it was still raining.

47   Canvas roofs reworked. In the reworking of the canvas roofs a band of lapped boards was introduced. This band was terminated with an upturned "hook," seen here at the west end of the drafting room. Photo courtesy of John H. Howe.

Rain was a challenge that could not be ignored. But nothing we did during the rain seemed to help matters. Nor for that matter did anything we did on sunny days help. After several weeks of rain and leaks Mr. Wright started a major reworking of the canvas roofs. He had the roof "trusses" taken apart saying that he was "going to fix them once and for all."

The roof trusses were an assembly of two-inch planks with one-by-twelve cheeks on either side. On the bottom was a two-by-six member, which projected about one inch on either side of the truss. The canvas-covered "flaps" rested on this projection. Into the top side of these projections, a small V-shaped gutter had been cut. This small gutter was not effective in catching and draining away the water from the sides of the trusses or the ends of the flaps. To replace these gutters, Mr. Wright had strips of thin galvanized steel, about ten inches wide, shaped with V-gutters at either side. These were placed over the top of the two-by-six bottom member of the trusses and did catch and drain away some of the rainwater.

This reworking of the canvas-covered roofs also involved the placing of a band of lapped, one-by-twelve, redwood boards between the trusses. The band extended the length of the drafting room and ended in an upturned hook outside the west end of the drafting room. Similar bands were also placed into the roofs of the "office" and the "living room" (Figs. 47, 48, 49).

Mr. Wright's fury at the rain may have been partly due to the fact that George Nelson, an editor at *Architectural Forum,* was in camp at the height of

48   South side of the drafting room, after roof was reworked. In the foreground, beds of yucca and prickly pear after weeding. Photo by author.

49   Interior of drafting room seen from east end after reworking of roof. Photo courtesy of John H. Howe.

this rainy season. My January 3 letter to George Beal had said that he was there working on a forthcoming issue, and a letter later that month to Verner Smith[50] indicated that the dummy for a forthcoming issue of the *Forum* was finished and that the Pauson house, which was then completed, was to be included in it. That forthcoming issue did not appear until January 1948. I do not know why it was forthcoming for such a long time.

Spring 1941

After the reworking of the canvas roofs was completed, construction of the apprentice wing, which had been started the previous spring, was resumed.

At about the same time Mr. Wright did a design for a series of small guest rooms, and construction was also started on these. Both the guest rooms and the rooms for apprentices were completed shortly after the first of March (Figs. 50, 51).

The guest rooms were built on the roof deck over the loggia east of the kitchen. Each of the rooms was not much larger than a sleeping compartment on a train. On the north side of each of these compartments was one twin bed and a narrow hanging space for clothing. There was a canvas door on the "clothes closet" and a drape that could be pulled to enclose the bed alcove. On the south side of the compartment there was a pair of canvas-covered doors. When these were closed, they formed the south wall of the room. When they stood open, as they usually did, the compartment was completely open to the "guest deck," and the person in it had no privacy. Some pairs of the compartments were open to each other so that they could be occupied by a couple. Otherwise they were separated only by a board wall covered with canvas.

Shortly after these projects had gotten under way we made our first of several trips to Flagstaff to ski. Fred Benedict was the organizer of the trips. He was the one person in the Fellowship who knew how to ski and who had skiing equipment. He had brought it to Arizona with a conviction, I suppose, that somehow and sometime during the winter he would be able to use it.

At that time, Saturday was Town Day. We did not have movies in camp on Saturday evenings because the interior of the Kiva, the small theater, had not been finished. As a result, Fred was able to get Mr. and Mrs. Wright's approval for the ski trips and for our starting them on Friday evenings after dinner. Our agreement with Mr. and Mrs. Wright was that we would be back in camp in time for Sunday evening dinner. This gave us a day and a half of skiing.

Those going on the trip would pack food, cooking equipment, and sleeping bags after tea on Friday. Then, after dinner, we would drive for a couple of hours to a camping place on the Verde River beyond Prescott. After an early breakfast we would then drive on to the ski area near the Snow Bowl in the San Francisco mountains northwest of Flagstaff.

50   Guest deck. A series of sleeping cubicles opening to the roof deck over the loggia east of the kitchen. Photo courtesy of John H. Howe.

51   Interior of sleeping cubicle. A small space for hanging clothes is at right of bed space. Photo courtesy of John H. Howe.

I described this first trip to Flagstaff in these enthusiastic words:

On Friday afternoon we left Phoenix with a lovely sunny temperature around 70, drove up to Jerome, camped on the Verde River, and the next morning, after a ride through Oak Creek Canyon, an unforgettable sight, we arrived in the Snow Bowl near Flagstaff. Three feet of snow, still sunny, and warm enough for skiing without heavy wraps, just a wool shirt. The landscape around there is terrific. It beats any picture postcard you can imagine. Huge pines and firs and aspen as thick as the pickets on a fence. Oak Creek Canyon is enough for anyone. The colors of the Grand Canyon. All of its beauty but more comprehensive because it isn't so huge as to be beyond your grasp. Through the bottom runs a creek with live oaks and peach orchards, irrigated from the creek, on either side. I decided that Oak Creek Canyon was a place where I could quite happily "eke out an existence."[51]

After a day of skiing, we drove into Flagstaff late on Saturday afternoon. There we rented two connecting rooms in a rather primitive tourist court where we could get in out of the snow and cold. In these we cooked our supper and breakfast on a wood-burning stove and rolled out our sleeping bags for the night. Some of us slept on the beds and some on the floor. After an early breakfast the next morning, we got in a half day of skiing and still made it back to camp for dinner at seven.

Early in February, a couple of weeks after our first trip, Mr. Wright was injured. He had gone to San Francisco with Blaine Drake to see the Bazett house, which had been completed the previous summer, and to visit several clients in the San Francisco area. On the return trip their Lincoln Continental had had an "encounter with a truck near Fresno." The details of the accident were never clear to me. I only know that midmorning one day word quickly spread that Mr. Wright and Blaine were back at the camp and had been in an auto accident.

Blaine, who had been driving, was not injured. But Mr. Wright, who had been resting on the back seat, was badly bruised and had some cuts on his leg. We did not see much of him for several weeks. He stayed in the family's quarters, flat on his back. I assume he refused to go to a hospital. His doctor came out from Phoenix to check on his condition frequently. And a masseur came out several times a week to give him physical therapy. It was about a month before he was back on his feet. But even then he did not have his usual energy.

We made three ski trips that winter. On the last one, near the end of February, I fell and severely twisted my ankle. We were very concerned that if Mr. and Mrs. Wright learned that I had been injured they might put an end to our skiing trips.

We were back in camp on Sunday in time for dinner. During dinner and the music which followed, I tried to walk and stand as though nothing had happened. At the time I was working on yet another of the many reworkings of the drafting

52 Interior of Kiva. The center of the room is filled with a stepped series of benches with ledges at the back on which to eat. A table for Mr. and Mrs. Wright and guests is at the back of this seating. Similar benches and ledges surround the room on three sides. Photo courtesy of John Geiger.

room roof. I was putting metal flashing under the ends of the boards in the lapped-board bands. Sitting on the roof all day meant that I didn't do much walking or standing. Whenever Mr. or Mrs. Wright was near and might see me, I managed to be standing still. Whether or not they ever knew of the injury, I don't know; nothing was ever said.

Also, at about that time, the rooms around the apprentice court were completed and with them the long-awaited shower room. It was now possible to take a hot shower before dinner. Completion of the shower room did away with one reason for Town Day.

It is misleading to say that the rooms around the apprentice court were completed. With each change of the occupants of those thirteen rooms, the rooms themselves were changed. Fireplaces were built to replace the small V-slots in the walls that were the original fireplaces. Closets and other built-in furnishings were moved and modified. Skylights were cut into the roof to let in more light, particularly in the north facing rooms. And glass was installed behind the exterior canvas flaps to make the rooms somewhat easier to heat on cold, windy nights.

After the apprentice rooms were completed the Kiva was also finished. This did away with another reason for Town Day. A small projection room was built onto the Kiva on its north side, and the interior of the theater was furnished. A

53   Group in Kiva. In front at left, Kay and Davy Davison. In middle, Mr. and Mrs. Wright and Wes Peters.
In back, left to right: Gordon Chadwick, Cary and Frances Caraway, Gene Masselink, and Gordon Lee.
Photo courtesy of Robert C. May.

screen was placed over the fireplace at the south end of the room. At the side of it
was a tier of three steps on which the chorus stood when it sang. An upright
piano was built into the east side of the room near the front. Benches were built
around three sides of the room. In front of these there was a twelve-inch-wide
ledge on which places could be set for dinner. In the center, at the back, was a
table with seating for Mr. and Mrs. Wright and a few guests. In front of this, in
progressively descending heights, were more ledges and benches. The people in
the front row sat on the carpeted floor. It was a bit cozy and crowded. The Fellowship was already larger than Mr. Wright had anticipated when the Kiva was
planned (Figs. 52, 53).

Town Day, however, had become a practice that could not easily be ended. It
had become a part of the week that the apprentices looked forward to. By com-
mon agreement between Mr. Wright and the apprentices, Town Day was shifted
from Saturday to Monday afternoon.

The Fellowship and the Draft

For a period after registration for the draft in the fall of 1940, none of the apprentices received a notice to appear for a physical exam, nor had any been drafted. But during the winter and early spring that began to change.

I had sought classification as a conscientious objector when I registered for the draft, and I later objected to receiving a 1-B classification. I wrote a letter to the Iowa County Board on February 12, 1941, appealing a continuance of this 1-B classification after a rejection of my first appeal.

It appeared that one by one the Fellowship was going to be reduced in size and effectiveness. Facing this possibility the Fellowship drafted a statement of its position; it objected to the Compulsory Military Draft and asked that we be allowed to work for constructive purposes as a group. I do not know now and did not know then by whom the statement was written. I assume it was a group effort of several of the seniors. Its sound suggests the influence of Mr. Wright, but there was a tendency for some apprentices to emulate Mr. Wright's manner of writing. I assume that he had read it and perhaps edited it before it was presented by Burt Goodrich in typed form at teatime to be signed by members of the Fellowship. (Burt Goodrich also wrote an article for the second issue of *Taliesin* magazine, published in February 1941, entitled "How to Stay Out of War the American Way.") He asked those who agreed with the statement to sign it. Twenty-five apprentices were listed on the statement. Three of those listed had not signed it.

THE TALIESIN FELLOWSHIP was founded in 1932 near Spring Green, Wisconsin, by Frank Lloyd Wright, American Architect, to accomplish the work herein stated:

1. To create upon the thousand-acre farm and in the architectural workshops and the home buildings of Taliesin a way of life firmly based upon the American tradition of hard work and yet establish a convincing example of indigenous American culture.

2. To assist young men to develop their creative capacities in building better buildings for America, buildings more truly expressive of the land we live in and of the people of our great Democracy.

3. To train such Builder-architects by continuous actual experience in planning and

building with every kind of tool and material, first upon the farm and buildings of the Fellowship, later by work and superintendence upon important buildings now in actual construction by ourselves in twenty-seven states throughout the country. Necessarily the endeavor of the Taliesin Fellowship is upon a completely legal, non-profit basis known as the Frank Lloyd Wright Foundation.

4. To this end every resource within the power of its leader has gone to build up not only the internal strength of the Fellowship work life but to get materials to work with and to extend the opportunities for the work and growth of the young men and women of the group. For the past eight years the energies and continual work of an average of twenty-seven worker-apprentices has gone into the Foundation. By the natural process of selection inevitable in the circumstances this group has been so knit together that it now stands well equipped to do the work it set out to do for our country.

To preserve for Americans what we must believe to be a true form of self-defense, we the undersigned members of the Taliesin Fellowship hereby go on record as Objectors to the Compulsory Military Draft which threatens not only to destroy us as a group but violates the deepest concern of our individual consciences.

To compel the breaking up of the consequences of these years of training is a far more serious loss to America at this time than the loss to the American army, of men whose convictions, education, and principles render them unfit for destruction and mass-murder called war. Therefore we respectfully ask that we be allowed to work as a group for interior defense than be compelled to waste our lives in jail. We ask that our services in preparing for war be used in the construction field in which we are already engaged in the effort to preserve our American Democracy. Compulsory conscription will only scatter us and render us impotent.

The Taliesin Fellowship

Anton Bek	Aaron Green
Frederic Benedict	Norman Hill
Curtis Besinger	John H. Howe
Peter Berndtson	Kenneth Lockhart
Alfred Bush	Rowan Maiden
Cary Caraway	John E. Lautner
Gordon Chadwick	Eugene Masselink
James Charlton	Robert Mosher
Allen L. Davison	William Wesley Peters
Benjamin Dombar	Charles F. Samson
Blaine Drake	Edgar A. Tafel
Herbert Fritz	Marcus Weston
Burton J. Goodrich	

The statement was sent to Clarence Dykstra, who was the president of the University of Wisconsin, and from 1940 to April 1941, Director of Selective Service.[52] In a letter I wrote to George Beal on March 28 I said:

> I wish that you could read a statement the Fellowship has made regarding conscription and military training. I hope no harm comes of it. I think that the Fellowship had to be put on record as objectors sooner or later and a group objection should certainly bear some weight. At least more than our "one-at-a-timers." We addressed the statement to Dykstra but since there is no longer a Director (of Selective Service) it may be just another "Arrow into the Air."

Kansas City, Spring, Summer, Early Fall, 1941

If there was any response from Dykstra or his successor to the Fellowship's statement, I didn't hear of it. Late in March 1941 I left the Fellowship to go back to Kansas City to work in Joe Radotinsky's office. I had spent about all of the money I had saved prior to joining the Fellowship. I had paid tuition for 1½ years, about $1,600. The rest had been spent for personal odds and ends.

I had worked in Joe's office for the greater part of the three years between my graduation from the University of Kansas and my joining the Fellowship. Joe needed a draftsman that spring and I needed money. He had sent me a telegram, about six weeks before I left, asking if I would be interested in working for him for a while. I was. I knew from conversation within the Fellowship that Mr. Wright was not inclined to support more nonpaying apprentices. In addition to replenishing my savings, working for Joe offered several other things: a vacation from Taliesin, an opportunity to see friends and family, and the chance to watch Community Church being constructed.

Taking my leave of the Fellowship was not easy. When I told Mr. Wright of my plans he offered no objection; he told me that he would be glad to see me back. There were many in the Fellowship with whom I had been closely associated (Fig. 54). I enjoyed their company and presence. We had shared many hardships with amusement and many pleasures with delight.

As I left Arizona I wrote in a notebook my thoughts and reactions.

As I ride on this train away from Taliesin in the desert a number of things are running through my mind. Thoughts concerning a year and one-half with Mr. Wright and the Taliesin Fellowship. Regrets for having to leave the Fellowship for a few months at this time when it was really expressing itself as a unified group, by taking a constructive stand with regard to the participation of the group in the present war and plans for war. Mixed feelings with regard to my friends in the Fellowship – regrets at leaving those whom I knew were really my friends and a peculiar feeling of pleasure and surprise and regret in the finding that I had some few friends in the Fellowship of whose friendship I wasn't aware.

54 Fellowship at lunch, spring 1941. Counterclockwise from left: Wes Peters, standing, Gordon Lee,
John Hill, Jack Howe, Marcus Weston, Davy Davison, unknown, Hans Koch, Karen Caraway, Kay Davison,
Tor and Cary Caraway, Kenn Lockhart. Gene Masselink, standing. Ted Bower, standing behind Cary. Jim
Charlton, seated on stone. Norman Hill, standing at back. Seated on grass, unknown and Aaron Green.

As I wrote George Beal late in March, shortly after my arrival in Kansas
City, one of my reasons for coming there was the "chance to watch the construction of the church, slow as it may be," but "unofficially and off-the-record," I was
also there "to see if I can find out what might be holding up construction. Mr.
Wright suggested that I try and find out." In this letter I also wrote that "I
strongly suspect that it is the same old machine at work," which of course was
difficult to determine.[53]

I began my investigation by asking Joe Radotinsky if he knew about anything that might be holding up construction. He said that all he knew was what
he had read in the papers. This convinced me that he knew more than he was
telling. I next talked with Bob Dunham, the friend who had gotten me my first
job in Joe's office. (He was no longer working there.) He said that the problems
were the result of incomplete drawings and poor supervision, that the architect
needed a more fully informed representative on the job. On March 31 I talked

with George Beal. He mentioned, among other things, that A. W. Archer had thought that the job was his until Mr. Wright had gotten it, and that resolutions had been proposed at a Kansas City A.I.A. meeting condemning Beal for urging the church committee to retain Mr. Wright as architect, and that the resolutions had not been approved due to the actions of Mr. Simpson, a partner in Keene and Simpson, Architects.

On the same day, I talked with Lloyd Roark, a classmate at K.U. He said that both architects and contractors were mad that the job had gone out of town, that many of the architects thought that the job should have been theirs, and that the plans for the church were difficult to read. On April 2 I managed to see Joe Cleveland. He said that much of the trouble lay with the building committee and its chairman, Arthur Adams, a lawyer who had connections with the Pendergast machine. When I talked with Professor Kellogg on April 20, he confirmed George Beal's statements about the resolutions proposed at the A.I.A. meeting. He said that the resolutions were introduced by A. W. Archer and waylaid by Mr. Simpson. On the same day, I talked with Professor Verner Smith who confirmed the statements of Beal and Kellogg. After talking with several other former K.U. students, I had a list of the names of most of the major architectural offices in Kansas City, all of whom believed that the commission for the church should have been theirs.[54]

In the middle of May, George Beal called and told me that Mr. and Mrs. Wright were in Lawrence, visiting overnight. I caught a bus to Lawrence early the next morning, had breakfast with the Beals and Mr. and Mrs. Wright, and then rode back to Kansas City with them. They were traveling cross-country in Mrs. Wright's Lincoln Continental with Herb Fritz driving them. During the ride from Lawrence to Kansas City, Mr. Wright, observing the countryside, seemed especially interested in the different kinds of roofs on the farm buildings and talked about their various characteristics. It was the shed roof in particular that seemed to catch his eye. It was a roof form that he had seldom used.

I assume that Mr. Wright spent a part of the day seeing the Sondern house, which was then complete. He also took care of problems connected with the Community Church; the footings had been poured, the concrete foundation walls were up to ground level, and the setting of the "tons of steel" which Commissioner of Buildings Frank Lloyd Lang boasted of requiring them to use, was under way (Fig. 55).

Late in the afternoon, I had a call from Gene Masselink. The Fellowship was in Kansas City. They were going to have dinner with the Sonderns. Could I come over and join them? Of course I could, and did.

The painter Thomas Hart Benton and his wife, Rita, lived just next door to the Sonderns and joined the dinner party. The Sondern house was one of the smallest of the Usonians, and probably the best in quality of construction. I don't know how we all fitted into the living room for dinner. After dinner we all moved

55   Community Church steelwork. Seen from the south side, the form of the building was beginning to take shape when this photo was taken on May 12, 1941, at about the time that Mr. Wright stopped in Kansas City. Photo by author.

next door to the Benton house, which was much larger than the comparatively small area of the Sondern house.

Mr. Wright and Tom Benton seemed to find great delight in each other's company, although I could not imagine a Benton mural or painting in one of Mr. Wright's buildings. It would not have met Mr. Wright's requirement that it stay flat on the wall. At that time Benton was in the process of being fired as director of the Kansas City Art Institute. He and his paintings were the center of much controversy. A painting of a female nude, "Suzanna and the Elders," and his comments regarding it, had offended the patrons of art in Kansas City. Mr. Wright was the center of a controversy about the building of Community Church. They traded the tales of their trials and tribulations with amusement. During the evening, the Fellowship, sitting on the floor of the Benton living room, sang almost all of the chorus's repertoire. Benton and his wife responded in kind, playing the guitar and harmonica for the Fellowship.

During the summer, I maintained contact with the Fellowship. I corresponded with several members of the Fellowship and was kept informed of activities.

Henry-Russell Hitchcock was at Taliesin, doing a book on Mr. Wright's work. Jack Howe was busy doing drawings for the book. Mr. Wright had done a preliminary design for a fraternity house in Hanover, Indiana. Working drawings had been started on the Florida Southern Library. One disturbing bit of news was that "all of the seniors" were leaving the Fellowship. As near as I could gather from the letters, they were leaving because of a change in policy. There had been an understanding that apprentices, at least senior apprentices, would be permitted to bring architectural projects of their own to the Fellowship and they would be done as Fellowship projects. Several had done this. Edgar Tafel, in addition to supervising the construction of several of Mr. Wright's houses – the Charles Manson house in Wausau, Wisconsin, the Bernard Schwartz house in Two Rivers, Wisconsin, and the Lloyd Lewis house in Libertyville, Illinois – was also supervising the construction of some houses which he had designed. Cornelia Berndtson had designed a house for her aunt, Hulda Notz. It was based on a previous house she had designed, using a hexagonal unit that was, according to reports, the source of Mr. Wright's use of the hexagonal unit in the Hanna house. Mr. Wright decided that this practice should stop. The reason for this decision, as Mr. Wright explained later, was that the houses designed by the apprentices were not as well done as those designed by him and that putting the energy of the Fellowship into these houses was in effect diluting and weakening his own efforts.

Those who left because they were unhappy with this change in policy were Peter and Cornelia Berndtson, Blaine and Hulda Drake, Edgar Tafel and his wife, Sally, whom he had married in mid-December, Ellis Jacobs and his wife, Phyllis, Bennie Dombar, and Burt Goodrich. That was not "all of the seniors," but it was over half of those whom I considered to be seniors. Those remaining were Wes Peters and Svetlana, Gene Masselink, Jack Howe, and Bob Mosher.

And yet, despite the news of this exodus, other news from the Fellowship was optimistic and ongoing: Mr. Wright had designed a house for Carlton Wall and working drawings were being done. Mr. Wright had had an exhibition in Milwaukee. There were new apprentices: Peter Sanford, Chi-Ngai Chau, and Gordon Lee.

During the summer Mr. Wright started writing and circulating the *Taliesin Square Papers,* subtitled "A Non-Political Voice from Our Democratic Minority." These were printed on newsprint and mailed at his expense to a rather large list including those who had subscribed to *Taliesin.* I received six of these during the summer. The first had been written in January in response to a request from the *News Chronicle of London* which asked if he "would be willing to write for publication exclusively in the *News Chronicle of London* an article of 1500 words on 'How I Would Rebuild London.'" The others were written in opposition to war. They were not only a protest against the increasing involvement of the United States in the European war; they were a protest to war in general as a means of solving social, economic, and political problems. Many of these papers were both a restatement and an elaboration of many of his beliefs, beliefs which had appeared much earlier in his writing and speaking; they were central to his larger vision of a way of life, his Broadacre proposals and his designs for buildings being only another form of that vision's expression. I had gone to Taliesin because I shared many of these beliefs as I understood them.

During this summer Mr. Wright and Lewis Mumford came to a shattering difference of opinion with regard to the war. Mumford had been a friend of Mr. Wright and one of his most understanding and appreciative critics. But a full-page ad appeared in the *New York Times* in which Mumford accused Mr. Wright of being an American quisling. (Vidkun Quisling was a pro-Nazi Norwegian who had betrayed his own country by aiding an invading enemy.) As a student I had become an admirer of Mumford's writing. I had read his books: *Sticks and Stones, Technics and Civilization,* and *The Culture of Cities.*[55] It seemed to me that he and Mr. Wright shared many of the same values. I wrote Mumford to protest his accusation. I hadn't expected a response, but much to my surprise we exchanged two letters. Neither of us changed our positions.

Mr. Wright had had vigorous and violent arguments about the war with other friends, including Bill Evjue, the editor of the *Capital Times* of Madison. These had been friendly quarrels and were soon patched up. But the fracture with Mumford was not to be soon healed.

The city's resistance to the building of the church seemed to continue during the summer when the city building commissioner required two structural tests. The floor system of the building consisted of steel bar joists, spaced farther apart than normally expected, with a thin floor slab of gunite concrete sprayed in place over a paper-backed steel mesh reinforcing. The building inspector insisted that there was to be no publicity on the test. We knew that if the test had failed there would have been much publicity. But the test was successful.

The city also required a test loading of the balcony of the sanctuary before the building could be occupied. The balcony is supported, in part, by two steel bars. These hang from and are welded to steel beams that span the sanctuary from front to back. These beams, which also support the roof system of the sanctuary, are supported by steel columns at the front of the sanctuary and at either side of the chancel, and by columns in similar positions at the rear. The building inspector insisted that the balcony be tested with a load several times that which it was designed to carry. It was loaded with concrete blocks and bags of sand. There was very little deflection under the load; the balcony did not fall. And again the city insisted that there was to be no publicity.

Except for these tests, contruction progressed rapidly, and by early fall gunite concrete was being sprayed on the wall, floor, and ceiling surface. Construction of Community Church was completed in mid-winter (Fig. 56). (The parking terraces and the chapel proposed in the original design were not built.) The dedication was held in January of 1942 on "the coldest day of winter." And again trouble arose. The city engineers had said that the heating system would not be satisfactory – and it wasn't. The building was cold for the ceremony. Those in the audience wore winter coats. The source of the problem with the heating system was

56 Community Church. The northwest side of the building as it appeared shortly before I left Kansas City in the fall to rejoin the Fellowship. Photo by author.

found only on the night before the dedication, too late to be repaired. The pumps that circulated the hot water through the pipe coils of the floor heating system were not properly connected and were running in reverse.

I was not present at the dedication. I saw the building in use for the first time in the spring of 1942, when I traveled to Wisconsin with Gordon Chadwick and Henning Watterson. We stopped in Kansas City to see the church. It was a great disappointment; it looked raw and unfinished. The sanctuary had seats but it lacked any other furnishings. The exterior had not been landscaped. During that summer I did drawings for suggested landscaping, for carpeting the interior, and for chancel furniture.

This was a building that did not receive Mr. Wright's finishing touch – the finishing touches were added by others. Mr. Wright told his version of the series of events that led to this circumstance in the second edition of his autobiography.[56]

It was characteristic of Mr. Wright to give intense attention to a building at the time of its design and during the preparation of the drawings for its construction. He gave his attention to it again as it neared completion. He appeared to lose interest during the construction process, particularly when the project was not nearby and he could not visit the building occasionally. Mr. Wright was impatient with the process of construction; he wanted to see the building taking shape quickly. It was and is a building that suffered as a result of Mr. Wright's not seeing it through to the finish.

The building as it stands today is something of an anomaly. Mr. Wright rejected it. Kansas City has accepted it. Henry-Russell Hitchcock included it as an unfinished project in *In the Nature of Materials,* but it has never appeared as an illustration in any publication on Mr. Wright's work for which he selected the illustrations. Kansas Citians seem to take some pride in it. They point to it as one of the three buildings in the city designed by Mr. Wright. The Community Christian Church, the present occupants, also seem to take a certain pride in occupying a building designed by Frank Lloyd Wright. But it stands as an aborted curiosity.

Toward the end of the summer I began to think of rejoining the Fellowship. I had come to Kansas City in the spring with some hope that I might be of help in expediting the construction of the church. I had gone over every week, following the process of construction, and had taken photos and sent copies of them to Mr. Wright. I had seen and talked with Joe Cleveland and his wife frequently. But there seemed to be nothing that I could do to effect the eventual outcome. I had received a letter from Mr. Wright which said, "You know how we feel about you here. We will be glad to see you back, Curtis." I had saved some money, about half of what I had earned. And with the buildup of war in Europe and the increasing restrictions on any building in the United States except that which was war-related, work in Radotinsky's office was slackening.

My plans to rejoin became firm in November when the migration to Arizona began. I received a letter from Gene Masselink early in November indicating that the migration was already under way.[57] This year they were not traveling in a caravan. Gene Masselink, in Mrs. Wright's Continental, picked me up on his way through Kansas City. We arrived at the camp before the end of the fourth week in November.

Winter 1941–1942

When we arrived at the camp I was told that I was to share a room on the apprentice court with Marcus Weston. Marcus and I were both seeking draft classification as conscientious objectors. I had gotten to know him when we were both assigned to work on construction projects at Taliesin in the fall of 1939. I enjoyed working with Marcus on these projects and learned something about carpentry from him. Marcus had learned carpentry from working with his father, Will Weston.

We were assigned a room near the northeast corner of the apprentice court. It was a pleasant, east-facing room. It was quickly warmed on cold mornings after we opened the canvas-covered flaps on the east side to let the sun in. The room was one of three which shared a diagonally positioned entry at a break in the concrete wall which defined the north half of the court.

I had not worked on building these rooms, but I was intrigued with their construction, particularly the way in which they were detailed. Except for a single layer of shiplap boards, covered with canvas, which formed a panel in the upper half of the partitions between rooms, there was little or no hidden construction. Every board counted both visually and constructionally. The west wall of our room was desert concrete. It absorbed heat during the afternoons. This heat helped to warm the room in the evening. There was a small V-shaped notch in this wall for a fireplace. It was large enough for only a very small fire.

The other three walls of the room were wood. The lower part of these walls were made of lapped, one-by-twelve redwood boards run horizontally. At desk or table-top height there was a two-by-six redwood ledge on the north and south walls. Above this were the canvas-covered panels. On the east side of the room the horizontal ledge was made of a redwood two-by-twelve. This made a broad continuous sill for the three openings above it. These openings were closed by pairs of horizontal, canvas-covered "flaps" that were hinged to allow control of sunlight and vision. They didn't keep out much of the cold night air.

The previous occupants of our room had built a clothes closet with canvas-covered doors, and a low desk or table on the south wall. Along the east wall was a platform for beds. It was long enough for two twin-bed mattresses, placed end to end, a luxury in the desert camp.

Shortly after my arrival in Arizona I had written Professor Beal:

Mr. Wright seems to have enough business to keep him busy. As busy as he can ever be; you don't think of Mr. Wright as being busy or rushed. He has a Defense Housing Project in the east somewhere; a hundred units I believe. It will certainly be interesting to compare this with those of Gropius, Raymond, and others that appeared in the *Architectural Forum* several months ago.

I suppose that you know about Mr. Wright's new books. The collected writings, edited by Fritz Gutheim, are already out. A book covering 50 years of his work edited by Henry Russell Hitchcock is supposed to be out sometime before Christmas. It should certainly be something of a source book for us lesser creatures.[58]

Thanks to our seasonal migrations Mr. Wright was able to view Taliesin and Taliesin West with a fresh eye each time he arrived at one of them. And before settling down to work on projects for clients, he immediately would launch a series of changes in the buildings. This winter he decided that it was time to replace the canvas on the roofs of his office and the drafting room (the canvas had been in place about three years and had become worn and dirty) and, while doing this, to make some more changes in the details of the roofs to eliminate leaks.

The Fellowship had settled into their tents or rooms, and work on the changes that Mr. Wright wanted were well under way, when word came over the radio in the drafting room on Sunday morning that the Japanese had attacked Pearl Harbor. This was disturbing news to a group in which there was already an undercurrent of differences of opinion about the war. Mr. Wright's position remained the same. If anything he became more vehement in his opposition to war in general and to this particular war.

In the early part of the winter, life in the Fellowship continued very much as usual. Wes and Svet's first child, Brandoch, was born on December 17, 1941. We celebrated Christmas with a feast at the long table in the drafting room and the opening of the Christmas Box.

I entitled the project that I did for the box "A Room with a Bath for Those without Roots." The "room" was one large space with a cooking arrangement, a bathroom, a sleeping porch, and a carport for two cars! There was a high, flat roof over the central space and a lower one over the carport. There were clerestory windows between the two roofs. The south wall was opened, with glass, to a terrace partially covered with a trellis and a garden beyond it. These units were arranged in a row. It was, in effect, a glamorized tourist court.

My drawings, a perspective, and a plan, were drawn on one 18"-by-24" sheet of tan charcoal paper and rendered in colored pencil. I was quite pleased with my effort. When Mr. Wright came to my project in the Box, he took one look at it and commented: "Oh wad some power the giftie gie us To see ourselves as others see us!" Without further comment he went on to the next drawing. It did not take me long to figure out that the comment was not favorable.

Soon after our arrival in the desert Henning Watterson began a weaving project that was to take more than a year to complete. Mr. Wright had designed a large rug for the central area of the Hillside living room. The design was based on a square unit of about three feet, a width that could be woven on Henning's, Svetlana's, and the Fellowship's looms. The design was made up of areas of dark brown, dark blue, bright orange, and black-and-white. The yarn for it was purchased from the Navajo Indians. It came in large loose hanks of naturally white and black yarn with some brown mixed in it. These were to be used for the white-and-black areas. The yarn had to be dyed for the other areas of color. The dyeing took a large part of the winter. It was done in large galvanized washtubs, in water heated over an open fire. Actual weaving did not get started until about a month before the spring migration.

Despite Mr. Wright's well-known objection to the increasing involvement of the United States in the war, he did talk optimistically of being asked to do two projects for government agencies. One of these was a portable field hospital. This never progressed beyond Mr. Wright's saying that he had been commissioned to do such a project. No drawings were ever made. The other was a defense housing project for Pittsfield, Massachusetts. He had signed a contract for this project in August. It did progress to a completed set of working drawings. (An insider's account of the death of this project was published in the *A.I.A. Journal* of February 1970 with the title "FLW versus the USA.")[59]

The preliminary drawings for this project were done in mid-January 1942, in only four days following receipt of the site survey. Some of the preliminary drawings for this project and Mr. Wright's account of the project were published in the January 1948 *Architectural Forum*.[60] Gordon Lee, an apprentice who had joined the Fellowship the previous summer, did the interior perspectives for the preliminary presentation. Gordon had designed a house for the Christmas Box and made very skillful drawings of it. His house was similar to a Swiss Alpine chalet, but it had some Wrightian characteristics. His drawings were meticulous and had a kind of *gemutlichkeit* charm; they were like illustrations that might have appeared in *Child Life* to illustrate the story of Heidi. It was probably because of these that Gordon was asked to do the interior perspectives of the Pittsfield housing units. He filled them with carefully drawn details of ordinary family life.

The project, called Cloverleaf, was based on the Suntop project which Mr. Wright had previously designed for Otto Mallory. The Pittsfield project, however, was designed to be built almost entirely of thin, precast concrete panels using "diatomaceous earth." Mr. Wright described it as a "house of cards." Some of the units were to have lapped-board parapets to introduce a variation into the scheme. Unlike the Suntop units, the four houses were separated to give each of the units an interior court.

We started working drawings for the project about a month later. On February 26, I wrote Professor Beal:

> We are in the midst of doing the drawings for a defense housing project now. Originally the project called for one hundred houses to be located near Pittsfield, Mass. While we were in the midst of doing the preliminaries Mr. Wright got a telegram from Washington calling the job off, changing the housing to demountables. I suppose that you may have seen this in the papers. I've never seen a supposed cancelling of a contract get so much publicity. Mr. Wright wired asking to be allowed to present his scheme before they called things off. So they wired back for him to come to Washington. He went rather expecting to be nicely brushed off. Instead the Gov. seemed interested in the scheme and sent him back to prepare the working drawings. They are particularly interested in their use around Washington, and perhaps elsewhere. In addition they want Mr. Wright to do a preliminary scheme for them of a demountable house. Mr. Wright was willing to do that and offered also to do a scheme for a demountable field hospital; the field hospital is out of the jurisdiction of the housing authorities, but they told him to do the scheme and they would sell it for him. So we're working for the government.

The drawings for the project were completed rather quickly early in March. There was little other architectural work to be done. Everyone who had had some drafting experience was assigned to the project. In order to work on the drawings at night when it was cold, we moved drafting into Mr. Wright's office. It was smaller than the drafting room and with a large fireplace and a gas heater could be more readily warmed.

In the February 26 letter to Professor Beal I also said:

> This defense housing scheme is no snap to do drawings for. The whole thing is practically an invention in building technic. Wall slabs of 2" thick diatomaceous earth, floor slabs of 2½" thick concrete. Everything is precast. There are some wood walls that come near to being in the realm of the usual construction.

The drawings for this project were quite complete; the panels were scheduled and the shape of each type of panel was drawn to show interlocking notches and slots. When this project did not proceed into construction, the Fellowship was quite disheartened. It had been an opportunity to put into practice the ideals put forth in the statement objecting to conscription.

At the same time that the preliminaries for the government housing project were being done, Mr. Wright also did the design for the fifty-unit Cooperative Homestead project proposed to be built near Detroit by and for auto workers who were to live in the houses. It was a very interesting scheme for low-cost housing, solving what Mr. Wright described as "mainly a drainage and landscape problem." A portion of the preliminary drawings for this project was also published in the January 1948 *Architectural Forum*.[61]

The houses consisted essentially of a simple flat-brimmed, hatlike roof hovering over a berm of earth banked against chest-height rammed earth walls. Sandwiched between the berm and the roof was a band of windows. A fireplace and massive piers of rammed earth were the dominant vertical elements. Working drawings for this project were completed by the end of February. Aaron Green, who, with Bob May, had done the drawings for the project, went to Detroit about a month later to start construction.

Construction was started; but the auto workers, who until that time had not been fully employed and had had time to do the rammed earth walls and piers, were now working overtime in the industrial plants that were gearing up for wartime production.

Spring 1942

Shortly after the completion of the Pittsfield drawings, near the end of March, four of us were told to get ready to go to Los Angeles. We were not told what we were going for except that we were to do some work on two houses that Mr. Wright had designed. The four assigned to go to Los Angeles were Gordon Chadwick, Kenn Lockhart, Marcus Weston, and myself. We drove over in a second-hand Model A Ford Roadster which Mr. Wright had bought earlier in the winter for Fellowship use.

We went first to the George Sturges house in Brentwood Heights west of Los Angeles (Fig. 57). This house, built about two years before under John Lautner's supervision, had exterior walls of single, lapped redwood boards, mitered at the corners. The redwood, probably unseasoned when the house was built, had shrunk, cracked, and discolored badly. Our job was to seal the cracks and to paint

57   Sturges House, Brentwood Heights, California. Photo by author.

the house inside and out with what would now be called a heavy-body stain. It was a mixture of iron oxide (red) barn paint and white lead that produced a rose color somewhat like that of freshly sawn or unweathered redwood. Before brushing on the paint we tightened all the screws that held the boards together and caulked the split boards and opened miters. Since the house projects rather dramatically from the hillside, scaffolding was something of a problem. Some areas could be reached with short ladders. But other areas, such as the underside of the balcony, which would have required elaborate scaffolding, was reached by a rather ingenious use of ropes and ladders.

It took us about two weeks to complete this work. The four of us lived with the Sturgeses, keeping our sleeping bags and luggage in one of their two bedrooms and sharing the one bath. We slept out on the balcony. The Sturgeses were amazingly tolerant of our presence. Mrs. Sturges fed us very well.

During the time we were at the Sturgeses' there was a blackout in Los Angeles. There had been reports of a sighting of a Japanese submarine off the coast of California. After hearing the sirens announcing the blackout we stood out on the balcony and from the hillside site of the house watched the lights of Los Angeles go out and heard the roar of the city go quiet. It was eerie to look out over the darkened city and hear only the occasional barking of a dog.

When our work at the Sturgeses' was complete, Mr. Wright met us in Los Angeles on a rainy Sunday afternoon, and took us out to Arch Oboler's. Arch had commissioned Mr. Wright to design a house for him in the Malibu mountains. The working drawings for the house, Eaglefeather, had been completed, but the house had not been built. The house was to have been on a high knob from which there was a view of the ocean. Instead Arch had built a small complex of buildings, also designed by Mr. Wright. There was a gatehouse and a stable at the entrance to his property and on another small knob was a small studio, "Eleanor's Retreat," for his wife. John Lautner had also supervised their construction.

But changes had been made in design and construction which had resulted in a complete change of the proportions of all the buildings. An extra fillip that further irritated Mr. Wright was a free-form swimming pool that Arch had added to the gatehouse, all without the architect's advice or approval.

It was clear that Mr. Wright had visited the gatehouse before. He knew precisely what he wanted done when we drove up to the gatehouse; even before we reached the house Mr. Wright had asked us to roll some white-washed stones, which were alongside the drive, down the hill. Without announcing himself to Arch, he asked us to knock out some stone walls that Arch had had built and to remove some wood pieces from the entrance gate. The gate had a pattern of mitered boards. With the addition of some extra pieces of wood the gates had become, quite literally, an eagle with wings outspread. Of course, Arch soon appeared and wanted to know what was going on. Arch has written his own high-

58   Eleanor's Retreat. The wall of "desert stonework" was extended out from the house about forty feet in order to "tie" the house to the ground. Without it the retreat was a bump on the top of the hill. Photo by author.

ly dramatized account of this event. It appeared in *Reader's Digest,* and bears some slight resemblance to my experience.[62]

We stayed at Arch's several weeks, living up in Eleanor's Retreat on the hill. Part of our time was spent adding two extra boards to the facia of all the buildings to make it a deep facia. This was Mr. Wright's effort to retrieve the proportions of the buildings. The remainder of our time was spent building walls and steps similar in construction to the 'desert concrete' of the camp. We built some low walls and broad steps to relate the swimming pool to the gatehouse. And we built a concrete and stone wall (Fig. 58) about forty feet long extending west and averaging about six feet high to relate Eleanor's Retreat to its site. Mr. Wright's design had shown it snuggled against the top of the hill, but it had been built perched like a birdhouse on top of the hill. This long horizontal mass was an attempt to settle that little "retreat" into the landscape; it also made for a more interesting approach. At the west end, and its highest point, the wall terminated in a ninety-degree bend. An opening alongside the terminating mass became a gateway to the retreat. We also planted a group of pine trees near the wall which, in addition to helping change the top of the knob visually, also reinforced the sense of apartness experienced in passing through the gate.

The concrete for that wall was all mixed by hand and on a piece of plywood. Much of it was placed at night under makeshift artificial light. We had received word to finish up the work and to return to camp as it was nearing the time for the spring migration.

We returned to camp in late April, leaving Los Angeles late in the afternoon in the Model A and driving all night to avoid the daytime heat of the desert.

It had become increasingly evident during the winter that, except for construction directly related to the war effort, there was going to be very little building. Rationing of some building materials had started before Pearl Harbor and the declaration of war. With this slowdown in non-war-related construction Mr. Wright was receiving less income from architectural fees. At one point, while waiting for the government check for the Cloverleaf project to arrive, our groceries were being bought on credit.

Coupled with this came a general lowering of Fellowship morale. Mrs. Wright was ill most of the winter. And members of the Fellowship had also been ill. Added to this was the fact that the engine of the Kohler generating plant had to go into the shop for three days for repairs. This left us without electricity and with a need to ration our water supply.

Toward the end of that winter Gordon Lee left. In less than a year Gordon had become a valued member of the group; but he had gotten a dog and because of some incident – which was never clear to me except that it concerned Mrs. Wright, who also had a dog – he was told to get rid of his dog. At about the same time, Jim Charlton left for a job in Phoenix. His draft number was coming up soon. Another person who was about to be drafted, Lock Crane, also left. And, because there were no new architectural projects coming in, others were also talking of leaving. I received word from the Iowa County draft board in Wisconsin that they had requested the Maricopa County Board to have me take a physical exam in Arizona, but I had not received a notice from the Arizona Board before the migration to Wisconsin began.

Music

Music and music making were essential ingredients in the life of Mr. Wright and, consequently, in that of the Fellowship. Music making was important to me as well; it was probably the presence of this activity that convinced me to join the Fellowship when I visited Taliesin in the summer of 1939.

I had started taking piano lessons when I was about six years old. With time and the development of some musical ability music making became an activity that I could share with others. Before I finished grade school I was playing the piano for the Baptist church choir. I also took up the violin and the alto horn so that I could play in the high school orchestra and the town band. By the time I graduated from high school I had become a competent pianist, but I had not learned to play the violin or the horn very well. I did, however, have some thoughts of becoming a professional musician.

When I joined the Fellowship in the fall of 1939, Svetlana Peters put together the informal music programs which followed Sunday evening dinners in the living room. Mr. Wright preferred that these evenings be casual, that they seem spontaneous and unrehearsed. An evening program might begin with a group of songs by the chorus and then be followed by a few numbers by the quartet or the ensemble. After this, Gene Masselink might sing a group of songs, accompanied on the piano by John Hill or Edgar Tafel. This could be followed by a piano solo; Edgar Tafel would play something by Brahms, or Frances Caraway would play a part of a Haydn or a Mozart sonata. If there were professional musicians present, such as the cellists Margaret Jean Cree or Sam Sciacchiatano, the evening might focus upon them. They would play several of Mr. Wright's favorites, perhaps one of Beethoven's cello sonatas followed by Fauré's *Apres un Reve,* and for an encore Mr. Wright was sure to request a solo version of the bumptious rondo of Bocccerini's String Quartette in C Major.

Svetlana knew that I played the piano, as there was a piano near her and Wes's apartment on which I practiced occasionally. She asked me to play Sunday evenings. Unfortunately, when it came to my performance, Mr. Wright did not like some of the flamboyant displays of technique, that I, as a high school teenager, had delighted in learning. I soon learned what to avoid playing and concentrated on movements from Beethoven's piano sonatas which I had also learned.

Although Mr. Wright sought to have professional musicians at Taliesin to enrich the life of the Fellowship, he encouraged the Fellowship to participate actively in making music as well as listening to it. He had grown up in an environment in which music was both nourishment and inspiration. His father was a musician of some ability, both as a composer and as a performer. His mother's family, the Lloyd-Joneses, had brought with them the Welsh tradition of choral singing.

As a child Mr. Wright had learned to play the piano and the viola. His first wife, Catherine, played the piano. All of their children were provided with instruments and encouraged not only to learn to play but to make music as a family. As he had become more deeply involved in architecture, his participation in music making had diminished. But his pleasure in hearing it had not. Nor had his recognition of the role that music and music making could play in the development of the ability to make architecture.

When Tony Bek returned to the Fellowship early in the winter of 1939 he became the leader of musical activities. Tony had been at Taliesin several summers before as a member of the Taliesin Quartette. He had organized the mixed chorus in the summer of 1939. This winter he started a men's chorus. Anyone who wanted to sing was encouraged to participate. His presence gave a bit more form to the various musical groups – the mixed chorus, the quartet, and the ensemble. The latter two were affectionately referred to by Mr. Wright as the "Farmer/Laborer Quartet" and the "Tout and Scramble."

This winter the quartet consisted of Svetlana and Bob May on violin, Tony Bek on viola, and Herb Fritz on cello. Its makeup was selective. But the makeup of the ensemble consisted of anyone who played some instrument, and wanted to participate. I sometimes played piano, sometimes violin. The pleasure was in the participation, not the quality of the performance.

During that first year of the men's chorus we concentrated on some of the motets of Palestrina and other composers of that period. Somehow this polyphonic music seemed appropriate to our untrained voices. A year later, in the fall of 1940, we knew enough of Palestrina's works to sing a half-hour program which was broadcast over WIBW, the Madison radio station. I did not buy a copy of the recording which was made of this broadcast. The sound of the first tenors was too embarrassing to me.

Much of Tony's time was occupied with searching for music that the various groups could perform, with rehearsing the groups, with transcribing and copying out parts, and with practicing for his own solo performances on the violin. But when not busy with musical activities he joined in the construction activities of the Fellowship. His wife, Honore, took her turn as a cook, and when not cooking spent much of that and the following winter tacking canvas on the flaps for the Garden Room and Mr. and Mrs. Wright's living quarters, or whatever part of the camp was then being constructed. In the fall of 1940 they both worked on models for the Museum of Modern Art exhibition, refurbishing existing models and painting the newly made.

Ordinarily Mr. Wright did not get involved in the selection and the preparation of the musical programs. However, those who performed were aware of Mr. Wright's likes and dislikes and his response to their performances, and they chose what they were going to perform accordingly. Fortunately, those composers whose music he did not like were few in number. He was open to hearing unfamiliar music.

Mr. Wright did not enjoy the repetitiveness that was necessary when practicing and rehearsing music. It seemed he liked to believe that performance came naturally, like the singing of birds. Annoyed by this necessity, he generally stayed away from chorus or ensemble rehearsals. However, during my first winter in Arizona it was difficult for him or Mrs. Wright to do this. The chorus met right after breakfast at the west end of the drafting room where the only piano in camp was located. Mr. and Mrs. Wright had their breakfast at the long table at the east end of the drafting room near the large fireplace and were sometimes still eating when chorus rehearsal began.

One morning, we were attempting to learn a Russian hymn in which "hospodi pomi liu" is chanted over and over accompanied by changing chords. Mrs. Wright could finally stand it no longer. We were getting the accent all wrong. She tried to correct it with no success. Mr. Wright suggested English words, but none seemed to fit. That chant was not added to our repertoire.

Sometimes Mr. Wright chose to intercede. It happened one afternoon when the chorus was rehearsing in the Playhouse at Hillside after tea. We were learning a Negro spiritual, "Children, Keep in the Middle of the Road," and Mr. Wright came by. Upon hearing the words of the song he objected to their message; he did not believe that a person should "keep in the middle of the road." Rather than saying that we should not learn this spiritual he tried to suggest other words that could be fitted to the music, such as "Children Keep A-Going," but he couldn't think of any words that actually fit, and he left without further comment. We spent no more time learning that spiritual.

Tony and his wife left the Fellowship late in the summer of 1941. With their departure Svetlana took over responsibility for the musical activity. About a month after Wes and Svet's first child was born in early winter, I was asked if I would take over direction of the choruses. I had had no experience with vocal training or vocal groups before joining the Fellowship other than playing the piano for church choirs. But since arriving at Taliesin I had been put in the position of learning to do many things for which I had had no preparatory training. And I was willing to try this (Fig. 59).

Svetlana continued to be very involved in the instrumental side of things. She played violin and piano quite well. And on her own she was learning to play the recorder and encouraging others to learn. During the summer of 1942 enough

59 The men's chorus, at the front of the Kiva, at the left of the screen. Several who appear in this photo did not sing in the chorus. Front row, left to right, seated: the author at the piano, Wes Peters, Davy Davison, Aaron Green, Cary Caraway. Standing, Gene Masselink, John Hill. Stacked behind Wes, Jack Howe, Lock Crane, Marcus Weston. Behind Gordon Lee are Jim Charlton and Norman Hill, unknown, Gordon Chadwick, Chi Ngia Chow, Bob Mosher, and Kenn Lockhart. Photo courtesy of Robert C. May.

people were playing recorders to form a recorder group. It was not long before recorder solos, duets, and quartets were part of the music on Sunday evenings.

Since the chorus had several works by Palestrina in its repertoire, I decided later in the year to do a small booklet on Palestrina for the 1942 Christmas Box. I wanted to do it somewhat in the manner of medieval illuminated manuscripts. I did some reading in Svetlana's set of *Grove's Dictionary of Music and Musicians* to get a better understanding of the polyphonic music of that period. I gathered together some dates, bracketing the lives of several artists, such as Michelangelo and Shakespeare, to give an idea of Palestrina's contemporaries and the era in which he composed. I wrote a brief essay and designed the layout of the pages with an elaborate initial letter starting each page and with a short musical quotation from Palestrina bordering the bottom of each page in a stylized musical notation. I typed the essay and other information on onion-skin paper, did the decorations in gold ink and watercolor, and bound the pages in a thin, copper-covered binding. I embossed the title and a geometric design in the copper and oxidized it to give it a weathered appearance.

Later that winter Mr. Wright asked me to do his "Work Song" in a similar manner as a cover for Book Five in the forthcoming edition of his *Autobiography*. In this poem (inspired, as I later learned, by Cyrano's "what would you have me do" speech from the second act of Rostand's play "Cyrano de Bergerac") Mr. Wright set forth many of the principles (confirmed by those of Cyrano) that would guide his own life. In his *Autobiography* Mr. Wright tells of submitting this poem to the editor Richard Watson Gilder of *The Century* magazine, and of receiving a letter of rejection saying, "The rhythm of the drum, Mr. Wright, can hardly be translated into poetry." A drawing of the "Work Song," done in the manner of a Japanese kakemono, hung in Mr. Wright's office at Taliesin. I do not know when the kakemono was done or who did it. (This drawing was reproduced on a foldout at the front of the 1938 *Architectural Forum* devoted to Mr. Wright's work.) On this drawing the date of the "Work Song" is given as 1896. But Mr. Wright, in a dinner conversation, after seeing the movie starring Jose Ferrar as Cyrano de Bergerac, stated that he had written his "Work Song" after seeing a performance of the play.[63] Mr. Wright felt that the Fellowship should have a work song. Several efforts were made to find one. These included "Joy in Work Is Man's Desiring," set to Bach's familiar hymn, and Mrs. Wright's setting of his work song which the chorus sang occasionally without much enthusiasm and which was the basis for the decoration of the cover of Book Five.

Spring and Summer 1942

In the migration to Wisconsin that spring I traveled with Gordon Chadwick and Henning Watterson in the Fellowship's station wagon. We left the desert camp amidst speculation that because of wartime conditions – such as the rationing of gas and tires – we would probably not return the following winter. We arrived in Wisconsin on May 12 after an uneventful trip. We had not had much car trouble although we had anticipated the worst.

My arrival in Wisconsin that spring brought with it for the first time a sense of returning home. I had enjoyed certain aspects of life in the desert, but life there did not provide the deeper kinds of satisfaction that I derived from that corner of Wisconsin, particularly from that farm in the valley, "that acreage where Wisconsin is most loveable." My easy explanation to myself and others was that I was a bovine creature that needed grass. But in another way, not so easily explained, I felt that I had begun to understand Mr. Wright's attachment to that valley. It was his home; returning to it was returning home.

Home was the valley where his mother's ancestors, the Lloyd-Joneses, had finally established themselves after migration to the United States from Wales in the mid-nineteenth century. It was a secure center for a boy who had lived with his restless parents in six different towns in four states before he was eleven years old. It was the place where, as a youth, working on an uncle's farm, he had learned to "add tired to tired." It was the place in which he had found seclusion after a mid-life crisis in which he had separated himself from his wife, his family, and his work and fled to Europe to sum up his career and to seek renewal. It was the place where, on land owned by his mother, he had built a house to live in with the woman who had shared his flight to Europe – and where he had buried her after the brutal tragedy in which she and others were murdered. It was the place from which he had gone to Japan to build the Imperial Hotel, seeking solace in his work as an architect. And it was the place at which he finally established a second family, living a Jeffersonian life on the land, surrounded by younger people wanting to learn from him and his work. This aspect of his life had become formalized as the Taliesin Fellowship in 1932.

When we arrived at Taliesin in May 1942, we were told that almost everyone was to live at Hillside that summer so that Taliesin would be quieter. Mrs.

Wright had told me during the winter that she felt there was too much activity around Taliesin. Although Mr. Wright seemed to enjoy living in the midst of construction, it seemed to have an adverse effect on Mrs. Wright. She attributed her illness during the winter, a nervous condition that seemed to affect her heart and digestion, to being surrounded by too much activity. All meals, except the evening meal, were to be served at Hillside even though the kitchen there was not yet in working order. Only Gene Masselink, Wes and Svetlana, and Davy and Kay Davison were to live at Taliesin. I was assigned to live below the house. After rejoining the Fellowship I had paid tuition for a half year but then had entered the ranks of the nonpaying apprentices. I was asked to take over some of the house chores, included keeping the fireplaces supplied with kindling and firewood and making sure they were laid ready for lighting, and keeping Mr. Wright's bedroom in order.

The fireplaces in the house required little of my time during the summer. But there were times on cool, damp evenings when Mr. Wright liked to have a fire. With the coming of fall and winter, the replenishing of firewood from the woodpile became a daily task, and fires were kept going all day.

Since Mr. Wright was an orderly person, keeping his room in order did not require too much time. I checked it after breakfast to make the bed and to pick up anything that might have been left lying about, which seldom happened. Once a week, generally on Friday or Saturday afternoon, I vacuumed the rugs, gave the room a light dusting, and checked to see which of his clothes needed to be laundered or sent to the dry cleaners. I also replaced flower or foliage arrangements when they began to lose their freshness. Those of us who were assigned these housekeeping responsibilities reserved the more thorough cleaning – waxing and polishing the floors, washing the windows and the like – for those times when Mr. and Mrs. Wright were away from Taliesin for a few days.

While taking care of Mr. Wright's room, I became aware of something I had not noticed before. All of Mr. Wright's shoes were exactly the same, except for color. They were made by the same shoemaker. There were brown shoes, white shoes, black shoes, and black patent leather shoes, in various states of wear from new to badly scuffed and worn. All had the same cut and the same added elevation in the heels, about three-quarters of an inch more than the normal heel height.

The same was true of his suits and shirts. His shirts, all white, were made by the same shirtmaker. The collars all had the same cut to stand high around his neck. The suits, though of different fabrics and colors, were rather few in number and were all made to the same cut by the same tailor. These, too, were in various states of wear, from fairly new to snagged and worn.

When I first arrived at Taliesin Mr. Wright still had some clothing that was the product of a more creative and picturesque period in his dressing style. But this had been put aside in favor of a more standardized way of clothing himself. Of course, on him it appeared to be anything but standardized. I never did figure out how he could take an ordinary tie and fashion it into his particular knot. Nor did I ever ask him how he did it.

About a week after our arrival in Wisconsin in May 1942, I was confronted with a personal problem. I received a letter from Tom Larrick. I had worked in Larrick's architectural office in Lawrence during the summer between my junior and senior years at the university. He had later closed his office and gone to Ohio University to teach in the architectural school. In his letter he explained that he was a reserve officer in the Engineering Corps and that he expected to be called into active duty during the summer. He asked if I would be interested in taking over his teaching position "for the duration" with an understanding that it might develop into something more permanent afterward. He seemed to think that I would not be drafted – because of my poor eyesight, I assumed.

I wrote Professor Beal on May 21 explaining my position and asking for his and Professor Kellogg's opinions. I didn't want to leave Taliesin. I hadn't discussed Larrick's proposal with Mr. Wright, but I knew his opinion on "academic" activity. I also knew that there was little or no income from architectural work and suspected that he might just welcome an opportunity to "get rid of me gracefully."

On June 18 I wrote to Professor Beal:

> I've decided not to try for Larrick's job in case he is called into the army. I don't think that I'm interested in teaching, at least not right now. Somehow I think that the work of the Fellowship is particularly important at this time; we've lost a lot of guys to the army and to defense jobs, and are bound to lose a few more.

Work that summer concentrated on getting Hillside into a more presentable state, both inside and out. And the day was put on a "wartime" schedule: breakfast at six; an hour for chorus; an hour in the garden; then work outside until lunch at 11:30; after lunch more work outside until 4:00 when we were to clean up for tea and to spend the time until dinner in the studio. For the first time in my Taliesin experience an effort was made to see that everyone had some project to work on in this studio period. As a part of this effort, Mr. Wright set one project much as it might be done in an academic setting. There were some glass display cases from the Hillside Home School which Mr. Wright planned to use in the new Hillside dining room for storaging dishes, tableware, and tablecloths. The doors of the cabinets had been removed and Mr. Wright proposed to replace the glass in the doors, much of which had been broken, with one-quarter-inch plywood and to hinge the doors together for use as folding screens in the dining area. He suggested that the apprentices do designs for the panels of these screens and that he would, as a critic, help them with their efforts.

I proposed a design based on a dragonfly silhouetted against a full moon – a large, gold-leafed circle with a thirty/sixty abstract pattern partially superimposed upon it. Mr. Wright's only comment was something to the effect that the two geometries didn't go together. I consoled myself with the knowledge that none of the proposed designs were made into screens.

With little or no architectural work to do and little money for construction materials the Fellowship spent the summer of 1942 marking time. Mr. Wright, having few clients and projects, started writing a revision and continuation of his *Autobiography,* which had been published in 1932, before the start of the Fellowship. In addition to the everyday maintenance work of the Fellowship, and work on the Hillside buildings, some apprentices were helping with farmwork.

Taliesin itself was an active farm and was surrounded by other farms owned by Mr. Wright or Wes Peters, all of which totaled about one thousand acres. A part of this was wooded hillsides, and a part was used for pasture for the dairy herd and the beef cattle. But much of it was under cultivation. Ben Graves, whom Wes had hired to manage his farms, was now managing the whole operation. During peak periods of farm activity the Fellowship had helped with the work. With a smaller group there was more work to be done by those remaining.

Toward the end of the summer Mr. Wright completed a change in the way one entered the guest wing below the house, a change which he had begun in the fall of 1939 when he had had the inside stair closed, and the only access to the guest wing had become an outside path around the northeast corner of the house from a terrace below the loggia.

Late in the summer of 1942 Mr. Wright opened up another access to the guest wing. He had a stair built that was outside but under the cover of the roof connecting the house to the studio. This change in the entrance to the guest wing seemed to be in anticipation of the fact that the Fellowship, reduced in numbers, would all be living at Taliesin during the coming winter. Of course this entrance was changed again several years later. It was made into an entrance that was much more gracious, less steep, and better lighted.

I received a notice of I-A classification from the Iowa County draft board in late June 1942. I immediately began an appeal with the State Board of Appeal. I heard nothing from the appeal board, but in the fall of 1942 I received a notice to appear in Madison on October 30 for a hearing with an officer of the Department of Justice. After this hearing, on December 3, I received notice that the State Board of Appeal had affirmed my I-A classification. But typed on this notice was a statement that the state director of Selective Service had appealed the Board of Appeals classification to the president. On January 16, 1943, I received notice that I had been classified IV-E, given classification as a conscientious objector by the president.

My experience with the draft board and the classification process was not unique. All of those remaining in the Fellowship who were eligible for the draft were undergoing similar experiences. By the end of December 1942 there were only eleven of us remaining at Taliesin. It was inevitable that these experiences were colored and affected by the attitudes of the local draft board and of the appeals board toward Mr. Wright and his open opposition to the draft and to American involvement in the war. Before Pearl Harbor his position had been somewhat shared; after Pearl Harbor it became the position of a small minority. The Fellowship, although always somewhat isolated from the surrounding community, had become much more so. External pressures on the Fellowship had begun to create internal tensions. These internal tensions seemed to find a focus that fall with the arrival of David and Priscilla Henken as apprentices.

David and Priscilla were from New York City. They had been active in and were well informed about the various pacifist and war-resistance groups based in New York. Though well intentioned, David was a bit ponderous and pompous in his manner. Priscilla, with her sharp wit, intelligence, and perceptiveness, was delightful and charming company.

Priscilla had not been at Taliesin long before Mr. Wright, always alert to the talents of those around him, knew of her background and capabilities. She had received a master's degree in English Literature from Columbia University when still in her late teens. Before coming to Taliesin, she had been teaching English literature in the New York school system. Working on a new edition of his *Autobiography,* Mr. Wright asked Priscilla to read a portion of his work with an eye toward improving the writing. There had been criticism of the style and syntax of the earlier editions of his autobiography. Priscilla read the part of the manuscript he asked her to read and tried to "correct" it. But she returned it to him "uncorrected." She told him that she found that as she tried to make changes to improve the grammar and sentence structure she also changed the style and meaning and that she thought it best that he say what he had to say in his own manner.

The Henkens arrived in the Fellowship at the time that Marcus Weston, unsuccessful in his desire to be classified as a conscientious objector, had been arrested and was awaiting trial for "failure to report for induction into the armed services." The Henkens were knowledgeable about organizations that could offer advice and support and were particularly interested in being helpful to Marcus in his encounter with arrest and his forthcoming trial and sentencing. Marcus was friendly with the Henkens and welcomed their support. But as new arrivals in the Fellowship their actions were regarded by some as pushy. They were trying to move across that invisible barrier too quickly. They encountered resentment from some members of the Fellowship, particularly from Kay and Davy Davison, who considered themselves Marcus's longtime friends in the Fellowship, and, as such, in a better position to advise him, particularly because of their closeness to Mr. and Mrs. Wright. As a kind of "maid-in-waiting" to Mrs. Wright, Kay seemed even closer to her than her own daughter, Svetlana.

In addition to this resentment, there was a suspicion that the Henkens were government agents planted within the Fellowship to gather evidence against Mr.

Wright and members of the Fellowship for their opposition to the draft and the war. Mrs. Wright seemed particularly concerned that the government might attempt some sort of action against Mr. Wright since he was so outspoken. The Henkens also expressed opposition to the draft and the war, but their memberships in antiwar organizations were regarded as part of their cover. In addition, David had received a IV-F classification from his draft board, having failed his physical exam. His not being subject to the draft was suspicious, although he was overweight and constantly snuffling from some sort of allergy. There also seemed to be an element of anti-Semitism in some peoples' attitude toward the Henkens. How prevalent this was I don't know.

Winter 1942–1943

The winter of 1942–1943 was a long one. We did not go to Arizona. The snow came early, lay deep on the ground all winter, and left late in the spring. The Hillside buildings were closed, and we all lived within the confines of Taliesin and in close proximity. We filled all of the rooms, including the guest rooms below the house.

Because of the snow and the cold much of our time was spent indoors; we could not work outside. But there were other things that closed us in, or were closing in on us. Increasingly we felt as though we were living on an island surrounded by unfriendly, if not hostile, forces: the war effort in general; gas and food rationing; the Selective Service System and its local representatives, the Iowa County draft board. These external forces generated both internal cohesiveness as well as conflicts.

In December, Marcus Weston, was tried in federal court by Judge Patrick D. Stone and in January was sentenced to prison. The trial and sentencing were surrounded by much publicity and by a public debate in the newspapers between Mr. Wright and those holding prowar sentiments. One of the casualties of Marcus's refusal to report for induction into the army was the longtime working relationship and friendship between Marcus's father, Will Weston, and Mr. Wright. Marcus's father and mother both felt that Marcus should have been willing to serve in the army and that Marcus had been unduly influenced by Mr. Wright. At that time, Will Weston was doing the carpentry work for the remodeling of Wes and Svet's apartment. When that was completed he did no further work at Taliesin. And an essential ingredient in the Fellowship as I had come to know it was missing.

The winter sentencing of Marcus was followed by the arrests in March of Jack Howe and Davy Davison for failure to report for induction. They were tried in June and sentenced to four years in Sandstone, a federal prison in Minnesota.

Living in such close conditions and subject to these external pressures, we did develop varying degrees of "fifth columns," which Mr. Wright referred to as "funft columns." In addition there always seemed to be an unacknowledged concern within the Fellowship about who was closest to the center without any clear understanding or definition of what this center was. Was it Mr. Wright? Mrs. Wright? Or both of them together?

60   A picnic late in the summer. Left to right: Mr. Wright, Iovanna, Gene Masselink, Howard TenBrink, Henning Watterson; standing, Ruth TenBrink, unknown, the author, Mrs. Wright, Burt Goodrich. Standing, Jack Howe, Priscilla Henken. Photo courtesy of Howard TenBrink.

There were some who were accepted as close to the center. Wes and Svet were in this group partly because Svetlana was Mrs. Wright's daughter, but also because she played a leading role in the musical life of the Fellowship. Svetlana, however, was not one to encourage "in" groups or cliques. She seemed instinctively to make efforts to bridge divisive boundaries. Wes did not seem concerned about such things. He worked closely with Mr. and Mrs. Wright in organizing the work of the Fellowship and he was very much in the center of activity, accepting the leadership role assigned to him.

Gene Masselink was also accepted as close to the center (Fig. 60). As Mr. Wright's secretary he seemed to know most overall about what was going on. He had a sense of humor – and a touch of grace – that seemed to keep him free of such a concern. Like Svetlana, he was a bridge-builder seeking to eliminate contention and to maintain harmony. Gene was not concerned about the draft – he had fallen and broken his hip sometime before my arrival in the Fellowship and had a IV-F classification. He was still troubled by his hip and walked with a limp.

Jack Howe was also accepted as being close to Mr. Wright; he worked closely with him in the drafting room. He spent much of his time during the winter making drawings for a forthcoming issue of *Architectural Forum* (which was destined not to appear for the duration of the war).

It was the most recent arrivals in the Fellowship who came to feel that they were well outside any inner circle. There were the onerous chores: boilers to be fired, dishes to be washed, kitchen work to be done. And because the Fellowship had become smaller, reduced to about twenty including two small children and Iovanna, who was still in high school, such chores were assigned frequently to the most recently arrived apprentices who felt that there were inequities in these assignments.

Since the group was smaller in number, only one person was assigned as kitchen helper. This did not mean that the work of the helper was proportionately reduced. There were still pots to be washed and vegetables to be prepared. And firing the boilers was an irksome, exhausting chore. There were three boilers to be fed. In colder weather they became increasingly ravenous. From five-thirty in the morning, when the boilers were fired up, until ten-thirty at night, when they were stoked for the night, the person responsible for firing them spent his day going from boiler to boiler. And still there were complaints that, although some radiators were whistling merrily, others, at the furthest reaches of the systems, were stone cold. By the end of a week the boiler tender was dragging himself from boiler to boiler.

Mr. Wright did not involve himself directly in these conflicts and with these cliques, but he did, at times when the Fellowship was together – at tea in the afternoon or at Sunday morning breakfast – express his disapproval of such "fifth column" activity. And he read to us that portion of Book Five of his *Autobiography,* on which he was working at that time, which was about the "liabilities of the Fellowship" and the "assets" of an Ideal Apprentice.

There were activities during the winter that served to counteract these stresses. The grand piano from Wes and Svet's apartment, which was being remodeled, was moved into the southeast corner of the Taliesin studio. The chorus and ensemble rehearsed there, as did the string trio, with Svet playing the violin, Ruth TenBrink the cello, and I the piano. We worked on, and performed, many trios that winter. We generally practiced after lunch when Mr. Wright was having his nap in the house. This was always a pleasant and satisfying time of the day.

We set up the movie projectors on the top of the vault in the studio and hung a screen on the east wall so that we could have movies there on Saturday evenings. With a fire crackling in the large fireplace it became a cozy movie theater on cold winter nights. We also had a Japanese print party in the studio. We all sat on the floor on cushions grouped around small Primus stoves on which we cooked the makings of a sukiyaki supper, after which Mr. Wright showed and talked about his Japanese print collection. We had an elaborate Halloween party with guests, skits, movie, and dinner at Hillside. Everyone went in costume. I dressed as an Indian Kachina, wearing a tall cardboard mask painted in a geometric pattern, a monk's cloth skirt with a painted border, worn over a pair of long Jockey underwear dyed brown, and brown makeup on my arms and torso.

The surprise of the party for me came when Mr. and Mrs. Wright, in long, braid-decorated Montenegran coats, took to the floor and danced ever so gracefully.

This surprise was followed by another that winter. Some of us had discovered that we could skate on the pond below Taliesin. One afternoon Mr. Wright appeared, donned some skates, and moved out across the ice. Compared with some of us who were trying to get back into practice, he moved as though he had been doing a lot of skating that winter.

That winter, also, much of the weaving of the rug for the Hillside living room was continued. Mr. Wright had drawn a design for it and Henning had spent much of the previous winter in Arizona dyeing the yarn for the colored areas of the rug. The rug, to be about twenty-five feet square, was designed to be made in strips that could be woven on a four-foot loom and then sewn together. Unfortunately, when the strips were completed and sewn together, the rug did not lie flat on the floor as desired. Mr. Wright then decided to use the long strips as drapes and hung them at the sides of the tall windows in the living room and the theater at Hillside.

During the fall of this period of increased tension within the Fellowship, I entered Wisconsin General's Hospital for the first of two operations on my eyes. I had awakened early one morning late in August with an irritation in one eye. It was inflamed and felt as though it had sand in it. At breakfast Gene informed me that Mr. and Mrs. Wright were already planning to go into Madison that morning, and suggested I join them. They took me to Wisconsin General's eye clinic. While being treated, I was asked by one of the young resident physicians if I would be interested in having my eyes operated on to correct a squint, a condition that I had had since early childhood. After the first operation which took place in September, a second one, attempting a better correction, was performed in late January. Each of these required that I be in the hospital for about ten days and, for the first few days, that I lie flat on my back.

Spring and Summer 1943

Mr. Wright had spent part of his time during the winter writing Books Five and Six of his *Autobiography*. Book Six, however, was not included in the new edition, which was published that summer. He had been advised, encouraged, and urged by Mrs. Wright, by friends whose opinions he valued, and, I assume, by the publisher that it should not be included. Publishing it at that time, when apprentices were being sentenced to prison for refusal to report for induction into the armed services, when Mr. Wright himself was in the news for his continued stand against conscription and the war, and when the war itself was not going well for the United States, would have only further antagonized those who did not share his views.

Book Six was published by Mr. Wright and the Taliesin Press. The Taliesin Press consisted of Gene Masselink and his little print shop beneath the north end of the stable. Gene had secured a small, second-hand press and fonts of type. To learn the technique of printing, he had gone to Spring Green several afternoons a week during the summer of 1942 and had worked with the publishers and printers of the Spring Green *Home News*.

When Mr. Wright finished writing his autobiography he shifted his interest to "the house." He began a process that later in the summer turned into preparation for an anticipated visit by Solomon Guggenheim and the Baroness Hilla von Rebay. They were coming to discuss the building of a museum to house Mr. Guggenheim's collection of nonobjective art. Preparation for any occasion always seemed to require, as a renewal, some architectural changes. Sometimes these were minor. But the prospect of a major architectural commission was a reason for major changes.

The changes began in the living room. The glass doors between the living room and the screened porch on the east side were taken out and the porch enclosed with windows and French doors. The porch became a deep alcove in the southeast corner of the living room and enlarged the area where Mr. and Mrs. Wright and their guests sat during Sunday evening dinners. While working on this change, I assisted George Haas and became involved in doing stonemasonry.

George had been trained as a mason in Germany. As a young man learning a craft, he had served the traditional and required apprenticeship. But after coming to the United States and Spring Green, he had, for some reason, owned and operated a butcher shop. With the war and ensuing food rationing, he complained that his quota of meat was not enough to enable him to keep the shop open and he threatened to close it. One day, when a government agent told him that he couldn't close his shop, George shut the door, locked it, and left. Not long afterward he was at Taliesin laying stone.

George was a happy and changed man laying stone. He loved rocks, which he pronounced with a guttural, rolling *Rrrr* in the German accent which he had never lost. A working relationship, very interesting to observe, soon developed between Mr. Wright and George. There was both mutual respect and affection in it. George picked up Mr. Wright's verbal directions quickly and laid up walls and piers that were admiringly approved. I learned something about rocks, about cutting and laying stone, from George, and I enjoyed working with him. There was something deeply satisfying in it. While George was laying up some stone piers for the living room porch enclosure, my job was to patch the existing stone piers where wood blocking for the door jambs had been removed leaving a vertical slot. The challenge to me was to fill in this slot and to make an inconspicuous patch, to find stones that matched those already in place in color and width, and to conceal or minimize the number of joints. I found that by throwing stone dust in the mortar I could hide many of the joints.

Having made this change in the living room, we moved to the entrance. It seemed that some students from Harvard had complained to Mr. Wright when visiting Taliesin that they had had difficulty finding the entrance. He was going to correct this.

A central pair of stone piers, at the right of the former entrance, where the steps down to the guest wing had previously been, was removed to make a wide opening for a pair of wide doors. An area of ferns and wildflowers was removed and replaced with stone paving and a broad band of a few steps leading up to the doors. These new doors were visually on the center of the garden court, and made a stronger connection between the interior of the entry area and the court. But after this was done, these doors were seldom used as the entrance. It was more convenient, when going into the house, to go either through the little kitchen entrance or through a single door in a recess at the left side of these wide doors, where the entrance door had originally been. Here my job was also patching the stone piers to conceal the vertical slot where blocking for the wood trim of the glass areas between the piers had been. While working, I became intrigued with the fragments of Chinese ceramics that Mr. Wright had had incorporated in the stonework of these piers when rebuilding Taliesin after one of the fires.

From the entrance the process of renewal moved to the loggia of the house and initiated a much larger project, the enclosure of the covered terrace that extended toward the hill garden and garden court, making it a library. The roof over this terrace had, in the original scheme for Taliesin, been a porte cochere;

the entrance drive coming up to the house from the south had passed under it. This entrance drive had been removed many years before. Its removal had probably contributed to the difficulty that the students from Harvard had in finding the entrance to the house. One no longer approached Taliesin from this direction or in this manner.

As a part of turning this roofed area into a library Mr. Wright decided that the fireplace that was on the west side of the loggia, in a lower-ceilinged area, should be opened through to this new room. This required much reworking of the fireplace and building of hoods on both sides. In working with George on this project I got my first opportunity to cut and lay larger stones. I got great satisfaction out of doing this, although after a day of working with a stone hammer and chisels, my hands were a bit stiff for playing the piano or the violin.

We had not completed the enclosure of the porch and the finishing of the interior of the library before a much larger project was started. The prospect of the Guggenheim Museum project had appeared. Mr. Wright decided to remodel the two small rooms and bath on the mezzanine of the house, Iovanna's rooms, into a suite in which Hilla Rebay would stay during her visit. Mr. Guggenheim was to stay in the main guest room, next to the living room.

To make Iovanna's small rooms, tucked up under the roof of the house, into suitable quarters grew into a major project. It required many changes over that part of the house where Mr. and Mrs. Wright's bedrooms were located. The roof over that part was raised and rebuilt (Fig. 61). A cantilevered, balconylike projection, with casement windows on the west and south sides, was built to enlarge the floor area of Iovanna's rooms. I was discovering that life at Taliesin was a continuous remodeling project. Nothing remained unchanged for long.

In May I received orders from the Iowa County draft board to report for a physical examination. It was ironic to me that I was appointed leader of the contingent of draftees who went by bus on May 24 from Dodgeville to Milwaukee for this examination at the induction center. I knew none of the others on the bus. As a person seeking classification as a conscientious objector I felt very much an outsider. After the waiting-in-line ordeal of the examination, I and the others on the bus, some of whom were less than sober, returned late that evening to Dodgeville. Not wanting to call anyone at Taliesin at that late hour, I decided to walk the fifteen miles from Dodgeville to Taliesin. There was little moonlight. Walking through the darkness, faintly seeing the shape of the highway and the surrounding landscape, hearing the sounds of the night and my own footsteps, evoked a strange sense of detachment which seemed to complete the day. I walked into the courts of Taliesin just as night was changing to day.

Having been found fit for alternative service at the physical exam in Milwaukee, I received a letter in June from the director of Civilian Public Service Camp #57 in Hill City, South Dakota, saying that I would receive notice from my local board to report to this church-operated camp on July 16.

61   Raising the roof over a part of Mr. Wright's bedroom to enlarge Iovanna's bedroom into a suitable place for Hilla Rebay to stay. Source of photo unknown.

I had heard that the government was going to open a camp for conscientious objectors and, not wanting to go to a church-operated camp, I wrote on July 1 asking that my assignment be transferred to this new government camp. On July 20 I received an order to report for "work of national importance." I had been assigned to the new government camp, C.P.S. #111, at Mancos, Colorado. I left Taliesin for Mancos, on July 26. Upon reporting for travel orders I became, in effect, an object being shipped across the country under the direction and control of the Selective Service System. My feelings about leaving Taliesin seemed to be balanced between regret and relief – regret over leaving friends whose company I enjoyed and activities which gave me satisfaction, and relief in knowing that I would be away from the tensions and animosities that had developed during the winter and that had neither lessened nor been eliminated by the arrival of spring and summer. I was leaving not knowing when or if I might return. I had been at Taliesin for two periods of time, totaling a little more than three years.

The Fellowship, which had seemed full of conviction about its future when I first arrived in Taliesin, now seemed somewhat in disarray. It had suffered two setbacks. Many of the senior apprentices had left in the summer of 1941 because they did not agree with Mr. Wright's decision to stop allowing individual apprentices to accept architectural commissions. (The fees from these were split three ways – a third to the apprentice, a third to the Fellowship, and a third to Mr. Wright.) Following this the Fellowship had been further reduced in size by the war. I was leaving a group whose main goal seemed to be survival.

I had gone to Taliesin in 1939 when I was 25 years old, after three years of experience in architectural offices. Mr. Wright had then been seventy-two. At that age most men would be looking back over their careers and seeking a less active life. Mr. Wright had himself said that as a young man he had thought that if he were going to accomplish anything in his life he would have to do it before he was forty. I was leaving Taliesin in 1943 when Mr. Wright was seventy-six. The Fellowship was much reduced in numbers and strength; its major effort seemed directed toward holding together those that remained and surviving the war. And yet, at the time I was leaving, Mr. Wright had, in effect, torn apart that part of Taliesin in which he lived and had started rebuilding it in anticipation of the visit of a prospective client with a major commission.

Interlude 1943–1946, "Work of National Importance"

I left Taliesin and the Fellowship in July 1943 and returned to Taliesin in June 1946. During those three years I was assigned to "work of national importance under civilian direction" in Civilian Public Service Camps: #111 near Mancos, Colorado, operated by the Bureau of Reclamation; #135 near Germfast, Michigan, operated by the Wildlife Services; and #148 near Minersville, California, operated by the Forest Service, all under the direction of the Camp Operations Division of the Selective Service System.

My work consisted of surveying, working as a draftsman and on the carpentry crew, maintaining and repairing dikes and roads in a wildlife refuge, serving as a camp infirmian, and even entering some architectural competitions.

I kept in touch with several people at Taliesin and managed to spend most of my furlough time there: Easter 1944 at Taliesin West, when Mr. Wright was urging people to read *The Fountainhead;* Christmas 1945 at Taliesin, when I assisted with the drawing for the model of the *Ladies Home Journal* "glass house"; and a three-week furlough in 1946 at Taliesin West before my impending discharge. The Fellowship had many new faces by 1946. Mr. Wright was busier than I had ever seen him. Mrs. Wright's brother and his wife, Uncle Vlado and Aunt Sophie, were there. Mrs. Wright seemed well and in a better frame of mind than when I had last seen her. Jack Howe and Davy Davison, who had both been released from prison, were also there.

I spent much of my time during this 1946 visit working on a model of the "Pergola" house which Mr. Wright had designed for Gerald Loeb to be built in Redding, Connecticut (Fig. 62). The design was a much enlarged version of the Ralph Jester house which Mr. Wright had designed to be built in California. Another version of this house was later proposed for Dr. Paul Palmer and his family in Phoenix, Arizona. Loeb was having the model made for an exhibition at the Museum of Modern Art. Richard Salter and Paolo Soleri were among the new apprentices working on the model. Paolo carved the small-scale figures that were placed around the circular swimming pool.

During my visit the question uppermost in my mind was whether or not I should return to Taliesin upon my release from C.P.S. And, although I did not discuss this with many that I knew, I sensed that most of them understood that I

62   Work on Loeb house model. During a visit to Taliesin West in April 1946 I spent most of my time working on a model of the Gerald Loeb house, to be built in Redding, Connecticut. Richard Salter is at left, the author at right. The scale figures around the swimming pool were carved by Paolo Soleri. The photo, courtesy of Lois Davidson Gottlieb, was taken during a later refurbishing of the model.

was wrestling with this question. Some knew that I was having doubts. I was also trying to determine their feelings about me and my return.

I knew that Mr. Wright felt that the question was settled; I was to return. I had a conversation with Mrs. Wright during which she asked me if I was going to return. I told her that I hadn't quite decided. She said that she would like to have me back, but that the answer to the question had to come from within and not from outside.

I applied for discharge from C.P.S. on June 1, 1946, when I became eligible, and I requested transportation to Spring Green, Wisconsin.

Summer 1946

I arrived in Spring Green on the four o'clock train. I had written Gene to tell him when I would arrive and I expected that someone would be there to meet me. I knew that when Jack and Davy returned to Taliesin after being released from prison it had been treated as a special event. I did not expect a party, but I did not expect to be left waiting at the station.

As I waited I wondered what I should do. There was no point in trying to call Taliesin. It was teatime and no one would be near the phone. I decided that if someone didn't show up soon, I would get on the next train to Kansas City. Marcus Weston finally appeared, friendly and apologetic. Gene had planned to meet me, but at the last moment Mrs. Wright had asked him to do something for her.

Being met by Marcus appeased my feelings somewhat, but I was irritated again when Marcus took me to the room that I was to stay in. It was next to the laundry in the kitchen wing. The room was hot and dusty, and it was bare except for a mattress and bed frame. Usually when a new apprentice arrived something was done to make the room he or she was to stay in pleasant. But this room had no arrangement of flowers or foliage and the bed was not made. There was no evidence of anticipation of my arrival. Gene appeared. He apologized for not having come to meet me, and explained that this room was only temporary and that other arrangements would soon be made. This soothed my feelings somewhat. But all affronts, imagined or otherwise, were set aside when Jack Howe told me that evening at dinner that Mr. Wright had told him that he wanted me to work with Jack in the studio at Taliesin on the preliminary drawings for the Rogers Lacy Hotel in Dallas. Mr. Wright wanted these drawings done at Taliesin rather than in the drafting room at Hillside so that he could work on them more closely as they developed. We were to work at Taliesin until the design had been developed to the point where the drawings could be traced for presentation to the client.

I had not kept many souvenirs from my three years in C.P.S. camps, but among the things I had brought with me was a small sand dollar. I had picked it up on the beach when several of us had gone with Dr. Habeggar to Eureka to see the redwoods and the northern California seacoast. I had kept this flat sea urchin because I thought it had architectural implications and I enjoyed the beauty of its delicate pattern. While unpacking my things I came across it, and it occurred to me that Mr. Wright would enjoy it. So I gave it to him. He put it on his desk in the office at Taliesin.

Shortly after this Mrs. Wright confronted me with a question: Why hadn't I brought her a gift? I was perplexed. I hadn't thought of the sand dollar as a gift. In much the same way that my musical activity was a sharing of something I enjoyed, I was simply sharing something with Mr. Wright and anyone else who might happen to see and enjoy it. It hadn't occurred to me that she might have expected a gift from me.

As I soon learned, the Fellowship had grown rapidly after the end of the war. There were now between fifty and sixty apprentices. Finding places for all of them to live was a problem.

Many of the new apprentices were GIs, but several were from foreign countries: Omar Mahoud from Egypt, Gira Sarabai from India (Mr. Wright had recently designed the Calico Mills Office Building for her family's company in Ahmedabad; it was not built), Ling Po from China, a couple from Hawaii, and a fellow from Colombia. Confronted with so many new apprentices, I did not get to know many of them, particularly those who stayed only a short time.

A few days after returning to Taliesin I moved into the room on the northeast corner of the upper floor of the stable wing. It was a pleasant room, which received morning light through a glass door opening out to a small balcony. There were windows with a four-foot-high window sill in the north wall, with a view toward the Wisconsin River valley. The room was sometimes called the "well room" since there was a light well in the hall outside that opened down to the hall below. The room was also called "Jack's room"; he had lived in it for several years and had built in its furnishings.

The drafting room was busier than I had ever known it to be. Working drawings for some of the larger projects – the Guggenheim Museum, the Johnson Tower, and the Adelman Laundry – had been completed. But there were houses, large and small, in various stages of production. And there were clients who were waiting for their houses to be designed – clients who had already sent in site plans, photos of the site, and other requested information. The project in which Mr. Wright was most interested and on which he focused his attention was the Rogers Lacy Hotel.

When I started work on the hotel project, Mr. Wright had already put his concept of the building on paper, and Jack had started sorting out this information into other drawings of the building, such as plans, sections, and elevations. This was my first experience working with one of Mr. Wright's conceptual drawings, and I was amazed at how fully developed the concept had become in Mr. Wright's mind before he had drawn it.

The drawing (Fig. 63) was not a plan, a section, or an elevation; it was all of these things combined. At the side of the drawing were small freehand perspec-

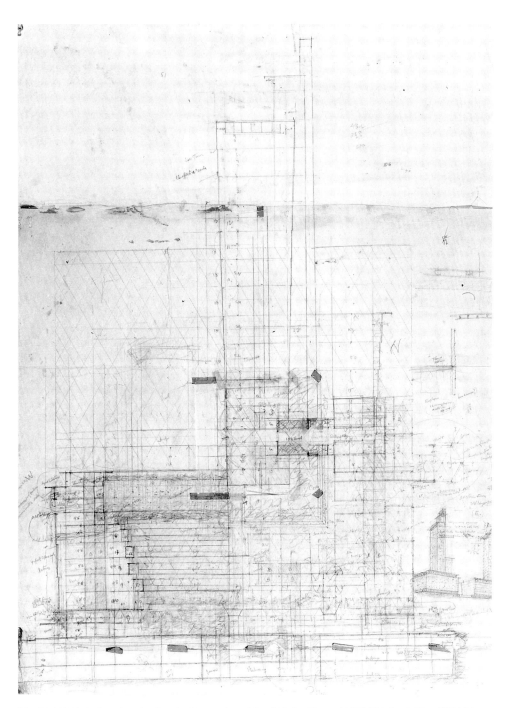

63   Mr. Wright's first drawing for the Rogers Lacy Hotel, Dallas, Texas. (4606.031 Frank Lloyd Wright Foundation Archives)

tives of the building's exterior. The essential drawing was drawn to scale and based on a module, a unit system that applied both horizontally and vertically. This unit seemed to be derived, in part, from the exterior "skin" that was proposed for the building, and also from the relation of floor heights and room dimensions. The "skin" was a fish-scale-like system of diamond-shaped panels of two layers of glass, with a layer of glass fibers in between for insulation and light diffusion. The panels were about 1½" thick and were to be bound at the edges with a lightweight metal channel. (A large triangular panel of this "skin" was in the Hillside drafting room.) The panels were to overlap each other vertically. As a result, each floor was stepped out slightly beyond the one below as the building rose. This stepping-out became most evident in the tall tower which was to contain suites and apartments (Fig. 64).

One feature of the hotel that intrigued me was the organization of the guest rooms in its lower block. In place of the usual double-loaded interior corridors with rooms on both sides, access to the rooms was from balconylike glazed galleries which surrounded a central court open to the sky. At the street level of the court there was a pool of water surrounded by the public functions of the hotel. The guest rooms were grouped in clusters of four accessible from the galleries by short corridors. The floors of the rooms were to be higher than those of the galleries. The rooms next to the galleries received daylight through a clerestory above the gallery. I had questions about just how all of this would work, but since the hotel never progressed beyond the preliminary stage my questions remained unanswered.

We worked in the studio at Taliesin on these drawings for about a month, producing many floor plans and sections, before Mr. Wright decided that we were ready to make presentation drawings to show the client. The final presentation drawings, done in the drafting room at Hillside, were traced on a Japanese paper which contained silk fibers. It came in a roll about twenty-four inches wide. Because of the height of the tower the drawings were organized vertically on the sheets. Drawing on this paper was a delicate operation. We could not erase since this destroyed the surface of the paper. We traced the drawings in brown ink. We could just touch the surface of the paper with a pen. Any pressure on the pen might catch the point in the silk fibers and cause a blot. To tint the drawings we used colored pencils applied to either side of the paper. Seeing the color on the reverse side of the translucent paper overlaid with another on the front side gave a kind of depth and airiness to the drawings.

The completed set of drawings consisted of about twenty sheets. Mr. Wright kept thinking of additional drawings that should be made and other apprentices were assigned to help us. Jack Howe did the main perspectives of the exterior and most of the plans. I drew most of the sections and several of the interior perspectives.

Mr. Lacy came to Taliesin for a weekend visit in mid-August to see the pre-

64   Perspective, Rogers Lacy Hotel. This drawing is one of the many from which the presentation
drawings were traced. (4606.072 Frank Lloyd Wright Foundation Archives)

liminaries. We had worked up to the last moment to complete them. The drawings were displayed in sequence on the walls of the Hillside drafting room so that Mr. Wright could walk around the room with Mr. Lacy and explain the proposed building to him. Mr. Lacy liked the building very much and returned to Dallas with the drawings rolled up under his arm. He intended to build it. But before we received word to start construction drawings, Mr. Lacy suddenly died. There was some hope after his death that the hotel still might be built to realize his intent, but this was not to be.

After the hotel drawings were completed, I was asked to start working drawings for the Lowell Walter house, "Cedar Rock," to be built on the Wapsipinicon River near Quasqueton, Iowa. The design for this house was an adaptation of the house for which I had helped to do drawings during my visit to Taliesin in December of 1944. It was referred to as the "glass house." Its living room was a square pavilion enclosed with glass on three sides. Mr. Wright called it "Opus 497."

On the last Monday morning in September an event occurred which was to have a major effect on the life and future of the Fellowship. This was the sudden, accidental death of Svetlana and her younger son, Daniel.

Alden Dow and his wife, Veda, were guests at Taliesin; it was a very pleasant weekend. The weather had been the delightful kind that occurs in Wisconsin in the fall. The musical program on Sunday evening had gone particularly well; Svetlana had been in charge of it. The living room was beautifully decorated with the wild purple asters that bloom along the roadsides in the fall. There was an aura of sweet melancholy; it was the end of summer and the beginning of fall.

On Monday morning after breakfast, the group I was working with was re-shingling the roofs over the tower rooms. From there we could see and hear the activity in the court outside Wes and Svet's apartment as people were getting ready for a trip to Madison. Wes was going to drive Mr. and Mrs. Wright to Madison and also take the Dows to the airport for their return to Midland. Svetlana was saying her goodbyes to the Dows and getting ready to go to Spring Green with her two sons, Brandoch and Daniel, in a Jeep.

The bustle of activity quieted and we continued laying shingles. We were enjoying the warm morning sun and the smell of the new cedar shingles. We had not worked long when we heard sounds of great urgency in the courtyards. Word spread quickly that the Jeep had gone off the road and overturned in the marshy area north of the Wisconsin River bridge. The State Highway Patrol was called to ask them to locate Wes on his way to Madison. It was not clear at first what had happened, but a picture finally began to be pieced together. The Jeep had over-turned completely in a slough. Svet's son Brandoch had been thrown clear of it, but Svet and Daniel had been trapped beneath it and probably drowned. Brandoch, then four years old, had climbed up the embankment to the highway. He was soaking wet and walking along the highway when he was picked up by a mechanic from the Bridge Service Station. He told the mechanic about the accident and the Richardsons, who ran the service station, had called Taliesin. An ambulance was called, and Svetlana and Daniel were rushed to a hospital in Madison. By lunchtime any hope for their survival was gone.

The Fellowship members, particularly those who had known Svet for any length of time, shared a numb, silent grief. Svetlana, with young Daniel in her arms, was buried the next afternoon. A brief service was held in the Garden Court at Taliesin. The chorus, which she had trained, sang. Mr. Wright read a poem which Iovanna had written as a tribute to Svetlana and Daniel. They were taken to the chapel yard for burial in the back of a horse-drawn "station wagon" which the Fellowship had used for picnics. The casket was banked with wild purple asters. Wes drove the wagon, with Gene Masselink beside him. The Fellowship followed on foot. Her going left a void in the Fellowship; it was a role that no one filled.

Svet had had a great sense of what was just. It was an innate part of her. If she felt that someone or some group was being done an injustice, she would quietly start putting things right. She did this with good humor and grace. There was no expression of righteousness or outrage. She was fearless and independent, and did not hesitate to take even Mr. or Mrs. Wright gently to task if she did not agree with them or if she felt that they were doing something she did not approve of. She was a builder of bridges. She maintained old friendships and made new ones with people both in the Fellowship and outside of it. Whenever cliques began to form in the Fellowship, she seemed instinctively to find ways to dissolve them. Mr. Wright had a great affection for her although she was not his daughter. And he admired and respected her.

The Fellowship, except for some of the recent arrivals, was slow to recover from Svetlana's death. Some of the newcomers, who did not know Svet and did not appreciate her role in the Fellowship, did not seem to understand our profound unhappiness.

To hasten the Fellowship's recovery and get it back into action, Mr. Wright made the decision to move to Arizona earlier than usual that year. In previous years we had stayed in Wisconsin until after Thanksgiving. An advance group was sent ahead to get the camp, particularly Mr. and Mrs. Wright's quarters, ready for our arrival. We did not travel in a caravan. I was among the last to leave. I stayed to complete the working drawings for the Walter house, on which I had been working. There were fourteen sheets of drawings in the completed set (Fig. 65).

In the original design for the house, metal doors and windows were to be used in the exterior walls. This was changed when construction started the following summer. John Hill supervised the construction. He revised many of the details after the decision was made to use walnut for the millwork and furniture. Wes did the calculations for the concrete roof slabs and for the steel tees which serve

65 "Cedar Rock," the Lowell Walter house, above the Wapsipinicon River, near Quasqueton, Iowa. Ezra Stoller © Esto.

as mullions and support the roof above the broad area of glass which surrounds the living room. The calculations for the roof slab over the living room were compounded by the higher ceiling over the clerestory at the center of the room; this required a large square hole in the center of the slab. This hole was covered by another slab with openings in it for skylights. This slab was in turn supported by steel tee mullions in the clerestory below it. I am still puzzled by the architectural magic by which all of this mass of concrete is made to appear to rest lightly above the room.

Winter 1946–1947

When the Fellowship ceased to travel between Wisconsin and Arizona in a caravan, the time spent changing locations lasted for several weeks. It was a period of loosely organized activity during which Mr. and Mrs. Wright might go to the east or west coast. His trip might include interviews with clients, past, present, or prospective, and a few lectures. It was a time during which apprentices could get away for visits with family or friends, or just get away, and when some apprentices might leave and others join the Fellowship.

I went to Arizona with Alex Mischelevich and Tom McEvoy in Wes's jeep. Alex had joined the Fellowship during the summer, Tom shortly before our departure. It was an uncomfortable, miserable trip. The weather was gray and cold. We drove in rain much of the way.

Shortly after our arrival, a group of the newer apprentices, including Tom McEvoy, left. The reason they gave was that they were not happy. They commented that no one in the Fellowship was happy. It was true – it was taking a longer time for some to recover from Svetlana's death than others. Despite the move to Arizona, Mrs. Wright, Wes, and Gene were slow in casting off this shadow.

I had a talk with Mrs. Wright in early December, on one of her better days. Mrs. Wright and I had never had any confidential talks, but somehow I felt that we understood each other. I happened to encounter her that day on the Sunset Terrace. She seemed to want to talk, and turned the conversation to the need for religion in life. My knowledge about Mrs. Wright's interest in Gurdjieff and his teaching was rather sketchy. She commented that during her twenty-two years – or more – with Mr. Wright she had been so busy standing by his side, encouraging him in his work, sharing with him the burden of his work and of the operation of the Fellowship, that she had at least partially lost sight of God. Her search for a meaning in life had been neglected, she felt, in the adventure of living. The loss of Svetlana had brought back to her the need for faith. Svetlana had been a companion to her as well as a daughter. Svet's cheerful nature had served as a balance for Mrs. Wright. It was faith that now was helping her heal the wound. She added that the desert was also a great help because in the desert she felt closer to a spiritual world, and that Unamuno and his *Tragic Sense of Life,* which Mr. Wright had read to her, was a great support during the first days following the tragedy.

It was Mr. Wright who, with his usual resiliency, set the tempo for the Fellowship's recovery. When he arrived in Arizona he immediately set out refurbishing the camp and getting it ready for the winter. He said that he was making up for the lack of materials and labor during the war, and started a process that took about two months to complete. New canvas was installed in some areas (Fig. 66). The changes in the drafting room which had been started the previous winter were completed (Fig. 67). He made changes in his office, in the family's living quarters, and in the interior of the small theater, which was too small for the growing Fellowship. He was trying to fit in a few more seats. By the time he had finished, he had made changes in every part of the camp except the apprentice wing and the service area.

One of the significant changes was the introduction of more glass. Mr. Wright had started adding glass in February 1945. Now he was adding even more, particularly on the north side of the drafting room and the east side of the living room (Fig. 68). I was very involved in putting most of this glass in place. Mr. Wright insisted that it be fitted carefully into each opening to eliminate the need for any trim that might be used to hold the glass in place, and that any devices be kept to a minimum and be nearly invisible. This required taking very careful and accurate dimensions of each opening and careful setting of the glass to avoid breakage. The glass was cut by the supplier in Phoenix to the dimensions we provided. We set it all.

Part of the refurbishing included new rugs and furniture in the living room. When in place, we joked that the living room looked like Korrick's furniture department.[64] It was full of blond wood furniture, with woven-webbing seats and backs, and pastel-colored cushions. In addition, many of the desert plants within the compound, such as staghorn and prickly pear, were removed and replaced with nursery stock.

With these changes the character of the camp changed. Some argued that it was for the better, some that it was for the worse. It had lost much of its large and bold, archaic quality. It was no longer a camp. Its scale had been changed by the introduction of smaller-scale elements. It had become domesticated and civilized.

These physical changes in the camp were accompanied by a change in the life of the Fellowship. Although we continued to call the place a camp, life became less and less camplike. There was much less "roughing it" and less of a sense of adventure. This change was due in part to a degree of affluence. The drafting room had become a very busy place. There was not only a change in the number of projects but also in their size. There were still small houses to work on but there were also larger ones. And there were some very large buildings which were not houses, particularly those for Edgar Kaufmann, Sr., and Huntington Hartford.

Gerald Loeb and his wife visited the camp on the first weekend in December, before we were ready for visitors. They came to talk about the large house that

66   New canvas in a new configuration, seen here on the roof of the office, was also placed on the drafting room and the Garden Room. Photo by author.

67   The south wall of the drafting room was pulled back to create this walkway. Photo courtesy of John H. Howe.

68   Living room refurbished. A new canvas roof in the new configuration was put overhead. Glass was inserted into openings on the east side, and the room furnished with new rugs and furniture. Ezra Stoller © Esto.

Mr. Wright had designed for them. In place of dinner in the living room on Sunday evening, we went up to Pinnacle Peak for a picnic. The cook and kitchen helpers and several other apprentices had gone ahead to start fires for baking potatoes and grilling steaks. The model of their house, on which I had worked during a furlough in the spring of 1946, was exhibited at the Museum of Modern Art, and the working drawings were started, but the house was not built.

Among the first guests to come after we were ready for visitors were Edgar Kaufmann, Sr., and his wife, and Edgar Jr. Edgar Kaufmann, Jr., had been an apprentice at Taliesin shortly after the Fellowship started and instigated his parents' construction of Fallingwater. Mr. Kaufmann brought with him a $250,000,000 project. It was not one for which Mr. Wright was to receive his regular fee. Pittsburgh was in the process of clearing the land where the Allegheny and Monongahela rivers meet, an area referred to as the Golden Triangle. The future use of this land had not been determined. Mr. Kaufmann wanted to contribute something of vision to the city, something that would stir the imaginations of those who were going to decide this area's future use. He had no particular project in mind. He wanted Mr. Wright to come up with a proposal and to make drawings that could be shown to the city to stimulate its thinking.

Although some architectural work had been done in the drafting room during this period of refurbishing, a large backlog of work had built up. We hardly dared to make a client list. The amount of work to be done was staggering. My first project was a rush job. I helped to get out a "very bad set of plans for a house for Ollie Adelman in Milwaukee." This was the first house designed for Ollie. (I later did working drawings for a much revised house, which was built.) Following this, I was asked to help do working drawings for the Grieco house for Andover, Massachusetts, and to oversee the working drawings for the Feenburg house which Bob Warn and Omar Mahoud had been assigned to work on.

Early in March, Mr. and Mrs. Wright went on a trip to the east coast. Mr. Wright was to attend a conference at Princeton University on March 5 and 6 on "Planning Man's Environment" and receive a Doctor of Fine Arts degree. When they returned, they brought with them Mrs. Wright's brother, Vladimir Lazovich, and his wife, Sophie, who had been living in New York City. They had visited the camp before but this time they came to stay. Aunt Sophie had been having sinus trouble and it was thought that the dry desert air would give her some relief. Some members of the Fellowship had met Uncle Vlado when they were in New York installing the exhibition at the Museum of Modern Art in 1940. Uncle Vlado and Aunt Sophie moved into two of the small compartmentlike rooms on the guest deck. They quickly adapted to and became a part of the life of the Fellowship.

A few weeks before leaving on this east coast trip, Mr. Wright did his first sketch for the Sports Club in Hollywood Hills for Huntington Hartford. I don't know how long he had been thinking about this project, but when he started to draw it was evident that the concept was clear in his mind. He could not draw fast enough. The contour map of the site, which Jack had drawn, was about four-feet-by-six-feet in size. It had been pinned on a four-by-eight sheet of plywood, which served as a large drawing board. A compass, with which he could draw large circles, was at hand. Mr. Wright stood up while drawing. Ordinarily he would have sat down, but he could swing the compass through the large circles more readily while standing. He seemed to run while drawing the long horizontal lines of the entrance drive along the T-square.

As I wrote to Marcus Weston early in March: It is the most exciting business of the winter. Three shallow, circular bowls, with shallow glass bowls over, fitting into the corners of a triangular masonry base. Over these is another shallow bowl, also with a glass cover. Below these on the crest of the hill are several other bowls perched on the hill to form the swimming pool, a tennis court, etc., and wrapping all around the hill are terraces stepping down. It outdoes Hollywood in a most pleasing way. It's my suggestion that they should get it built as a permanent set for "The Fountainhead."[65] (The last sentence was a reference to the fact that Mr. Wright was being approached to do sets for the movie. Although he was not interested and was being further discouraged by both Mrs. Wright and his son Lloyd he enjoyed joking about it, saying that for $250,000 – the price reportedly being offered – he would not only design the sets, but play the leading role.)

From this drawing Jack Howe made other drawings – plans, sections, and elevations – on which Mr. Wright drew more detail and on which he made one major change. The stone base supporting the shallow concrete bowls was tilted off a vertical axis. The source of the idea for this project was evident in this first sketch. It was based on the modest memorial to Svetlana, which was standing on the Sunset Terrace (Fig. 69). Steel disks from a disk harrow (an agricultural implement used by farmers to turn the soil and kill weeds) had been placed at various places around the camp. They were used as large, shallow bowls to hold fruit and for arrangements of flowers. Mr. Wright had taken three of these and had them mounted on a low triangular base with inward sloping sides made of redwood boards. The centers of the disks rested on the three corners of the base. Their edges just touched. The disks were painted a rusty Cherokee red, the same red that was used on Mr. Wright's automobiles. Gene Masselink carved Svet's name into the base just below the bowls, and gold-leafed the small incised letters. When it was completed and put in place on the Sunset Terrace near the rooms in which Wes and Svet had lived, a handsome chunk of red stone covered with lichen was placed in the center. (The preceding winter Svetlana had done some beautiful drawings based on close-up details of lichen-covered rocks.) One of the bowls was filled with water, one with fruit, and one with flowers. The bowls were kept filled and fresh by Gene Masselink.

Jack Howe did the presentation drawings for the Sports Club, the first of several projects that Mr. Wright designed for Huntington Hartford during the following year. All were related to the proposed development of a large, unspoiled 130-acre site in the Hollywood Hills. The nature of this development did not seem to be clearly determined at the start. The drawings for the various projects had varying titles – Country Club, Play Resort, Sports Club, Resort Hotel. The development, as eventually drawn on a master plan, included the sports facility on the highest point, a house for Huntington Hartford on another point, and a central hotel facility near the entrance to the property at the lower end of the canyon. The central building was a support facility for cottage suites located nearby and residences to be built on the hillsides. Two different schemes for this hotel were done, one on the east side of the canyon, another on the west, during the sum-

69   The memorial to Svetlana on the Sunset Terrace. The memorial was made from three disks of a harrow. Photo courtesy of John H. Howe.

mer of 1947. All were to be connected with a system of roads culminating in the sports club facility. The road system had bridges spanning the side canyons at critical points and providing lookout points.

I made the preliminary drawings for Hartford's residence early in the fall of 1947. The design was an adaptation of the Jester house. I started the presentation drawings; Jack added the finishing touches. I also did the presentation drawing of the master plan. Jack and I collaborated on one of the overall perspectives of the site.

Early in February former apprentices Gordon Lee and Gordon Chadwick, both of whom had been living and working with Fritz Benedict in Aspen, came to Arizona. Gordon Lee was rejoining the Fellowship. Gordon Chadwick came to make arrangements with Wes to go to Pecos, New Mexico, to start construction of the Friedman house, which Mr. Wright had asked him to supervise.

In addition to Chadwick, there were other former apprentices who came for a visit during the winter. Among them were Bill Comer, Howard TenBrink, and David Henken. Howard and David had left the Fellowship in 1943 under somewhat strained circumstances. During their visit I became aware of an attitude toward them that disturbed me. They were treated by some apprentices, who regarded themselves as part of the inner circle, as being less desireable. Though I had recently become a senior apprentice, my relation to the inner circle was ambiguous and uncertain. And I got a certain pleasure and satisfaction out of it being this way. I had been friendly with these apprentices when they were in the Fellowship and had no reason to treat them differently now that they were not in the Fellowship.

During the winter there were other guests who were more hospitably received: George Nelson to discuss and work on the forthcoming issue of *Architectural Forum;* Anne Baxter, Mr. Wright's granddaughter and "a great little actress," and her husband, John Hodiak; Wes's mother for a week or so; Gene's brother and his wife for a few days; Walter Lippman for a Saturday evening dinner and a movie in the small, crowded theater; and Dorothy Liebes, "the world's greatest weaver," who was staying near Phoenix, for several short visits. But the guests who were the highlight of the winter were the well-known German architect Eric Mendelsohn and his wife.

The Mendelsohns came for a weekend toward the end of March. We had a somewhat spontaneous and elaborate costume party on the terrace along the south side of the drafting room (Figs. 70, 71). Mr. Wright and Mendelsohn enjoyed each other's company very much. They sat long after breakfast and lunch conversing. We had the usual dinner and movie in the theater on Saturday evening and dinner followed by music in the living room on Sunday evening. After Svetlana's death I was again asked to be responsible for the musical activity. I do not know what the program that evening consisted of, but I do remember that I played a Beethoven piano sonata, the Pathetique, opus 13.

Other winter visitors were people staying at the Arizona Biltmore Hotel in Phoenix. Mr. Wright had an understanding with the hotel's social secretary that if hotel guests came with a note from the hotel on Saturday afternoons, they would be shown around the camp without charge. This practice came to an abrupt end late in the afternoon on February 22.

We had had quite a few visitors that afternoon, some from the hotel. What they saw of the camp depended on who happened to show them around and the nature of the visitor's interest. There was no set policy. Some were walked out to the point of the desert garden where they could get an overview of the camp. Some were taken on a slightly longer tour.

Late that afternoon, when some of us were still working in the drafting room, a man, his wife, and his daughter started to enter the room. An apprentice intercepted them and ushered them toward the point for an overall view of the camp. But the little girl caught sight of Mrs. Wright's dog and started after it, heading for the entrance to the camp. The man pursued his daughter, but when he caught sight of Mr. and Mrs. Wright, who were just returning from Phoenix, he headed for them instead. He followed them into the office, where he proceeded to intro-

70, 71   Party pictures taken at the impromptu masquerade party for Eric Mendelsohn and his wife. Jack Howe, Kay Davison, and John Hill. Andrew Devane. Source of photos unknown.

duce himself and his family to Mr. and Mrs. Wright and to otherwise make a nuisance of himself. Mr. Wright had seated himself at his desk to read his mail. The man began looking over his shoulder and indiscriminately taking pictures. Mrs. Wright became upset; she particularly resented curiosity seekers. She shouted at them to get out. Those of us in the drafting room, hearing the shouting, came out to see what was happening. A letter went to the Biltmore Hotel that afternoon saying that since we were so busy, the Saturday afternoon visits would have to be discontinued.

Mr. Wright did his first sketch for Pittsburgh's Golden Triangle project late in March, after his return from the trip to the east coast. I assume that he had been thinking about this project since Kaufmann's visit early in February. Mr. Wright proposed that the land be used as a civic center. It was an imaginative and challenging proposal. It included facilities for all of the activities that one might consider locating in a civic center. Drawn at a scale of one inch to thirty-two feet, the plan was near the size of the four-by-eight sheet of plywood that was used as a drawing board. Again he was swinging circles with a compass (Fig. 72).

The central feature was a great spiraling ramp. On top of the space enclosed by the ramp was a nine-acre park with a large fountain in its center. Beneath this park was a large coliseum partially open to the sky but having a sheltered playing area surrounded by sheltered seating. Beneath the coliseum and within the space enclosed by the spiraling ramp was a park with a sports arena, convention facilities, an opera house, a symphony hall, and a cinema which was divided into smaller theaters.

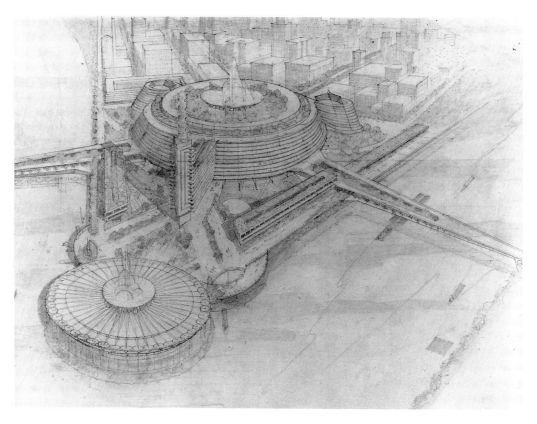

72 Pittsburgh Point Park Project. An overall aerial view of the proposed Civic Center. (4821.004 Frank Lloyd Wright Foundation Archives)

Attached to the periphery of this central feature was a building for city offices, bridges spanning the two rivers, and two smaller spiraling ramps for quicker egress from the structure. At the point where the Allegheny and the Monongahela meet, the apex of the Golden Triangle, was another large water feature containing an aquarium, restaurants, and swimming pools. The remaining area was a great landscaped park. Beneath the entire area was more parking – there was also parking along the spiraling ramp – and a system of roadways for collecting and distributing the vehicular traffic, that which crossed the bridges as well as that generated within the structure and the adjacent streets.

Jack Howe and Gordon Lee worked with Mr. Wright in the development of the many preliminary drawings. Others were asked to help with the final presentation drawings. I traced one of the sections through the entire structure and drew and traced a one-sixteenth-inch-scale drawing through the structure containing the aquarium.

This proposal was much more than Mr. Kaufmann had anticipated or hoped for. The scope and complexity of it was overwhelming. He suggested that Mr.

Wright do a simpler proposal. The result was a second proposal done during the summer of 1947, in which the emphasis was upon the two essential bridges. The bridges spring from the base of a central pylon. From the pylon, webs of cables extend to help support the bridges. The facilities for most of the activities included in the prior proposal are clustered in a landscape park around the base of the pylons.

Although the movement of traffic was a major concern in planning both proposals, its handling had not been emphasized in the presentation drawings of the first proposal. In the set of drawings for the second proposal were diagrams which Gordon Lee had carefully studied and drawn of the various kinds of traffic – pedestrian, auto, and truck – and how each of these was to be handled on separate levels of the bridges and within the complex. These drawings were completed in the fall of 1947.

During the spring of 1947 there were several departures from the Fellowship that were attended with some heat and more than the usual stress. Greg Affleck and Hiram Middlebrook were asked to leave in early April. The sheriff had come to camp to see Mr. Wright about Alex Mishelevich and the Model A that Alex had driven to town. Neither Alex nor the Model A were licensed. Alex spent the night in jail. While discussing Alex's offense the sheriff mentioned that it was not as bad as another offense. The sheriff told Mr. Wright that Greg and Hiram had gotten drunk in Phoenix, and on their way back to camp had stopped at El Chorro for another drink. Refused admission they had started throwing rocks at the inn.

Alex had taken his turn in the kitchen at about Christmastime and was assigned to serve Mr. and Mrs. Wright. During this time in the kitchen he began to assume a familiarity with Mrs. Wright, patting her on the shoulders. I don't think he had reached the fanny-slapping familiarity with her that he had assumed with Antoinette Prevost and probably Kay, who was the cook. After some episode to which Kay had taken exception, Alex had a session with Mr. Wright.

About a month later, a group representing Huntington Hartford was at Taliesin West to discuss the resort project. Alex managed to hitch a ride with them when they returned to Los Angeles. During the ride, Alex presented himself as Mr. Wright's representative on the project, saying that he would come to Los Angeles and handle the construction of the project and that he thought he could live on about $300 per month. Mr. Wright's son Lloyd was associated with his father on this project. The client, suspicious of Alex, asked Lloyd about Alex's proposal. Lloyd wrote his father concerning Alex's activities. Again Alex was called on the carpet for his actions and, as I understood it, was told to leave the Fellowship. Somehow he managed to stay on until the Fellowship left for Wisconsin.

Spring and Summer 1947

This spring I was a member of the advance party sent to Wisconsin to open the house for Mr. and Mrs. Wright's arrival. Opening the house in Wisconsin was much more than unlocking a few doors. In addition to dusting and vacuuming and airing it out, there were dustcovers to be removed from the furniture, rugs to be unrolled, furniture to be put back in place, beds to be made, and plants to be moved back to the loggia from the heated area where they had been kept over the winter. There were valves in the water system to be opened and closed, and pipes and plumbing fixtures to be checked for any leaks or breaks during the winter due to freezing.

When we arrived, I moved into the room on the upper level of the stable wing where I had lived during the previous summer and fall. John Hill was back in his room at the west end. And Peter Matthews moved into the small room on the north side of the hall. The three of us were viewed by some as a clubby clique. And we were. We enjoyed our "set-up" and each other's company. Johnnie was the host of the group. His room was comfortably and handsomely furnished. He had a small grand piano and a record player and he seemed always ready to serve a cup of instant coffee. Peter was the raconteur. It seemed his room was always being worked on, but was never finished. No matter what work he was assigned to during the day he seemed to find in it the makings of an interesting tale, which he recounted in the evening when we were getting ready to go over to Hillside for dinner. My role in the group seemed to be to enjoy Johnnie's hospitality and Peter's stories, and to keep the bathroom clean. I also did some chauffeuring for the occupants of the stable wing. I was in charge of the Fellowship's Jeep that summer and frequently used it for trips between Taliesin and Hillside, especially in rainy weather.

My responsibilities in connection with music were considerably lightened that summer by the presence of a group of professional musicians. Through John Rosenfeld, the music critic of the *Dallas Morning News,* Mr. Wright had met and asked Anatol Dorati, the conductor of the Dallas Symphony, to find a group of young musicians who would be interested in spending the summer at Taliesin. (Rosenfeld had been instrumental in Mr. Wright's being asked to design the Rogers Lacy Hotel.) A group of four came: a violinist, Ann Purcell; a cellist, Signe Sandstrom; a violist, Ernst Wallfisch; and a pianist, Lory Wallfisch, Ernst's wife.

Ernst had studied with George Enesco. He and his wife had come to the United States from Rumania after World War II, assisted by Yehudi Menuhin.

Mr. Wright had mixed feelings about having professional musicians at Taliesin. He was concerned that it might discourage and reduce the music-making efforts of the amateurs. But he did enjoy the higher level of performance of the professionals. This contradiction was partly resolved by the participation of the professionals in the efforts of our amateur ensemble and by some of the amateurs taking lessons with the professionals.

John Hill and Brandoch took cello lessons with Signe. I took viola lessons with Ernst. I had started playing the viola at Svetlana's urging before the war and used Mr. Wright's viola. I never heard him play it, but I did understand that he had played it as a young man.

Early in the summer, when I went into the living room at Taliesin one Sunday evening for dinner, Gene Masselink asked me to sit with two guests who had arrived that afternoon. They were Henri Cartier-Bresson and John Malcolm Brinnin. During dinner I learned that they were on a cross-country photographic tour, finding artists, all in the country, away from cities. They stayed overnight in the guest rooms below the house.

The next morning, at breakfast, Gene asked me if I would accompany them as they spent part of the day following Mr. Wright around while Cartier-Bresson took photos of him in his activities. I assumed that Brinnin was to take notes and perhaps write something to go with the photos. I stayed with them all morning, but it was not a morning in which Mr. Wright followed his customary pattern of activity. Usually he went to his office after breakfast to respond to any mail that might have arrived late the preceding afternoon. After that he might walk to Hillside with Mrs. Wright and arrive at about ten-thirty or eleven. Mr. Wright would work until lunch in the drafting room on whatever might be needing his attention. This morning he decided he wanted to check out the no longer active quarry from which most of the stone for the construction of Taliesin had come. I assume he was going to reopen it to take out more stone.

This quarry was on a hilltop northwest of Taliesin. It was a spot to which we had gone on Fellowship picnics or to pick gooseberries or raspberries. The road up to the quarry was partially overgrown. It wandered across a pasture and then up the southwest slope of the hill on a somewhat easy grade. We had followed this road when taking food and supplies for picnics up to the quarry in a Jeep or a pickup truck. Ordinarily I think Mr. Wright would have had someone drive him up to the quarry to check its condition, but this morning he chose to go on foot, and not by the easier route on the road but by the steeper slope where there were outcrops of stone. He led the way, thrashing through the tangle of scrub oak, hazel brush, and raspberry bushes. I went behind him, followed by Cartier-Bresson and Brinnin. We arrived at Hillside just in time for lunch. We had walked the entire morning.

I have seen only one photo from that morning's expedition. It was published in the March 1948 issue of *Harper's Bazaar*. It was taken in the shade of the north wall of the living room at the east entrance to Hillside. The entrance doors are slightly out of focus in the background, but the whiskers on Mr. Wright's face are in sharp focus. He had not shaved that morning. He had a brown beret pushed down over his hair, which had not been combed or brushed after the morning of thrashing through the brush. He was wearing a light wool, tan and brown tweed suit which he had begun wearing as an everyday suit. It still had sticktights and cockleburs attached to it and a few snagged threads where it had caught in the brush.

Mrs. Wright did not like the photo and questioned why a magazine would choose to publish such a picture. I won't speculate as to how Mr. Wright felt about it, but I do believe that Mr. Wright knew who Henri Cartier-Bresson was and that he was familiar with the nature of his photographic work.

In addition to rehearsing the chorus, working in the garden for an hour each morning, and taking my turn as breakfast cook, my time was divided that summer between work in the studio and work outside on stonemasonry.

Several projects for Huntington Hartford, as well as the second scheme for Pittsburgh, were done during the summer. Interspersed between these were houses, both large and small, but mostly small. The largest was that for Dr. Paul Palmer and his family in Phoenix. Mr. Wright designed the master plans for two housing projects near Kalamazoo, Michigan – Parkwyn Village and Galesburg Country Homes. These master plans were not based on a rectangular grid, as in previous master plans for housing, but on a curvilinear motif. The sites for the individual houses were circular. The areas between the circles were to be filled with native plants. Ideally, the circles would have just touched at their perimeters, but, due to the conditions of the entire site, some individual sites overlapped or were not complete circles. These two projects had begun as one cooperative project, but the group had split into two when the members could not agree upon one site.

The master plan for Usonia Homes, near Pleasantville, New York, was also done that summer. It was also based on circular sites for the individual homes. Mr. Wright designed many of the homes for the Kalamazoo projects, but for Pleasantville he agreed to design only three houses; however, the designs of all the other houses were to be subject to his approval.

Working by myself during the summer, I did the working drawings for the Douglas Grant house in Cedar Rapids, Iowa. This was one of my favorite houses (Fig. 73). It was essentially a simple house, but it had a spatial richness that was achieved in other houses only with a more complex form. Its construction and many of its details were similar to those of the Walter house, so the drawings were done relatively easily. John Hill supervised the construction. I went with

73   The Douglas Grant house, Cedar Rapids, Iowa. Photo courtesy of Sidney Robinson.

him to Cedar Rapids several times during its construction, once when they were just ready to pour the concrete slab. The formwork for the slab was supported on a forest of poplar poles. The Grants were doing much of the work themselves and were quite ingenious in getting it done.

In the working drawings I had shown the stone walls and piers as being stonework similar to that of Taliesin. But the Grants had a readily available source of gray limestone which was unevenly bedded and broken into small, thin pieces. Lacking any skill as masons, they developed a way of laying this stone which resulted in a tweedy texture with which Mr. Wright was quite happy. They made a form that was small enough for them to move and set in place easily. Then they put in layers of stone, about a foot deep, against the exterior and interior faces of the form, set the insulation core in place along with wall ties to hold the faces together, and grouted the entire section. This resulted in an appearance similar to that of a dry stone wall, one laid without mortar. They moved into the house before the interior wood partitions were in place and did much of the finishing themselves. Mr. Wright had a high regard for clients like the Grants.

In the drafting room that summer, Jack Howe and I developed a working relationship that went on to become a fixed pattern. I became, in effect, an assistant to him. If he was doing a set of presentation drawings, he might ask me to complete blocking in a perspective and to draw some scale figures. He said that I was better at drawing people and cars than he was. Then he would block in the entourage and trace and render the final drawings.

During the several years Jack had been in prison, he developed a beautiful drawing technique consisting of ink lines of various weights and dots of differing density. This technique was used on many of the presentation drawings that he did that summer, particularly the perspectives of the two schemes for the Cottage Group Resort Hotel for Huntington Hartford. These drawings, seen just as ink drawings before the color was added, although they were somewhat different in technique, easily rivaled the best drawings in Wright's *Ausgefuhrte Bauten* folios of 1910.[66] Mr. Wright acknowledged the quality of these drawings as ink drawings but, quoting his old chief, Dankmar Adler, asked Jack to color them: "Put some color on it, Frank; the client likes color."

Jack had become a very quick and productive draftsman by setting goals for himself. For example, he would decide that he would complete a certain drawing before lunch or teatime or before he could leave the drafting room to do something else. This sometimes created problems for the people working with him. He was reluctant to take time from whatever he was doing to answer any questions that another person might have. That summer I assisted Jack with the presentation drawings for the Self-Service Garage in Pittsburgh, the Huntington Hartford projects, and several projects for the Valley National Bank of Phoenix.

For Mr. Wright's Birthday Box that June, I designed a house which I called "Fantasy Impromptu." I took some of the ideas in the Huntington Hartford Sports Club project a step further into something that would have been technically even more difficult to build. It was a house consisting of three glass balls supported at different heights on a massive central masonry element. One of the balls was the living room, another was an enclosed swimming pool space into which all of the other rooms opened. The pool itself was to be a glass bowl! The third ball, as Mr. Wright pointed out in his comments during the opening of "the Box," was extraneous.

Early in the summer Mr. Wright started construction of a foyer addition to the west side of the Playhouse at Hillside. I was assigned to help with laying the stone walls and piers. We had just gotten started on this project when Mr. Wright asked me to start another wall nearby. It was to extend west from the southwest corner of the Dana Gallery. He indicated where he wanted it to end, its configuration, and the location of a plaque that he wanted to include. The plaque (Fig. 74) was to be a memorial to his Aunts Jane and Nell who had founded the school. I found a stone slab large enough for the plaque and laid out the lettering for it at one-quarter full size on tracing paper. After getting Mr. Wright's approval of this layout, I drew it full size on a piece of brown paper and used this to transfer the lettering to the stone for carving. While carving the letters sans serif, since Mr. Wright disliked Roman lettering, I developed a theory about how the "serif" might have developed through the act of cutting into stone. It was much easier to

74   Memorial to Aunts Nell and Jane. Photo courtesy of Steve Padget.

get a crisp, clean letter with that extra cut. Cutting and laying stone did not benefit my work in the studio or my musical activity. Gripping the handle of a stone hammer for several hours tended to stiffen my right hand and wrist; holding a chisel with my left hand, particularly if I made a mislick and hit my hand, did little to improve my left hand's flexibility. But I did get great satisfaction out of this work. Before this project was completed I started acquiring my own set of stoneworking tools.

While sandstone was being taken out of the quarry that summer for masonry work at Hillside, Wes asked the quarrymen to break out a slab large enough to be used to cover Svetlana's grave. A slab about twelve inches thick and about three-by-seven feet in area was broken out. It was dragged behind the caterpillar tractor to the chapel yard near Svetlana's grave. Later in the fall, when the weather was cooler, I spent much of my time between tea and dinner at the chapel yard, squaring and dressing the stone. The slab was set in place before I left for Arizona, with its top surface only a few inches above the level of the ground. I continued to do some stonework during many of the following summers and sometimes indulged in the fantasy that I could live quite happily as a stone-mason. I questioned this fantasy only in the fall when it sometimes took me – and my back – a month or more to recover from the soreness brought about by overly optimistic stone lifting.

Most festive occasions at Taliesin required at least a week of planning and preparation, but there was one weekend in mid-August which turned into a gala event without much effort on anyone's part. On Friday Prince Rana Mansinhji from India, who had joined the Fellowship in February, dressed himself in clothing which we had never seen him wear, and went to Madison to celebrate Indian independence with students from India at the university. He must have created a sensation on the bus going and coming. He was dressed in trousers fitted tightly below the knee, a long gray coat buttoned to the collar band, and a flamboyant silk turban that he had wound with humps of folds over the left eye and the free end of the fabric flowing out behind.

On Saturday we spent the day getting ready for the usual influx of weekend guests. But before dinner, Mansinhji, again dressed in his native dress and looking quite handsome, gave a party in the Hill Garden in honor of India's independence. He served punch and Indian delicacies which consisted of vegetables and many different kinds of flowers, dipped in an unfamiliar flavored batter and deep fried in hot fat.

During the summer of 1947 I became aware that the Fellowship consisted of a larger number – as well as a larger percentage – of apprentices from outside the United States. Near the end of the summer a reporter and a photographer from the *Capital Times* of Madison came out to do a story on the Fellowship. The article, which appeared on Sunday, September 28, referred to the Fellowship as a "League of Nations." This "league" included Gershon Kohn from Israel; Albert Friedlander from Germany – his concentration camp number tattooed on his arm; Paolo Soleri from Italy; Mansinhji from India; Omar Mahoud as well as Salah Zeitoon and his wife and small daughter from Egypt; the Wallfisches from Rumania; Shao Fang and Sheng Pao, who had recently arrived from China joining Ling Po; Hans Lubbers from Holland; and Tor Bjornstad, who still spoke with a Norwegian accent. Although this summer appeared to be an exception, there had always been several apprentices from other countries. Some stayed only a few months, others stayed for several years (Fig. 75).

Early in October, when I went to the office late one afternoon to check for mail, I encountered Mr. and Mrs. Wright and John Hill in the studio admiring and discussing the model of the Guggenheim Museum (Fig. 76). It had been damaged in shipping and Johnnie had spent some time that summer restoring and refurbishing it in anticipation of a visit in mid-October from Solomon Guggenheim. The model was displayed with a marble Greek male torso nearby. Mr. Wright was pointing out the similarity in concept between the two: the twist of the torso and the turning of the spiral, the monomaterial and the articulation of the forms. Somehow the conversation shifted from the model to Louis Sullivan, his ornament and his ideas about architecture. With this shift Mr. Wright went into the vault and brought out the collection of sketches for ornament which Sullivan had given Mr. Wright three days before his death. He casually spread them out on the several drafting tables in the studio so that we could look at them. It was exciting to be able to handle and study these germinal notations done on bits and

75   A picnic at Borglum Rock. In foreground at left, Shao Fung; left to right: Aunt Sophie, Mrs. Wright, and Mary Lim. In background left to right: Ernst and Lory Wallfisch, Donald Brown, and unknown. Photo courtesy of John Geiger.

76   Brandoch Peters with model of Guggenheim Museum. The model could be opened to reveal the interior. Source of photo unknown.

pieces of office stationery. I had seen reproductions of Sullivan's drawings, including those in *A System of Architectural Ornament,* published by the A.I.A. But I had not seen any of these drawings before. They were still crisp and sparkling after forty years or more. Drawn at small scale, they suggested amazing detail. They were like steel engravings, yet still rhythmic and filled with poetry. Seeing these drawings I realized how much was lost in reproductions of Sullivan's drawings.

Early in November, several staffmembers of *Architectural Forum,* including Paul Grotz, the art editor, came to Taliesin to work with Mr. Wright on the layout and text of a special issue of the magazine, the January 1948 issue, published on the tenth anniversary of the 1938 special issue.

I was among the last to leave Wisconsin for Arizona that year, staying on to do another revision, the second, of the working drawings of a house for Ollie Adelman. I stayed also to help Wes close up Hillside and parts of Taliesin. Construction of the Johnson Laboratory Tower had started and Wes was making trips to Racine to check on this. I enjoyed being at Taliesin after most of the group had left. And I enjoyed getting a real taste of winter. I wrote John Mitaraky about one of these winter experiences:[67]

> Last Friday nite as I walked over the hill between Hillside and Taliesin I saw the most wonderful spectacle of a winter night. The moon was nearly full, filling the snow with a slightly yellow inner glow. Great clouds of almost rose and grey were moving across a sky that was a blue as distant and dark as eternity – yet luminous, and casting violet shadows on the snow. The hills, almost surrounded by halos when the light struck them full, were cleanly etched with deep brown and blue trees and bushes. The whole effect was sharp and clear – with all of the essence of winter nights that one could ask for compressed into one intense experience.

Winter 1947–1948

Getting settled into camp in Arizona took much less time that winter than it had the previous winter. Viewed in retrospect, the general refurbishing of the year before had been a preparation for the photos of the camp taken for the special issue of *Architectural Forum* which was soon to make its appearance. But there were always changes to be made when Mr. Wright saw his work with a fresh eye. And, despite the seeming prominence of the masonry walls, there was always maintenance to be done.

Each year the process of settling down to work was interrupted by the holiday season. The trappings of Christmas seemed out of place in the desert. They were something Mr. Wright tolerated. Mrs. Wright and Iovanna felt that we should have a Christmas tree complete with decorations, but Mr. Wright insisted that if we were going to decorate something it should be a cactus. Mrs. Wright and Iovanna thought we should sing Christmas carols, but that we shouldn't rehearse them. But as director of the chorus, I knew that if we were going to sing them, particularly when guests were present, we should at least know the words and, I hoped, be able to sing them in four-part harmony.

This year the holiday season was accompanied by cold and sunless days. It was a spell that lasted well into February. There were several mornings when there was a skim of ice on the pools in the camp and a dusting of snow on the mountains north of camp. During these months it was uncomfortable working in the drafting room. Early in the morning the only source of heat was the large fireplace at the east end. As the day progressed, if it was sunny, the sun warmed the space somewhat. During this cold spell Mr. Wright commented that he should have oriented the camp differently so that the sun's rays would reach the drafting room earlier in the morning. To be warm, those of us who were working in the drafting room bundled ourselves in sweaters, jackets, and scarves. It was difficult to draw wearing gloves or mittens.

On one of these mornings when I had bundled myself in a sweater and an old suede jacket, and wrapped a wool scarf around my head, I met Mr. Wright coming out of his office as I was going in to check the mail. Seeing me so bundled, he said to me, "Curtis, you look like hell. I should give you some money so that you can get some decent clothes." If he had paused I would have told him that I also felt like hell. A recurrent sinus problem had flared up.

I spent most of my time in the drafting room that winter. There was a steady stream of preliminary drawings to be done for houses, most of them small, and an increasing number of working drawings. Wartime constraints on construction had been lifted. And some clients who, following the war, had expected a recession and with it a decline in building costs, had now decided there was not going to be a recession and that they should no longer wait since building costs were continuing to rise. Shortly after the holiday season, I received a letter from Professor George Beal, who had, following the war, become chairman of the department of architecture at the University of Kansas. The letter offered me a teaching position, on a trial basis, for the spring semester of 1948, which was to start in mid-February. It was a tempting and unsettling letter. I had thought that I would like to try my hand at teaching. This was an opportunity to do it, and to earn some money. I had emerged from three years of "work of national importance" with no savings and owing money, which I had borrowed from my parents and brother.

As a senior apprentice I was receiving a monthly stipend of thirty dollars. Sometimes, among ourselves and depending on the mood we were in, the seniors referred to the stipend as a "pittance" or "thirty pieces of silver." Thirty dollars covered my personal needs. But it did not enable me to save any money or to live in a manner comparable to that of some of the seniors who seemed to have other sources of income. It had been easy to live a Spartan existence when Mr. Wright had had little income. It was difficult and sometimes irritating to do so when he was living more affluently, particularly when there were comments such as the one about my cold-weather garb. While trying to decide how I should respond to Professor Beal's offer, I talked with Mrs. Wright about it and showed the letter to Mr. Wright. To my relief his response was a definite no. He said that I should stay at Taliesin. He was also somewhat annoyed with George for not having written directly to him, for trying to take me away from him behind his back. My reply to Professor Beal's letter explained my reasons for not accepting his offer:

> We are very busy now – and doing work that is probably as interesting as any in his career. The *Forum* will give you a taste of that. That aspect of it holds me. There is the fact that I've worked with Mr. Wright long enough now to be somewhat useful to him. . . . I've had one or two other "feelers" which I've felt that I had to turn down too. . . . The Fellowship has become my home and that too stands in the way of any thought of leaving it.[68]

Although I had decided to stay at Taliesin, largely because of my interest in the work being produced, I continued during the winter to question whether or not I had made the right decision. There were other things that contributed to my unsettled state of mind. There was the strong prospect of war with Russia and the

77   Sunday lunch on steps near pool on south side of drafting room. Left to right: Lee Kawahara, Lois Davidson, John Pell, Donald Brown, Sheng Pao, Ling Po, Gordon Lee, Bob Brevick, Mansinh Rana, Bob Cross, the author, Joan Frazier, John Hill, Shirley Oliver, Shao Fung, Polly Lockhart. Photo courtesy of John Geiger.

possibility of my going to prison or spending another spell on "work of national importance." There was also the increasing size of the Fellowship. It had gotten too large for the camp (Fig. 77). Mr. Wright was looking for ways in which the camp might be enlarged, particularly the Kiva which seated only about forty-five people comfortably. In addition to being physically too large, the Fellowship had ceased to be a close-knit group; it was becoming impersonal and institutional. There had been a continuous, large turnover of new apprentices after the war, but what I missed most was the sense of adventure that had permeated the Fellow-ship in the years before the war. Although Mr. Wright's work was still interesting and fresh, getting out drawings for the projects was becoming somewhat routine.

A project on which I spent a good part of my time during this winter was a set of working drawings for a house for Albert "Ollie" Adelman. I had already been involved in two revisions of drawings for a house for Ollie. Construction prices seemed to be rising faster than we could revise drawings. This, the third try, was successful. The house was built in the summer of 1948. It was published in the January 1951 *Architectural Forum*. This house was to be built of concrete block, and was designed for a long and relatively narrow site, 136 feet wide and 800 feet long. Most of the site was treeless and flat, but at the west end, away from the street, the site sloped down into a tree-filled ravine.

Mr. Wright had redesigned the house into a long, in-line plan placed diagonally across the site. The main entrance to the house was on the north side near the living room and also near the middle of the site. The bedroom wing extended toward the northeast corner of the site. The bedrooms faced south southeast. The service wing extended toward the southwest corner. A gallery facing southeast led to the dining room at the far end, overlooking the ravine. A covered walkway, which made an L shape of the overall plan of the house, connected the garage to the house at a service entrance near the kitchen and maid's room.

When working drawings for any house were started one of the first drawings Mr. Wright wanted to see after the plan had been laid out was a cross section of the house, drawn at three-quarter-inch scale. This was a scale at which it was possible to show details of construction. As work on the drawings progressed, this section was complemented with details drawn at a larger scale, one-quarter full-size sections of windows, doors, cabinetwork, etc.

Mr. Wright insisted that we made too many drawings, that there was no need to detail all of the special conditions. He said that a good builder should be able to understand the grammar of a house's construction and would be able to work out these special conditions, as and where they occurred.

This house had a roof unlike any of the houses I had worked on up to this time. It had a hipped roof, but the pitches of the opposite sides of the roof were not the same. The ridge of the roof was located over the partitions separating the circulation space from the rooms adjacent to it. Circulation in the east wing was on the north side. It was on the south in the west wing. The shift in the location of the ridges was accommodated by the two-story-high space of the living room and entrance. The ridges stopped against the masonry walls which surrounded this high space, over which there was a flat roof with a skylight above the entrance area.

I blocked in the construction section for Ollie's house following the details of other houses on which I had worked and which had interior board and batten walls. When I showed this drawing to Mr. Wright, he reworked it completely, changing the details of the ceilings, the interior walls, and the soffits at the eaves of the roof. The result was a grammar unlike any that I had previously worked on, and a different way of making the windows and the exterior glass doors.

In the house for Lowell Walters Mr. Wright had wanted to use steel windows and doors in combination with the mullions made of steel T's. In this house for Ollie, he also wanted to use steel T mullions, with windows and doors having top and bottom rails of wood but with stiles made of small, aluminum T-sections. This would have reduced the width of the mullions and given greater emphasis to the

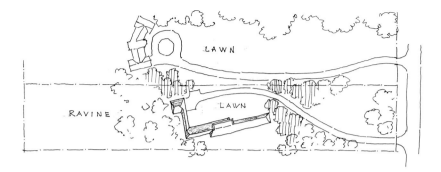

78   Site plan, Albert Adelman residence, Fox Point, Wisconsin. The house is set at an angle on the narrow site to provide generous views from the centrally located living room. Otherwise these would be available only on a wider lot. Drawn from memory by author.

horizontal sweep of the bands of windows and doors. The leg of the T was to be let into a notch in the rails and held in place with countersunk bolts.

In the completed set of working drawings, the doors and windows were detailed to be made in this manner, but when the builder tried to get sub-bids for the millwork he encountered a problem, a conflict between two labor unions. Since the stiles were shown as metal, the metalworkers insisted that the windows should be made by metalworkers. Since the rails were to be wood, the woodworkers insisted that the windows should be made by woodworkers. The problem was resolved by making the doors and windows of wood.

While writing about this project I would like to interject one other experience related to it. In the summer of 1948 I went to Milwaukee with Mr. Wright and Wes to stake out the house on the site. In doing this I learned something about the house which had puzzled me but which I had never questioned when working on the drawings: why was it placed diagonally on the site? The answer to this question became clear to me when we located the stakes for the corners of the house (Fig. 78).

The house on the lot north of Ollie's site was set well back from the street. In front of it was a large, nicely landscaped, and well-tended lawn. There was a border of planting along the boundary between the two sites. But there was a wide opening in this band near the middle of the properties and just at the point where the entrance to Ollie's house was to be. This resulted in a visual widening of Ollie's relatively narrow site at that point. The lawn of the house to the north became, in effect, a lawn in front of Ollie's entrance. With this diagonal placement, when approaching the entrance, you entered the site on a drive at the southeast corner of the lot, came around the house at the east end, and arrived at this open space in front of the entrance.

Now that I understood the placement of Ollie's house, I began to understand the statements Mr. Wright had made when I first joined the Fellowship about the Rebhuhn house in Great Neck, Long Island, that the design of the house had made the site seem larger than it was. I began to look at Mr. Wright's work for other ways in which the design might make the site appear larger, ways in which elements of the landscape were or could be "pulled into the design." I began with Taliesin West. I knew that I enjoyed being in the camp and particularly walking through it. And I saw that the camp was rich with visual axes, extensions of paths along which one moved. These extended to elements on the horizon, reaching out and grabbing some as far as forty miles away – the visual axis extending toward mountains near Chandler. There was also the one that extended toward Camelback Mountain about fourteen miles away, one toward the McDowell Mountains north of the camp, and one toward the peaks four miles east of the camp, the axis which began at the west end of the pergola-covered walk north of the drafting room (Fig. 79). Many of these axes have since been blocked, modified, or muddied by construction or planting within the camp itself as well as by construction in the views from the camp. The result has been, in effect, the destruction of the architectural work that the camp was in its origin.

Phoenix was a place to which many people came to escape the rigors of a northern winter. At the peak of the season we had a regular series of visitors to the camp.

Early in February we made elaborate preparations for the visit of Edgar Kaufmann, Sr.[69] He came to see the preliminary drawings for the second proposal, the two suspension bridges, for the Golden Triangle in Pittsburgh. He brought with him the industrial designer Raymond Lowey. Mr. Wright and Lowey had something of a set-to during breakfast one morning.[70] It resulted from Mr. Wright's comment during breakfast that "streamliners" stood in the way of any real progress in design. Lowey had recently designed the "streamlined" Studebaker which was very much in the news.

At the end of February, Raymond Duncan,[71] the brother of the famous dancer Isadora, and a prime example of "the individual," came for Sunday evening dinner with his secretary. Both came dressed in heavy, hand-spun and handwoven wool togas, and wore sandals. (I assume that they wove the wool for the togas and made the sandals.) He wore his graying hair in a long bob with a headband, and heavy, horn-rimmed glasses. If he hadn't been so authentic he would have been a sad, but amusing, object. If his dress had been part of a pose it would have been highly entertaining. But it wasn't. His dress was normal for Raymond and Mr. Wright accepted it as such. He and Mr. Wright were deep in conversation with each other all through dinner. Mrs. Wright was disappointed in him. She had hoped for a man of "some spiritual development."

The following week the Rubicons came to dinner. Mr. Rubicon was the head of one of the largest advertising agencies in the United States. He and Mr. Wright spent the evening on the verge of blows arguing over going to war with Russia. Mr. Wright was not in favor of it. In the middle of March Artur Rodjinski, the con-

79   A visual axis which begins in the walk along the north side of the drafting room and extends to mountain peaks four miles east of the camp. Photo courtesy of John H. Howe.

ductor of the Chicago Symphony, and his wife came to Sunday evening dinner.[72] He and his wife had come out to see the camp late in February. Gene Masselink had shown them around and was quite enthusiastic about them after the tour. Rodjinski was the first musician of some importance whom he had encountered who was as appreciative of Mr. Wright's work as Mr. Wright was of music. That evening was a very pleasant and agreeable affair. On the first Sunday in April a Mr. Donnard, from whom Mr. Wright had bought an A.C., an English sports car, was invited to dinner.[73] This also turned into a very interesting evening.

In the second weekend in April Gerald Loeb and his wife,[74] for whom Mr. Wright had designed the large house in Connecticut, came for the weekend. In preparation for their visit I helped refurbish the model of their house which I had helped build in the spring of 1946 when I was on leave from the C.O. camp in Minersville. The Loebs were interested in having Mr. Wright design the sets of the movie *The Fountainhead.*

Late in March, Mr. Wright began to talk about being in Wisconsin before the end of April and to make definite plans. During the last five or six years he had made the trip by train. This time he wanted to drive, probably in the A.C. that he had recently acquired. He marked the itinerary he proposed to take on a map. But then Mr. and Mrs. Wright went by train, and I rode with Gene Masselink who had been assigned to drive the A.C. We arrived in Wisconsin with sunburned faces the first week in May.

Summer 1948

The summer of 1948 was an active and productive time, architecturally. When we arrived in Wisconsin, the Johnson Tower was well under way; the maze of underground construction, including a tunnel connecting the tower to the factory, was up to ground level. In connection with this project Mr. Wright and Wes made frequent trips to Racine. And Ben Wiltscheck and his assistant, John Halmah, spent many weekends during the summer and fall at Taliesin; they came to go over drawings for details for the building and to get these approved by Mr. Wright.

The Lowell Walter house was under way and John Hill, who was supervising it, made frequent trips to Iowa to check on its progress. It was about half completed by fall. The second house for the Jacobses, the hemicycle being built near Madison, was beginning to take shape. When we went to Madison we stopped at the site coming and going, to observe its progress. It was nearly completed that fall. With these projects and others under construction, Mr. Wright was frequently away from Taliesin. We had been in Wisconsin about two weeks when Mr. Wright left for New York, where he was to see a client, taking with him the preliminary sketches for a tourist resort on the edge of Meteor Canyon in northern Arizona. The drawings were completed just before his departure.[75]

As soon as we were settled in the drafting room, Jack and I started work on the construction drawings for the Morris Shop in San Francisco. We had done the preliminary drawings for this remodeling project while still in Arizona. I had peopled these drawings of the shop with scale figures based on my idea of what San Francisco matrons might look like when shopping for fine wedding gifts. To speed up this process, we decided to use these preliminary drawings as part of the working drawings. The client had asked for no changes in the plans and we saw no need to duplicate them. We simply added some sheets of details: of the front facade, of the ramp connecting the two floors, and of typical details of display cases and cabinetwork (Fig. 80). Wes took these drawings to San Francisco to get construction started. He hadn't been there long before he discovered that some of the dimensions of existing construction with which we had been provided – specifically, of floor and ceiling heights – were inaccurate. Rather than return the drawings to Taliesin, he asked Mr. Wright to send someone to San

80   V. C. Morris Shop, San Francisco. The interior is an investigation of circles. Maynard Parker, photo, copyright Maynard L. Parker Estate.

Francisco to help him revise the drawings. Mr. Wright sent Ling Po. At about the same time, Mr. Wright began a search for Manuel Sandoval, who had been an apprentice and who had done some of the cabinetwork for the Kaufmann house. He wanted him to do the cabinetwork for this shop. This remodeling project was nearing completion when we left Wisconsin for Arizona that winter.

The other major architectural project on which I worked with Jack and Wes during the summer was the Unitarian Church for Madison, Wisconsin. We continued a practice we had begun to develop: Jack did the general plans, the elevations, and the small-scale sections; I did the larger-scale sections and details; Wes did the structural calculations for which I drew the plans and details.

The preliminary presentation drawings had been done by Jack during the previous winter in Arizona. When the Unitarians asked Mr. Wright to design a new building for them, they were meeting in a church in the downtown area. They were considering buying a site away from downtown, but the site was, in Mr. Wright's opinion, not far enough out and it was too small. He urged them to go farther out and to buy a larger site, which they did. Madison soon surrounded it.

Many of the details of construction were similar to those of the houses on which we were working. The interesting and puzzling aspect of this project to me was the roof over the sanctuary. I was puzzled by what seemed to me to be a very unwrightian characteristic of the roof. Its external shape did not conform to the ceiling on the interior. Internally, the surfaces of the ceiling sloped from low horizontal eaves up to a central ridge which in turn sloped up to a peak beyond the chancel area. Externally the roof over the sanctuary did not have a central ridge; it had a wide triangular area which, from its base at the ridge of the adjoining wings, continued the roof slope of these wings and diminished to a point over the peak of the interior. This central flat area was, in a sense, folded down on either side, somewhat like the wings of a bird folded against its body. I couldn't accept the idea that the roof was like "hands folded in prayer," which, apparently, was Mrs. Wright's suggestion. This and the triangular unit system did not seem appropriately Unitarian but more "trinitarian." It was not like Unity Temple in Oak Park which was to me essentially Unitarian.

When we began work on this project I doubted that this contradiction between the interior and exterior shapes of the sanctuary was what Mr. Wright intended. The ceiling surfaces that resulted from lines connecting the horizontal eaves, which were converging on a point, to the ridge which was rising to a point over the convergence of the eaves, resulted in two double-curved surfaces, sections of hyperbolic paraboloids. These double-curved surfaces did not seem to me to be something that Mr. Wright would knowingly do.

To help us figure out how to build this roof – and to resolve in my mind whether this was what Mr. Wright intended – we made a model of the roof over the sanctuary. The model confirmed that this was indeed Mr. Wright's intention.

81　Unitarian Church, Madison, Wisconsin. Roof under construction. Photo by John Newhouse. Courtesy of State Historical Society of Wisconsin. (WHi (N48) 17119)

While making the model I calculated the dimensions and determined the shape of each roof truss according to its location in the configuration of the roof, and made a drawing of each of them. Each had a different shape. Wes figured the sizes of the members in each truss. The resulting construction was a series of parallel trusses located on the unit system; they were not steel trusses, but wood. Mr. Wright insisted that they should, for reasons of economy, be wood trusses that could be built on the job by the carpenters. I later derived much satisfaction from the fact that the carpenters encountered no problems in framing the roof with these drawings (Fig. 81). The model also proved useful later in the process of getting a building permit from the Wisconsin Industrial Commission. They had questions about the construction of the roof. Wes used the model, plus his calculations, to explain the structure of the roof to the commission.

Early in the summer, Ernst and Lory Wallfisch, whose music making the previous summer had been so well received and who had left with the invitation to return the next summer, arrived from Dallas. But their return was not as warm and friendly as their departure had been the previous fall. Mrs. Wright insisted that this summer they should take their turn as kitchen helpers and doing dishes, and spend an hour or so in the garden each morning. None of the professional musicians had done these things the previous summer. The Wallfisches didn't expect – or want – to do them this summer; they felt that this would interfere with their practicing.

Mrs. Porter, Mr. Wright's sister Jane, became aware of this disagreement and asked the Wallfisches to stay at Tanyderi. This made for a strange and strained relation between the Porters and Taliesin. The Porters didn't attend any social events at Taliesin that summer. At the end of the summer, Ernst and Lory gave a recital in the Porters' living room. Mrs. Porter invited the Fellowship to this recital. Some of us went. It was on a Sunday afternoon and did not conflict with any Fellowship activity. Although we anticipated some reprimand from Mrs. Wright, none was forthcoming. Friendly relations with the Porters were resumed the following summer.

Our musical activity that summer was supplemented by Marcel Grandjany, the distinguished harpist, and his wife and son, who spent the summer at Taliesin. They had been at Taliesin once before, in the summer of 1946. Iovanna had started learning to play the harp while in high school. She went into Madison once a week for lessons with Louise Cooper. When she was in New York for a year or so during the war studying French she was also taking lessons from Mr. Grandjany. The Grandjanys stayed in the new guest apartment into which the little dining room and former Fellowship dining room had been remodeled.

In addition to the architectural projects on which he worked during the summer, Mr. Wright continued his writing about Louis Sullivan. He had started this project in the fall of 1947, not too long after the conversation with Mrs. Wright, John Hill, and me concerning Sullivan and during which he had gone into the vault and brought out the collection of Sullivan's drawings. The manuscript had several titles while he was working on it, including "When I was a Pencil in His Hand" and "Mobocracy and Genius." But in the fall, when the manuscript was near its final form and he talked of taking it to New York, he was calling it "Genius and the Mobocracy."[76] Several times during this writing Mr. Wright raised the question, in talking with the Fellowship and with visitors, as to whether he should write the book he could write or whether he should let Sullivan "rest in peace." He chose the latter.

This was a summer in which I became more aware of the fact that the Fellowship had in its midst a good many objects which, were they in an art museum, would be protected in glass cases or displayed behind velvet ropes with "Do Not Touch" signs before them. These objects were sometimes accidentally damaged when not moved out of harm's way during a remodeling project or during Mr. Wright's continuous practice of rearranging the objects on the decks or shelves to "make eye music."

One afternoon, during tea in the tea circle, Tal (Kay and Davy Davison's child) and Brandoch were playing and romping about in the Hill Garden nearby. During their romping they knocked over a large Ming tea jar that was standing on the point of the stone outcrop in the garden. The jar rolled down the hill, toward the house, and was shattered into hundreds of pieces when it struck the low retaining wall at the east edge of the garden. There was a silent moment of suspense and an expectation that Mr. Wright would be angry. Instead, he appeared to accept this philosophically as one of the hazards of living with works of art and, particularly, with small boys.

Nineteen forty-eight was the year in which we had the largest influx of new apprentices. Many of them arrived at the beginning of the summer, after the migration from Arizona. One whose arrival I particularly remember was that of Roland Rebay.

Roland was the nephew of Baroness Hilla Rebay, the director of Solomon Guggenheim's Museum of Non-Objective Art. For this reason some thought he got special attention, but it may have been because he was so personable. He was with the Fellowship for two years, leaving in the spring of 1950 to live with Aunt Hilla in New York and to attend Pratt Institute before returning to Germany two years later.

Soon after Roland's arrival Iovanna took an interest in him. They spent much time together. This was facilitated by his volunteering to take care of the horses, to become a sort of stableman. Of course, taking care of the horses also provided him with opportunities to go riding with Iovanna.

That summer Mr. and Mrs. Wright had their two riding horses kept in the stable at Taliesin. There was a hired man who cleaned the stables, but Roland often happened to be there to saddle up the horses when Mr. and Mrs. Wright decided to go for a ride. Sometimes in the morning, after Mr. Wright had completed his work in the office, he and Mrs. Wright would go for a short ride that ended up at Hillside, where he would work in the drafting room until lunch. Sometimes they would go for a ride after tea in the afternoon. This ride often ended at Hillside also, and just at that time when some of us, who had been working there all afternoon, were planning to leave to attend to personal errands. Their arrival would interrupt our plans – you couldn't very well leave if Mr. Wright wanted to check some project on which you were working.

Roland lived at Hillside. And, although he sang a hearty baritone in the chorus, I did not become well acquainted with him until his second year in the Fellowship. This was in the summer of 1949, after Iovanna had spent a few months at the Gurdjieff Institute in Paris and had, after her return to Taliesin, lost interest in Roland.

Late in the summer of 1948 Gordon Lee decided to leave the Fellowship for the second time. He had first joined the Fellowship in the summer of 1941 and had left less than a year later, in January 1942, because he was told that he could not keep a dog he had bought. He rejoined the Fellowship in January 1947 when he and Gordon Chadwick came to visit so that "Chad" could talk with Mr. Wright about supervising the construction of the Friedman house in Pecos, New Mexico.

Gordon was personable, well mannered, well liked, and self-contained. He kept his thoughts to himself. He was a meticulous, dependable draftsman who drew beautifully. And, although he had not been with the Fellowship for a long period of time, he had proved to be a valuable member of it. For this reason, he was accepted and regarded by the seniors as a member of their group. As a token of our regard and affection for him, we decided to give him a going-away party. We held it in John Hill's room on the upper floor of the stable wing.

That winter I did not have a project which had to be completed before I could leave for Arizona. The migration started early in December.

Winter 1948–1949

The migration to Arizona took place as usual before the holiday season. And, as usual, after our arrival we were involved in making changes in the camp. But this year, in addition to these minor changes, Mr. Wright was planning to make a major addition to the camp, a new theater. It was to be about twice the size of the Kiva, seating about one hundred people. When this new theater was completed, the Kiva was to become a library and sitting room for the Fellowship. Mr. Wright was also hoping to complete another project, one that had been started late the previous winter season and on which the group who had stayed at the camp over the summer had continued to work. It was to be a place for Iovanna to live; the crew working on it referred to it as the "son-in-law trap." It was being built on the site of the former Suntrap and included some of the elements of its construction, such as fireplaces. It was to contain a suite of rooms for Iovanna and another suite sometimes referred to as a place for guests or for Uncle Vlado and Aunt Sophie. This winter it was also being suggested that it be used as a schoolroom for the little boys, Brandoch and Tal, who were now of school age. Iovanna's suite included a living room, a bedroom, a small kitchen, and a bath; the other suite, a large sitting room, two small bedrooms, and a bath.

When we arrived, the group who had stayed at the camp over the summer to take care of it and to work on Iovanna's living quarters were commended for the appearance of the camp. It looked better than it ever had. This group had been larger than usual; it included Uncle Vlado and Aunt Sophie, Betty Mock and her son, Fritzli, Mark Mills, Charles Montooth, Ling Po, Verne Rouillard, Paolo Soleri, and Richard Salter.

Since the camp had been so well cared for, we were surprised, shortly after our arrival, to hear that several of this group had been told to leave the Fellowship. It was never clear to me what had occurred to cause this. Whatever it was, it seemed to center around Paolo Soleri. He and several of his friends left.[77]

Work in the drafting room that winter consisted mostly of preliminary drawings of house designs, and working drawings for their construction. There was, however, one interesting exception – work on a small theater for a group in Hartford, Connecticut. Kirk Douglas, the movie actor, was a prime mover in this project; he visited the camp several times in connection with it. The design was based on an earlier design by Mr. Wright for the "New Theater" for Woodstock, New York. A model of the Hartford Theater was made and the model and photos of it were used for promotional purposes, but the project went no further.

Mr. and Mrs. Wright went to New York early in February. Iovanna went with them, primarily to meet Georgi Gurdjieff, the Russian mystic with whom Mrs. Wright had studied. He was there in connection with the forthcoming publication of some of his writings. Iovanna became interested in him and his work, and decided to go to France to study with him. She went directly to Paris, and did not return to Wisconsin until the following summer.

In the middle of March, Mr. Wright went to Houston, Texas, to be awarded the Gold Medal of the American Institute of Architects. He went with some misgivings and reluctance. He had never become a member of the institute. And, moreover, he had long been critical of it, particularly of its members who did not practice in accord with its code of ethics. After receiving notice that he had been selected to receive the medal, he considered turning it down. But he knew that many of his friends and admirers had put much time and energy into preparing his nomination and supporting his selection – which he felt was long overdue (but not, as he suggested with some malice, as long overdue as the Gold Medal awarded posthumously to Louis Sullivan, only twenty-four years after Sullivan's death!). So, he decided to accept it. In his acceptance speech, he expressed his gratitude for the award, and then reminded those at the convention that, although he had never become a member of their group, he had always practiced in accord with its code of ethics.

That winter I spent most of my time – except for turns as breakfast cook and time devoted to the chorus and ensemble rehearsals – working on the construction of the new theater, which Mr. Wright was then referring to as "the cabaret theater." I was in charge of the project. I say that I was "in charge" with this caution: Mr. Wright was also there and directing the work. I was the one in charge of the crew working on the project when he wasn't there.

Mr. Wright was in a hurry to get construction under way. When it started, the only drawing for the theater was a rough plan that Mr. Wright had drawn. The rest of the concept was still in Mr. Wright's mind. As he described it, the theater was to be built on the northwest side of his studio office. It was essentially a long hole in the ground with a flat roof over it. At its highest point this roof was to be only about seven feet above ground level. Due to the slope of the ground, at its far end, one would be able to step up on the roof easily. To a person approaching the camp from the entrance court, the theater would appear to be only a long low wall of desert concrete. In a sense it had no exterior elevations.

Mr. Wright rented a bulldozer and hired an operator to come out and dig the hole. We put in stakes to mark the far corners of the proposed construction. Even with a bulldozer the digging was not easy. The ground beneath a very light skim of soil was mostly caliche. It was like a low grade of concrete made with large chunks of granite bound together with deposits of lime. When Mr. Wright was satisfied that the hole was close to the desired shape, he sent the bulldozer and operator back to Phoenix.

At that point Mr. Wright did some more work on the plan, and I drew some quick sections based on floor elevations that Mr. Wright had put on the plan. The datum for the floor levels was the square court area at the east side of the office. The entrance was to be at the northwest corner of this court. From an entrance vestibule one was to go up a few broad steps to a long, glass-enclosed gallery along the east side of the theater (all of the steps in the camp had a four-inch rise and a sixteen-inch tread), then to a foyer at the far end, the rear. Here one was stopped by a broad, generous fireplace and went down a few steps to the floor level of the foyer, which was the same level as the entrance vestibule. From this level one went down a few steps to a single aisle, paralleling the gallery above, which sloped toward the front of the theater and the movie screen. From this single aisle one entered rows of built-in seats. The rows of seats were canted at a slight angle; one did not sit looking directly at the screen. The rows of seats were to be made of concrete and cast in place. The seats were to have cushions attached to individually hinged plywood flaps that could be lifted for easier access to the seats.

After looking at the sections I had drawn, Mr. Wright decided to increase the slope of the floor in the seating area to improve the sight lines. There was no raised stage in the theater, but there was to be an area in front of the screen where the chorus could stand, or the ensemble could sit, when performing. He decided to lower the floor in this area to make this into a kind of orchestra pit. These changes required that the bulldozer and its operator be brought back. Even after we had started to form and pour the walls of desert concrete, he continued to think of changes he wanted to make.

Since we had already started construction, much excavation had to be done by hand. It was slow and frustrating work. Being in charge of the crew, I was the subject of many questions and complaints from those assigned to do the digging. And the continuing questions were annoying: why was Mr. Wright making changes? Couldn't he have thought of these before? Wouldn't it have been easier to do this with the bulldozer? Couldn't this all have been done more efficiently?

As the walls were going up I asked Fred Liebhardt to make a drawing for the piers that were to support the roof along the west side of the gallery. Mr. Wright had indicated that these piers were to have a decorative pattern somewhat similar to that of the concrete block of the Arizona Biltmore Hotel. Fred and his wife had been in the Fellowship less than a year. He had not worked much in the drafting room during that time. He was having difficulty interpreting Mr. Wright's sketch for the piers and in getting the pattern to work satisfactorily on the shape Mr. Wright had drawn. I didn't want to take time to do the drawing myself so I suggested that Mr. Wright take a look at it. Mr. Wright sensed that

82   Construction of Cabaret Theater. Wes Peters is helping set molds for piers supporting roof in place. Source of photo unknown.

83   Pouring roof slab of Cabaret Theater. Source of photo unknown.

Fred was having problems, so he sat down and completely changed the piers, making them much simpler (Figs. 82, 83).

We started forming the roof slab in mid-April. We set the reinforcing in place and poured the slab just before we left for Wisconsin near the end of April. The reinforcing of the slab was experimental and controversial. The slab was to be only about six inches thick. Wes had designed the reinforcing with bars of conventional sizes at conventional spacing. But reinforcing at this spacing would have meant that we could not use any large stones in the roof slab. Mr. Wright insisted that the roof slab should have large stones to give it a continuity of appearance with the walls. He replaced the conventional reinforcing with only two large bars, about one inch square, in each bay. They were placed to make an X in each bay. The bars were bent at each end to be parallel with the side walls to get anchorage at the ends. After we finished pouring the slab we decided to leave the formwork in place during the summer so that the concrete might achieve close to its ultimate strength before the forms were stripped.

The Fellowship had continued to grow in size during this winter season. And with this growth came an increasing resentment toward the "seniors." Before World War II the Fellowship had consisted of two groups, the "seniors" and the others. There wasn't, however, a clear line of demarcation between them. But after World War II there was a clear line of demarcation between the seniors, who had all been at Taliesin before the war, and those who had arrived afterward. But even among those who had arrived after the war, there began to be another line of demarcation. Some of those who had joined after the war – and who had stayed on after their initial year – had acquired a degree of seniority. They had shown some leadership in getting the construction work done and were being assigned to work in the drafting room more frequently in order to keep up with the increasing number of commissions. This group had a much closer association with the seniors than did the more recent arrivals. And the newcomers felt that this intermediary group was simply another barrier between them and Mr. Wright.

This resentment took a surprising turn. On a Sunday afternoon, a few weeks before we were to leave for Wisconsin, Mr. and Mrs. Wright called a meeting of the entire Fellowship to discuss openly a statement that had come to their attention – that all of the seniors were homosexuals. They wanted to know who was making the statement and what the basis for the statement was.

It was an embarrassing situation for everyone present. Most were reluctant to talk. There seemed to be a general assumption that any male who was not married or in pursuit of women was a homosexual. Comradeship and close friendships were presumed to be based on sex. Conversations heard through the paper-thin partitions between the rooms in the apprentice court were assumed to be sexual in nature. And comments and actions by a senior toward a newcomer had been interpreted as an invitation to homosexual activity. There was some resentment that Mr. Wright had chosen to air the statement openly before all of the Fellowship.

I sometimes think that Mr. Wright was as naive about homosexuality as I was. During the following summer, when Oscar Stonorov was at Taliesin beginning plans for the large exhibition that became known as "Sixty Years of Living Architecture," he came to Gene in the office one day after having lunch with Mr. Wright. Stonorov was both amused and amazed. During lunch Mr. Wright had asked him, "What is a homosexual?"

As a result of this session several of the newcomers chose not to migrate to Wisconsin, but to leave the Fellowship. I was not aware that anyone was asked – or told – to leave. The ill feeling that had developed was somewhat mitigated by the semi annual migration and the shifting of our activities back to Wisconsin.

Summer 1949

The migration to Wisconsin began at the end of April. After getting settled, the event uppermost in the minds of Fellowship members was the forthcoming celebration of Mr. Wright's eightieth birthday on June 8. The event itself was accompanied by the usual quarrel between Mr. Wright and his sister, Jane, about the year of his birth. He insisted he was born in 1869. She maintained it was 1867. She knew that he was older than she was, and she knew the year in which she was born.

It seemed to me that this shifting of the year of his birth was done to tease – and to annoy – his sister and to start an argument. During my years in the Fellowship I had begun to believe that verbal contention was the indoor sport of the Lloyd-Joneses, an exercise of wills. It took various forms. Sometimes it was sister versus brother. Sometimes it was father versus son. And sometimes it was "Truth against the World." Recurring examples of this were the arguments between Mr. Wright and his son, Lloyd. Whenever Lloyd came for a visit, not much time elapsed before the two of them were into an argument about something or other. It might happen when Mr. Wright and Lloyd would go for a walk around the Arizona camp. Mr. Wright would be pointing out recent improvements, and Lloyd would be explaining and commenting on those things that should have been done or were not done properly. The argument would rise in intensity until one wondered if it were coming to blows. But tempers would soon cool and they would again be on the best terms with each other.

More guests than usual were invited for this birthday. The release of Mr. Wright's book on Sullivan, *Genius and the Mobocracy,* had been planned to coincide with the event. Ben Raeburn, the publisher, was one of the guests and brought copies of the book with him. This year's birthday celebration seemed less the private, familial affair that it had been in previous years. With all the reporters and photographers present, the opening of the Fellowship's Birthday Box seemed more of a public event.

Iovanna returned from Paris to Taliesin in time for the birthday celebration. Her return marked the beginning of a series of changes in the Fellowship that eventually led to my decision to leave. She had gone to Paris to work with Gurdjieff and had not been back at Taliesin long before she began an effort, with Mrs.

Wright's support, to introduce some elements of his practices into the activities of the Fellowship. I know that some will argue that many of these, such as shared gardening and kitchen work, were already present in the Fellowship, even that they had been there from its beginnings. But prior to Iovanna's going to Paris to study with Gurdjieff I had not been much aware of the effects of his teachings on the ongoing life of the Fellowship. Of course we all knew that Mrs. Wright had spent several years at Gurdjieff's Institute for the Harmonious Development of Man, had met Mr. Wright when this group came to the United States in 1924 to give demonstrations of "movements" in Chicago and New York, and that Mrs. Wright had not returned to Paris with the group but had remained in the United States. There was also the story about Gurdjieff's visit to Taliesin at a time when Mr. Wright was seriously ill with pneumonia. It seems that Gurdjieff had demonstrated his great, esoteric wisdom by cooking a hot, spicy brew, the ingredients of which were a mystery to everyone except Gurdjieff, miraculously curing Mr. Wright.

Not long after the birthday celebration Mr. Wright began what was to be a series of readings from the writings of Gurdjieff. Everyone in the Fellowship was to meet on Thursday afternoons at teatime in the living room at Hillside, but after only two weeks, Mr. Wright discontinued them. In a later Sunday morning talk he explained that he had discontinued the talks because he was too busy with his own work. I suspected otherwise.

At the same time that the readings were started Iovanna began a series of meetings, held after dinner in the evening, to teach "movements." Participation in "movements" was not mandatory, just as participation in the ensemble and the chorus were not mandatory. But there were subtle – and not so subtle – pressures from Iovanna and indirectly from Mrs. Wright for everyone to participate. In some of his Sunday morning talks, Mr. Wright commented that these "exercises in coordination" might help some of the less coordinated members of the Fellowship, those whose actions were awkward and ungraceful.

I was not directly involved in doing "movements," but I did play the piano to accompany the practice sessions and therefore was, in a manner, participating. The music, copied on manuscript paper, was referred to as "Mr. Gurdjieff's music." It was, so we were told, music that he had remembered from his experiences in the monasteries and lamaseries of the east and which had been transcribed for piano by Thomas de Hartmann. The music was not interesting to play, particularly when it was played over and over for these practice sessions. The value of "movements," as I saw it, lay in the degree of intense concentration required to learn them.

The Adaskins, who had given a concert at Taliesin West the previous winter, which resulted in their being invited to spend the summer at Taliesin, arrived shortly after the birthday celebration. They stayed until late in the summer when they returned to Vancouver for the beginning of university classes. Mr. Adaskin was on the music faculty of the University of British Columbia. They played for the Sunday evening concerts and, if requested, before the movie on Wednesday evenings. (We were having midweek movies thats summer.) In addition, they proposed to give a weekly series of lecture recitals. Their first and only lecture recital was given on a Wednesday evening in the Playhouse at Hillside, but Mr. Wright stopped them and suggested that they just play the music and not attempt to give an academic explanation of it. The Adaskins took this suggestion in stride.

I spent much of my time in the drafting room that summer. Jack Howe was away most of the season; he was supervising the construction of several houses in Michigan and would return to Taliesin on some weekends to have Mr. Wright approve supplementary drawings that he had done, such as those for cabinet-work and furniture. He also returned to do the presentation drawings of projects for which Mr. Wright had done preliminary sketches. One of these, which I assisted Jack with, was the Self-Service Garage for Pittsburgh, which Edgar Kaufmann had commissioned. I drew the sections and the scale figures – cars and people – on the perspectives.

At about midsummer Mr. Wright did preliminary sketches for a Y.W.C.A. in Racine, Wisconsin, which Herbert Johnson had commissioned him to do. This was the first project for which I translated Mr. Wright's first drawings into the plans, sections, and elevations on which he would do further work before the presentation drawings were made.

The site proposed for the project was rather small. The largest spaces required were those for the gymnasium and the swimming pool. Mr. Wright made the swimming pool the major feature of the scheme. It was placed on an upper level, over some of the social spaces and within a faceted green houselike enclosure. This enclosure also extended over a central, multistory lobby surrounded by balconies with ramps connecting the several floors.

The number of facilities to be accommodated on the small site made for a tightly fitted and complex layering of spaces. I was never certain that I had all of these properly sorted out into plans, sections, and elevations. Except for the feature of the glass-enclosed swimming pool with its rooftop terraces, I didn't feel that this was one of Mr. Wright's better projects. Nor did I feel that my set of presentation drawings, complete with plans, sections, elevations, and perspectives of the interior and exterior, was a very good set of drawings. A perspective that Jack drew, a revision of one of mine, greatly improved the appearance of the proposed building and my set of drawings – and also my feelings about both.

On one of his weekend visits to Taliesin Jack suggested that I start a preliminary design for a house in Michigan for Howard Anthony and his wife. They were anxious to get construction started on their house. Mr. Wright had not yet done a design for it. The suggestion intrigued me. Mr. Wright had designed three one-room cottages for his sister, Maginel Wright Barney, the previous summer. Each was based on a different geometry. The triangular one interested me the

84   Howard Anthony residence, Benton Harbor, Michigan. View of house from across street. Entrance to house is at center of photo. Carport is at right. Laboratory wing is at left. Ezra Stoller © Esto.

most. So I decided to try to work out a design for the Anthonys based on this thirty–sixty design. I proposed to put the laboratory and the guest room and extra bath which the Anthonys desired in a wing that would be attached to the hypotenuse of the triangular plan. A carport could be attached at the shorter side of the triangle (Fig. 84).

The Anthonys' site was a difficult one. There was an open, rectangular area near its center. Its major dimension was east–west. The ground sloped away from this central area on three sides, on the south to the street, on the east and north into a heavily wooded area. Through the wooded slope on the north there were views toward the river. The site presented problems that were difficult to resolve. Opening the house to the north and views into the woods made for large areas of glass on that side. Opening it to the south for winter sun made for openness to the entrance drive and the street and loss of privacy. Since the Anthonys had selected the site for its bird-watching potential, I felt that any extensions of the living space, such as terraces to the exterior, should face into the woods. So I placed the right angle of the triangle pointing into the woods. The laboratory and guest-room wing were extended from the hypotenuse on the south side. The cooking area was placed at the southeast corner of the triangle where it would receive morning light and have a view of the entrance drive. A flat roof covered the cooking area and extended toward the east over the carport.

Jack looked at my plan and suggested a few changes, which I made. When we showed the drawings of this plan to Mr. Wright he changed the flat roof over the cooking area and carport into a pitched roof and made the hipped roof which I had drawn with equal slopes into one with unequal slopes.

After the Anthonys had approved the design for their house (they first asked for a few changes) I started on the working drawings by myself. They were nearly complete when one afternoon Gene told me that the Anthonys were coming the next day to pick up prints of the drawings. Apparently they had been promised completed ones by that date. Davy Davison, who was working in the drafting room at the time, volunteered to help me finish the drawings that night. They were complete the next morning, after Davy and I worked on them all night. Mr. Wright signed them without further changes.

While I was working on these preliminary drawings for the Anthony house, Jack suggested that I take over work on the construction drawings for the Henry J. Neils house in Minneapolis (Fig. 85). Preliminary drawings for the house had been done in Arizona earlier in the year. After our arrival in Wisconsin, John Geiger had been asked to work on the construction drawings. He started them, but while working he felt that there were elements of the design that needed to be improved. He asked Jack to have Mr. Wright look at the drawings but Jack was unwilling to do this; a revision would slow down the process of getting the drawings out.

The Neilses were persistent in asking for their drawings and anxious to get construction started. Steve Oyakawa was assigned to work on the drawings, and toward the end of the summer, when they were completed and were shown to Mr. Wright for his approval and signature, he didn't sign them. Instead he revised the design. He made many changes simplifying it. It was at this point that I was asked to take over the working drawings. I do not remember whether I made changes on Steve's work or whether I started a completely new set, but I do know that I felt the drawings could have been more quickly produced by starting afresh. Mr. Wright often insisted that we make revisions on the drawings on which he had worked and made changes. Many of these changes, ones that would have been of interest to students of Mr. Wright's work, were erased in this process.

An important change in this house was the change from a hipped to a gabled roof which had unequal slopes. With this change the door-height soffits at the eaves of the roof were eliminated. The roof became one simple, asymmetrically folded plane. These door-height soffits had helped to produce many characteris-

85   Henry J. Neils residence, Minneapolis, Minnesota. View of interior of living room looking toward open gable. Doors at left open to terrace and view of lake. Photo by Pedro E. Guerrero.

tics of the so-called prairie houses: the intimate scale, the horizontal layering of the space, its spatial contrasts, and also the spatial continuity between the exterior and interior of the houses. The openness of the gable and the elimination of the eave-height soffits as well as the simplification of the setting of the glass enclosure gave a new sense of openness and freedom to the occupants of this house. It also eliminated the horizonal layering of the interior space and gave it increased plasticity. But it also made for problems in the structural framing of the roof. Gone was that space between the soffits and the roof joists in which horizontal structural members could be concealed. Any structural reinforcement of the roof – with steel beams or channels – now had to be handled within the roof thickness. Framing the roof became an intriguing problem. Several of the houses designed at this time had this characteristic.

One of my responsibilities in the drafting room that summer was to keep the room in order. Since only a few people were working there it did not require much of my time. But it did lead to a conflict with Wes.

Wes had established his working area in the northwest corner of the drafting room behind the seat by the fireplace. He had a large desk there on which he kept his engineering books and notebooks for his structural calculations, and on which he could spread out the drawings of projects he was working on. But not everything that accumulated there was related to work in the drafting room. Much of it was related to his interests in other areas, such as sports cars. Wes's corner had gotten rather cluttered and Mr. Wright had commented that it needed to be put in order. I suggested to Wes a few times that he might straighten up his corner and he had said that he would do it. But nothing happened, so I took it upon myself to do it. I didn't remove anything – I simply put things in orderly piles.

I was working in the studio the following morning when Wes came in. Mr. Wright was the only other person there. Wes immediately became angry. He started walking back and forth and rubbing his hands together as he did when he was annoyed. He demanded to know who had moved things around on his desk. I told him that I had because it needed straightening up. We were immediately shouting at each other. Mr. Wright sat there with a twinkle in his eyes, saying nothing. He was obviously amused by this verbal fray between two seniors. It was his silent amusement that quieted us and settled the dispute.

On a cold, rainy Sunday afternoon in late October, Auguste Perret, the distinguished French architect, came for a visit with Mr. Wright. This was a visitor in whom I was greatly interested. As an architectural student I was particularly intrigued by his church at Le Raincy. But I was also aware of his earlier work, such as his Rue Franklin apartment house, his Garage Ponthieu, and his Champs-Elysées Theatre in Paris.

Perret's pioneering use of concrete paralleled in time several of Mr. Wright's early projects that were also to be built of concrete: the studies for a monolithic concrete bank, the design of a fireproof house for *The Ladies Home Journal*, Unity Temple, and the concrete block houses of California. But they were not parallel in manner. Perret's buildings were based on a rational, clearly expressed, elegant structural system. The enclosing elements were thin, sometimes transparent, panels in-filled between the structural elements. Mr. Wright used the concrete as massive planar elements and piers that enfolded and defined the spaces. Enclosure was completed by glass elements inserted between the concrete elements.

Perret visited Taliesin at a time when his projects for rebuilding war-damaged cities, such as the reconstruction of Le Havre, were being published and criticized. They were urban-scale projects and made much use of standardized, prefabricated, reinforced concrete elements. His critics said that in his old age he was reverting to the classicism of his Beaux Arts education and of his teacher Gaudet.

Perret had been invited for lunch with Mr. and Mrs. Wright. After lunch in the Taliesin living room, Mr. Wright decided to entertain his guest by showing him a film. This may have been partly due to the frustration of trying to converse through Mrs. Wright or the interpreter who was traveling with Mr. Perret. But it may also have resulted from the fact that Mr. Wright enjoyed showing the Playhouse to his guests. He was quite proud of it. A phone call from Taliesin to Hillside got the film rewound for showing and a fire started in the fireplace in the theater to counteract the chill of the day. The lights of the theater sparkled in the gloom of the afternoon. It had been cleaned, the floor had been waxed, and fresh foliage had been put in the day before for the Saturday evening dinner and film.

Gene Masselink brought Mr. Wright, Mr. Perret, and his interpreter to Hillside. By the time they arrived, a group of apprentices had gathered in the Playhouse, attracted by the presence of Mr. Perret as well as the opportunity to see the film.

Mr. Wright, age 82, was wrapped in a bulky, light brown tweed cape. It was worn over a tan tweed suit. On his head was a brown felt beret pushed casually to one side. Mr. Perret, age 75, was wearing a more trimly tailored, heavy black serge cape with a velvet collar over a trim black suit. On his head was a black, flat-brimmed felt hat with a band of black grosgrained ribbon. It was a study in contrasts: Mr. Wright in the robust tweediness of a country gentleman; Mr. Perret in the tailored elegance of French urbanity.

After the film was shown and as Mr. Wright and Mr. Perret were preparing to leave the theater, Mr. Perret, as translated by his interpreter, remarked that Mr. Wright was not only a great architect, but a great artist. He had made his life into a work of art.

Winter 1949–1950

Upon our arrival in Arizona, I was assigned to live in the room on the east side of the north entrance to the apprentice court (see Fig. 41). It was an oddly shaped, five-sided room and one in which I had wanted to live. I immediately made plans to remodel it.

When I had finished making changes I was quite pleased with the room; I felt that I now had one of the better rooms on the apprentice court.

Although there were still a few stragglers, most of the apprentices had arrived and were settled in the camp by the middle of December. The most pressing project upon our arrival was the completion of the new theater. We had poured the roof slab for this the previous spring just before our departure for Wisconsin.

When we started to remove the shoring and the formwork, which had been left in place over the summer, rather large cracks began to appear in the slab. We were concerned that the roof slab might collapse. Confronted with the possible failure of this reinforcing experiment, Mr. Wright, "snatching victory from the jaws of defeat," designed a series of inverted beams to be poured above the slab.

After the roof had been made secure we started work on the completion of the interior. We were ready to pour the concrete floor in the theater when Mr. Wright decided that the orchestra pit at the front had to be dug several inches deeper, again, by hand. This was done, in part, so that a plywood floor could be put in the orchestra pit. Mr. Wright felt this was necessary for the acoustics of the room.

I was asked to make a plan for the serving kitchen in the theater. It was located near the entrance, just behind the movie screen. Food, prepared in the main kitchen, was brought here to be served on Saturday evenings. Having made the plan for the kitchen, I was put in charge of the crew that built it.

Although Mr. Wright was impatient to have the theater completed, it was not ready for use until early the next season in Arizona. And even then the apprentices who were working on the finishing touches were picking up their paintbrushes and stealing away to get dressed for dinner as guests were beginning to arrive. Mr. Wright was quite proud of this new toy. And he took great delight in showing it to guests or visitors, often asking Gene to show a movie even to midday visitors (Figs. 86, 87).

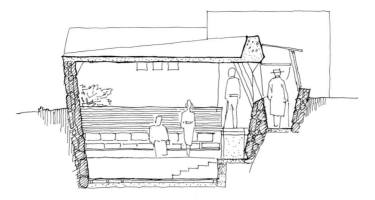

86   Cross section of Cabaret Theater.

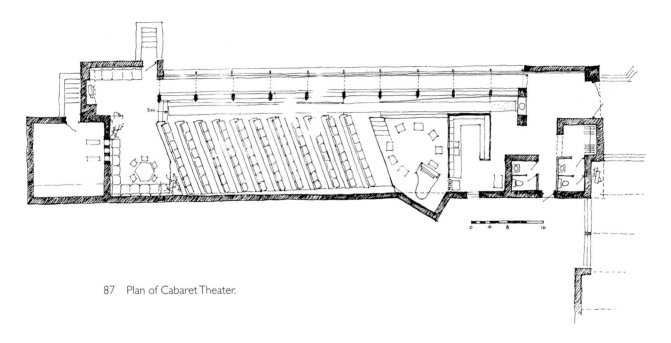

87   Plan of Cabaret Theater.

For me this theater was an interesting architectural lesson. Seen only in plan, it might appear that the space is tunnellike, too long and narrow, and perhaps too simple and uninteresting. The room *is* simple, but not uninteresting. And what produces its interest? The more obvious answers to this question can be given first: the texture and color of the surfaces defining the space (though the room is made essentially of one material, a course-textured concrete with a random pattern of gray, black and rusty-red stones); the change of level between the gallery and the main space; the diffuse, almost shadowless, light from one side during the day; and the equally diffuse, but more mysterious, light of evening, coming from multiple sources.

But these obvious answers alone do not account for the room's interest. The source of its interest resides elsewhere, in the dynamics of the space itself and not in the surfaces that define it. The sources of its dynamics, its vital quality, are several. The first of these is the direction of the room itself which is reinforced by the parallel vector of the gallery. These are reinforced by a built-in forced perspective. Due to the slope of the side walls the room is wider at the ceiling than it is at the floor. And due to the slope of the floor from the rear toward the front the floor becomes narrower at the front. This built-in convergence augments the normal visual convergence of parallel lines. Countering this lengthwise thrust is the slight cant of the seating. Its lines are not perpendicular to the parallel walls. These directional lines establish a slight rotation, another vector in the space. Against these are played other directional thrusts which one encounters when moving about in the room.

This theater meant much to me, not only because of my involvement in its construction but also because it was such a clear architectural lesson in how a building – one that did not have an interesting site with attractive views, that did not have an interesting exterior, and which in plan appeared to be a long, narrow hole in the ground – could be made into a place that was deeply satisfying to be in.

During the winter I was also in charge of a crew that formed and poured a simple, concrete-slab bridge across the wash at the east side of the apprentice wing and on the path that led to Iovanna's cottage, the Suntrap. We also poured a concrete slab at the east side of the Suntrap.

An interesting thing happened while I was working on this project. I had tried to align the forms with the outside walls of the Suntrap. We had placed dividers in the slab to enable us to screed it level and had aligned one of these dividers with the center of a pair of doors on the east side of the living room.

We had finished pouring the slab and were cleaning up the area around it when Mr. Wright came over to inspect. He came through the living room of the cottage and through the open pair of doors on its east side. He immediately called our attention to the fact that the divider which we had placed at the center of the doors did not line up with a divider in the interior floor slab. We had not thought of aligning the exterior slab with the interior. I was happy when a rug on the interior floor covered up this fault. Mr. Wright had a sharp eye when he walked onto a construction site. He could spot a floor that was out of level, lines that were out of plumb, and surfaces, such as brickwork, in which there might be a very slight bulge or cavity.

When I first saw Scottsdale in the winter of 1939, the town consisted of a few commercial buildings clustered near an intersection on Scottsdale Road. It grew very little during the war years and immediately afterward. But when we arrived in the desert the winter of 1949, there were signs of sudden growth. There was another drug store, a new pool hall, gift shops, and several chic decorating shops.[78] This growth, especially the development of residential areas on land that had been grapefruit and orange groves, stimulated Mr. Wright to think about how one might build in this particular area. And it revived his interest in the question of how a middle-income family that felt it could not afford his services, particularly the veterans of World War II, might, in fact, be able to build.

One product of this stimulation was the revival of the "textile block" system of construction which he had used for several houses in Los Angeles in the 1920s. He now called this system the "Usonian Automatic" and believed that a family using it could design and build its own home. To test this belief, he urged the apprentices to design houses based on the use of this system. In response to this – as well as to the question of what to do for the Christmas Box – I designed a small Usonian Automatic. The design, based on a two-foot, eight-inch module, consisted of two intersecting, rectangular volumes. The living space was in one of these; two bedrooms, a kitchen, and a bath were in the other. The floor level of the bedrooms and bath was to be two feet above the floor of the living room and the kitchen. This made a taller space at the intersection of the two volumes. I was pleased with the result, but there were many technical problems, especially in the system of glazing that I proposed, that remained unsolved. Mr. Wright's comment during the opening of the Box did not make an indelible impression on my memory.

During this winter Mr. Wright had an opportunity to try another idea for building a low-cost house. Raymond Carlson, the editor of *Arizona Highways* magazine, asked Mr. Wright to design a home for him. The site was a corner lot in a typical, flat residential development to the northwest of central Phoenix. In this instance Mr. Wright chose to use a system of construction which, in effect, brought the English half-timber system up to date. The design was based on the use of a four-foot, four-inch unit system. It consisted of four-by-four posts with an infill of one-and-a-half-inch Cemesto panels, a product used primarily for enclosing industrial buildings. The panels were a layer of fiber insulation faced on both sides with asbestos cement panels. The posts were to be painted a turquoise blue. The gray panels were to be left unpainted.

The low-cost houses being built in the Phoenix area at that time were ranch houses. All rooms were on the same level. The Carlson house was to be a split-level house of multiple stories. The living room was at ground level and about a story and one-third in height. The kitchen and the dining area were about two-thirds of a story below the floor level of the living room. A part of the dining room was a "well" that opened up to the living room. Two bedrooms and a bath were one-third of a story up from the level of the living room. The ceiling of these rooms was at the same height as that of the living room. Above the bedrooms was a study that opened out onto a roof garden above the living room. From their roof garden the Carlsons were to have a view over the orange groves and to the mountains surrounding the desert valley. (In Mr. Wright's mind one of the flaws of the ranch houses being built in the Phoenix area was the absence of a view.)

This was the winter during which several of us, primarily friends of Roland Rebay, often borrowed Wes's Jeep and went on excursions into the Arizona landscape on Sundays, after breakfast. When we returned from one of these excursions late one Sunday afternoon we saw Mr. Wright working at a drafting table outside his office. It was a cool day, and he had moved outside to work in the sun's warmth. He was just finishing putting on paper the concept for another way of building among the orange groves and was pleased with his afternoon's work, which he labeled "How to Build in the Southwest." Jack Howe did a set of presentation drawings of this design. A year later when asked by his son, David, to design a house for him, its design was based on this house.

I did not work all winter on construction. After we had poured the slab at the Suntrap, Jack asked me to start working drawings of the house designed for Mrs. Clinton Walker. It was a small house but on an exceptional site, a small promontory in Monterey Bay. It was the only building site on the ocean side of the road around the bay (Figs. 88, 89). Eric Wright, Mr. Wright's grandson, who had been in the Fellowship for about two years, was assigned to work with me.

I was interested in doing the drawings for this house, particularly for its living room with its outward-stepping system of glazing. The purpose of this glazing was to prevent the spray of the waves, which often break around this rocky promontory, from being blown into the room. There are sliding vents in the horizontal members of the offsets which can be opened for ventilation. Mr. Wright had proposed a similar glazing system for the living room of the 1931 "House on a Mesa" project. A model of this project was shown in the international exhibition of Modern Architecture at the Museum of Modern Art in 1932. Eric and I completed the drawing before the first of March, when Mr. Wright signed them.

The roof of the living room, often described as "floating" – it appears to have no visible means of support – is described by some as being cantilevered from the masonry mass of the tall living room fireplace. This daring idea is readily accepted by those who fail to see the thin cast-iron posts, which have a triangular section and a budlike pattern along their sides. These posts, which slope slightly outward, rest on the top of the low masonry wall that forms the back of the seating which surrounds the room. They support a collar beam which surrounds the living room and is anchored in the masonry masses of the house. There was a kind of "magic" – as well as magician's tricks – in much of Mr. Wright's later work.

That winter, following the death of Gurdjieff in October 1949, there seemed to be an effort and intention to establish Taliesin as a center, of a kind, for the teaching of Gurdjieff philosophy. Mme. Jeanne de Salzman, who had been Gurdjieff's secretary for many years, visited the camp during the winter and asked to meet with all the senior apprentices. In the meeting she asked if all of the seniors were

88 Mrs. Clinton Walker residence, Carmel, California. Ezra Stoller © Esto.

89 View from living room. Thin cast iron columns with budlike pattern on sides support the roof.
Ezra Stoller © Esto.

seriously interested in Gurdjieff and his work. I commented that I didn't think they were. I wasn't asked to expand on my statement, but I knew that some were participating in "movements" not because of their interest but because they did not want to be uncooperative. Mme. de Salzman apparently relayed my comment to Mrs. Wright, who soon let me know that it was not appreciated.

Shortly before the spring migration to Wisconsin, a demonstration of Gurdjieff "movements" was given on Easter Sunday in the living room following the evening dinner. The demonstration was a major part of the after-dinner program. Before the "movements" began the chorus sang a group of songs. This probably included "Cool, Clear Water" which had become one of Mr. Wright's – and Brandoch's – favorites. Gene Masselink had prepared a blue-printed, hand-lettered and hand-decorated program for the demonstration.[79] It contained an introduction, written, I assume, by Iovanna, with Mrs. Wright's approval. It stated that an introduction was "necessary to assure a correct understanding" of the demonstration. The demonstration consisted of "sacred gymnastics," "sacred dances," and "religious ceremonies preserved in temples of Turkestan, Thibet, Afghanistan, Kafiristan, Chitral." There were quite a few guests, including Serge Koussevitzky, the conductor of the Boston Symphony, and his wife, and friends of Mr. and Mrs. Wright's from Phoenix.

Summer 1950

That spring I returned to the east room on the upper floor of the stable wing where I had been living. My life in that room was soon affected by a campaign begun by Mr. Wright that summer to clean up the exterior of Taliesin and to get it into better shape. A part of this campaign was the removal of an "excrescence" on the north side of the stable wing, the side seen by visitors in the entrance court. It consisted of the closet in my room, and one in Brandoch's playroom, which was below my room.

That year, as my contribution to the Birthday Box on June 8, I measured this "excrescence" in Brandoch's room and mine. I drew up plans of these rooms and the north elevation of this part of the stable wing. To the drawings I attached an envelope containing a pencil and an eraser. Although Mr. Wright had not spoken directly to me about removing this closet space, this was my way of letting him know that I agreed to his doing it. On June 12, which was both Wes's birthday and mine, we "celebrated" by removing the "excrescence." After tea that afternoon, we put a chain through some holes in the wall which we had cut, and attached the chain to the Caterpillar tractor. With Mr. Wright looking on we pulled the "excrescence" away from the building. Following that, Mr. and Mrs. Wright took the two of us, plus a few other seniors, to dinner at the hotel in Mineral Point where we continued our birthday celebration.

Shortly after this celebration Mr. and Mrs. Wright left on an extended trip to England. Mr. Wright had been invited to be the guest of honor at the prize-giving of the School of Architecture of the Architectural Association in London. Before leaving, Mr. Wright gave us instructions for repairing the "wound" caused by the removal of the excrescence and for remodeling the roof over the parking stalls between the stable wing and the stable. He also set a crew to work on the demolition of the old Home building. He wanted the site cleared and leveled before his return. Mr. Wright's decision to remove that building came as a surprise. He had started the remodeling of this house, the first building of the Hillside Home School, in the early years of the Fellowship, and had attempted to change the building (credited to Silsbee but believed to have been designed by Mr. Wright while working in Silsbee's office) into one resembling the buildings he had designed for his aunts in 1902. The roof had been reconfigured and given red tile like that of other Hillside buildings. During the previous winter George Haas, the stonemason, had started building a sandstone stairway in the interior, a replacement for a central wooden stair. This had led us to believe that Mr. Wright was going to resume work on the building. Some apprentices had moved into it, planning to live there that summer. But the site was clear when the Wrights returned.

Upon their return Mr. Wright put a crew to work on another aspect of his campaign to clean up the exterior of Taliesin. He started to enlarge his own bedroom. He extended it to the south onto the balcony/terrace at that side of the room. This extension was covered on the west side by an existing hipped roof. He put a flat roof over the east side. This enlargement of his room was covered with a low flat ceiling. Into this ceiling he introduced a raised skylight beneath which he placed his desk and worktable. These were moved out from the east side of the room where his desk had previously stood next to the windows. In addition he opened up the west side of the room, which had previously been secluded and private, to a new terrace and pool on this side and to a view of the Hill Garden.

Construction of the Unitarian Church in Madison was well under way that summer. And, since I had been involved in the details of the working drawings, I was asked to do many of the supplementary drawings for this project. While Mr. and Mrs. Wright were in England, I started a drawing for the steeple under the roof at the "prow" of the church. Marshall Erdman, the builder, had completed the framing of the roof and wanted to start construction of this feature. On the preliminary sketches and in the working drawings this feature had been shown as being built of special patterned concrete block with inserts of stained glass (Fig. 90).

I had blocked out larger-scale drawings of the plan, sections, and elevations of this feature on which Mr. Wright could work when he returned from England. Soon after his return he went to Madison to check on the progress of construction of the church. The next morning, when he came into the drafting room, I asked him to look at the drawings that I had started. He sat down at my desk and said that he had changed his mind, that he wanted to keep the effect of having the "prow" open rather than blocked by the steeple. On the drawings I had laid out he quickly drew a section of the wall of glass as it now exists, with the sloping two-by-twelve wood louvres in the glass (Fig. 91).

Wes, who was in the studio, came over to look on, and immediately raised the question as to how these two-by-twelves were to be supported. Mr. Wright replied that they would be supported by the glass. Wes immediately challenged this, and a contest of wills emerged.

I was annoyed with Wes for challenging Mr. Wright at this time and creating this contention. I believed that had he not been challenged, Mr. Wright, having drawn the sloping boards, would have continued to think about this change he had just put on paper and would have come up with his own question about support and his own solution to the problem.

90   The steeple at the "prow" of the Unitarian Church, Madison, Wisconsin, as originally designed.

91   The steeple as built. Ezra Stoller © Esto.

In my supplementary drawings of this wall – made at Wes's urging and with my own doubts as to whether the one-quarter-inch plate glass was sufficient to support that area of glass and boards – I showed thin steel supports located on the unit lines. These supports, with their width perpendicular to the glass, were two inches wide and one-quarter inch thick. Equivalent plates were welded to their tops and bottoms. These plates were to be let into the planks and secured with screws. Mr. Wright saw these details and approved them. But the following summer, 1951, when the Fellowship put several intense weeks of work into completing the building, Mr. Wright spotted those supports and directed me to personally remove them from the inner wall of glass above the choir loft. These supports created a disturbing pattern when seen against similar supports that were in the exterior wall. These he did not insist that I remove.

A bit later in the summer I was asked to do a detailed layout of the horizontal battens on the copper roof of the church. In laying out the roof plan I discovered a ticklish problem in the spacing of the roof battens. Those on the steep roof at the sides of the chancel could not be spaced the same as those on the shallower pitched roof. The problem lay at the line where the central roof folded down at the sides of the auditorium. I worked out a solution to the problem that was satisfactory to Mr. Wright. And I went into Madison with prints of my drawing to explain the layout to the workers on the job. While we were on the roof talking about this layout, the owner of the roofing company drove up and instructed his workers to get down off the roof, to stop wasting time. Since I had taken the time to drive into Madison to make certain that the workers understood the scheme, his comment made me angry. Without saying a word, I got down off the roof and drove back to Taliesin. I do not know what transpired then, but the next morning I was asked to go to Madison again to help the workers lay out the pattern of the battens on the roof. There was no mention of the previous day.

Nineteen fifty was the first summer of the Crosley Hotshots. Mr. Wright decided to equip the seniors with transportation. Wes was already well equipped; he had a Jeep, a pick-up, and a Mercury. For the rest of us Mr. Wright bought Crosleys from Smart Motors in Madison. For Gene Masselink, Jack Howe, John Hill, and me he bought Hotshots. For Davy and Kay Davison and for Kenn and Polly Lockhart he bought Crosley station wagons; they had families to transport. For Mrs. Wright and himself he bought a slightly fancier version of the Hotshot. The Davisons soon disposed of their station wagon in favor of a Studebaker.

I was quite happy with my Hotshot. Though I had had personal use of the Fellowship Jeep for the previous two years, this was the first car I could call my own. I washed and waxed the Hotshot faithfully on Saturday afternoons. And I enjoyed driving it. It was like a large mechanized roller skate. One sat in it on a low platform about a foot above the ground, enclosed in a shoelike shell. I always felt that if the brakes failed in an emergency I could drag my foot to stop. A portion of the shell, over the cast-aluminum motor, lifted off for access to the engine.

A small amount of luggage could be placed behind the seat, under the shell.

During the summer, Mr. Wright put some apprentices to work restoring and freshening the models that had been shown at the Museum of Modern Art in the fall of 1940. These models, plus several others, such as the Guggenheim, which had been made since that exhibition, were to be shown at an exhibition which was to be held in Italy in the spring of the following year. Oscar Stonorov, an architect from Philadelphia, was helping to organize and assemble the exhibition material. He spent a great deal of time at Taliesin that summer working with Mr. Wright to select the material to be included.

Before being sent to Italy, the exhibition was to be shown at Gimbels Department Store in Philadelphia. Arthur C. Kaufman, Executive Head of Gimbels Brothers, was sponsoring and providing generous financial support for the exhibition. It was also being fostered by the United States Department of State as part of a public relations battle over Italy's position in the Cold War with the Soviet Union.

"Movement" rehearsals continued during the summer. The group, under Iovanna's direction, met two nights a week. After breakfast on Sunday, June 18, Mr. Wright talked to the Fellowship about "doing movements." His comments were directed toward those who were not "in movements." The talk was taped by Bruce Pfeiffer, who had begun making tapes of all of Mr. Wright's Sunday morning talks. (When Bruce began recording these talks he used amateur, home-recording equipment. It was not long before he was using professional quality equipment provided by Edgar Kaufmann, Jr.) This tape was later transferred to "Frank Lloyd Wright Talks to His Taliesin Fellowship," made by the American Recording Company in Chicago. I don't know the purpose of these records; they were not made available to the public.

Later in the summer Mrs. Wright and Iovanna began urging members of the Fellowship to buy copies of Gurdjieff's book *All and Everything,* which had just been published.[80] I bought a copy, but I never managed to read it. It was a book which some of us facetiously referred to as "All about Everything." During one Sunday morning talk Mr. Wright asked which apprentices had read Emerson's essay "Self-Reliance." He returned from Madison one afternoon with a box filled with copies of the Modern Library edition of the *Writings of Ralph Waldo Emerson.* There were enough copies so each member of the Fellowship could have one. The box was placed near the Fellowship mailboxes.

Gurdjieff's name does not appear with those of Emerson and Whitman in the lists of "influences and inferences" that are included in Wright's *Autobiography* and in his Testament. I felt that he accepted "movements" as an activity that Iovanna and Mrs. Wright were interested in and supported them primarily for this reason.

Toward the end of the summer, three Irishmen who had sailed the Atlantic in a small boat to join the Fellowship and who had been received with much acclaim by the New York press finally arrived at Taliesin. They were Desmond Dalton, Tony Jacobs, and John (Sean) Kenny, and were immediately assigned to work with a crew that was clearing a path for telephone lines along the ridge of the hills to the east of Taliesin. Mr. Wright had been working for several years to get the poles and wires along the highway out of the valley and out of sight, and had finally gotten the telephone company to agree to move the lines. Mr. Wright's contribution to the agreement was to clear a right of way for the lines.

The removal of these lines was only one part of a much larger project on which Mr. Wright had been engaged for many years. It was a large-scale landscape project that might be called "The Remodeling of the Lloyd-Jones Valley." The removal of the Rieder house and barn during my first fall in the Fellowship was my introduction to this project. But before this he had moved a house and a barn, which had been down near the highway, up onto the side of Midway Hill. Mr. Wright was still at work on this project at the time of his death. It is one that should be thoroughly researched, documented, and published.

Toward the end of summer I was told that I was to move from my room in the stable wing at Taliesin to the apartment at the north end of the Midway Barn. This end of the barn had been made into an apartment the summer before. It consisted of two small bedrooms, a bath, a living room with a stone fireplace at the north end, and a small kitchen alcove tucked in behind the fireplace on its left side. There was a sink, a gas stove, and a refrigerator in the small kitchen. At the right side of the fireplace a door opened out to a small screened porch projecting beyond the end of the barn. As I later described it I was living with several not-quite-realized luxuries. My moving to the barn apartment was part of Mr. Wright's plan for the operation of the farm, which was to become a more integral part of the Fellowship's life. We were to do more than just occasionally help to get the crops in.

When I first joined the Fellowship there was a hired man, with a wife and several small children, who took care of the cows. The husband, driving the small Bantam pick-up, brought a five-gallon can of milk to the milk room every day and, when requested, supplied the kitchen with rich cream for table use and for churning butter. Except for the occasional help getting the crops in, that was the extent of the Fellowship's physical involvement with the cows. Otherwise the herd of Guernseys was a visually decorative element that Mr. Wright enjoyed seeing in the pastures.

Now the Fellowship was going to take over the operation of the farm, without any "hired men." Wes was to be in charge of the fieldwork: the plowing, planting, cultivation, and harvesting of the crops. John Hill and Kenn Lockhart were to be in charge of the cows. Eric Wright was to be in charge of the chickens, and Larry Martyn, a new apprentice, was to be in charge of the pigs. All of these men, except Wes, were going to stay at Midway during the coming winter and run the farm. Other apprentices were to be assigned to take care of the milk room at Midway on a weekly basis, keeping it clean, separating the cream from the milk, and churning the butter. My role at the barn was never clearly defined.

On Sunday, October 29, the anniversary of Gurdjieff's death, a "movements demonstration" was given in the Playhouse at Hillside. Before the demonstration Mr. Wright gave an address, a tribute to Gurdjieff. It was tape recorded and later transcribed, then edited by Mr. Wright, and printed by Gene. This was done "for the benefit of those who were unable to be with us." To me this seemed to be part of an ongoing effort to associate or to connect Mr. Wright with Gurdjieff. Mr. Wright's address was unique in that Mr. Wright did not speak in his usual first person "I," but in a collective "We." It was not like him to do this.[81]

Early in November Mr. Wright sent several of us, including John Hill and me, to the Lowell Walter house in Iowa. We went to paint the soffit and fascia of the house a flower-pot red so that photos of the house could be taken for a special section of the January 1951 issue of *Architectural Forum*. This section was to be reprinted and distributed in connection with the Italian exhibition of Mr. Wright's work, which Oscar Stonorov was assembling.

Ezra Stoller, who was to do the photography, arrived while we were working. The cold weather created problems for him, particularly in taking photos of the interior. The humidity level in the house was quite high due to the watering of plants in the top-lighted planting area near the center of the living room. It was difficult to keep the large areas of plate glass cleared of condensation long enough for Ezra to get photos taken with a view toward the exterior.

During this month Mr. Wright decided that this year the Fellowship was again to travel to Arizona in a caravan, led by Wes. We left near the first of December, I in my Hotshot, a day before the caravan did. I wanted to make stops to visit my parents and also to see friends in Kansas City and Lawrence.

Winter 1950–1951

Mr. Wright had become ill on a trip to Michigan late in October. His illness during November had kept him confined to the interior of Taliesin until near the end of the month when he ventured over to Hillside to check on the models before they were sent to Philadelphia. But with his arrival in Arizona his health appeared to be much improved. He was looking forward to the publication of the *Architectural Forum* with the special section and to the opening of the exhibition in Philadelphia near the end of January. Although he was still on a very strict diet and not quite as chipper as usual, he was up and about, checking on the work in the drafting room and pushing work on the new theater. He was determined to have it completed and ready for use by Christmas. We did have dinner there on Christmas Eve, a Sunday, after two intense days of work.

With the theater completed, Mr. Wright shifted his attention to the backlog of work in the drafting room; on the Monday following Christmas he put his design concept for a house for John Gillin on paper. The design was developed and the presentation drawings completed a couple of days before New Year's.[82] Jack Howe did most of the work on these drawings but I helped by laying out one of the perspectives, an aerial view of the house as seen on the garden side, the side away from the street and open toward a creek which runs through the property. It was a large house with three wings radiating out from a central hexagonal living room: a wing for entertaining, a service wing, and a bedroom wing.

As soon as Mr. Gillin had seen and approved these drawings, we started working drawings. Mr. Gillin was eager to start building as he feared the government might decide to stop this kind of construction following North Korea's invasion of South Korea the preceding summer.[83] Not long after we had started the drawing Wes went to Dallas to lay out the house on the site. Construction had started before the first of February. We hoped to be able to keep the drawings ahead of the construction process.

At about the same time that we started the construction drawings for the Gillin house we also started working drawings for a house for Mr. Wright's son, David, and his wife.[84] The design that Mr. Wright had titled "How to Live in the Southwest" was, with a few changes, the design of David's house (Fig. 92).

David was the sales representative in the Phoenix area for the Besser Manu-

92   Garden Court of David Wright residence seen from north side. Ramp up to entrance starts below the master bedroom which is above at left. Projected bay of living room is above at right. Maynard Parker, photo, copyright Maynard L. Parker Estate.

facturing Company, an outfit that produced machinery and equipment for making concrete blocks including molds for the various kinds and shapes of blocks. One of the constraints in making the drawings for David's house was to use only those blocks that could be produced with Besser molds. We used only one special block, the one with a decorative pattern that forms the edge of the elevated concrete slab on which the house rests. The drawings for David's house were completed by mid-February and David began arrangements to start construction. Mr. Wright proposed that Gordon Chadwick supervise the construction and contacted him in Aspen to see if he would be interested. Gordon came to Phoenix, and he and David reached an agreement about the terms under which he would oversee the project. Gordon returned to Aspen for several weeks to complete some work there and then returned to Phoenix to start building. He did not live at the camp but he was there very often going over the details of the house and its construction. The house was completed about a year later.

Shortly after we had started the drawings for David's house, Mr. Wright made a sketch of a design for a house in Palm Springs, California, for Edgar Kaufmann, Sr. The Kaufmanns had a house in Palm Springs that Richard Neutra had designed for them about five years earlier. In contrast with the rectangular geometry of the house by Neutra, the house Mr. Wright proposed was based – as seen in plan – on segments of circles. But the concept was more than this; the copper-covered roofs were to be segments of spheres and other doubly curved surfaces. He called the house "Boulders," a reference to the terrain in which the house was to sit and to the stones which were to be built into the masonry base of the house.

Toward the end of January, after weeks of ideal weather, we had a flood in the camp.[85] It started raining on a Monday afternoon. After dinner on Monday evening some of us went into Scottsdale to see a movie. When we came out of the theater we had doubts about whether we would be able to make it back to the camp. I was driving my Hotshot. Charles Montooth, who was driving a pick-up truck, stayed behind me to make sure I didn't get into trouble when going through the washes. It continued to rain through the night.

The next morning at about six o'clock there was a sudden heavy downpour. I was awakened by it and got up and dressed.[86] I went outside to check on the level of the water in the ditch on the northeast side of my room. Water was running in the ditch but there didn't appear to be any particular danger. I walked along the east side of the apprentice court and crossed the bridge back into the court. There I encountered John Paul. John and his wife were living in John Hill's room, next to mine. He asked, "What's that roaring sound?" I knew then that the worst was about to happen and rushed to my room. Water was already flowing down the steps outside the entrance to my room. It made a pretty – but tawny – cascade. And it was beginning to flow into my room through the doorway. I put everything that was on the floor up on the bed and on the sill around the room. In no time at all there were about five inches of water in my room. Luckily I had gotten most everything up and out of the wet. John Paul had taken a board and made a dam at the doorway. It took me most of the rest of the day to get the water out of the room and to clean up the silt that had settled on the floor.

Much of the camp was in a condition similar to that of my room, except that in some places the water simply ran through without leaving a deposit of silt. The new theater, however, was in danger of being inundated. Mr. Wright spent the morning there protecting it. A pump he had bought with the idea that it would be used to fight fires with the water from the triangular pool near the drafting room was put to work in the theater pumping water out of the orchestra pit.

During the last week in January Mr. and Mrs. Wright went to Philadelphia for the opening of the exhibition "Sixty Years of Living Architecture," at Gimbels.[87] (It was to go to Italy later.) Mr. Wright was very pleased with the exhibition as it had been installed by Stonorov. He said that it was worth going miles to see. Of course the idea of going miles to see it was immediately accepted, and there was talk of chartering an airplane to take the Fellowship to Philadelphia. Nothing came of this proposal as there was too much architectural work waiting to be done.

Work in the drafting room focused on houses and more houses. Some were large, some were small. They had different geometries. Some were rectangular, some triangular, and some circular. In this steady flow of houses through the drafting room I began to see that the process by which they were designed could be placed in one of three general categories. First were those that were essentially a new concept, perhaps of geometry or construction. In this category were those which Mr. Wright, after consideration of the client's requirements and site, put on paper in an almost completely realized form. From this first sketch, plans and elevations were extracted and, after few or no changes, presentation drawings were made to be shown or sent to the client for their approval.

Second were those for which Mr. Wright, after studying the client's site plan and requirements, would draw on the site plan the overall configuration of the house in its intended location, showing the approach drive to the house. He would then ask one of the senior apprentices to work out the plan in detail in accord with the client's needs, and to make it like such and such a house – one for which the client may have expressed a preference. Mr. Wright would then work on these drawings. He might make only minor changes in the design – or it might be completely changed before presentation drawings were made.

The third category consisted of those houses which Jack or one of the other apprentices would design when Mr. Wright couldn't, especially if the clients were becoming impatient. These drawings would then be shown to Mr. Wright for further work. He might make only minor changes or he might reject it by revising it completely. After this the revision would be developed and presentation drawings made.

One of the houses for which I did working drawings was the W. L. Fuller house near Pass Christian, Mississippi. The house was similar in construction and detailing to the Carlson house in Phoenix. It was a larger house, nestled among tall pine trees and located in an area with high potential for damage from flooding and winds during the hurricane season on the Gulf Coast. Because of this, the main living level of both the house and the guest house was raised a full floor above ground level and supported on concrete masonry piers. The small guest house was attached to the main house by a generous outdoor terrace.

Concrete masonry cores, incorporating fireplaces and containing utility and workspace areas, started at ground level and gave a supporting massiveness to the house. Two bedrooms and a bath were supported one floor above the living level by the masonry core of the main house. These bedrooms had access to a rooftop terrace above the living room.

Although the possibility of damage from hurricanes was anticipated in the design of the house, the vicious force of Hurricane Camille in 1969 was not. The Fuller house, like many others in the region, was destroyed by this hurricane's fury.

Early in the winter Thomas de Hartmann and his wife, Olga, came to the camp. They had become interested in Gurdjieff and his teachings and had joined his group in Russia in 1917, remaining with the group until 1929. During these years, Mrs. de Hartmann had served as Gurdjieff's secretary. Mr. de Hartmann had played the piano for the group's rehearsals and performances. He had worked with Gurdjieff on the music used for the performances. And he had also worked on some of Gurdjieff's own compositions, writing down the melodies which Mr. Gurdjieff whistled or picked out on the piano with one finger. The de Hartmanns left the group in 1929 when Gurdjieff "made conditions impossible" for them. They settled in a town near Paris and although no longer directly associated with him remained devoted to him and his teaching.

The de Hartmanns lived in the guest apartment of Iovanna's cottage. There was a grand piano in the apartment and Mr. de Hartmann continued to work at his compositions there. He gave several talks to the Fellowship about the relatedness of the various arts.

Toward the end of April the migration to Wisconsin started. Davy had gone ahead to start the garden and the van had been packed. This year I chose to travel with John Geiger again. I was driving my Hotshot. He was driving Mr. Wright's Continental convertible. And again we chose to take a scenic route – through Salt River Canyon, Sante Fe, Taos, and Cimmaron Canyon. After we left Taos it started to rain. When we reached Cimmaron Canyon it was raining heavily. Work had been started on improving the narrow and winding canyon road. That ride through the canyon in my Hotshot was like driving down a rushing mountain stream. Fortunately Geiger and the Continental were behind me and pushed me through several pools.

Summer 1951

When I arrived in Wisconsin I settled into the apartment in the barn, into which I had moved the previous summer, and I resumed feeding the calves. I became very much aware of the personalities of the different cows. This awareness began with one particular calf among those that I had fed the previous fall. I fed the calves after the morning and evening milking each day, giving each of them a portion of the milk that had been set aside for them. Teaching newborn calves to drink from a pail was part of this job. As they got a little older, hay became part of each feeding. One particular calf had no interest in hay. She always wanted more milk. During the winter this calf had been sickly and had gotten special attention from Kenn, Johnnie, and Harper Harrison, the veterinarian. She survived the winter. When I arrived in Wisconsin she was out in the pasture with the other cows. But one day, when I happened to walk by the cow pasture, much to my surprise, this calf – now actually a full-grown cow – came running over to me seemingly expecting special attention and favors. She continued to do this whenever I went near the pasture.

Near the end of May Mr. and Mrs. Wright and Iovanna left on an extended trip to Italy for the opening of the exhibition "Sixty Years of Living Architecture" in Florence. They were away most of the month of June.

Mr. Wright returned from Italy much invigorated by the experience. He was still basking in the warmth of his and the exhibition's reception in Italy. The exhibition had been handsomely installed in the rooms of the Strozzi Palace. The traditional richness of the setting and of the ceremonies attendant on the opening of the exhibition and on the bestowing of honors upon him had struck a resonant chord in his love of drama and display. He did not hesitate to remind everyone that the Star of Solidarity, which the Venetians had awarded him in the Doge's Palace, had been given to only a few other artists, among them Dante. Being awarded the de Medici Medal by Florence was a recognition by the city whose citizens had also been patrons of Brunelleschi and Michelangelo.

Mr. Wright resumed work on the Guggenheim Museum with new vigor. This project had been languishing for several years. During the war a model had been made and a set of working drawings started with the intent that the construction would begin with the war's end. But at the end of the war Mr. Guggenheim, believing that there would soon be a recession and with it lower building costs, was not willing to start construction right away. As an interim measure for housing and displaying the collection, Mr. Wright designed and did working drawings for a building referred to as the Annex. This building was to serve as a temporary museum until the Guggenheim Museum itself could be constructed, and would then serve as an annex to the Guggenheim. The Annex was to be built on a small parcel of land facing 88th Street in New York City and connecting to the property Mr. Guggenheim then owned. But before this building could be started, Mr. Guggenheim died.

With his death and the formation of a foundation and the appointment of a board of trustees by his heirs, a fresh start of a sort was made. The trustees purchased two properties, a town house and a tall apartment building – which were south of the property already owned – at the northeast corner of 88th Street and Fifth Avenue. The purchase of these properties gave the foundation the complete frontage on Fifth Avenue between 88th and 89th streets. It was now possible for the major space of the museum, the spiral gallery, to revert to the position that it had occupied on Mr. Wright's very first sketch for the museum, so Mr. Wright flipped the plan.

With this flipping of the plan in the summer of 1951, Mr. Wright asked us to start a complete new set of working drawings for the museum. I was asked to work with Jack on them. This was the beginning of my on-and-off involvement with this project, which would continue for the next four years.

During the following four years I made what I considered one small contribution to ease the construction of the building. This was a system for dimensioning the ramp. In the previous drawings the ramp had been dimensioned as arcs of quadrants of circles with a separate center for each of these quadrants. The radius of each of these quadrants was increased a given amount with each complete cycle of the ramp. I proposed instead that the ramp be dimensioned as an arithmetic spiral. By this time the ramp was thought of as consisting of twelve structural bays of thirty degrees each. In two of these segments the floor needed to be level, at the elevator and the stair landings. I proposed that the rise of the ramp and its increase in width could be taken care of by a note on the drawings explaining that with each ten degrees of turn the floor would rise a fraction of the total floor to floor height and that the radius of the outer wall of the ramp would increase by a similar fraction of the total increase in the width of the ramp in one full cycle. I understand that this was the system that the builder followed.

The origin and development of the design for the Guggenheim Museum during the three years between the summers of 1943 and 1946 have always been something of a puzzle to me. I was not at Taliesin during those years and I do not know the circumstances under which the various drawings or sketches were made. Mr. Wright's first sketch was followed by other drawings rendered by persons unknown: plans and elevations of buildings with different geometries, with different elevations, with floors that are level, with ramps that taper in as well as out, and which are built of various materials. The very fact that these drawings were made is untypical of Mr. Wright's way of working. They seem more like the design studies that are and were done very often in other architectural practices.

These design studies lend credence to Hilla Rebay's statements that the idea of the museum was hers and that she gave it to Mr. Wright. I heard her make such a statement when I went out to dinner with her and her nephew, Roland, during one of her many visits to Taliesin and Taliesin West. During our dinner conversation she said that she had had the idea of a continuous, spiraling museum many years before Le Corbusier had had his.[88]

Toward the end of July Mr. Wright decided that the Fellowship should take on the job of completing the Unitarian Church in Madison. Construction of the building had started in 1949. When the building was dedicated in February of 1951, the work had progressed to the point where the building was enclosed but incomplete. The small congregation which had contributed much of its time and energy to the building had run out of both money and energy. Mr. Wright was embarrassed and annoyed that the building was being used in this state. It was not a credit to him or his work. Much work remained to be done.

At the start of this project only Wes and I went to Madison. We would leave Taliesin after breakfast, go to Madison in his pick-up, and after a day of work return to Taliesin in time for dinner in the evening.

We started by bulldozing in the drive to the entrance along the north side of the parsonage. One afternoon, when Wes was using the Fellowship's bulldozer to knock out the existing steps and a toe wall at their base, the bulldozer went over this wall. As it did so, the front end of the dozer suddenly dropped, and in a see-saw action the rear end, where Wes was seated, was lifted. Wes was caught between the seat of the dozer and the eave of the roof. He managed somehow to turn the motor off and to extricate himself. His breath had been knocked out of him and he was in considerable pain. I helped him into his pick-up and drove him to the nearest hospital to be examined and treated. Several ribs were cracked or broken. He left the hospital with his chest heavily taped. That ended work for that day.

After about a week of only the two of us going in to work on the church, a few more people were added to the crew. Day by day more and more were added, until only a few people remained at Taliesin (Figs. 93, 94). Mr. Wright was scheduled to give a talk at the church, at another dedication, on August 14. Admission was to be charged to help defray the costs of completion. But it soon became evident that the work was not going to be completed by the 14th. The talk was rescheduled for the 21st, a week later.

93   Work at the Unitarian Church in Madison. Apprentices removing scaffolding after the plastering of the ceiling was completed. John Newhouse photographer. Photo courtesy of the State Historical Society of Wisconsin. (WHi (N48) 17116)

94   Interior of the Unitarian Church when completed. Ezra Stoller © Esto.

During a weekend early in August, I drew up a seating plan for the church similar to that shown on the preliminary drawings and designed a two-person seating unit for it. Mr. Wright approved this seating plan and unit. The seating unit was based on the use of four-by-eight sheets of three-quarter-inch plywood. Each unit was four feet wide. The back rest was hinged to the seat and held in an upright position by chains attached at the ends of the back and seat. Thin seat and back cushions, covered with an inexpensive fabric, were to be attached to the plywood.

I was quite pleased with the design of the seating unit. It made very economical use of the plywood. A truckload of plywood was taken to the mill where the pieces were cut out and a truckload of pieces was hauled away. The only waste was the sawdust created by the cutting. These units were assembled, finished, and upholstered by the crew working at the church.

Mr. Wright became very concerned about the acoustics in the church's auditorium while we were working there. Because of the noise level and the reverberation, apprentices to whom he was trying to give directions could not understand him. Talking louder or shouting did not help. Disturbed by this, Mr. Wright decided to put a tympanum over the rostrum and the choir loft. He made a drawing for it on a piece of board and supervised its being put in place. It was designed in two pieces, so that it could be built on the floor of the auditorium and lifted into place and assembled. He also added large panels of fabric which hung in front of the glass walls at the sides of the two stone piers at either side of the rostrum. Fortunately, as the furniture was put in place, the acoustics improved.

Only a few members of the Fellowship were not working at the church on the weekend preceding the Tuesday on which the talk had been rescheduled. We worked all day Saturday and Sunday. Gene Masselink, who seldom got far from the telephone or the typewriter, was there doing the lettering – in gold leaf – which Mr. Wright wanted done: the names of noted Unitarians which were placed on the wood facia of the lower ceiling of the hearth room and a quotation over the opening to the hearth room at the rear of the auditorium. The source and the wording of the quotation presented a problem. Mr. Wright insisted it was from "an ancient Persian," but a search of several references did not produce either a source or an exact wording. Mr. Wright resolved the problem by writing his own paraphrase of this bit of advice to the congregation and the minister and attributing it to "an ancient parable." It read,

> "Do you have a loaf of bread
> Break the loaf in two
> And give one half for some flowers of the narcissus
> For the bread feeds the body indeed
> But the flowers feed the soul."

There was one bit of lettering that the minister and the spokesmen for the congregation would not accept. That was the word *Unity* which Mr. Wright asked me to carve in the face of the large stone which serves as the lectern. I was grateful that this bit of carving was not accepted. I had worked all of Monday night – before the Tuesday of the talk – completing the stonework around the rostrum and did not look forward to spending part of Tuesday flattening the face of the stone and carving *Unity* into it. As it was, we did not finish cleaning up the interior of the church until late Tuesday afternoon. Little time was left. Since Mr. Wright wanted the chorus to perform before his talk, we had to rush out to Taliesin to shower and dress and hurry back to the church.

I did not get up for breakfast the next morning, but at about eight o'clock someone came knocking at my door. Mr. Wright was up, had had his breakfast, and wanted us all to go back to the church in Madison again. He had scheduled another fund-raising talk for the next Tuesday, the 28th. There was more work he wanted done before this second talk.

Early in the fall, when Mr. Wright went to Detroit to give a lecture, Mrs. Wright went with him. When they returned Mrs. Wright told me that she had met a young violinist there who was interested in "movements" and who wanted to join the Fellowship. He was going to come to Taliesin to play on a Sunday evening and I was to accompany him. She added that she hoped Mr. Wright would accept him and that, if he was accepted, he would be responsible for the ensemble, relieving me of this responsibility. I resented this message. It seemed to me that Mrs. Wright was intruding into the musical activities which I thought were Mr. Wright's province.

The violinist, John Amarantides, arrived on a Saturday morning. That afternoon we worked on some pieces, and got together again on Sunday afternoon for another rehearsal and to decide what he would perform that evening. Although I resented him at first, I found that I enjoyed playing with him. We seemed to share an understanding of the music. On Sunday evening we played a group of pieces to end the concert. Mr. Wright enjoyed John's music and invited him to join the Fellowship. He joined later that fall.

The completion of the church presented another opportunity for a demonstration of "movements" in Madison. Ostensibly, this would be another fund-raising event to help offset the costs of the completion, but it seemed to me that fund-raising was not the main purpose of this event. It was an opportunity to publicize and to proselytize for Gurdjieff's teaching with the hope that a "group" might be established in Madison.

With the demonstration out of the way, plans were made for the migration to Arizona. By the middle of November the move was under way. Mr. and Mrs. Wright were going to New York for a few days on their way to Arizona. Mr. Wright was hoping to present the revised plans for the museum to the board of trustees for their approval.

Winter 1951–1952

Early in March of 1952 I wrote Marcus Weston saying:

> This winter will go down in Fellowship history as the winter everyone was sick. I've never seen so much of it. Hardly anyone has escaped. It has generally taken the form of a kind of "cold" or flu. Someone who isn't sniffling, having a sore throat, or having a temperature is a rarity.[89]

The weather during the first half of the winter was of no help in alleviating this condition. It was cold and rainy. And in March, when pleasant, resortlike weather was expected, it was still cold.

The winter in camp did not begin with any major changes or major construction projects. There were the usual minor changes, repairing and freshening things here and there.

Because of the continued cold, Mr. Wright decided that the living room (sometimes referred to as the Garden Room) should have a fireplace. This was built on the east side, near the south end. At the same time, the exterior balcony, to which this end of the room could be opened, was enclosed and made part of the room. The alcove created more seating. The construction of the fireplace shifted the focus of the room from the openings out to the garden to the fireplace.

There was one change that winter that did not visibly affect the camp but did much to affect life in the camp. For several years, Mr. Wright had resisted having the camp connected to the public power system – he did not like the idea of power poles along the roads. But it had become possible to bring power in from the west, underground for a part of the way, and otherwise in such a manner that the line was not visible from the road up to the camp or from within it.

With the elimination of our own generator and the fumes and noise that went with it, the shop area of the camp began to receive some of Mr. Wright's attention. A roof was built over the area where a wall had been built and a floor slab poured the previous winter for a pottery shop. And a gas-fired kiln was installed. This shop, which had support from Mrs. Wright, appeared to be Steve Oyakawa's project. He was the only one who made any pots there that winter.

During the later part of the winter a locker room was built. It provided much needed storage, shower, and toilet facilities for the apprentices who were living in tents. The men's shower and toilet facilities in the apprentice court had been much too small for many years. They were always crowded in the evening when apprentices were getting ready for dinner.

I did very little outside construction work that winter. My time was divided between work in the drafting room and music-related activities. Some visitors, aware only of my musical activities and not of my work in the drafting room, assumed that I was a musician and not an architect. In addition to making certain that Brandoch practiced the cello, practicing pieces that John Amarantides wanted us to play, and rehearsing with the chorus and ensemble, I was also searching for works that could be added to the chorus's repertoire. It was not easy to find music that would work successfully with the chorus's assortment of untrained voices. Strange as it may seem, the a cappella motets of sixteenth- and seventeenth-century composers such as Antonio Lotti, Tomás Luis de Victoria, Heinrich Schutz, and, of course, Palestrina (whom Tony Bek had focused on when he was directing the chorus) seemed to work best.

We did learn a few "westerns" such as "Cool Clear Water" which was a favorite of Brandoch, Wes, and Mr. Wright. We made an attempt to learn "Tumbling Tumble Weeds" which Mrs. Wright requested, but it didn't work. We added a few Bach chorales and Negro spirituals. One of these, "Were You There When They Crucified My Lord," with Iovanna singing the solo part, was favored by Mr. and Mrs. Wright. But there was one motet by Victoria, "O Vos Omnes," which appeared to have a profound effect on Mr. Wright; during the singing of this motet Mr. Wright appeared to be mentally in another world from which he returned with a start at the motet's end.

During this winter I no longer was a breakfast cook; I became instead the supervisor of the breakfast cooks. I was asked to take over this job when Kenn Lockhart, who had been doing it, was asked to stay in Wisconsin during the winter to help take care of the farm. Now instead of taking my turn as a breakfast cook, I was responsible for training and breaking in new breakfast cooks. Whenever a new breakfast cook was assigned, I got up at five-thirty every morning to steer him or her through their first week of cooking. Every Sunday morning, regardless of whether the cook was new or experienced, I was in the kitchen helping with the cooking and serving, and trying to make certain that there were no disasters, particularly when guests were present.

At the beginning of the winter, work in the drafting room focused on two things: the usual small houses and working drawings for the Guggenheim Museum. By the middle of March I was complaining in letters to friends that the paper was wearing thin from all of the changes. Some of the changes were the result of negotiations with the New York City Building Department. (The process of applying for and securing a building permit had begun, and Mr. Wright had associated himself with the firm of Holden and McLaughlin to assist him in this process.) Some of the changes resulted from Mr. Wright's continuing effort to resolve certain purely architectural problems chief among these being how to terminate an upward-rising, outward-expanding spiral once it has been started. But there were other architectural problems as well: Should the parapet wall of the roof of the ramp be horizontal or continue the slope of the ramp? Should the outer wall of the ramp be in one surface, that of an inverted cone, or should these walls be separate surfaces stepping out at each revolution? Finally, some changes were the result of efforts to reduce the cost of the building, such as the elimination of the glass tubing dome over the central space of the museum and the winding strip of glass tubing in the outer wall of the ramp which was to provide natural light for the ramp.

During the winter I also worked on three other projects: preliminary drawings for an apartment building for the Edgar Kaufmann Charitable Trust, preliminary drawings for the Anderton Court Shops for Nina Anderton, and working drawings for the Charles Glore, house which were completed in mid-February.

The apartment project, called the Point View Residences, was to be built on Mt. Washington in Pittsburgh. Two different designs were done for this project. The first of these was based on the apartment project in Los Angeles which Mr. Wright designed for Elizabeth Noble in 1929. This was a project that Mr. Wright wanted to see realized.

The Elizabeth Noble Apartment project was a step beyond the houses that Mr. Wright and his son, Lloyd, had built in the Los Angeles area: the textile block houses of Mr. Wright, such as the Millard and Ennis houses, and the houses with plain plaster surfaces encrusted with geometric growths of precast patterned block designed by Lloyd, such as the Snowden and the studio/house which he designed for himself and his family. The surface ornament and the massive encrustation of these houses were replaced, in the Noble apartments, with a cubic and crystalline growth of glass and steel. This fenestration contrasted with the plain surfaces of the massive concrete elements.

The Point View project was to be about twice the size of its Los Angeles predecessor. I did many of the developmental drawings on which Mr. Wright worked to adapt the Noble scheme to the requirements of the Point View Residences. And Jack Howe and I did a very complete set of presentation drawings. I laid out and drew most of the much published perspective view of the apartment as seen from the northeast. Jack and Mr. Wright put on the finishing touches.

When these presentation drawings were completed, they were sent to Mr. Kaufmann for his study and approval. A response to these drawings was very slow in coming. The delay was partially explained by Mrs. Kaufmann's illness and death that year. Much later in the year, Mr. Wright received a letter from Edgar Junior, suggesting changes in the plans. It was not until sometime later – in 1953 – that it became clear to Mr. Wright that the reworked and warmed-over Elizabeth Noble design was not acceptable.

Two slightly different schemes were done for the Anderton Court Shops. Both schemes were based on the idea of a complex of small shops grouped around a central court and organized vertically instead of horizontally. The shops were to be in a split level arrangement with half levels on alternate sides of the court. The half-level rises were to be connected by gently sloping ramps that spiraled up around a spire, located near the street and terminated by a decorative lighting element. The top level, at the left, was to be an apartment for Eric Bass, who was to own one of the shops and to manage the entire complex.

In the first scheme proposed, the right-hand shop, which was a half level below the street, presented a massive wall to the street. This was not acceptable; all of the shops were to have as much glass front as possible. In the second scheme this massive element was replaced by the glass front of a two-level shop. The lower floor of this shop faced into a sunken garden, a half level below the street.

Although I worked on both sets of preliminary drawings and on the working drawings for this complex, I never did like it. On a larger site this complex of shops could have been a rich and marvelous mix, an interpenetration of ramps, foliage, crystallic glass fronts, and light and shade. On this narrow site it became crowded, cramped, and much too complicated. It was evident that the motive was to crowd as much rental space as possible onto the site. When built, the complex confirmed my opinion of the scheme. Additions and alterations since its completion have only strengthened my dislike.

One of the small houses in the studio that winter was of particular interest to the Fellowship. It was a Usonian Automatic house for Arthur Pieper's father, built on a site north of Scottsdale. Arthur, an apprentice from St. Louis, had joined the Fellowship in 1949. Shortly after joining the Fellowship he married Bodil Hammergard, an apprentice from Denmark, who had joined the Fellowship at about the same time. Construction was well along when we left the desert that spring.

Another point of interest that winter was the construction of David Wright's house (Figs. 95, 96), which was enclosed and nearing completion. It was only a block or so off Camelback Road, one of the cross streets that could be taken into Phoenix. This house, supervised by Gordon Chadwick, was very well built. What particularly impressed me was the carpentry work on the ceiling of the master bedroom. The roof of the bedroom wing was another of those that had different pitches on each side. The ridge of the roof was over the partition separating the corridor from the bedrooms. The steeper pitch was on the corridor side. The roof, however, did not terminate in a gable as might be expected. The end wall of the master bedroom was a half circle. The eave of the roof was horizontal and a hipped roof here made a transition between the different slopes of the sides. The ceilings of the bedrooms reflected the external form of the roof. They were made of lapped mahogany boards. But that of the master bedroom was like the construction of a boat. It was a conicallike surface with the boards becoming increas-

95   David Wright living room seen from the entrance. Maynard Parker, photo, copyright Maynard L. Parker Estate.

96   Master bedroom of David Wright residence. Fireplace is at left. Note pattern of lapped boards on ceiling. Maynard Parker, photo, copyright Maynard L. Parker Estate.

ingly narrow in making the transition from their spacing on the shallow side to their spacing on the steeper pitch of the other side.

Mr. Wright had resumed his correspondence with Lewis Mumford during the summer of 1951 and continued it during the winter. These letters appeared to be an effort by Mr. Wright to reestablish the relationship with Mumford that had ended ten years before in a fiery and furious disagreement over the need for the United States to enter into the war against Germany. Mr. Wright wanted to repair the damage caused by this disagreement and to resume the friendship which both had previously enjoyed.

During the winter Gene Masselink showed me some of these letters, which he had begun to refer to jokingly as "Mr. Wright's love letters to Lewis Mumford." Unless Mr. Wright chose to talk about it, the members of the Fellowship were not, in general, privy to much of Mr. Wright's correspondence, even to that related to architectural projects on which one might be working. He often mentioned that he followed the advice Dankmar Adler had given him: "to keep his office in his hat."

I assume that Gene showed me some of these letters because of my interest in Mumford's writing. I had acquired some of his books as a student, and while in the Fellowship had acquired others as they were published. I also looked forward to reading his "Skyline" articles in the *New Yorker*. Mr. Wright's letters to Mumford included affectionate invitations to Mumford and his wife, Sophie, to visit. They were open invitations to come whenever it was convenient, either to the camp in Arizona or to Taliesin in Wisconsin. Much to Mr. Wright's disappointment, although Mumford did respond to his letters, he and his wife never came for a visit.

At the end of March, Mr. and Mrs. Wright and Iovanna went to Paris for the opening there of the "Sixty Years of Living Architecture" exhibition. It had already been shown in Florence and Zurich, and was scheduled for Munich and Rotterdam after Paris. They were going to be away for several weeks. Gene Masselink took advantage of their absence to go to Rochester, Minnesota, for an operation on his hip. Also during their absence, several of us decided to go on a trip up to the Indian country in northeastern Arizona. We got permission to use the Fellowship pick-up from Wes, who had been left in charge of things during Mr. and Mrs. Wright's absence, and packed our sleeping bags and enough food supplies for a week in the back of the truck. Our first night out was spent camping on the south rim of the Canyon de Chelly, above Chimney Rock. The next day we drove down into the canyon, waded across the river, and climbed up into the White House ruins. From there we headed northwest toward Monument Valley. We camped there for several days simply enjoying the scenery, the setting for several of our favorite movies. The camping trip lasted about a week.

In late April we got word that there had been a fire at Hillside in Wisconsin. This unsettling news did not offer many details. We had started packing the van for the move to Wisconsin a few days earlier. Now, not knowing quite what to expect when we arrived, we started on the trip in small groups. I was driving my Hotshot. John Rattenbury, who had arrived a year or so before, was assigned to ride with me.

Summer 1952

When we arrived at Taliesin early in May the cause of the fire and the extent of the damage became clear. Mr. and Mrs. Wright had gone directly to Taliesin when they returned from their trip to Paris. On Saturday afternoon, April 26, Mr. Wright organized a crew to clean up the grounds around the Hillside buildings. This was an area that had not been mowed the previous summer and which had become covered with a high, weedy growth. Mr. Wright was trying to start a fire to burn away this overgrowth. He had run out of matches and had sent Davy to get more matches and some gasoline. While Davy was away, Mr. Wright left the area where he had been trying to start the fire. The wind, which had been blowing away from the building, suddenly changed direction. The fire flared up quickly and was driven by the wind toward the building. How the fire got inside the building was not too clear.

The fire spread quickly through the upper floor of the classroom section and into the theater. It destroyed the roof and walls of the upper level of this central section, and most of the theater. Only the stone walls and a portion of the roof on the north end of the theater were left standing. Fortunately the fire was stopped at the east end of this central section. If it had not been stopped, it could have spread into the living room and the northern section of the building, including the drafting room and the apprentice rooms alongside it.

The remains of the fire had not cooled Sunday morning when Mr. Wright was at a drafting table making plans for the rebuilding. On Monday morning he started the work of clearing away the debris.

The repair of the damage done by the fire and the rebuilding of the portions destroyed was the main construction project of the summer. Kelly Oliver was assigned to be in charge of this project, more or less (Mr. Wright was there directing the work much of the time; Fig. 97).

The replacement of the dining-room roof went rather quickly. Its construction was interesting. Mr. Wright wanted to make it fireproof. It was framed with heavy Douglas fir timbers. These were spaced at the same interval that the oak beams of the previous floor had been. The sandstone walls on which the timbers were to rest were about twenty-one inches thick at the top. They were even thicker at the floor level since the outside surface battered inward toward the top. To

97 Reconstruction of Hillside after the fire. Mr. Wright and Kelly Oliver on scaffolding for rebuilding roof of the theater. Completed dining room roof is in background at left. Photo by Pedro E. Guerrero.

counteract the outward thrust of the sloping roof (there were no cross ties) Mr. Wright had wood haunches put beneath the roof timbers. These extended out several feet from the inside face of the wall and redirected a part of the outward thrust of the beams downward into the wall, giving the room a vaultlike section. The stone piers which had been previously built to support the floor above were removed. Though the dining room still had the same floor area, with its new ceiling it now seemed larger.

The construction of the roof over the theater went more slowly. Mr. Wright seemed uncertain about how he wanted to rebuild this. Iovanna, with Mrs. Wright's backing and with the help of the "movements" group, was insisting on a larger stage for the practice and performance of "movements." Mr. Wright wanted to retain the charm and intimacy of the former Playhouse, but at the same time he wanted to make a change. The roof of the theater was not framed until the middle of October. The theater was not covered over until shortly before we left for Arizona early in November.

I had arrived in Wisconsin about a week after the fire and was assigned to live at Taliesin in a room below the bridge. Except for the fact that it had no kitchen facilities, it had the potential of being a small studio apartment. I had followed its renovation the preceding summer with a covetous eye and was happy to be assigned to it. I immediately began making plans to remodel it for my use. My plans were still in a nebulous state when John Geiger returned from supervising the construction of the Zimmerman house in Vermont. He was assigned to share the room with me. I had worked with him on several different projects and did not object to this.

One afternoon early in July, while working on this remodeling project, I cut the index and middle finger of my right hand rather badly. I was ripping a board on the table saw in the shop area and not watching what I was doing. Someone who happened by volunteered to drive me to Spring Green so that Doctor Wahl could take care of it. He cleaned the cut and bandaged my fingers. But that evening after dinner John Hill came by my room and proposed that he take me to Dodgeville to have the doctor at the hospital there check the extent of the damage. I gathered that he had talked with Mr. and Mrs. Wright and that they were concerned about my fingers. The doctor at the hospital removed the bandage, cleaned the cut again, and rebandaged my fingers.

There were two major projects in the drafting room that summer: the design of an office building for the H. C. Price Company of Bartlesville, Oklahoma, and the design of a country residence for Raul Bailleres in Acapulco, Mexico. (In addition to these projects there was also work on the design and construction of several smaller houses as well as drawings for the Guggenheim Museum.)

Bruce Goff had recommended Mr. Wright to the Prices. Goff, at that time, was the chairman of the School of Architecture at the University of Oklahoma as well as a practicing architect. He was also an admirer – but not an imitator – of Mr. Wright's work.

Mr. and Mrs. Price and their sons came to Taliesin early in June in their company's plane. This made an impression on Mr. Wright. Harold Price, Sr., was the kind of man Mr. Wright admired. He had developed a small electrical welding shop into a major contracting company, one active in building gas and oil pipelines. He wanted to construct a building that would be a contribution to this small city which had been a major factor in his success. Mr. Wright assured him that he had come to the right architect. He was soon calling Mr. and Mrs. Price "Harold" and "Mary Lou." Shortly after their visit they sent Mr. Wright a site plan and other data needed for their project. But after this was received there was little visible evidence that Mr. Wright was working on their project.

At about the same time, Mr. Wright was corresponding with Raul Bailleres about the possibility of designing a house for the Bailleres family in Acapulco.

Mr. Wright accepted this project and was invited to Mexico by the Baillereses to see the site of their proposed house. He and Mrs. Wright went to Mexico for about a week in the middle of July, visiting Mexico City, Cuernavaca, and Acapulco. When they returned from this trip Mr. Wright already had a design for the Bailleres house in mind. It was simply a matter of putting it on paper.

According to Mr. and Mrs. Wright, Acapulco was a delightful place and the Baillereses had a beautiful site near and overlooking the ocean. They were a wealthy family; they had a *palacio* in Cuernavaca which required many servants to operate. Mr. Bailleres favored Cuernavaca. It was Mrs. Bailleres who wanted a house in Acapulco. Mrs. Wright described Mrs. Bailleres as an extremely attractive woman who conducted herself beautifully.[90]

The central feature of the house was a large space, circular in plan and covered with a thin shell concrete dome with a large circular opening at its center. Mr. Wright called it a patio. It was an open, partially shielded, living room. At one side of the space, a particularly large boulder was to become part of a major feature of this living space. This feature was a boulder-shaped concrete shell, a cove of more intimate space, which would be heated on cool evenings by a large fireplace and cooled on hot days by the evaporation of water sprayed over it. On the side toward the ocean, the patio opened to a series of terraces which cascaded down to the water. One of these was a grassy lawn. Another was a brimming, fresh-water swimming pool whose overflow splashed onto the boulders and into the ocean below. The house was entered from a large, graveled entrance court defined and partially enclosed by the wings of the house.

With the completion late in August of the preliminary drawings for the Bailleres house, Mr. Wright shifted his attention to the office building for the H. C. Price Company. The concept that Mr. Wright put on paper was not the three-story block that the Prices had envisioned. Their building was to be a tall tower standing on the prairie. It was based on the St. Marks Tower in the Bouwerie project, the apartment building Mr. Wright had designed for Norman Guthrie back in 1929. The major difference between the Price Tower and St. Marks was that offices were to occupy three of the quadrants of the tower. Only one quadrant was to have apartments with interpenetrating mezzanine bedrooms.

An office block, which was to be occupied by the public service company, was pulled away from the base of the tower and placed at one side of the site. This gave their offices a separate entrance and a separate identity. Two floors of rental space for small shops connected the two-story public service office block to the elevator lobbies at the base of the tower. There were to be separate entrances for the offices and the apartments. The lobby space at the ground-floor level was to be the equivalent of two floors' height. Mr. Wright felt that the ceiling of the ground floor of the Johnson Tower was too low.

The building was planned on a thirty–sixty, diamond-shaped unit system. But since the scheme was a pinwheel, the unit system rotated ninety degrees in each quadrant of the tower. The parallel lines of the unit were thirty inches apart. In doing the developmental drawings, those of us who were assisting Mr. Wright questioned this dimension of the unit system. We proposed that it should be a little larger, that it was too small for a public building. The unit system being used made many situations in the plan somewhat tight and cramped. He rejected our proposal and insisted that the tower was to be tall and slender.

We completed the presentation drawings in about a month. When they were nearing completion Mr. Wright invited the Prices to come to Taliesin for a weekend visit to view the plans. They were surprised and delighted and perhaps a bit uncertain about the proposed design. It was different from, as well as more than, what they had expected. They proposed that they fly Mr. Wright to Bartlesville to see the site and to further discuss the design.

There was another construction project at Taliesin during the summer which at times rivaled the rebuilding of the sections of Hillside destroyed by the fire. This was the boat project. Early in June Wes had convinced Mr. Wright that he should buy a large wooden boat with an inboard motor, which was for sale at one of the lakes in Madison.

The boat was bought, and was put into the Wisconsin River just north of Taliesin. But it was soon discovered that the boat's motor needed either a major overhaul or replacement, and that there were no docking facilities. So the boat was moved to the upper pond at Taliesin with the idea that it would be converted into a "three-masted schooner" that could be used on the pond and in connection with a party that was to be given later in the summer. Party plans and preparations were the province of Mrs. Wright and those who worked most closely with her.

Several people were surreptitiously put to work on what started out to be a three-masted schooner. I say surreptitiously because those pushing this project, primarily Wes and Mrs. Wright, knew that Mr. Wright would not approve of people working on this project while work on the rebuilding at Hillside was lagging.

While Mr. and Mrs. Wright were on the trip to Mexico in the middle of July, Kay conceived the idea that we should have a surprise party for them when they returned, a "pirate party." I described this in a letter to Roland Rebay:

> Well, so far we've avoided having the "pirate party." Mr. and Mrs. Wright returned from Mexico and Acapulco last Thursday afternoon. Kay and some of the esoterics were all set to try and have a Pirate Party that night. There was much talk of a push to get the Galleon finished – in any fashion – so that the party could proceed. Wm. Wesley – to whom the Galleon is most dear – managed to forestall this. He wants the Galleon to enter the water in full splendor.[91]

We did have a party on the evening of their return – a picnic on Midway Hill. And after the picnic, Wes set off some of the fireworks he had laid in for the pirate party.

The pirate party was held later in the summer, shortly before the summer guests were to leave. Among these guests were several of Mr. Wright's grandchildren; Mrs. Barney, Mr. Wright's sister; and Dr. and Mrs. Masselink, Gene's parents.

I did not begin to enjoy this party until the galleon arrived, in full sail and in all of its splendor, at the scene of the party, the west side of the pond, under oak trees at the edge of the pasture. I was told that the galleon's arrival, with music coming across the water, just as the late afternoon sun was breaking through the overcast sky was a "breathtaking event."[92] I couldn't say; dressed as pirates, John Amarantides and I were providing the music. We played a Corelli barcarolle over and over. I accompanied John on the harmonium, a small organ pumped by foot. The boat was laden with pirates and their exotic loot, including several dancing girls stolen from the harem of some Arabian chieftain – Heloise Schweizer, Shirley Oliver, and Maxine Pfefferkorn. Of course, Iovanna was the most splendid of the stolen beauties.

My resentment of the time and energy that had gone into the preparation for this particular party came to a full boil following the party on September 14, a Sunday evening. During the preceding weeks I had become increasingly irritated by the conflict between chorus rehearsals and work on the boat. Some of the chorus members excused themselves from attendance at rehearsals by saying that they had to work on the boat or go in search of materials for the boat; others seized on this excuse to go on personal errands. I had said that if we didn't rehearse, the chorus would perform without me as the conductor. That evening I didn't go to dinner. Gene Masselink came looking for me when it was time for the music to begin. I reminded him of my threat and stayed away. On Monday I was called over to Taliesin for a meeting with Mr. and Mrs. Wright.

As a result of this meeting, the time for chorus rehearsal was changed from after tea to after breakfast, and Mr. Wright assembled the entire Fellowship for a talk. I described this meeting in a letter to Roland Rebay:[93]

> It was something of a "revival meeting" in which Mr. Wright discussed the ideals, means and methods of the Fellowship, including "kitchen-helping," etc. The desire for a spirit of "fellowship" in the Fellowship. The desire not to see "clicks" established. The sense of working together of the "seasoned" members (instead of "seniors") and the newer apprentices. The desire for a sense of "cultivation" and culture. The absence of table manners. General uncouthness. That we were set on a pedestal in the worlds' view and should live up to it, etc. The fact that not much had been accomplished during the summer. The desire to have the theater finished, etc. As instruments of "cultivation" he named "music" and "movements."

Those who were involved in fashioning the boat into a Spanish galleon were not the only persons involved in surreptitious activity at Taliesin that summer. In addition to being in charge of the "movements" group at Taliesin, Iovanna was also starting a Gurdjieff group in Chicago and went to that city once a week under the pretense that she was shopping.

During the summer, Iovanna threatened to leave Taliesin unless by fall she had a place for "movements" at Taliesin. Early in October the idea was proposed to Mr. Wright that the Chicago group should come to Taliesin once a week for their meetings instead of Iovanna going to Chicago. This idea was vetoed by Mr. Wright. Iovanna was cross with him and with Gene Masselink.

Iovanna's irritation with Gene and Mr. Wright was only a symptom of the schism that was developing within the Fellowship. It was more than just a question of cliques, though these also were present. Unlike previous schisms based on seniority and closeness to Mr. and Mrs. Wright, this one had a different base: it was a division between those who were in "movements" and those who weren't. It was between those whose primary interest was in architecture and who looked to Mr. Wright for leadership and those whose major interest lay elsewhere and was focused on "movements" and Mrs. Wright's interest in Gurdjieff and his teaching.

Those who were not participating in "movements" were a readily identifiable group. Those who were participating consisted of at least two groups. There were those who accepted "movements" simply as exercises in coordination and rhythm – they were participating because it was expected of them. But there was another group who regarded "movements" as something more, as an activity that would eventually lead to the possession of esoteric knowledge, a higher level of being, and increased spirituality. They acted as though their closeness to Mrs. Wright and Iovanna and now Kay was an indication that they were already well on their way to becoming superior beings.

Mr. Wright's calendar for October was filled with travel, and did not include a slot for a "demonstration" in memory of Gurdjieff on the date of his death. Planned were a trip to Cornell University for a lecture and to discuss the possibility of designing a house for the president of the university and a trip to Salt Lake City to meet with a group that wanted him to plan a small college for them. A week-long trip to Mexico City as the guest of honor at an October 19 meeting of the Pan-American Congress of Architects was also planned.[94] (The "Sixty Years of Living Architecture" exhibition, which had been shown in various cities in Europe, was also to open in Mexico City at this time.)

The migration to Arizona started early in November, but not as early as Mr. Wright had hoped. Mr. Wright was an active member of an honorary committee supporting Adlai Stevenson's campaign for the presidency. Some of us felt that we should stay in Wisconsin until after the election. Mr. Wright insisted that we could mail back our votes to Wisconsin. I was among the last to leave.

Early in the fall, Mr. Wright had traded in Gene's, Jack's, and Kenn's Hotshots for Hillmans. When Iovanna's M.G. was being traded for a Hillman, Wes

suggested that I ask Mr. Wright if I could have it. I told him that I wasn't interested in Iovanna's M.G. It had been poorly driven, and it already needed a second
set of bearings which I couldn't afford. John Hill's Hillman, not painted Cherokee red, arrived late in October; mine arrived a week later.

A few days after its delivery I started for Arizona with Kenn and Polly Lockhart and their son, Brian. Since my Hillman was not yet broken in I could not
travel over fifty miles an hour. We spent the first night at my parents' house, and
headed west for Denver the next morning.

Winter 1952–1953

Before the migration began, Mr. Wright said that there wasn't going to be much outside construction work that winter, that we were all going to work in the drafting room. There was not the customary period of tearing the camp apart. We settled down to work in the drafting room more quickly than usual. Something called "Stormy Weather" was brushed on the canvas roofs. It was tested by rain shortly after its application, and very little water came through. The drafting room became one of the pleasanter places to be in inclement weather.

During the winter Mrs. Wright started giving a series of weekly talks. The talks were taped by Bruce Pfeiffer and later transcribed. Mrs. Wright's book, *The Struggle Within,* published in 1955, is an edited compilation of these talks.

The talks were given in the middle of the week, in the evening after dinner, in the living room of Iovanna's apartment in the Sun Cottage. The group would assemble at about nine to wait for her arrival. She spoke for about an hour without notes and without much modulation in her voice, almost as though she were reading from a text. The mood was solemn; there was no discussion after she finished talking. I assumed that these evening meetings were patterned after evenings at Gurdjieff's Institute for the Harmonious Development of Man.

In addition to the usual small houses and the continuing revisions to the Guggenheim plans, there were two major projects in the drafting room that winter: the Price Tower and the first proposal for the Point View Residences for the Kaufmann Charitable Trust. I worked on both; but except for the time that was given to rehearsals – of chorus after breakfast, of the ensemble after lunch, and with the violinist John Amarantides – most of my time was devoted to the Price Tower. There was more pressure to get these drawings out.

We followed what had become customary procedure on larger projects. Jack Howe did the general plans and elevations. I did the small-scale sections and the larger-scale details. And Wes did the structural calculations and details. He was assisted by other apprentices who transferred the results of his calculations into the structural plans and details.

Charles Laughton, the actor, was in the Phoenix area during the last half of January. He had arrived a couple of weeks before the opening of the road show *John Brown's Body,* in which he was appearing. Early in this stay he came out to visit with Mr. Wright and to see the camp. During this visit he volunteered to give an evening of readings for the Fellowship. This evening of readings, from both serious and humorous literature, was so warmly received that he offered to give another. All together he gave us three evenings.[95]

In return Mr. Wright decided to give Laughton an overnight picnic at Schnebly Hill near Sedona. Preparations were made and on a Thursday afternoon, the first week in February, Uncle Vlado and an advance party went up to roast a lamb. The rest of the Fellowship, except for Mrs. Wright and several who chose to stay in camp with her, went up on Friday afternoon. We had the roast lamb that evening. After the repast we built up the fire, sat around its circle, and sang a good part of the chorus's repertoire. We spent the night there sleeping on the ground in our sleeping bags.

Mr. Wright, Laughton, Uncle Vlado, and Wes chose not to rough it; they went to a Sedona motel for the night and returned to the picnic spot the next morning for a breakfast of hamburgers cooked over an open fire. After breakfast we packed the cooking equipment in the pick-up, cleaned up the campsite, and started back to camp, returning by way of back-country roads. It was a day of delightful scenery, but not always delightful driving. Several of the cars were stuck in unexpected mud holes. It was my impression that this was not Laughton's idea of fun, but he was a good sport about it all.

In the middle of what had started as a pleasant and productive winter a tragic event occurred. During a quiet Sunday afternoon in the middle of February, Roger Pond, the 1½-year-old son of Bob and Ann Pond, was found floating face down in the triangular pool on the south side of the drafting room. No one knew how long he had been there. He had been playing in the apprentice court and had apparently wandered off to investigate this pool. Efforts at resuscitation were made but they were unsuccessful. Roger's death was a great blow to Bob and Ann and to the entire Fellowship.

I had become a close friend of Bob and Ann during the early part of that winter, largely through Roger. He was then a little over a year old. During the day he spent part of his time in a playpen in the apprentice court near Bob and Ann's room. He was a chipper and cheerful little character. I enjoyed seeing him and stopping to "chat" with him in going to and from my room on the apprentice court during the day.

Late in the afternoon, after the drowning, there was some feeling on the part of the Fellowship that we should not continue with our Sunday evening dinner and concert as though nothing had happened to interrupt our routine. But there was a mutual agreement between Mr. and Mrs. Wright and Bob and Ann that it would be better to continue, that being with the Fellowship would offer some support and comfort. The music that evening, some of Bob and Ann's favorites, took on new meaning and significance.

Bob and Kelly Oliver spent part of the next morning in the shop making a small redwood coffin. Late in the afternoon of the following day, the Fellowship assembled at the base of the hill, about a half mile from camp, where there was a large flat-topped pictograph rock. Ann had selected this spot. It was one of the places that she liked to walk to in the desert in the evening. It was higher than the camp and provided a wide sweeping view over the desert and to the western horizon. John Geiger and I had gone there in the morning to bring in more desert flowers and yet to try to leave the spot looking undisturbed. We took the little folding harmonium from the camp up to this spot for music. Bob and Ann had requested that the chorus sing the *Cherubim Hymn* and César Franck's *Panis Angelicus*. Gene sang the solo and John Amarantides, Brandoch and I played the accompaniment. Mr. Wright read a section of a Walt Whitman poem which Ann had selected. As we turned to walk back to camp, we faced the distant view and a setting sun.

This was an occasion when many in the Fellowship saw a Frank Lloyd Wright that they had never seen before, a side which was not congruent with the public image of the man. They saw that even at a time when Mr. Wright's own work was at a peak and making great demands on his time and energy, he could set it aside and give his support to those who needed it.

Toward the end of February Mr. Wright asked Kenn Lockhart to start making a three-eighths-inch scale model of the Price Tower. The Prices wanted the model to be displayed at a Petroleum Exposition in the middle of May, where they were going to announce their plans for building the tower. Kenn asked me to help with the model as I was familiar with the details of the tower. As a result I was splitting my time between work on the working drawings for the tower and the model of it. For this model I made replicas of all of the patterned copper panels with which the spandrel walls of alternate floors of the building are faced and of the panels between the spandrels that enclose the utility spaces on each floor. To make the patterned panels I made a three-eighths-inch drawing of the pattern. From this drawing Kenn had a machine shop in Phoenix make a steel die. With this die and an ordinary shop vise I proceeded to stamp, by hand, rows of the panels onto strips of thin sheet copper. These were then glued to the wood with which the model was being made. The panels for the utility rooms were made individually by scribing their pattern on the copper sheets.

The model was not quite finished in late April, when Joe Price came to take photos of it. While he was there, Mr. Wright left for a week-long trip to Salt Lake City and San Francisco.[96] He was unhappy with the appearance of the model when he left, but it was not clear to us just what was making him unhappy. The model was finally completed to his satisfaction after he returned. It was shipped off before we left for Wisconsin.

The working drawings of the tower were completed in mid-April but not without our calling on several other apprentices for help and an exhausting all-night session of drawing.

Summer 1953

I arrived at Taliesin in the middle of May, well after the advance party had opened the house and the Fellowship had resumed its daily pattern of activity. I settled into the room that John Geiger and I had shared the previous summer and fall and resumed my usual routine. I intended to complete the fireplace in my room this year.

During the last week in May, Mr. Wright went to New York to receive the National Institute of Arts and Letters Gold Medal for Architecture. He returned to Taliesin for the weekend and went back to New York on Monday of the next week for a hearing concerning an appeal for a building permit for the Guggenheim Museum. He was back at Taliesin the following weekend for the usual celebration of his birthday – a birthday breakfast with the Fellowship and the opening of the Birthday Box. It seemed that he was in New York City every other week during the summer.

We had not been in Wisconsin long before John Hill left Taliesin to go to New York to become the architecture editor of *House Beautiful*, replacing James Marston Fitch.[97] (John later became editorial director.) The leading article of the April issue of the magazine, entitled "The Threat to the Next America," had been, in effect, an attack on modern design and its leading proponents, the Bauhaus and the Museum of Modern Art. Elizabeth Gordon, the editor of the magazine, had joined forces with Mr. Wright in his war on the International Style. An article he had written in February attacking the International Style had been printed and mailed to those who had been receiving the series of Square Papers which, over time, he had written and published. A similar article by him was published in the June *Architectural Record* and in the July *House Beautiful*.

I was sorry to see John leave. He was one of my close friends in the Fellowship. I had enjoyed working with him on many projects and in participating with him in many of the Fellowship's activities. Mr. Wright was reluctant to let him go, but he was the person who had suggested to Elizabeth Gordon that John might be a good replacement for James Fitch. Mr. Wright explained that he was not losing an apprentice, but sending him to serve on another front.

Mr. Wright returned from one of his trips to New York with a new design in mind for the Point View Residences, the apartment building for the Kaufmann Charitable Trust. It was to contain twelve apartments as the prior scheme had, but this one was based on a triangular module. And although the first proposal had several apartments that occupied two floors, in this proposal all of the apartments, except the top one, which was a penthouse apartment for the Kaufmanns, were to occupy one complete floor. Presentation drawings were done and working drawings were started before the end of the month.[98] The drawings were nearing completion when Mr. Kaufmann decided not to proceed with construction. This decision came as something of a relief. Construction had started on the Price Tower and I was doing drawings, for changes and details.

In June the energy of the Fellowship began to go in two different directions, into two different activities, both of them major. One was Mr. Wright's plan to hold the "Italian exhibition" in a temporary building to be set up on the empty lot adjacent to the two buildings owned by the Guggenheim Foundation, the site of the future museum. The other was Mrs. Wright's plan to hold a "movements" demonstration in Chicago.

As I wrote to Marcus:

> He is determined to have an exhibition in NYC – as a part of the present war in Architectural circles between the "organic" and the "international." The frame work would be pipe, the covering plywood and corrugated glass. There is a small, full-size house included as a part of the scheme. I don't know exactly how he plans to finance it, except that U.S. Plywood seems willing to supply the plywood – for free. So I suppose there may be others.[99]

About a week later I wrote Bob and Ann Pond:

> I must admit that the more I hear of this "demonstration" the more fearful and wonderful it all becomes: special costumes, special sets to be designed by Gene and Wes – and approved by Mr. Wright, special lighting, special music. I first heard "eight harps – " then I heard "six harps – " alternating with yours truly. The Goodman Theater in the Art Institute as a possible place to have it. If not there then some other theater.... Etc. ... I must admit that it does sound a little exciting – and terrifying...and I suppose that if I was an Ardent "mover" it might seem the most wonderful thing in the world...but it doesn't seem the most wonderful thing in the world...because there are other things that seem more wonderful to me...things like a noble building...or perhaps exquisite music. But I don't always like to play the "spoil sport."[100]

Early in the summer Heloise Fichter Schweizer and I started working on costumes for the demonstration: she as designer, I as tailor/seamster. We set up a sewing machine in the unfinished "space for goats" at the west end of the Taliesin complex, beyond the chicken house and pens. And so, my day had one more fragment added to it: It began with cooking breakfast (it was my turn). Following breakfast, the chorus rehearsed. Then, when the majority of the Fellowship went to work in the garden, I went to Taliesin to practice cello with Brandoch, which meant making certain that he did his exercises, scales, and pieces with the proper fingering and also playing the piano accompaniment for the pieces. Then the violinist John Amarantides and I rehearsed for about an hour. After this I went out to the "goat pen" to work with Heloise for a while on the costumes for the demonstration, attempting to solve any constructional problems of cut and fit. This meant that I got to the drafting room at Hillside at about eleven o'clock, with the hope of getting in about an hour of work before lunch. Following lunch the ensemble rehearsed for about an hour. I could then get in about two hours of work in the drafting room before teatime. If Mr. Wright came into the drafting room after tea, I would stay and work until about six, leaving in time to shower and shave. Dinner was at seven. After dinner, two nights a week, there were "movement" rehearsals from eight o'clock until ten or so.

There was the usual flow of visitors during the summer. Llewellyn Wright and his family had come in late June. Helen, Lloyd Wright's wife, was there at the same time. There was one particular Sunday evening during their visit that had the atmosphere of a pleasant family gathering. I described this evening in a letter to Bob Pond written on June 28:

> The before dinner drinks in the Loggia created a pleasant frame of mind. . . . Mr. Wright entered (the living room) musing over the fact that after all we might as well face it: the "weaker sex" is actually the stronger sex and that men are only tolerated as an accessory to the continuation of the breed – the strutting and preening of the peacock, etc.
>
> After dinner Mr. Wright read a take off on Saroyan by Wolcott Gibbs, called SHAKESPEARE, HERE'S YOUR HAT. It was very funny – but the funniest thing about it was the way that Mr. Wright gets himself nearly in tears from laughing so that he is unable to read. . . . After that he read a little from Whitman. . . . And then into the music . . . [101]

On the Fourth of July Walter Bimson (Valley National Bank, Phoenix) and his wife arrived to stay overnight. Mr. Wright seemed to regard the Bimsons' visit as a special occasion. I wrote the Ponds concerning this:

> I don't quite understand this. Bimson certainly doesn't seem inclined to build any design of Mr. Wright's (of which we have made several) but perhaps he rates as a "patron of the Arts" [I seemed to be ignoring the fact that Bimson was Mr. Wright's banker in Phoenix] and as a big wheel in Phoenix. So we've done some sprucing up

around the place. . . . All of which is to the good . . . some corners have gotten cleaned that might otherwise have been missed for another year . . . not that there aren't plenty of corners that still need taking care of . . .[102]

During the last weekend in August, after Sunday morning breakfast with the Fellowship, Mr. Wright went to the drafting room and asked to see the drawings Jack Howe had done for the house that was to be erected as a part of the exhibition on the Guggenheim site in New York. He sat down at his desk and proceeded to make changes in the design. When he finished working on the drawings he asked me and John Geiger to make the revisions to the drawings. He wanted prints to be made and sent to New York early the next morning. John and I spent a very intense afternoon erasing and redrawing. As we worked we realized that what had been a rather routine house had been changed into an exceptional one. The general layout of the plan had not been changed, but the overall form had been simplified, strengthened, and given a nobility that it had lacked. Much of this was due to changes in the living room, the major space of the house.

Unfortunately, as was true of many such revisions of Mr. Wright's work, no record of the changes survive. John and I did not make another set of drawings, nor did we make prints before starting work. As we erased and redrew we eliminated any record of the previous house, including Mr. Wright's work on the drawings. What remained was the result of the changes and not a record of the changes themselves. While we were working on the drawings we encountered many questions about how details should be handled, questions which we did not have time to resolve that afternoon. Faced with the lack of time, we jokingly suggested that "they" could figure this out in New York. We didn't realize that within three weeks both of us would be in New York to help with the construction of the house and the temporary pavilion, and with the setting up of the exhibition.

On Saturday of the first weekend in September, Mr. Wright returned to Taliesin from one of his many trips to New York that summer. He was quite pleased with the progress being made on the house and the temporary building, which were being constructed by David Henken.[103] He said that the exhibition was to open on September 20.[104] The walls of the house were going up in red Brikcrete. The walls, ceilings, and floors of the house were to be oak plywood. All of it – as much as he wanted – was being supplied by U.S. Plywood. The exhibition material, last shown in Mexico City, was on the dock in New York and awaiting unpacking.

Mr. Wright returned from this trip with plans to send some apprentices to New York to help with the construction and to set up the exhibition. He told Kenn Lockhart and Tom Casey that they were to go. This started an argument with Mrs. Wright. She did not want anyone who was going to be in the "movements" demonstration in Chicago to go. It was now definite that this was going to be held at the Goodman Theater on November 2 and 3.

Kenn Lockhart and Tom Casey left for New York on Tuesday afternoon. They were going to remodel the Guggenheim Museum model, to bring it up to date. Later the same week John Geiger, Robin Molny, and Morton Delson were also on their way to New York. They went in the Fellowship's station wagon. On September 18, Mr. Wright returned from another trip to New York.[105] He then said that the exhibition was to open a week from the coming Tuesday, on September 29. On Monday morning John Rattenbury and I were told that we should get ready to go to New York. We were put on a plane that afternoon.

With our arrival in New York there were now seven apprentices there. A week after our arrival Kenn Lockhart and Tom Casey went back to Taliesin to prepare for the demonstration. At about the same time, Mrs. Wright called me and asked me to tell Mr. Wright that I wanted to return to Taliesin to help with the music for the demonstration. I was not to tell him that she had asked me to do this. I told her I couldn't do this, that if the exhibition was to open when planned it was more important that I remain in New York. Before the exhibition was finally to open, another six apprentices were sent to help: Kelly Oliver, Edward Thurman, Jim Pfefferkorn, George Thompson, David Wheatley, and Herbert de Levie.

Our workday in New York had a strange pattern. We would get up in the morning, dress in our street clothes, have breakfast in the hotel coffee shop, and go to the Guggenheim site. We had a work area in the street level floor of the fourteen-story apartment building, which then stood at the northeast corner of 88th Street and Fifth Avenue. This room had been an exhibition space when Hilla Rebay was the director of what was then called the Museum of Non-Objective Art. The two lower floors of the town house, the next door north of the apartment building, was being used as the Guggenheim Gallery, then under the direction of James Johnson Sweeney.

Arriving at the site, we changed into our work clothes and started work. At the beginning we could not work outside on the construction site; the carpenters, members of the union, would not work if we were on the job. Some of the models that needed repairing had been brought from the dock to the site, as well as some of the exhibition panels. Since we could not work outside on the job when the union was there, we worked, at first, inside in this temporary shop. We were prefabricating parts which were to go into the house.

We would work inside until lunchtime, then change into street clothes and go to lunch. A delicatessen, nearby on Madison Avenue, seemed to receive most of our business. However, I do remember one occasion when all of this somewhat motley crew went to lunch with Mr. Wright at a nearby Schrafft's. I use the words "motley crew" because in that fashionable neighborhood a group of Taliesin apprentices with their long hair and their notion of "street clothes" was an unfamiliar sight.

After lunch we would change back into our work clothes and work inside until teatime. After tea, we would go out on the site to work, since the union carpenters stopped work at that time. The union did not seem to work an eight-hour day. They started work at about nine and quit before four, taking an hour for lunch. We worked outside until dinnertime. Dinnertime got later and later after we had rigged up some lights so that we could continue to work after dark.

At the end of the day we changed into street clothes again and went to the hotel to clean up for dinner. During the month or more that I was in New York City we tried a great variety of eating places. Some of the time, John Hill, who was then an editor for *House Beautiful,* would join us. Very often, Bill Short, who was with Holden and McLaughlin's office and who was "piloting" this project as well as the Guggenheim Museum through the unfamiliar waters of New York City building codes and regulations, was our "pilot in" seeking out places to eat.[106] Betsey Barton joined us for dinner occasionally.[107] One Sunday evening a few of us had dinner with Mr. Wright at the Oak Room in the Plaza Hotel. And there was one evening when the more senior members of our group went to Betsey Barton's father's town house in the East Fifties for drinks and then out to dinner.

Eventually our practice of working on the site after the unions had left and late into the night began to wear down the union's opposition to our working on the site while they were there. We were soon working alongside members of the union – and doing more work. We also eroded the city's regulations against noise and working on Sundays. The policemen on the beat seemed to have a great interest in our activity. They did come by in the evening and on Sundays a few times to chat and to ask that we keep the noise down. Apparently someone living in the apartments on the three sides of the site had complained. Many of the people who lived in the vicinity displayed a great curiosity about our activity.

Progress on the construction of the building was delayed several times by tests and changes required by the city's building codes. Originally Mr. Wright had thought that the temporary building would be enclosed with plywood and have strip skylights of translucent corrugated plastic. To conform with the building code it was first proposed that the plywood be replaced with corrugated cemesto panels. In actual construction this became 1½-inch-thick, four-by-eight insulated cemesto panels. The proposed skylights of corrugated plastic were replaced with corrugated wire glass following a fire test required by the city. In this test the reputedly fire-resistant plastic panels burned quite merrily. The supporting structure of the temporary building was constructed of stock, pipe-scaffolding members and connectors (Fig. 98). After a test loading of the structure, required by the city, some of the structural members were doubled, particularly those supporting the roof and skylight panels. The roof structure had deflected considerably during the loading, but to our surprise it sprang back into shape when the loading was removed.

One of the questions we encountered during the work on the exhibition was "Who is Mr. Wright's public relations agent?" The questioners would not believe that he did not have one. The forthcoming exhibition had been receiving much

98   The interior of the north end of the exhibition pavilion about a week before the exhibit was to open. Photo by Pedro E. Guerrero.

publicity in the magazines and newspapers and on radio and television. The Guggenheim model had been taken to a television studio for an appearance by Mr. Wright. He had been interviewed by Jinx Falkenburg for her radio show. People familiar with public relations activity would simply not believe that he did not have an agent – and a very good one.

About a week before the exhibition was scheduled to open, Oscar Stonorov appeared on the site ready to install it. He had designed the exhibit and supervised its installation in Philadelphia and at the other sites at which it had been shown. He was dismayed to find the building still incomplete. Several nights later Stonorov and Sweeney, the director of the museum, showed up. This was only a few days before the press opening. They asked me when we were going to install the exhibit. There was still work being done on the building. Having since seen the more leisurely and carefully studied ways in which museum exhibitions are installed, I can now understand their concern. At that time, I heard their question as simply added pressure on me and the others from Taliesin, who were, by then, after longer and longer working days, reaching exhaustion.

99   The interior of the south end of the pavilion after an arched opening was cut in the north wall of the town house in which the museum was then housed. The opening was cut to make an entrance into the exhibition pavilion. Photo by Pedro E. Guerrero.

During our weeks of work on the exhibition pavilion and the house it had become increasingly evident that the exhibition was being held without the museum director's full and enthusiastic cooperation. A clear example of this occurred on the Saturday before the opening. Mr. Wright wanted the entrance to the exhibition to be through the entrance hall of the town house whose two lower floors served as galleries for the museum. Mr. Sweeney was resisting this. It meant knocking an opening through the north wall of the town house and installing a fire door at the opening. And to Sweeney's annoyance it meant the noise and debris of knocking a hole in a thick brick wall. Mr. Wright was there on the job early Saturday morning. He had the arched opening that he wanted laid out on the wall. A jackhammer crew and its equipment were there ready to break through the opening. By late afternoon the opening had been made and the fire door installed, and the cleanup of the debris was under way (Fig. 99). Mr. Wright seemed to know whom to call and what levers to push to get things done.

100   The northeast corner of the living room of the exhibition house, seen here from near the entrance to the house. Dining area is at right of photo. Ezra Stoller © Esto.

On the Sunday morning before the opening of the exhibition, John Hill came to the site and told me that Mrs. Wright wanted to see me that afternoon at his apartment. I met her there, and after some polite conversation she and I went in a cab to the Plaza Hotel. In one room of their suite in the hotel, she again asked me to tell Mr. Wright that I wanted to return with her to Taliesin so that I could take over the organizing and conducting of the music for the demonstration that Bruce had been working on during the summer. From her statements I gathered that somehow the music was not going well. During our conversation, such as it was, I told her that I would not go back to Taliesin until the exhibition was open.

A few days before the preview for the press, Mr. Wright began to install the exhibition and to supervise the furnishing and decoration of the exhibition house (Fig. 100). He directed the placement of the eight-by-eight-foot panels of large photos of buildings and drawings and the placement of the models on their specially made model stands. He marked out with his cane, on the asphalt floor of the Pavilion, the shape of areas around the panels which he wanted filled with gravel. (The "Pavilion," as the temporary building was referred to, was built on an area that had been paved for a parking lot.) And he indicated where he wanted the pots of ferns, chrysanthemums, and other greenery to be placed in these

101   Mr. Wright at the Steinway grand which he had placed at the north end of the pavilion. Photo by Pedro E. Guerrero.

gravel areas. He borrowed a small Calder mobile from the Guggenheim collection and had it hung from a corner of the roof of the house near the entrance to the exhibition house. He borrowed two massive stone Chinese lions from a dealer in fine Oriental art which were placed in the pavilion, one near the entrance to the house. And he convinced the Steinway Piano Company that it should loan him a concert grand which he had placed on a low platform which was built at the north end of the pavilion (Fig. 101). The purpose of the grand piano intrigued me. Was Mr. Wright going to sit down and improvise at odd moments as he did at Taliesin? Was he going to perform some of the pieces he remembered from his childhood? Were there to be formal concerts? Or some sort of soirees by musicians who might happen to come to see the exhibition? I still do not know the answer to the puzzle of the piano's presence.

Work on the installation continued until the moment on Wednesday evening of October 21 when people began to arrive for the press opening. There was still more to be done before the formal opening on Friday evening, the 23rd.

On the evening of the press opening Mrs. Wright informed me that she had tickets for the two of us to return to Taliesin the following afternoon. Wes and Gene met us at the Madison airport. We arrived at Taliesin a little after nine o'clock. Since I was exhausted from the previous weeks of intense work, I went directly to my room and to bed.

The next morning, after breakfast, I encountered Brandoch in the courtyard outside my room. He indicated that he had not been practicing the cello very consistently during my absence. We went into the living room of Wes's apartment to resume his practicing. While I was working with Brandoch, Mrs. Wright came in and furiously demanded to know what I was doing. I probably muttered the obvious reply, that I was working with Brandoch, whereupon she asked why I wasn't working on the music for the demonstration. Why hadn't I been up all night working on the music like Bruce and John A.? I have no idea what my response to that question was, but I do know that at that point I lost my temper too.

During the remainder of that week and into the next, I lived like a person in quarantine, in semi-isolation. Though I ate my meals with the Fellowship, I felt like I was caught behind enemy lines. The apprentices who had been in New York returned toward the end of the following week. I assume that I must have resumed work in the drafting room with Jack Howe – when he could be spared from preparation for the demonstration. Early the next week Gene and Wes approached me and suggested that I apologize to Mrs. Wright. In my mind I had no reason to apologize. But they finally convinced me that I should do this, so I went through the motions of an apology.

Although conditions continued to be strained, I was asked and did begin to play the piano for "movement" rehearsals. Several people who dared to speak to me commented that they were glad I was playing for rehearsals again. It seemed that when Bruce was playing he wouldn't – or didn't – stick to a steady beat, that his beat was erratic and threw their concentration and movements off.

Toward the end of the week I heard, through Gene, who was my means of communication with Mrs. Wright and the group, that it had been arranged for Arthur Zak, the conductor of the Rockford, Illinois, symphony orchestra, to conduct the orchestra for the demonstration. Mr. Zak came to Taliesin on November 1. That afternoon, in order to give him an idea of the music, I played the piano for a run-through of the complete program of "movements" for the demonstration.

On Monday afternoon I drove to Chicago in my Hillman and checked into the hotel, north of the river, where the group was staying. That evening, Mr. Wright took several of the seniors, Mrs. Wright, and Iovanna to dinner at the Cliff Dwellers Club. I was included. The next morning I walked down to the Goodman Theater for a sketchy dress rehearsal with the orchestra.

The matinee performance was the first and only full dress rehearsal.[108] During the break between the two sections of the program, I played Gurdjieff's "Great Prayer" as a piano solo.

That evening the program was repeated to what appeared to be a full house.

For both performances the orchestra was in formal dress; I wore the black velvet jacket Mr. Wright had given me the previous year. He had gotten himself a new black velvet jacket.

If there were any reviews of the performance in the press I did not stay to see them. I left Chicago the next morning. When I returned to Taliesin about two weeks later, I found that most of the Fellowship had left for Arizona.

My state of mind at that time is best understood by a letter I wrote to Marcus Weston:

> Frankly, I'm in no hurry to get to Arizona – I'm going to have to cultivate some new friends – or be a "lone wolf" – this winter. Last winter I depended on Johnnie Hill, John Geiger, and the Ponds for most of my pleasant associations. Johnnie is in New York, now. John Geiger is there now and for the duration of Mr. Wright's show – which threatens to be extended – and even then I'm not sure that Geiger will return to Taliesin. Between you and me – he has about had his fill of the "soul searching" establishment that we are turning into – via "movements" etc. I don't go along with it – in spite of the fact that I am useful to it. And since "soul-searching" is waxing here and "Architecture" is waning, I wonder just what my status is going to be. . . . You see Mr. Wright's philosophy and Mrs. Wright's do not mix. As near as I can tell they are in direct opposition. The division of the effort of the Fellowship into two camps regarding Mr. Wright's show in New York – and Mrs. Wright's show in Chicago is an example of this. Mrs. Wright was strongly opposed to Mr. Wright's having the show in New York. But the show in Chicago was only possible through the fact that Mr. Wright was in New York – allowing them the time necessary to rehearse, make the costumes, etc. Outside of the show in New York – and the show in Chicago – very little was accomplished here this summer. The theater at Hillside is still unfinished – and at the present rate will not be finished until sometime next summer.[109]

Winter 1953–1954

I left Taliesin early on Sunday morning, November 22, and drove to my parents' home in Stanberry, Missouri. Wes and the Lockharts were to meet me there on Tuesday. As things developed my parents, Kenn and Polly, Brian and Leslie, Wes and Brandoch, and I had Thanksgiving dinner with my sister and her family at their house. After Thanksgiving dinner we left for Arizona.

Kenn and Polly had seen the little house that Mr. Wright had designed for Dr. Miller in Charles City, Iowa. They had suggested that the Millers send photos of the house to Mr. Wright. Shortly after we arrived in Arizona, Mr. Wright received the photos. He was delighted with the house; it was "just what he would have done himself" (this was a reference to the series of stone terraces, steps, and walls leading down to a boat dock on the Cedar River, which the Millers had designed and built by themselves). Mr. Wright included many photos of this house in his book *The Natural House,* published in 1954.

For me, all this enthusiasm for the house had an ironic quality. Originally, Dr. Miller and his son, both dentists, wanted two houses connected by their dental office. They had received the preliminary sketches before the war. During the war they had built this elaborate bit of stonework and had started other landscaping. After the war, and after much waiting, they had finally received their working drawings. I had the impression from comments in the drafting room that there was not much interest in the Millers or their project. But the Millers were persistent. The son had done most of the carpentry and had built the furniture. It had all been done with care. And as a result, "we" were delighted – willing to claim credit – and a little baffled by those uninteresting people who, somehow, hadn't seemed equal to – or capable of – a Frank Lloyd Wright house.

The drafting room was a busy place that winter. Soon after I arrived in Arizona I was dividing my time between finishing the working drawings for the second design for the Point View Residences for the Kaufmanns and doing revisions and supplementary drawings for the Price Tower. Wes was spending much time in Bartlesville. In early January the foundations were up to sidewalk level. The working drawings for the apartments were finished early in January and prints were sent to the Kaufmanns. A few weeks later, when Mr. Wright returned from one of his many trips to New York, he reported that the Kaufmanns were pleased with the drawings.

During the winter, Mr. Wright continued to make revisions in the drawings for the Guggenheim Museum. He was hoping to get the plans approved so that construction could start in the spring. I was doing some work on these drawings. On December 11, 1953, I wrote Bob Pond:

> The Guggenheim Museum is undergoing another treatment with erasers and scissors. Everything that was along the back property line is being eliminated: the Historical gallery; the caretakers apartment and the storage rooms. The whole building is being moved back on the lot. And the broad band that extended across the front is being lengthened. The whole design is being much improved by this process of elimination. Too many things were going on before.

Later that winter Harry Guggenheim, chairman of the board of directors of the Guggenheim Foundation, came to the camp with James Johnson Sweeney, the director of the museum who had replaced Hilla Rebay after Solomon Guggenheim's death. They came to make a proposal to Mr. Wright that he design another museum based on Sweeney's conception of what a museum should be. Mr. Wright would be paid his full fee for the museum he designed for the previous director, as well as for the new design which was to replace it. Mr. Wright rejected this proposal. He insisted that Solomon Guggenheim, though dead, was his client and that he was going to build the design that had been approved and accepted by Solomon.

In mid-January, after I finished work on the Kaufmann apartments, I started the working drawings of a house for Mr. Wright's son Llewellyn and his family. Mr. Wright had designed the house the previous fall. Llewellyn wanted to start construction in the spring. I had finished the drawings by February 11. This was a house that I enjoyed doing the drawings for; I liked the house and I liked Llewellyn and his family. His children had spent several summers at Taliesin. The boys had played in the ensemble. I described the house in a letter to George Beal as "a simple house – if you will admit that a house consisting of arcs of circles can be simple."[110]

While I was still working on the drawings for Llewellyn's house, Mr. Wright did the design for a winter home in Arizona for Mr. and Mrs. H. C. Price, Sr. Mrs. Price insisted from the start that it be a "grandma house."

Before the Prices asked Mr. Wright to do this house for them, he had made a sketch of another house, for no one in particular, in answer to the question "How to live in the Southwest." It was a small, flat-roofed house, with an open but roofed-over living space, which he labeled a "patio," as its major feature. The patio had an enclosed bedroom wing on one side. And offset on the opposite side was an enclosed space for living, dining, and cooking. It was a concept that interested me very much – that of a house in which activities could be contracted into a smaller space in unfavorable weather or expanded into a larger space in fair weather, when neither heating nor cooling is required. This idea became the basis for the Prices' "grandma house."

When the preliminary drawings for the Grandma House were completed in mid-February, Mr. Wright started work on the design for the synagogue for the Beth Sholom congregation in Elkins Park, Pennsylvania. He had received this commission in December. By early January it was clear that he had a concept for this building in mind, but he was not yet ready to put it on paper. When he did put it on paper he indicated that it was not fixed in size, that it could be adapted to different sizes of congregations. On February 22 I wrote Bob Pond:

> Mr. Wright is still designing the Synagogue. It seems that they have about $500,000 to spend on the building – not including the furnishing. And Mr. Wright seems to think that they will get more if necessary. It's getting to be an interesting design. A rather richly surfaced triangular pyramid of copper and glass coming out of a base that is six-sided – but not hexagonal – the corner angles are not all equal – although it is symmetrical about an axis. Does this sound beautifully clear to you? . . . It's hard to describe. And even Jack has had difficulty finding out what shape and form it is – but it seems to be coming along to everyone's satisfaction now. . . . Otherwise . . . work in the drafting room is centered on the Museum.

I did some work on the preliminary drawings for the synagogue, most of it on the development of the site plan. These drawings were finished in mid-March.

When the presentation drawings for the synagogue were completed, Mr. Wright did a design for a house for Harold Price, Jr., and his growing family. It was to be built in Bartlesville, Oklahoma, on land near his parents' home. The working drawings for this house were started and completed before the spring migration to Wisconsin. During the winter, Mr. Wright had also done designs for several small houses and for an auto showroom for Jaguar cars for Max Hoffman. It was to be built inside the ground floor corner of a building on Fifth Avenue near Lever House. Essentially an "interior decoration job," it had a circular mirror on the ceiling over a shallow ramp for the display of cars.

There was one other project that winter in which Mr. Wright had a great interest and into which he put much time and energy. This was the showing of the "Sixty Years of Living Architecture" exhibition in Los Angeles.

The exhibition in New York had been very well attended and its showing had been extended into December. John Geiger was part of the group sent to New York to help build the pavilion and to install the exhibition. Mr. Wright had asked him to stay on as a caretaker for the exhibition and for the pavilion, and so he had remained in New York after the other apprentices had returned to Wisconsin. This temporary building had been conceived as a fair-weather building, not for winter weather. And with its extended use into the winter, problems had developed.

When the exhibition finally closed, John oversaw its being packed into shipping crates and forwarded to Los Angeles. The major question was the cost of shipping the exhibition across the country and installing it in Los Angeles – between $16,000 and $20,000.

In mid-February, there was some talk that the Los Angeles exhibition might not be held. But a few days later it was definitely on. John Geiger, still in New York, flew to Minneapolis to pick up his car, then drove to Arizona, and from there went on to Los Angeles.

On March 6 I wrote Marcus Weston:

> John Geiger has come and gone on to Los Angeles to supervise the installation of the exhibition there. Mr. Wright seems to be maintaining a very definite hands off policy there. Luckily there is no house to build there – the Pavilion to house the exhibition is being built in conjunction with the Barnsdahl Residence on Olive Hill. The Park Dept. of L.A. now owns Olive Hill – but they are permitting the Art Dept. to use the Residence – and the pavilion is being built as a "permanent" structure for use in other exhibitions. A sort of toe-hold for a museum, since L.A. has no museum.
>
> It's going to have a welded pipe frame – none of the clamps as in New York. It is going to have Corrulux – where the N.Y. pavilion had glass – but it's still cemesto. The section of the building is in general the same except that it is a narrower room – only about 24 feet – but longer.

The exhibition opened on June 1.

There was not much outside work on construction during the winter, except for what was largely instigated by Mrs. Wright and the "movements" group: one was Mrs. Wright's new room; the other was the beginning of a "movements temple," sometimes referred to as a theater. This new room for Mrs. Wright was built at the east end of the family's quarters. Its design and construction contributed to my growing concern about the future of the Fellowship. In my December 11 letter to Bob Pond I wrote:

> Mrs. Wright's room is finished now, although some little fussing is still going on in there. It's finished like a house – not a part of the camp. The walls are plastered and painted; the ceilings are mahogany plywood; the cabinet work is mahogany plywood. It has real wood sash and doors – with glass – no canvas. It has carpeting all over, cork floor in bathroom. All very finished. But somehow it does not seem like a room of Mr. Wright's. Too many architects on the job.
>
> As I've now learned it was a "committee" design. When I arrived in camp, according to remarks, Mr. Wright was being simply horrid, changing things,

etc. . . . Now I've learned the reason. And all of the other architects should have known why. . . . Mr. Wright had laid out the plan so that there were three pairs of full length glass doors. The "committee" while he was gone decided that more protection was needed around the fireplace so they eliminated one of the pairs of doors and replaced it with masonry – leaving Mr. Wright, the architect, with two pairs of doors on either side of a central mullion. Keeping the center open is lesson "A" in architecture. Faced with a central mullion "which he couldn't take" he started changing things to try and save the day. He had to eliminate the central mullion – and in order to do it had to revise the roof framing which is exposed. And yet when I arrived here it seemed – from reports – that Mr. Wright was simply being nasty and changing things without rhyme or reason. I would have thought that the "committee" might have understood the reasons for his changes. Something so basically wrong – architecturally – simply couldn't be allowed to remain. As a result the room does not still feel right – and it isn't right. It is dark where the extra pair of doors would have made for more light. It seems unsettled and restless . . . and all that it needs is wall paper to make it seem like a real imitation.

The other construction project of the winter was the "movements" theater. Early in the winter, Jack had drawn a plan and section based on a sketch Mr. Wright had made, but these drawings did not represent what "the group" wanted. In my December 11 letter to Bob Pond I also wrote:

Today Dick Carney and Steve (Oyakawa) were in the drafting room worrying about the design of the Theater. It seems that what is really wanted is a duplicate of the stage of the Goodman Theater in Chicago: lighting, cyclorama, curtains and all. Mr. Wright's sketches do not include this – except in equivalent area. The stage is to occupy most of – about two-thirds – the present badminton courts. The seating is on the sloping ground toward the mountains – a stepped up floor with seats for about 200 people. I'm rather alternately amused and irritated by this project. Construction hasn't started yet, but the "group" is eager to start now that Mrs. Wright's room is complete.

About a month later, on January 13 – and in the same state of mind – I wrote to Marcus Weston:

Right now work outside is involved with starting construction on a "movements" Temple. They are just getting started on the pouring of walls, piers, etc. . . . The whole building isn't going to be that large . . . and it doesn't have a stage just like the Goodman Theater. . . . But they do want it arranged so that they can have performances. . . . It is right here that I begin not to understand the whole point and purpose of "movements." A strange mixture of "theater" and "religion." . . . And yet supposedly – it pertains to "inner" development. Now the "inner" life cannot be "demonstrated" on a stage – at least not as they comprehend it – or as I understand that they think of it.

A religion doesn't think of itself in terms of "performers" and "audience" – not even the Catholic Mass with all of its "drama" is conceived in these terms. There is no "audience" – they are all participants. . . . But I suppose that in this strange disjointed age anything is possible. . . . Tourists go to watch the Indians dance – their dances are at least partly religious in nature. . . . I suppose that the "tourists" can come to Taliesin to watch the Fellowship dance – with Iovanna playing the role of the little white priestess. . . . But I will never understand making a public exhibition of one's religion. . . . Hardly even in a Church – and never in a Theater – even if it's called a "temple."

The division of the Fellowship into two groups, which the two "shows" – one in New York and one in Chicago – had made evident, continued during the winter. My relation to Mrs. Wright was, on the surface, civil. But beneath that surface it was unsettled and strained. My attitude toward her was not improved by several brief conversations that I had with her during the winter. In one she told me that the Fellowship, as it then existed, was only a scaffolding for what it was to become after Mr. Wright's death. I was bothered by her suggestion that the Fellowship could be something more without Mr. Wright than it was with him. To me, he and his work were the heart of the Fellowship.

In another exchange she told me that I should work more closely with her, that she could be of help to me in improving my effectiveness in the drafting room, and that it was important to improve my work there since "architecture was how we made our living." I was disturbed by the idea that "architecture was how we made our living," and that those of us working in the drafting room were "making a living" for the "movements" groups. I was not inclined to try to explain to her that I thought architecture was our life, not how we made our living. It was certainly Mr. Wright's life; it was not how he made his living. In working with Mr. Wright, it had become clear to me that he was, in effect, "possessed" by architecture in much the same way that any genius is "possessed" by his work. As John Hill's father had once observed, Mr. Wright had a compulsion to build and would be building even if he had no clients and if he had only mud and sticks to build with.

Made aware that Mrs. Wright was beginning to make plans for the future of the Fellowship, I also became alert to instances in which Mrs. Wright seemed to be making an effort to move out of her prior role in the Fellowship, that of directing the domestic and household dimension of Fellowship life by deciding in which rooms guests should stay, which people should live where, who should be the cooks and kitchen helpers, what the menu should be, etc., and to exercising more control over other aspects of our lives. Mr. Wright's increasing age – he was now eighty-six – and his deep involvement in several major projects – the museum, the Price Tower, the synagogue, and several large houses – appeared to provide her with this opportunity. The instances I remember were in themselves trivial, but they began to add up.

The Fellowship had its usual mixture of guests on Saturday and Sunday evenings during the winter: Willem Dudok, the Dutch architect, visited Taliesin West before I arrived in Arizona. I was sorry that I had missed his visit. As a student, I had been very interested in his work, particularly in his Hilversum Town Hall. Edward Everett Horton, who was acting in a play at the Sombrero Playhouse, came out one evening; so did Grady Gammage, president of Arizona State Teachers College and his wife; Anne Baxter, Mr. Wright's granddaughter, who was visiting David Wright and his wife at their new house, came one afternoon and stayed for dinner. (Mr. Wright was obviously pleased with and proud of his granddaughter and her success.) She was followed by Arch Oboler and his secretary; they showed up in a blue Volkswagen bus. Arch had come to discuss the addition of a larger and more luxurious living room to his Gate House, which was gradually to become his house. He had brought with him his latest movie, which he insisted on showing to Mr. Wright. Called *The Twonky,* it was something about a visitor from outer space who was masquerading as a television set. And Karsch, the photographer, was there on a Sunday evening and came back on two of the following days. Mr. Wright was hoping for a photo to replace the cigarette-in-mouth and the cigarette-in-hand photos which had been available. He no longer smoked, but more importantly he had received a letter from a mother whose son had cited Mr. Wright as his model when she had protested her son's smoking.

Toward the end of March a crew of photographers with moviemaking equipment spent a week following Mr. Wright around. They were hoping to get casual pictures of Mr. Wright as he went about his work. They photographed the camp and Fellowship activities at various times of the day. I spent a morning playing sections of Beethoven's piano sonatas on the living room piano which they recorded for background sound. They shot a great deal of footage, but we saw only a brief cutting of this at Taliesin the following summer. That seemed to be the end of that project.

A few weeks after the photographers left, the annual migration began. My trip was uneventful.

Summer 1954

By the first of June we were fairly well settled in Wisconsin – "as settled as we ever get" – and work in the drafting room was under way. The frequent trips Mr. Wright had made during the winter continued into the summer. These began at the end of May when he went to Detroit for a lecture. From there he went to Los Angeles for the opening of the "Sixty Years of Living Architecture" exhibit, and then back to the east coast to receive an honorary degree at Yale, to Philadelphia to give a lecture, and to New York where he was to meet Mrs. Wright and Iovanna. They were back at Taliesin for his birthday on June 8.

Mrs. Wright had encouraged the apprentices to do designs for wallpapers, fabrics, and furniture for the Birthday Box. It seemed that Mr. Wright had an agreement with a few producers that he would do such designs. But confronted with a backlog of architectural work – mostly small houses – he was not finding, or taking, the time to do them. Some apprentices did try their hand at doing such designs, but these did not generate much interest or enthusiasm from Mr. Wright.

I did a design for what was essentially a one-room residence for a single person. It consisted of one large football-shaped living room placed at one side of a circular court which also contained a small plunge pool. The court was surrounded by a low masonry wall. Spaces for cooking, sleeping, dressing, and bathing were sequestered at one side under a low, flat roof. Over the living room was an inverted orange-peel shaped roof. I had inverted this roof as a flippant gesture. I wanted to know just how Mr. Wright would respond. His response was negative and indicated – more by what he didn't say than by what he did say – that he knew he was being tested.

There were about seventy people in the Fellowship at the beginning of the summer. Finding places for all of them to live was becoming a problem. People were living in five or six different places: at Taliesin; at Hillside; in the house and the barn apartment at Midway; at Tanyderi and in Mrs. Porter's cottage; at Aldebaran, Wes's farm; and at "River House." The last was the house in which Glenn and Ruth Richardson had lived when they operated the Bridge service station and cafe. Mr. Wright had bought this property and was making plans to build a restaurant there.

Soon after getting settled in the drafting room we revised the working drawings for Harold Price, Jr.'s, house. Haskell Culwell, who was building the Price Tower, had made an estimate of the cost of the house. It was $100,000 more than the $150,000 which Harold Jr. wanted to spend. The major revisions were in the construction of the floors and roofs. These had been designed to be concrete, poured in place. They were changed to wood framing.

When we finished these revisions we started the drawings for the Grandma House for the Prices, which was to be built near the Paradise Valley golf course. It was the only house designed during the past winter that was a new concept. It was going to be a "palatial affair – only about 240 feet long." There was a certain "classic simplicity" in its design. The exterior walls were to be built of standard concrete block and to have steel window sash and doors with a two-foot-high glass transom above them. The interior partitions were to be mahogany plywood. The roof was to be framed with steel beams that supported ceiling panels of "Tectum." (This was a roof deck material consisting of wood fiber and a cement binder used in industrial buildings.) Over this deck a layer of insulating concrete was to be poured. I did all of the sections, both small and large scale, and all of the detailing. In detailing the steel sash and doors with the transoms above I got a certain satisfaction out of working out details, which Mr. Wright approved, based on the use of the manufacturer's stock sections. Haskell Culwell started construction of this house soon after the drawings were completed.

Off and on during the summer I did supplementary drawings for the Price Tower, "trying to keep ahead of construction" – such things as quarter full-size details of the stamped copper spandrels, the bronze plaques in the center of each floor of the tower, and the slender, copper sheathed columns which help to support the roof over the carports of the apartments.

We did not start working drawings for the synagogue in Philadelphia until after the middle of August. Part of the slowness and difficulty in doing the drawings for the synagogue stemmed from the fact that it was not designed on a unit system as had been all of the other buildings by Mr. Wright on which I had worked. In the previous buildings, all dimensions were established by the unit system. All exterior and interior walls were located in plan in relation to a unit system. And in many projects, vertical dimensions – in elevations and section – were also determined by a unit system. For example, in the Grandma House for the Prices, the horizontal and the vertical units were determined by the use of concrete block. These unit lines, in addition to being shown in the small-scale plans and elevations and sections, were also shown in the larger-scale details in order for the location of all components of the detail to be clearly understood.

Mr. Wright's first sketches for the synagogue and the subsequent development drawings and presentation drawings had not included a unit system. Nor did we, in starting the working drawings, attempt to establish one. As a result, much of the time I spent on these drawings was devoted to working out three-dimensional trigonometry problems. These were done to locate certain critical points and the baselines connecting these points. For example: the legs of the "tri-pod," the main structural element of the glass and metal superstructure, when seen in an elevation of one side of the basic triangle of the plan, appeared to be at an angle of sixty degrees with the horizontal. But the legs themselves, when seen in a direct elevation, were not at a sixty-degree angle.

The drawings for the synagogue had not been finished when I left for Arizona early in November. Mr. Wright went to Philadelphia in mid-November for a ceremonial ground-breaking, confident that the drawings would soon be finished.

I also worked on drawings for several small houses during the summer as well as revisions of the drawings for the Guggenheim Museum. On October 11 I wrote Ann Pond:

> Mr. Wright has been spending a great deal of time in the drafting room this past week. Almost too much. He has been working on the re-designing of the Guggenheim Museum, and as long as he is working re-designing we can't get caught up with the drawings. He can change things much faster than we can draw them. But he is going to New York this coming week so that we may have a chance to do a little consolidation.

Two weeks later, on October 27, I wrote Marcus:

> We have nearly finished the redrawing of the reworking of the Museum plans. Bids on it ran too high. Mr. Wright came back from New York filled with the idea of getting out a new set of plans in ten days. But that was several weeks ago. Wes has done nothing about reworking the structural plans. Architecturally the museum is now much improved. Somewhat simplified – and a lot of the odds and ends that were never quite eliminated in former revisions have now been cleaned out. I never felt right about it before; it seemed needlessly complicated, and full of unresolved loose ends and lacked any sense of organization that would make building it possible. Now it seems to me possible to build with some sense. It still looks essentially the same.

My correspondence with friends during the summer and fall indicates that I was beginning to think of leaving the Fellowship. Several events during the summer and fall served to reinforce this line of thought. The first of these was the marriage of Iovanna and Arthur Pieper in a Russian Orthodox service in Chicago. I was not invited to the wedding or the reception. I was the only senior who wasn't. All of those who were most devout and active in "movements" did go to Chicago.

I was both irritated and amused by the obvious snub. And it caused me to think about my future in the Fellowship, particularly about my relation to Mrs. Wright and Iovanna. Early in the third week in August I received a letter from Bill Short, who was then working in Philadelphia. He wrote that he and another fellow were making an architectural excursion and planned to be at Taliesin the following weekend. Bill had visited Taliesin West for about a week the previous winter. The other fellow, Bob Venturi, had worked with Oscar Stonorov in arranging Mr. Wright's exhibition in Philadelphia. He had also worked with Eero Saarinen. They were planning to see some of Saarinen's work. In his letter Bill suggested that I might make the return trip to Philadelphia with them. His suggestion appealed to me. I had an urge to go traveling. I was considering applying for a Fulbright grant in order to enable me to get away from Taliesin for a while and to see something of the world. I felt a need for fresh contacts and fresh problems, something to keep me from getting "sour." But we were just starting the working drawings for the synagogue. And I didn't feel that I should ask Mr. Wright if I could make this trip to Philadelphia.

At about the same time that Bill Short and Bob Venturi were at Taliesin, Gene unveiled a portrait of Mr. Wright on which he had been working during the summer. After this painting was unveiled I wrote Ann Pond on September 7:

> I suppose that it is all right — except that it isn't Mr. Wright. It was "unveiled" initially about two weeks ago — at which time Mr. Wright commented, in effect, that the subject of the picture as painted didn't look like a man who could build a building. In my more sarcastic moments I say that it is Mr. Wright dressed as the Dalai Lama. Mrs. Wright had supervised the painting of the portrait rather closely so the resemblance to the Dalai Lama may be intentional. In my "negative" moments (which can stretch into hours) I think of the portrait as a part of the procedure which I call "The Preparation of the Myth." Gene wants to paint a portrait of Mr. Wright in a white suit. This one is in a Chinese red dressing gown.

Toward the end of the summer the rebuilding of the theater at Hillside reached the point where the theater was usable, and an interest in theatrics was revived. The Thornton Wilder play *A Happy Journey* was performed by a cast that included Jack and Lu Howe, Shirley Oliver and Timmie Wright, and Maxine Pfefferkorn and Elihu Sutta. This performance went very well, except that during the performance Mr. Wright was heckling them about their position on the stage — they weren't "with the floor boards." I didn't understand what he was referring to. My only explanation was that he wanted them seated in a row parallel to the direction of the oak flooring.

Another group, under Mrs. Wright's direction, started rehearsing Oscar Wilde's play *Salome*. Iovanna, of course, was to be Salome; Eric Wright, John the Baptist; Arthur Pieper, the Captain of the Guard who kills himself for the love of Salome; and John Rattenbury, Herod. Bruce Pfeiffer was doing the music for it, including a dance of the Seven Veils.

Mrs. Wright asked me to attend a rehearsal. During this rehearsal, when

Iovanna was writhing on the floor of the stage wanting to "kiss the lips" of John the Baptist in a cell below and telling him of her love through an imaginary grate in the floor, I started laughing. Iovanna was doing a stellar imitation of the heroine, Jennifer Jones, of her favorite movie, *Duel in the Sun,* which we called Lust in the Dust. (In this movie, which also starred Gregory Peck and Joseph Cotten, Jennifer Jones plays the role of a half-breed Indian girl who comes to live in the home of a wealthy cattle baron and falls in love with both his sons.) This struck me as outrageously funny. I think what made it seem so funny to me was the potential outrage of Mr. Wright if he were to see Iovanna, who was Eric's aunt but about the same age, portraying lust for her nephew. I couldn't stop laughing so I left the theater. *Salome* was not performed. Nor did Mrs. Wright ever speak to me about or reprimand me for my laughter.

In my October 11 letter to Ann Pond I wrote:

A week ago Sunday Morning Mr. Wright in musing about something to talk about came up with the idea that the Fellowship should do some of the talking so he proposed that a different person should take the chair each Sunday and start a discussion. (This was not a new idea; it had been tried in the years before I joined the Fellowship.) He then asked for "volunteers." Of course there were no volunteers. So then he proposed that the next Sunday Iovanna should lead the discussion. Yesterday (Sunday) morning Iovanna was ill. Somehow I'm a little skeptical of these illnesses of Iovanna's. In a sense they are probably very real – at least she probably doesn't feel well. But it has happened to me so often that I've had her scheduled to play on a Sunday evening – or to sing – or something. Then suddenly she isn't feeling well. She has a headache or something. It's a "way out."

Well, look who's talking... I sometimes think I'm one of the world's No. I cowards in certain respects – in a way it probably accounts for the fact that I'm still at Taliesin. Remaining here is a kind of evasion too. If I was the sort of man that I really would like to be I'd be trying to build my own buildings, instead of remaining here and more or less kidding myself into thinking that I am really helping a great ideal along. You see, the Great Ideal got along without me for a good many years – and will get along without me. Should I leave. So where are we...

So much of what is done around here is done with the general idea that Mr. Wright mustn't know what is going on that I get more than just a little fed up with it. The whole thing at times seems like a group of adolescents hiding out behind the barn smoking their first cigarette or indulging themselves in some kind of petty vice. It's all too juvenile – or something – and one doubts that people who feel that they have to live this way will ever do much in Architecture.

A certain evasiveness, slyness, cleverness and general skill at lying is held up as something to be achieved. Almost as a way of Life. I suppose that it is a "way of life." But I am sure that it is not a way to practice architecture. Not certainly a way to build Good Buildings.

On a cold, wet October afternoon, when I was at work in the drafting room, I got a call from Gene Masselink saying that Mr. and Mrs. Wright wanted to see me at Taliesin. I drove over to Taliesin and went to the loggia in the house where Mr. and Mrs. Wright were waiting. With them were Iovanna, and Kenn and Polly Lockhart. Of course, I was curious as to what was up. Mrs. Wright took the lead. I was being accused of using vulgar language and being, in general, vulgar. As an example, Iovanna cited my use of the words "ladies" and "gents" when, during chorus rehearsals, I called upon different sections to rehearse their parts. To her "ladies" and "gents" were vulgar expressions for men's and women's restrooms. Kenn was there to cite an instance when during preparation for Easter breakfast I had lost my temper with him and accused him of being willing to "change the diapers" of the apprentice who had done the shopping for the ingredients for the paschal cheese and had returned with the wrong form of cottage cheese.

The meeting had come to the point where I assumed that Mr. Wright was expected to become angry with me and where I was expected to either defend myself or to confess and apologize. But none of this happened. At that point Brandoch came into the loggia in tears. He had just returned from school and had found Corinius, his sparrow hawk, dead. He had captured this small hawk in Arizona the previous winter. Mrs. Wright rose to console Brandoch and left the loggia. Iovanna followed her. Kenn and Polly excused themselves and left. This left me and Mr. Wright sitting in the loggia.

Mr. Wright ended the discussion. He suggested that in the future I should be more cautious in my use of language, saying that "Sometimes you may get caught with your pants down." He then added, as he rose to leave, "Put your trust in your work; not in your friends. It will never betray you."

In my October 27 letter to Marcus Weston I wrote:

Talk of the migration to Arizona is in the air. Last Sunday morning at breakfast Mr. Wright announced that it would start around the first of November. And added that he would allow about two weeks for it.

Interpreted, this means that he is going to be travelling around for the next three weeks. . . .

I'm planning to go through Kansas City and investigate what might be necessary for me to be registered in either Kansas or Missouri or both. It's time that I was registered as an Architect someplace. I don't think that I would have much difficulty in either of these states – mostly a matter of filling out forms and paying a fee. After that I might try for the National Registration Board. That would require some work on my part.

Winter 1954–1955

On November 21 I arrived in Arizona, about a week before Mr. Wright did. I had been on the road for two weeks. I visited my parents for two days, and was in Kansas City and Lawrence for two days, seeing friends and looking into the requirements for architectural registration in Kansas and Missouri. It was my intention to become registered as an architect in one or both states during the winter. In Kansas City Joe Radotinsky proposed that I come and work in his office. In Lawrence, Professor Beal suggested that I might combine part-time teaching with an architectural practice.

During my trip to Arizona I began to wonder just what I might discover when I arrived in camp. Friends I visited on the way were asking about newspaper articles reporting that Mr. Wright was going to leave Wisconsin because of his tax problems. These problems were not a new development; they had begun many years before when Mr. Wright established the Frank Lloyd Wright Foundation and began refusing to pay county, state, and federal taxes.[111]

As long as Mr. Wright had little income from his architectural practice or from his writing and lectures, the various taxing agencies showed little interest in trying to collect these taxes. Their interest changed when it was evident that his practice was flourishing. In the summer of 1953, after Iowa County had attempted to collect taxes on Taliesin and Mr. Wright had refused to pay them, a judge ruled that the foundation was a business and not a tax-exempt educational institution. During the past summer the tax problem had also flared up at the state level. Mr. Wright's threat to burn Taliesin and to leave the state had been caused by the refusal of the State Supreme Court to give tax-exempt status to the foundation and the Fellowship. The federal governemnt had not yet become publicly involved, but an agent of the Internal Revenue Service had spent the summer of 1953 going through bank accounts and canceled checks attempting to discover just how the income of the foundation had been spent. Gene had been cooperative with the agent, giving him the use of his room as a temporary office for his investigation.

With regard to this I wrote Bob Pond on February 1 that:

Gene is doing "hard time" (a "con" term – for feeling low). It seems that he is now beginning to get the blame for losing the tax case. We used to joke about the fact when he was going to Dodgeville (the county seat of Iowa County) and going through the check books with the lawyers that he would eventually be blamed for something or another. . . . Well . . . it has arrived.

When I arrived in camp, no one knew much more about what was going on than I did. Wes was still in Wisconsin. Mr. Wright was in New York. There were reports that other states, such as Michigan and New York, were making offers to induce Mr. Wright to relocate to their areas. There was speculation about sites in the Adirondacks in upper New York State and about an island in the Thousand Island group in the St. Lawrence River. Some of the reports, such as one saying that he was going to burn Taliesin and leave the masonry ruins as a memorial to his ancestors, were unbelievable.

This talk of relocation was intriguing, but I doubted that anything would come of it. Several years before, when there were reports of a power line being built within our view from the camp, Mr. Wright had threatened to sell the camp and move to Tucson and start another there. He had gone to investigate sites near Tucson, but nothing had come of it. He was now over eighty years old and deeply involved in major projects. I doubted that he and particularly Mrs. Wright and Iovanna, who were now enjoying the luxuries of his revived practice, would be willing to undergo the hardships that had accompanied the construction of the camp.

Following an interview with Mr. Wright, an article written by Bill Evjue, editor and publisher of the Madison *Capital Times,* convinced me that we were not going to relocate. It stated that Mr. Wright was not going to burn Taliesin – that he would do that only as a last resort in the settlement of the tax problem.

At the same time that Mr. Wright was losing the battle with the county and the state for tax-exempt status, he was winning a small battle in Madison. On November 1, shortly before our move to Arizona, the citizens of Madison had voted favorably on a referendum composed of three issues: whether or not to issue four million dollars in bonds to build a civic auditorium, whether the site of the auditorium should be at the foot of Monona Avenue, and whether Frank Lloyd Wright should be the architect. The issuing of the bonds had received the largest majority, the site a smaller one, and Frank Lloyd Wright as architect the smallest.

Mr. Wright's involvement with proposals to build on this site began in the summer of 1938, before I joined the Fellowship. He was asked to make some sketches for a civic center on it. He called his proposal Olin Terrace. The scheme included offices and jail facilities for the city and county, an auditorium, a railway station, docking for boats, and much parking for autos. All of these were to be placed beneath a park, which would terminate Monona Avenue and provide views over Lake Monona. This project was not commissioned by the city or county but by a group of citizens. The project received both favorable and unfavorable publicity, but soon became dormant. It was revived and revised during the summer of 1941, when there was a move to build an auditorium in Madison.

The revised scheme received much publicity, but with the onset of the war, again became dormant. It was revived by yet another group of citizens in the summer of 1954, when the city was again considering building an auditorium.

After this favorable vote – the referendum was advisory only – Mr. Wright decided to help generate more interest in his proposal. Early in January he started a group of apprentices working on elaborate presentation drawings and a large model of the project.[112] In the middle of January the drawings were still in a rough state and the model was only beginning to take shape. A week later the drawings and model were being worked on night and day.[113] Mr. Wright wanted these finished by the first of February, when he was planning to make a trip to the east coast. His plans included the opening of the Jaguar showroom in New York City and a testimonial dinner in Madison, where he planned to exhibit the model and drawings. He also wanted to take the working drawings for the synagogue in Philadelphia with him.

On February 1, I wrote Bob Pond:

There is to be a "Testimonial Dinner" for Mr. Wright in Madison on the 7th of February. Would you like to attend? It costs only $40 per plate. . . . If you can't attend you can still send $40. They hope to get 400 persons present at $40 per, and $40 apiece from another 400 who can't attend, the proceeds to be used to pay off the delinquent taxes. Also the dinner is to prove to Mr. Wright that he really is appreciated in Wisconsin – and to prove to him that he should not carry out his threat to leave the State. Also the "Testimonial Dinner" is to call the attention of the State Legislature to the need for special legislation to put the Frank Lloyd Wright Foundation in a tax exempt classification. Cary Caraway is chairman of the dinner Committee.

At the same time Mr. Wright is going to take the model of the Madison Civic Center and renderings of the plans and perspectives with him for presentation. The crowd working on the model and the drawings are working pretty steadily. There is even a "nite crew" of four or five, who works during the wee hours – and sleeps during the day. Practically everybody in the Fellowship is working on the drawings and the model – except for a few of us who are working on the Synagogue. We're about half way on them (the working drawings) now. Unless Mr. Wright moves something. If that happens we may all blow what few brains we have left . . .

. . . The Civic Center model is nearly finished. It is supposed to be shipped tomorrow. Mr. Wright and Wes are going Friday, I understand. And with Wes's going to Wisconsin, also go our plans for finishing the Synagogue drawings during Mr. Wright's absence. . . . Oh, well. . . .

The Testimonial Dinner was held on February 10. The Master of Ceremonies was Bill Evjue, not only the editor and publisher of the *Capital Times* but also a friend of Mr. Wright. Ralph Walker, past president of the American Institute of Architects, was the principal speaker. He read a special tribute to Mr. Wright. Other speakers included Governor Kohler of Wisconsin and Cary Caraway, the former apprentice who had organized the dinner. He presented Mr. Wright with a check for $10,000. Mr. Wright, overwhelmed by the testimonial, responded: "I would never have known the fine esteem of my fellow citizens, if it had not been for the adverse tax decision."

On the surface my relations with Mrs. Wright remained civil. But there were several instances during the winter when the civility was interrupted. One of these instances occurred early in December when a strange dog appeared in camp. A group, including Mrs. Wright, had gathered around the dog and was speculating about where it might have come from and what kind of dog it was. I said that it was a weimaraner. Mrs. Wright immediately said that it wasn't, that she knew a weimaraner when she saw one. Her tone of voice implied that she was always right. In this instance she wasn't. However, she took a fancy to this dog and after many telephone calls and trips to town involving Wes and Gene she came to own either this dog or one just like it. (There was an air of deception and mystery around the acquisition of the pet. To avoid Mr. Wright's anger over buying an expensive dog, he was encouraged to believe that it was the same dog that had appeared in camp.)

During the winter there seemed to be a sense of purge in the air, directed toward those who were not in "movements." Some of the faithful who had the same faults as those against whom the purge was directed were found to be acceptable and their presence justifiable. The purge was not always overt, nor was it something new in the Fellowship. There seemed always to be a way to make life unpleasant for those who were deemed undesirable.

Mr. Wright seemed to be in an angry and irritable state much of the winter. My awareness of it began on Sunday evening, December 12. It was a grim evening; nothing, including the music, went right. Mr. Wright had returned from Bartlesville on Saturday. I don't know what may have happened there to make him angry, except that he did see Bruce Goff's first design for Joe Price's studio. He commented afterward that it looked like an aircraft accident looking for a place to happen. He had returned from Bartlesville in the Prices' plane. Since the cabin of the plane was not pressurized and since the flight had to be made at a high altitude, he had had to wear an oxygen mask. This had been uncomfortable for him and had contributed to his general state of irritation.

Early in the week following his return from Bartlesville Mr Wright went to check on the "grandma" Price house (Fig. 102). (When I arrived in Arizona late in November the roof had been framed and the roof deck was being put in place.) When he returned to camp he was furious with Wes; he accused him of wasting

102 H. C. Price, Sr., residence, Phoenix, Arizona. The atrium, the outdoor living room and reception hall. This space which is open on all sides connects the living room and bedroom wings. Glass doors at left open into the living room. Maynard Parker, photo, copyright Maynard L. Parker Estate.

the Prices' money, of spending ten thousand dollars for copper flashing over the inverted roof beams. He had intended that the roofing should just be run up and over these beams. It was not possible to convince him that the flashing cost was less than ten thousand and that it included at least one thousand lineal feet of a rather elaborate stamped and perforated copper roof facia.

Part of Mr. Wright's irritation seemed to stem from his feeling that there was an effort afoot to put things over on him. He commented that he was being asked to approve and sign drawings when he didn't have the time to check them thoroughly. And he was. We had begun, quite consciously, to wait for advantageous times for Mr. Wright to check and sign drawings, times when he was in a good mood or when he was pressed for time – on his way to keep an appointment in Madison or Phoenix or when he was leaving on an extended trip.

A few weeks later, when the interior partitions were being put in place, he again returned from a visit to the Price house in a furious state. He walked into the drafting room, where a few of us were working, and shouted, "Get that crapper out of the living room." It soon became clear that what had made him mad was a coatroom and lavatory for guests that was in the southeast corner of the living room space of the house. He wouldn't accept the argument that this coatroom and lavatory had been shown there in the preliminary drawings and in the working drawings and that he had seen and approved both. He insisted that the "crapper" had to be removed. Jack asked me to see if I could find another place for it. My explanation to myself was that this facility for guests had not been shown on the preliminary drawings and that Mr. Wright, without giving it much thought and intending to take care of it later, had put it there when the Prices had asked for such a facility. After some study I found an unobtrusive location for this "powder room," and it was relocated.

Mrs. Price arrived in Arizona near the end of January. She wanted to get started on the furnishings for the house. At this time the cabinetwork was being put in place and some wood finishing had been started. Although there was still much work to be done outside the house, rugs were going down inside by the end of the first week in February. During this furnishing and finishing I did several more supplementary drawings, based on sketches by Mr. Wright, for the copper hoods over the fireplaces in the living room and the atrium and for the hemispherical light fixtures in the living room. One drawing that Mr. Wright made for the furnishing was a sketch for modifying two overstuffed reclining loungers which Mr. and Mrs. Price insisted they had to have in the living room.

During this furnishing of the Prices' house Mr. Wright also did some sketches for three lines of furniture to be produced by a manufacturer. Each line was based on a different geometry, one circular, one rectangular, and one triangular/hexagonal. Jack asked me to make the drawings of the triangular line. Other apprentices were assigned to the other two lines. I made plans and elevations of such things as chairs, tables, chests of drawers, etc. And I also made several perspective drawings of the various pieces as they might be grouped in different rooms. The furniture which was later produced by Henredon was based on a modification of this triangular/hexagonal design.

I wasn't much interested in this project. Nor did it appear that Mr. Wright was. His actions seemed perfunctory. I suspected that his sketches were made at Mrs. Wright's urging, and that furniture design was part of Mrs. Wright's plans for the future. Mr. Wright's previous designs for furniture had all been done as furnishings for a specific building and as a complement to the architecture of those buildings. He had designed the furniture for these buildings not because he was particularly interested in the design of furniture as such, but because the furniture which was available on the market did not contribute harmoniously to the whole which he was seeking to create, and, indeed, detracted from it.

Over time I had gotten the impression that Mr. Wright did not have much regard for the furniture that he designed. It was simply more acceptable than that which was available. He often commented that he was black and blue from living with his own furniture and that when friends or clients came to see him he welcomed them by suggesting that they "Please be crated."

About a week before Easter I accompanied Wes on a trip to San Francisco. We went in a pick-up truck to get parts of a glazed-tile Chinese gateway that Mr. Wright had purchased from a dealer in Oriental art objects. I welcomed this opportunity to get away from camp for a while. After picking up the parts of the gate and packing them in the truck we spent a day sightseeing. We stopped by the Morris Shop and the Beuhler house, over in Orinda, both of these projects I had worked on. I was happy to see them completed, and was particularly interested to see the translucent plastic ceiling of the Morris Shop and the large disclike planter which was hung beneath it. Mr. Wright had added both of these features when the construction of the shop was nearing completion. When Mr. Wright made his drawing of the ceiling of plastic hemispheres and shallow discs I thought it was going to be a bit too much, but the result was like clouds on a serene summer day.

Although our drive to San Francisco had taken one long day we decided to make a leisurely return. We spent most of one day driving south on the coastal highway, through Monterey and Carmel and the Big Sur country. At Carmel we managed to see only the exterior of the Walker house, as no one seemed to be home. We turned inland toward Bakersfield just above San Luis Obispo. When we arrived in camp Mr. Wright soon began happily distributing the parts of the Chinese gate in various places about the camp where he wanted them installed.

As I wrote to Marcus on April 19, Easter that year was

the usual fertility festival with all of the eggs in various forms: Baba, Paschal cheese and dyed and painted hard-boiled eggs. The preparation of the breakfast was the usual emotional affair. I've yet to understand how the simple process of making a bread can become such an emotional affair – verging on hysteria.

There were lots of guests: Aaron Green and wife, Ben Raeburn of Horizon Press, John Lloyd Wright and his wife, Arthur and Iovanna were here as house guests – also Kelly Oliver, now down in Dallas supervising a house, Kathryn Wright Baxter was here for breakfast with David Wright (David's wife was noticeably absent. "We" haven't been on speaking terms this winter for some reason). Also the Rubicans, the Stillmans (Fifi McCormick's son) and family, a Mr. Marek and wife – who does a music column for *House Beautiful*. All in all there were over 100 people at Easter Breakfast. And all in all it was a memorable occasion – I guess. Tables nicely set with lots of flowers. . . . The chorus sang from the guest deck, etc.

The drawings for the synagogue were not finished when we left Arizona, nor were the drawings for the Guggenheim Museum. In the same letter to Marcus I also wrote:

> We are in the midst of revising the Museum drawings again – for the last time, I hope. There has been a consulting engineer from NYC working with Mr. W. and Wes on the Project. Also a contractor has more or less been selected. And some suggestions have been taken from him to make the thing more feasible. So all in all it seems to be coming within the realm of possibility. And might – I hope – get started this summer.

Summer 1955

On April 19 I wrote Marcus Weston that "in a week or so the migration to Wisconsin will be imminent." Two weeks later, on May 3, I wrote George Beal:

> The season here is at an end. Mr. and Mrs. Wright have already left, going to New York to be there until about the middle of May. Mr. Wright has several lecture dates in the East.
>
> About half of the Fellowship is already en route to Wisconsin by various and devious routes. By the end of this week Taliesin West will be down to its summer "staff" of Uncle Vlado and Aunt Sophie and one apprentice – Bill Owen.

I left Arizona on Thursday, May 5, arriving in Oklahoma City on the evening of the 7th. I stayed overnight there with Haskell Culwell and his wife. In addition to a full-size mock-up of an office chair for the Price Tower, I was also carrying prints of more supplementary drawings that I had made for the finishing of the tower and of the house for Harold Price, Jr., prints that I was to deliver to Culwell. On the following day I drove on to Bartlesville to deliver the mock-up of the proposed office chair to Mr. Price for his testing and approval. I stayed overnight with the Prices. The day after that I drove to my hometown where I stopped for a day to visit my parents. I arrived at Taliesin on the evening of Sunday, May 11. Fortunately, Mr. and Mrs. Wright were away so there was no formal Sunday evening to prepare for.

Haskell Culwell was an interesting person. I had gotten to know something about him while working on the several projects for the Price family. He had gotten his start in building as a brick mason. After working as a mason for several years, he became a contractor for masonry work. From his work as a masonry contractor he moved into general contracting. As a successful general contractor he had several men on his staff whom he assigned to be in charge of other projects that he had contracted to build. But he reserved for himself the buildings Mr. Wright had designed. He was personally interested in them; he enjoyed the challenge they presented.

Culwell was a builder, the kind that every architect would like to work with. He was interested in getting the building built well and in getting it built economically. He didn't hesitate to suggest changes in construction if he believed that these would achieve the same end at less cost. For example he had suggested that a full basement be built under the Price Tower and its two-story wing. He said it would cost no more to excavate the full basement and to extend all foundations down to the same depth than to excavate and build the partial basement and crawl space which we had shown on the drawings. And doing this gave the plumbing, heating, and air-conditioning contractors more space in which to install and maintain their equipment. He was proud of the concrete block work on the "grandma" Price house, particularly of the fact that he had been able to lay out and build the many outward stepping piers without cutting any block. In an effort to hold down costs on many subcontracts, such as painting, plastering, and tilework, he personally took off the quantities of work involved and provided these to the subcontractors as a basis for their bids. He suspected that many such bidders could not read drawings and overestimated the quantities in their take-offs to protect themselves from potential errors.

Mr. Wright was away from Taliesin about half the time that summer, but he generally returned for the weekends. There were frequent trips to New York in connection with the Guggenheim Museum; he was hoping and trying to get its construction started. There were trips to Bartlesville which were related to the tower and to work on Harold Jr.'s house. And there were trips to San Francisco and Washington, D.C.

Mr. Wright was at Taliesin for the celebration of his birthday on June 8. This year's celebration was more lavish than any that had preceded it. In order to accommodate all of the guests invited for dinner that evening, the dinner was served in the Hillside drafting room. The drafting tables were moved to the sides of the room, much to Mr. Wright's annoyance, and the furniture from the dining room was moved to the drafting room. The room and the tables were decorated with crepe paper, balloons, flowers, and candles.

The dinner was preceded by drinks in the living room at Taliesin. It was followed by music and a movie in the theater at Hillside. In a June 15th letter to Marcus Weston, who had attended the dinner with his wife, I wrote:

> I'm wondering how the dinner, music and movie seemed to an "outsider." To me it all seemed a little like a bad dream that simply wouldn't end. Somehow we manage — I think it's a real "gift" — to arrange large scale "entertainments" that are no fun for those helping to arrange them. . . and I'm curious as to whether any of the guests actually "enjoy" them, or just politely say that they do. The general opinion here seems to be that the only pleasant moment of the day was in the living room at Hillside when Margaret Jean played for the group assembled there, more or less extemporaneously. [Margaret Jean Cree, a cellist, John Amarantides, and I had rehearsed a Beethoven trio in the living room after lunch. And after this rehearsal Margaret Jean and I were running through some of Mr. Wright's favorites that she might, if requested, play that evening.]

The Federal Bureau of Internal Revenue was waiting for the Foundation when it arrived in Wisconsin. They (he) are here now going through check books, bills, receipts, etc. . . . back to 1942. It seems that even tax-exempt Foundations are supposed to file reports on income and expenditures. And now — in addition to the township and county getting their claims for taxes very well established — the State is beginning to poke its head in the door and is wondering if they can't have some too.

Mr. Wright's trips to Washington, D.C., were connected to the possibility of his being involved in the design of the Air Force Academy near Colorado Springs. He had been approached the previous year by Pace Associates of Chicago. They were interested in his being affiliated with them in seeking the commission for this project. Surprisingly, Mr. Wright had agreed, and the union became known as Kittyhawk Associates. Mr. Wright went to Washington two different times in July in pursuit of the project. It was clear that he was interested in designing it, and that he had begun to think about the design. He had asked Gordon Lee, who was then practicing in Denver, to secure topographic maps of the area selected for the site of the academy. It was also clear that the various meetings Mr. Wright had been asked to attend had led him to believe that Kittyhawk Associates would be selected to design the project. But there was a limit as to how far Mr. Wright would go in pursuit of this commission.

I went into the Taliesin living room one Sunday afternoon early in August. Mr. Wright was pacing about the room, clearly angry. He had just gotten word that he was expected to go to Washington one more time for the selection process. Kittyhawk Associates was among the finalists. He had refused to go, saying, "If they are not familiar with my work by now, then to Hell with them." I do not know what other firms may have been among the finalists, but clearly Skidmore, Owings and Merrill (which Mr. Wright referred to as "the three blind Mies") was. And it was they who received the commission.

Work on two major architectural projects went on during the summer. The drawings for the synagogue were completed before the end of the summer and the search for a builder began. Estimated costs from builders in the Philadelphia area were much too high. Faced with unfamiliar construction they were estimating high to protect themselves. Haskell Culwell, who had by then built three of Mr. Wright's projects, was eventually selected as the builder.

Work on the Guggenheim Museum continued, off and on, during the summer, as revisions continued to be made. Mendel Glickman was at Taliesin most of the summer, assisting Wes with the structural calculations for the synagogue and the museum. One change that Mr. Wright made quite quickly — and with only a swing of a compass — made several weeks of Mendel's calculations obsolete. This was the change by which Mr. Wright added a semicylindrical protrusion at the south end of the broad band which extended uninterrupted across the museum's

Fifth Avenue side at the first level of the ramp. This external protrusion made an internal space which he labeled "architectural archives." Confronted with this change, Mendel, with no sign of exasperation, quietly collected all of the calculations he had been making, and the details of reinforcing steel which he had drawn for this wall (it was in effect a deep beam), and put them carefully aside. Having done this he got out a fresh pile of paper and started a new set of calculations for this corner of the building.

In addition to the synagogue and the museum I also worked on three houses during the summer: a Usonian Automatic for Mr. and Mrs. Toufic Kalil in Manchester, Vermont; a house for Max Hoffman in Rye, New York; and a house for Willard "Bud" Kelland, Herbert Johnson's son-in-law, near Racine, Wisconsin. I had designed a Usonian Automatic for the Christmas Box when Mr. Wright had suggested that the apprentices try their hand at this. And I had continued, whenever I had an idea for one, to put it on paper. That summer Jack suggested that I design one for Toufic Kalil. After studying the Kalils' requirements and the photos and topographic plan of their site, which they had sent, I soon arrived at an overall scheme and quickly developed it in detail and in terms of their requirements. After Jack had looked at the drawings and made some suggestions for changes, I made a set of presentation drawings for the client, which Mr. Wright checked and signed.

After Mr. Wright received approval of the design from the Kalils I proceeded to do working drawings for the house. If I remember correctly, Eric Wright assisted me with these. When they were complete, Mr. Wright checked them and signed them. He made only a minor change in the fenestration of the living room.

After I had finished the Kalil drawings, Jack asked me to assist him with the working drawings for a house for Max Hoffman. This was the third design Mr. Wright had done for a house for Hoffman. It was not as large or as complex as the two previous ones, but it was still a large house. The construction and the details were comparatively simple and the working drawings were quickly done.

With these drawings complete, Jack asked me to check the working drawings for a house for Willard "Bud" Kelland on which John Rattenbury had worked the previous winter. I assumed that these drawings were nearly ready for Mr. Wright to check and sign. I agreed to do this, thinking that at most it might take a couple of hours. Instead it required several weeks of work. I now think that Jack must have known or suspected that more than a "quick check" was required. I had checked other drawings on which apprentices had worked and generally found only a few minor errors which were quickly corrected. These drawings, however, were filled with major errors. None of the drawings seemed to be in agreement. The elevations didn't match the plans. The sections weren't in agreement with the elevations. There was an upper level over a portion of the house; the stairs to this upper level simply did not work. The detail drawing of the stairs did not agree with the stairs shown in plan. And so it went. The changes were compounded by the fact that Mr. Wright became interested in the house while I was making the corrections, and changed the roof. This was a change that needed to be made as the roof had been something of a mess.

The easy solution – and the quicker one – would have been to have started a fresh set of drawings. But Mr. Wright – and Jack – insisted that the corrections be made on the drawings that John had started.

On warm, humid Wisconsin afternoons the Hillside drafting room was not a pleasant place to work. It was not air-conditioned, nor were there any fans. Mr. Wright was susceptible to drafts and objected to air-conditioning. Only on the hottest of days would he remove his jacket and appear in shirt-sleeves. He would appear in the living room on a warm and humid Sunday evening dressed in his white wool suit. By the end of the evening he still appeared comfortable even though I would have sweated through my shirt and summer dinner jacket. On one summer day when I went to Milwaukee with Mr. Wright and Wes, he insisted, on our return trip, that the windows of the car be kept closed. While Wes and I sweltered in the front seat he napped in the back, comfortable in his wool tweed suit.

While I was sweltering in the drafting room making the changes and corrections on the drawings for the Kelland house, my irritation with John Rattenbury was compounded by my knowing that he was at the upper pond working on the annual renovation of the boat for the elaborate summer party Mrs. Wright was planning (Fig. 103). Mr. Wright objected to devoting so much time and energy to these affairs. He insisted that they should be more spontaneous and that any preparation for them should be done after tea, in the apprentices' free time.

There were other surreptitious activities at Taliesin that summer. Iovanna's "Chicago group" was coming to Taliesin for the weekends and meeting with Mrs.

103   The boat for the elaborate end-of-summer party.

Wright on Sunday afternoons in the living room of Wes's apartment. There was concern that Mr. Wright not learn of these meetings. And there was concern on my part that anyone at Taliesin should learn of my plans to leave the Fellowship. On June 24 I wrote Marcus Weston:

> I haven't broken the news to anyone at Taliesin – yet – so don't you. . . . But I'm planning to leave here this late summer. I'm taking a teaching job at the University of Kansas. I don't consider it permanent; it's a try-out. And something of a bridge.

> There was a time when I thought of Taliesin as my life: I don't think in these terms now. In fact I haven't thought in these terms for about two years. About a year ago I decided to begin the transition. Some of the seeds planted then are beginning to grow. I've got my license in Kansas. I take an oral exam for the Missouri registration this fall. The Missouri license is more desireable since it "enjoys" reciprocity with more states. The teaching job will only take about half my time, but it will give me enough to live on. In the meantime a few clients might come my way. Who knows? When I began to think of leaving here Joe Radotinsky asked me to come back with him, and take over the designing and getting out the drawings; he would get the jobs. After part time teaching came into the picture he seemed willing to have me work part time for him. That would certainly help fill the purse, which is tragically empty . . . but I think that I may wait for any action on this until I see just how much of my time is otherwise occupied.

> . . . I don't know when I'm going to break the news. Probably about the middle of July. Then if there is a scream of "Get out," I will get. . . . If it is accepted otherwise I'll probably be here until about the middle of August.

> This hasn't been a snap decision. I've had about two years to think about it. And there have been a few moments when I thought that I might be making a mistake. . . . but they have become fewer.

At the end of July I had not yet told Mr. Wright of my decision to leave, but I was already making plans to go through Michigan on my way to Lawrence. I was planning to see Professor Beal and his wife who were visiting a Lawrence friend at her summer cottage on the eastern shore of Lake Michigan, and to visit Bob and Ann Pond in Ann Arbor. I planned to arrive in Lawrence near the end of the first week in September in order to get settled before the beginning of the fall semester. And I had made arrangements for my sister to come to Taliesin with her station wagon to pick up my books and other things I had accumulated over the years; there wasn't room for all of this in my car.

The summer party was held during the first week in August (Fig. 104). It was an elaborate affair with many invited guests in addition to those who had spent

104 The party. At left, Iovanna as one of the maidens dispensing treasures. Photo courtesy of Special Collections, Kenneth Spencer Research Library, University of Kansas.

the summer at Taliesin. The party had a Venetian Renaissance theme. It began at the west side of the upper pond with the arrival of the boat. On it was Marco Polo returning from a trip to the Orient. The boat was filled with his crew and with glamorous and exotic maidens bearing marvelous treasures. After the maidens had distributed the treasures as gifts to the women guests, dinner was served. Following dinner the party moved to the theater at Hillside. There a program of music, poetry, and dances from the time of the Renaissance, and a skit – a takeoff of *The Merchant of Venice* – were presented. After this program the party moved back to the pasture at the west side of the pond for a fireworks display. These were shot off at the east side of the pond so that they could be seen against the hills and reflected in the pond on which lighted candles were floating, moved by the slow currents of the pond.

In the week following the party I decided that I could no longer put off telling Mr. Wright of my intention to leave Taliesin. I was reluctant to do this. I had spent much time rehearsing in my mind just what I might say and how it should be said. And I had spent many nights, before finally going to sleep, trying to write a letter or a statement to explain to Mr. Wright just why I had decided to leave.

One morning, I went in to see Gene to tell him that I was going to leave and to ask him when might be a good time to tell Mr. Wright. Gene did not seem surprised by my news. I had given Mr. Wright as a reference in my applications for registration as an architect, and Gene told me that Mr. Wright had written letters in response to inquiries from the registration boards of Kansas and Missouri. Gene told me that that morning was a good time to talk to Mr. Wright, that he was in a good mood and had just finished with the morning's mail.

When I went into his part of the office, Mr. Wright looked up and asked me what it was I wanted to see him about. He had probably heard me talking with Gene. I told him rather directly that I was going to leave the Fellowship. To my great surprise – and relief – he was neither hurt nor angry. It was as though he had been expecting this and was prepared to hear it. He did not protest or inquire as to why I was leaving. It seemed that I did not need to explain, that he understood clearly. I left his office feeling that he had been aware of my inner turmoil for some time, that he had been wondering what I might do.

On Sunday morning, I was in the kitchen at Hillside, helping, as usual, to prepare and serve breakfast. After breakfast, when Mr. Wright had begun his Sunday morning talk, Mrs. Wright came into the kitchen, where I was cleaning up. She was angry, and demanded to know why I had told everyone but her of my intention to leave. She insisted that I should have discussed it with her before telling anyone else. I replied that I had told only Gene and Mr. Wright and that I assumed that they would tell her. I didn't tell her that I felt no need to discuss it with her.

Toward the end of the following week it was generally known that I was going to leave. My sister and her two sons arrived with their station wagon on Thursday afternoon to pick up my things. On Saturday evening I was invited to the Lockharts (they were living in the guest cottage at Tanyderi) for a before-dinner drink. There the members of "the group" presented me with a going-away present, a tan, nubby-silk, summer-weight suit. This was unexpected, embarrassing, and somewhat annoying. (I assumed that Iovanna and John Amarantides had done the shopping. It was not something that I would have selected for myself. Shortly after I arrived in Lawrence I gave it to a friend who admired it.)

That Sunday morning I was, as usual, in the kitchen at Hillside helping with breakfast. When Mr. and Mrs. Wright arrived at the dining room, Mr. Wright noticed that a flower had fallen from the flower arrangement on their table. When someone started to fix this he asked them to leave it as it was. And he sent word that I should come and sit at the family's table with them.

After breakfast Mr. Wright began his talk by saying that a flower had fallen from the bouquet and announced to the Fellowship that I was leaving. In the talk that followed I heard reverberations of arguments that must have gone on between Mr. and Mrs. Wright and Iovanna, echoes of statements indicating that I was not warmly regarded by members of the "movements group." During his talk Mr. Wright responded to this by saying, in effect, that it was not necessary for a person with my responsibilities in the Fellowship to be popular, but rather to be respected.

The music that evening was for me an emotional leave-taking. As my contribution to the program I played the Largo movement from Beethoven's piano sonata, Opus 10, number 3. It was something that I had played several times before and which Mr. Wright liked to hear. I followed this with the theme of a set of variations by Schubert, the Third Impromptu of a set of four. This seemed to convey something that I could not put into words.

I left Taliesin the next morning, August 22, shortly after breakfast.

Notes

Introduction

1. James O. Maloney, ed., *A History of the School of Engineering at the University of Kansas, 1868–1988.* Privately funded work.

2. "Wright Apprentices," *Time* Magazine (September 5, 1932,) 33.

3. Frank Lloyd Wright, *Modern Architecture, being the Kahn Lectures for 1930,* Princeton, New Jersey: Princeton University Press, 1931. Lecture 2, "Style in Industry."

4. Frank Lloyd Wright, *The Disappearing City,* New York: William Farquar Payson, 1932, 76.

5. Frank Lloyd Wright, "The Hillside Home School of the Allied Arts: Why We Want This School," a 16-page prospectus dated October 1931.

6. Frank Lloyd Wright, "An Extension of the Work in Architecture at Taliesin to include Apprentices in Residence," an announcement brochure, published in the *Capital Times* (Madison, Wisconsin), August 7, 1932, and included in Frank Lloyd Wright, *An Autobiography,* New York: Duell Sloan and Pierce, 1943, 390–94.

7. "Wright Apprentices,"33.

8. "Frank L. Wright Will Be Assembly Speaker January 15," *University Daily Kansan,* January 3, 1935, 1.

9. Frank Lloyd Wright, *An Autobiography,* London, New York and Toronto: Longmans, Green and Company, 1933.

10. Frank Lloyd Wright, *Ausgefuhrte Bauten und Entwurfe von Frank Lloyd Wright,* Berlin: Ernst Wasmuth, 1910. Seventy-two plates, twenty-eight with tissue overlays, in two portfolios.

11. Wijdeveld, H. Th., ed., *The Life Work of the American Architect Frank Lloyd Wright,* Holland: C.A. Mees, 1925.

12. Fries, H. de, ed. *Frank Lloyd Wright, Aus dem Lebenswerke eines Architekten, mit uber 100 Abbildungen und 9 Farbentafeln,* Berlin: Verlag Ernst Pollak, 1926.

13. See William Miller, *A New History of the United States,* George Braziller, Inc., for a brief discussion of the New Deal, 375–81, 394.

14. Meyer Levin, "Master-Builder, Concerning Frank Lloyd Wright, Stormy Petrel of Architecture," *Coronet* III (December 1937), 171–84.

15. Frank Lloyd Wright, "The Man St. Peter Liked," *Coronet* III (December 1937), 91.

16. Frank Lloyd Wright, "Frank Lloyd Wright," *Architectural Forum* (January 1938), 1–102 (special issue).

17. Talbot F. Hamlin, "F.L.W. – An Analysis," *Pencil Points* XIX March 1938, 137–44.

18. Letter to Eugene Masselink, January 5, 1939, in Frank Lloyd Wright Foundation Archives.

19. See letters received from Joseph Hudmut, Dean of the Graduate School of Design, Harvard University, in Special Collections, Kenneth Spencer Research Library, University of Kansas.

Fall 1939

20. Letter to Eugene Masselink, September 26, 1939, and telegram to FLLW, October 6, 1939.

21. Letter to George Beal, December 30, 1939.

22. Letter to George Beal, December 13, 1939.

23. *Ibid.*

24. *Ibid.*

25. Letter to my parents, Mr. and Mrs. Wray Besinger, November 21, 1939.

Winter 1939

26. Letter to my parents, November 21, 1939.

Taliesin West

27. Letter to George and Helen Beal, December 30, 1939.

The Suntrap

    28. Letter to George Beal, March 12, 1940.
    29. Letter to George Beal, April 20, 1940.

The Los Angeles Trip

    30. Letter to George Beal, April 20, 1940.

Spring 1940

    31. Letter to George Beal, March 12, 1940.
    32. *Arizona Highways,* May 1940, vol. XVI, no. 5.

Migration To Wisconsin – 1940

    33. *Taliesin,* vol. I, no. 2, p. 5.

Summer 1940

    34. Mary Ellen Chase, *A Goodly Fellowship,* New York: the MacMillan Company, 1939. Chapter IV, "The Hillside Homeschool," provides a vivid description of the school, its faculty, and its students.

Movies

    35. Such a list, an inventory of all the films shown at Taliesin and the dates of their showing, can now be constructed, with the information made available by the publication of *Frank Lloyd Wright, An Index of the Taliesin Correspondence,* edited with an introduction by Anthony Alofsin, New York and London: Garland Publishing Inc., 1990. The names of many film distributors, including those of foreign films, appear in this index. The films were booked by Mr. Wright's secretary, Eugene Masselink, and by Karl Jensen who had preceded him. Most of the booking was done by mail, although some was done by telephone and confirmed by mail.

Summer and Fall 1940 – Work in the Drafting Room

    36. Letter to my parents, November 21, 1939.
    37. Letter from Lloyd Roark, November 22, 1939.
    38. *Kansas City Star,* April 9, 1940.
    39. Letter to George Beal, April 20, 1940.
    40. Letter to George Beal, September 5, 1940.
    41. *Kansas City Star,* December 3, 1940.

The War in Europe

    42. Letter to George Beal, July 22, 1940.

The Exhibition at the Museum of Modern Art, New York

    43. Letter to George Beal, September 5, 1940.
    44. Henry-Russell Hitchcock, *In the Nature of Materials,* New York: Duell, Sloan and Pearce, 1942.

    45. This question was partially answered in a letter that Alfred Barr, the director of the Museum of Modern Art, wrote in response to a review of the exhibition written by Milton Brown, "Frank Lloyd Wright's First Fifty Years," *Parnassus* XII, December 1940, 37–38. Barr's letter appeared in the following issue of the magazine *Parnassus* XIII in January 1941, p. 3. "Mr. Brown's surprise that there was no catalogue is natural enough. For six months the Department of Architecture had been planning and working upon a catalogue which would have comprised a great deal of factual and critical material, including essays by a half dozen of the foremost architects and architectural historians in this country. Mr. Wright, insisting upon 'no prejudgements in advance of the show,' refused to permit the publication of the catalogue as planned, although it had been intended as a tribute to him." The question then became, and still remains, which of the "essays" was the source of Mr. Wright's anger.

    46. See the 1970 BBC talks by Lionel March, "An Architect in Search of Democracy: Broadacre City," published in H. Allen Brooks, *Writings on Wright,* Cambridge, Massachusetts, and London, England: MIT Press, 1981, 195–206. Also, Rich Ahern, "The Neglected Legacy of Frank Lloyd Wright," *Journal of the Taliesin Fellows,* no. 2, Fall 1990, 8–12.

    47. For a sampling:
    E. F. Schumacher, *Small Is Beautiful,* New York: Harper & Row, 1973.
    Wendell Berry, *The Unsettling of America, Culture and Agriculture,* New York: Avon Books, 1977.
    Thomas Berry, *The Dream of the Earth,* San Francisco: Sierra Club Books, 1988.
    Frank Bryan and John McClaughry, *The Vermont Papers: Recreating Democracy on a Human Scale,* Post Mills, VT: Chelsea Green, 1989.

    48. The exhibition was open from November 13, 1940, until January 5, 1941. In addition to the review by Milton Brown mentioned in Note 45, other reviews included: F. A. Gutheim's "First Reckon with His Future," *Magazine of Art* XXXIV, January 1941, 32–33; H. R. Hitchcock's "Frank Lloyd Wright at the Museum of Modern Art," *Art Bulletin* XXIII, March 1941, 73–76; "City for the Future," *Time* Magazine, November 25, 1940, 58; "Fall exhibit," *Pencil Points* XXI, October 1940, 58; and Talbot Hamlin's "Frank Lloyd Wright," *Nation,* November 30, 1940, 541–42.

Winter in Arizona, 1940–1941

    49. Letter to George and Helen Beal, January 3, 1941.
    50. Letter to Verner Smith, January 20, 1941.

Spring 1941

51. Letter to Verner Smith, January 20, 1941.

The Fellowship and the Draft

52. A carbon copy of the original of this statement is in the Frank Lloyd Wright Collection, Special Collections, Kenneth Spencer Research Library, University of Kansas.

Kansas City, Spring, Summer, Early Fall, 1941

53. Letter to George Beal, March 28, 1941.

54. Notes made shortly after these conversations are in the files of the Frank Lloyd Wright Collection, Special Collections, Kenneth Spencer Research Library, University of Kansas.

55. Lewis Mumford, *Sticks and Stones, A Study of American Architecture,* Boni and Liveright, Inc., 1924; second revised edition, Dover Publications, 1955. Lewis Mumford, *Technics and Civilization,* New York: Harcourt Brace and Company, 1934. Lewis Mumford, The Culture of Cities, New York: Harcourt, Brace and Company, 1938.

56. Frank Lloyd Wright, *An Autobiography,* New York: Duell, Sloan and Pearce, 1943, 482–86, "The Church of the Future." Mr. Wright's account of the design and construction of Community Church agrees in overall form with mine. It varies somewhat in detail. A fuller account based on research into the now available archives remains to be written.

57. Letter from Gene Masselink, Novermber 7, 1941.

Winter 1941–1942

58. Letter to George Beal written shortly after arrival in Arizona, winter 1941.

59. Talbot Wegg, "FLW versus the USA," *AIA Journal,* February 1970, vol. 53, no. 2, 48–52. This engaging article about the Pittsfield housing project was written by Talbot Wegg, AIA, an architect who was Chief of the Planning Section of the Division of Defense Housing of the Federal Works Agency. In brief, the project died when the senator from Massachusetts, John W. McCormack, majority leader of the House, asked Clark Foreman, the director of the Division of Defense Housing, why he hired a Wisconsin architect for a Massachusetts project. Foreman had selected Mr. Wright for this project because he was determined that the housing program should not merely be a contribution to the nation's defense but also to its architecture. It appeared that the House and the House committee that was responsible for housing and related facilities generated by the defense program was controlled by Southern Democrats who were more interested in the political aspects of such facilities than in their social and design aspects.

60. *The Architectural Forum,* January 1948, vol. 88, no. 1, 80–81. An issue devoted to the work of Frank Lloyd Wright.

61. *Ibid.,* 82–83.

Spring 1942

62. Arch Oboler, "He's Always Magnificiently Wright," *Reader's Digest,* 72-49-54, F 58.

Music

63. The play was written in 1896 and published in the United States in 1898. Richard Mansfield played the role of Cyrano when it opened at the Garden Theater in New York City on October 3, 1898. Mansfield played Cyrano exclusively throughout the 1898–99 season. The play left New York after an eight-week run; it moved to Chicago early in January 1899. Mr. Wright probably saw the play then. I suspect that the date given on the drawing was based on his imprecise memory.

Winter 1946–1947

64. Korrick's was the department store in Phoenix from which the new furniture had been purchased.

65. Letter to Marcus Weston, March 1947.

Spring and Summer 1947

66. Frank Lloyd Wright, *Ausgefuhrte Bauten und Entwurfe von Frank Lloyd Wright,* Berlin: Ernst Wasmuth, 1910.

67. Letter to John Mitaraky, November 30, 1947.

Winter 1947–1948

68. Letter to George Beal, January 1948.

69. Letter to John Mitaraky, February 4, 1948.

70. Letter to John Mitaraky, February 9, 1948.

71. Letter to John Mitaraky, March 7, 1948.

72. Letter to Marcus Weston, March 21, 1948.

73. Letter to John Mitaraky, April 17, 1948.

74. Letter to Marcus Weston, April 11, 1948.

Summer 1948

75. Letter to John Mitaraky, May 19, 1948.

76. Frank Lloyd Wright, *Genius and the Mobocracy,* New York: Duell, Sloan and Pearce, 1947.

Winter 1948–1949

77. Since I was not involved I can only speculate about the reasons for their being

asked to leave. There may have been several. Paolo was the "guru" of a small group of his friends who admired him and his talent. He did very interesting drawings on yards of butcher paper which he put in the Birthday and Christmas boxes. One of these was a drawing for a bridge which Betty Mock included in the book on bridges she was working on at the time (*The Architecture of Bridges,* New York: Museum of Modern Art, 1949). Soleri's later published writings indicate that he may have been philosophically at odds with Mr. Wright. He has also suggested that he resented being asked to work in the kitchen, and particularly to being assigned to wait on Mr. and Mrs. Wright and their guests. However, all that I know about these occasions was that he did very interesting and ingenious flower arrangements. I have reason to believe, based on more recent reading in *Letters to Apprentices,* edited by Bruce Brooks Pfieffer, that there may have been difficulties during the summer, disagreements with Uncle Vlado and the group about who was in control of the camp and about who was telling whom to do what. I refer to the letters to "Dear Boys:" p. 110, June 13, 1948, and p. 11, July 3, 1949.

Winter 1949–1950

78. Letter to Marcus Weston, December 19, 1949.
79. A copy of this program is in the Frank Lloyd Wright Collection, Special Collections, Kenneth Spencer Library, University of Kansas.

Summer 1950

80. G. Gurdjieff, *All and Everything,* New York: Harcourt Brace and Company, 1950.
81. Special Collections, Kenneth Spencer Research Library, University of Kansas.

Winter 1950–1951

82. Letter to Marcus Weston, February 4, 1951.
83. *Ibid.*
84. *Ibid.*
85. *Ibid.*
86. *Ibid.*
87. *Ibid.*

Summer 1951

88. A statement by her, that the idea of the Guggenheim Museum was hers and that she gave it to Mr. Wright, appears in a chronology of her career which is in the catalogue of an exhibition of her paintings and collages that was held at French and Company, Inc., New York City, in 1962. An article written by William J. Hennessey and published in *Arts* Magazine, April 1978, pp. 128–32, proposes that the idea

that Hilla Rebay gave to Mr. Wright was really Rudolph Bauer's, and that it was at her insistence that Mr. Wright gave form to Bauer's ideas. Rudolph Bauer was a painter whose work Hilla Rebay admired and exhibited, and which she encouraged Solomon Guggenheim to buy.

Winter 1951–1952

89. Letter to Marcus Weston, March 3, 1952.

Summer 1952

90. Letter to Roland v. Rebay, July 29, 1952.
91. *Ibid.*
92. Letter to Marcus Weston, September 11, 1952.
93. Letter to Roland v. Rebay, September 24, 1952.
94. Letter to Roland v. Rebay, October 10, 1952.

Winter 1952–1953

95. Letter to Marcus Weston, March 2, 1953.
96. Letter to Marcus Weston, April 27, 1953.

Summer 1953

97. James M. Fitch became an editor with *House Beautiful* in 1949. During his five years with the magazine he was heavily involved in its Climate Control Project, a forerunner of the effort to conserve energy through the effective design of houses. Before moving to *House Beautiful,* Fitch had been an editor of *Architectural Forum.* During his three years with the *Forum* he wrote his first book, *American Building, The Forces that Shape It,* (Boston: Houghton Mifflin, 1947). This book was later revised and enlarged, and published as two separate volumes. After leaving *House Beautiful* Fitch began teaching at Columbia University, in New York City. In 1964 he established Columbia's pioneering Program in Historic Preservation. He also published two other notable books: *Walter Gropius,* in the Master of World Architecture Series (New York: George Braziller, Inc., 1960), and *Architecture and the Aesthetics of Plenty,* (New York: Columbia University Press, 1961).

Frank Lloyd Wright's association with *House Beautiful* began early in his career. He and a client, William Herman Winslow, "During the Winter Months of the Year Eighteen Hundred and Ninety Six and Seven," printed by hand at the Auvergne Press – in the stable of the Winslow House – in River Forest a small, limited edition book, *The House Beautiful,* written by William C. Gannet. A magazine bearing the title of the book began publication in February 1897. Included in it were illustrations of Mr. Wright's own house in Oak Park.

98. Letter to Marcus Weston, June 20, 1953.

99. *Ibid.*

100. Letter to Bob and Ann Pond, June 28, 1953.

101. *Ibid.*

102. Letter to Bob and Ann Pond, July 4, 1953.

103. David Henken and his wife, Priscilla, had been apprentices at Taliesin during World War Two. David was also one of the organizing forces in Usonia Homes, Incorporated, a cooperative housing project, near Pleasantville, New York, for which Mr. Wright designed the site plan (1947). He also agreed to design three of the houses and approve – or disapprove – the design of other houses to be built in the project by other architects. Nine houses had been built by 1953. Others have been built since then. David and Priscilla have written their own account of this project, *Realizations of Usonia: Frank Lloyd Wright in Westchester* (Hudson River Mus., Westchester, 1985). It has also been the subject of a Master's thesis by a University of Pennsylvania student, Ciorsdan Conran, 1991.

104. Letter to Bob Pond, September 8, 1953.

105. Letter to Marcus Weston, September 21, 1953.

106. William H. Short studied architecture at Princeton University. In 1953 he was working with the architectural office of Holden and McLaughlin. In 1947 Mr. Wright had asked this well-established firm to associate with him on the Guggenheim project in order to assist in the process of getting the plans approved and getting a building permit issued. Bill Short was the "legman" for much of this activity as well as for getting an occupancy permit for the temporary exhibition pavilion and the house. When construction of the museum building finally started in 1957, Mr. Wright asked Bill to assist with supervision. After completion of the building, Bill became a partner of Robert Venturi. During this partnership (1960–63) several of Venturi's early projects were built including the house for Venturi's mother in Chestnut Hill, Pennsylvania. After this partnership ended Bill began practice on his own and was soon recognized for his work in the area of historic preservation. In 1974 he established the partnership of Short and Ford. This partnership soon became known for its sensitive design in adding new buildings to older complexes and for additions to and renovations of historic buildings. Its work has received many awards for design excellence. And Bill himself was made a Fellow of the American Institute of Architects. He died in April 1991, at the age of 66.

107. Betsey Barton was the daughter of Bruce Barton, who was a principal partner in a successful advertising agency (Batten, Barton, Durstine and Osborn) and the author of numerous books, including *The Man Nobody Knows*. Betsey, also the author of several books including *The Long Walk*, had been injured in an accident and had lost the use of her legs. She was a frequent guest at Taliesin West during the winter seasons of the early 1950s; she had become a friend of Mr. and Mrs. Wright and of some of the apprentices, particularly of Gene Masselink, Wes Peters, and John Hill.

108. A program for this demonstration, "Music, Ritual Exercises and Temple Dances by George Gurdjieff," is in Special Collections, Kenneth Spencer Research Library, University of Kansas.

109. Letter to Marcus Weston, November 20, 1953.

Winter 1953–1954

110. Letter to the Beals, January 15, 1954.

Winter 1954–1955

111. The history of the foundation should be carefully researched and fully documented. I know, for example, that as a member of the board of the foundation before World War Two, I was asked to sign a document prepared by Mr. Randolf Conners, Mr. Wright's lawyer in Madison.

112. Letter to Marcus Weston, January 23, 1955.

113. Letter to Bob Pond, February 1, 1955.

Personae

This is by no means a complete list of persons who were in the Fellowship. Nor is it even a complete list of those who were there during the years that I was. Rather, it is an attempt to identify some of those who played a part in my experiences.

The biographical data given here are based primarily on information included in the Directory of Members of the Taliesin Fellowship 1932–1982, and its Supplement. This directory was compiled by Elizabeth B. Kassler (Betty Mock) in anticipation of the 50th anniversary of the founding of the Fellowship. It was privately printed in an edition limited to 450 copies.

Barney, Maginel Wright; Illustrator
> The youngest sister of Mr. Wright and a frequent summer visitor at Taliesin. Recognized as one of America's finest illustrators, as well as a painter and fashion designer. Illustrated many classic children's books. Her work appeared in leading magazines as well as in one-person shows in New York galleries. Author of *The Valley of God-Almighty Joneses,* 1965.

Bek, Anton J. (Tony); Musician, and Honore, his wife
> At Taliesin during the summers of 1938 and 1939 as violist with the Taliesin String Quartette. He and his wife joined the Fellowship during the winter of 1939–40 and remained until the end of the summer of 1941.

Benedict, Frederic A. (Fritz); Architect, FAIA
> Born in Medford, Wisconsin, 1914; received his B.S. in 1936 and his M.S. in landscape architecture from University of Wisconsin in 1938. In U.S. Army 10th Mountain Divison from 1941 to 1945. In Fellowship from 1938 to 1941. In 1945 he began practicing in Aspen, Colorado, specializing in the planning and design of mountain resort communities. Retired in 1992.

Berndtson, Peter; Architect
> In Fellowship from 1939 to 1940 and from 1942 to 1946. Practiced in Pennsylvania from 1946 to 1957 with his wife, Cornelia. After divorce, ran his own practice in Pittsburgh from 1958 until his death in 1972. Designed over 90 buildings, mostly residential. His drawings now in Hunt Library, Carnegie Mellon University. Book by Donald Miller and Aaron Sheon, *Organic Vision, The Architecture of Peter Berndtson,* Hexagon Press, 1980.

Brierly, Cornelia; Landscape Architect, ASLA
> In Fellowship from 1934 to 1941, from 1942 to 1946, and from 1957 to present. Architecture practice with her husband, Peter Berndtson, from 1946 until 1957 when divorced. From 1959 to date, on staff of the FLLW Foundation. Interior designer and landscape architect with TAA; instructor in FLLW School of Architecture.

Caraway, Jesse Claud (Cary); Architect
> Born in Texas. Attended University of Texas. In Fellowship from 1935 to 1942. Supervised construction of residences for Theo Baird, Amherst, Massachusetts, James Christie, Bernardsville, New Jersey, and J. C. Pew, Madison, Wisconsin. Was University of Illinois Architect, Chicago.

Cary was organizer of Frank Lloyd Wright testimonial dinner in Madison, Wisconsin, 1955. He was also involved in Frank Lloyd Wright Day in Chicago, September 17, 1956. Died 1994.

Chadwick, Gordon, Architect
Born in Red Bank, New Jersey, 1916. B.A. Princeton University, 1938. In Fellowship from 1938 to 1942. Supervised construction of Loren Pope residence, Falls Church, Virginia. In U.S. Army monuments, architecture and fine arts section during World War Two. With Fritz Benedict, designed a studio for Herbert Bayer and several houses in Aspen, Colorado, 1946. Supervised construction of Arnold Friedman residence, Pecos, New Mexico, 1946. Supervised construction of David Wright residence, Phoenix, Arizona, 1951–52. In his own practice, designed residences and information center at colonial Williamsburg, 1955. Partner of George Nelson. Died 1980.

Charlton, Jim; Architect, AIA
Born in Reading, Pennsylvania, 1919. In Fellowship from 1939 to 1942. U.S. Air Force fighter pilot, 1942–45. In private practice 1956–65 in California. Waikiki, Hawaii, office 1968–75.

Cuneo, Lawrence (Larry); Photographer
In Fellowship from 1939 to 1940. Married Kay Schneider, summer 1939. Divorced spring 1940. Now living in or near Los Angeles.

Cusack, Victor A.; Architect, AIA
Born 1915. Attended Yale University from 1935 to 1938 and 1943 to 1944. In Fellowship from 1938 to 1940. Served in U.S. Navy from 1943–45. Design architect in Los Angeles and San Francisco offices 1945–46. Since 1965 has been with William L. Pereira Associates, Los Angeles; vice-president since 1974.

Davison, Allen Lape (Davy)
In Fellowship from 1938 to 1974. Married Kay Schneider, 1941. Father of Tal and Celeste Davison. Supervised construction of several houses including Bulbulian and Keys residences, Rochester, Minnesota, and Thaxton residence in Bunker Hill, Texas. Delineator of many nighttime renderings of FLLW projects, including Madison Civic Center, Guggenheim Museum, Arizona State Capitol, twin cantilevered bridges in Pittsburgh, Pennsylvania, Pittsburgh Civic Center. Member of staff of FLLW Foundation and TAA from 1959 until his death in 1974.

Davison, Cornelia "Kay" Schneider
Born in Hamburg, Germany, 1918. In Fellowship from 1935 to date. Married to Larry Cuneo from 1939 to 1940. Married to "Davy" Davison in 1941. Mother of Tal and Celeste Davison, Secretary to Mrs. FLLW. Personnel Coordination at FLLW School of Architecture; staff member FLLW Foundation; Costume designer and lecturer on painting.

Dombar, Benjamin (Bennie); Architect, AIA; NCARB
Born 1916. In Fellowship from 1934 to 1941. In Army Air Corp. from 1942 to 1945. Private practice since 1948. Supervised addition to Rosenbaum residence, Florence, Alabama, 1948, and original and addition to Cedric Boulter residence, 1954 and 1958, Cincinnati, Ohio. Associate Editor *Ohio Architecture* Magazine; President Cincinnati Architecture Society; Vice-President and President Cincinnati Chapter AIA.

Drake, Blaine; Architect
Born in Ogden, Utah, 1911. Attended University of Southern California at Berkeley for three years. In Fellowship from 1933 to 1941. Designed and constructed residences, offices, and clinics, a school, a church, and a chapel. Associate Architect with Alden Dow, Phoenix Art Museum. Exhibition of work in Roswell, New Mexico, Museum and Art Center, 1958. Died 1993.

Drake, Hulda Brierly; Designer
Born in Pennsylvania, 1911. Received a B.A. in art at Carnegie Tech. In Fellowship from 1934 to 1941. Worked in studio with husband, Blaine. Interior design of many of their projects. Died in 1992.

Fritz, Herbert (Herb), Jr.; Architect

Born in Sioux City, Iowa, 1915. Student at University of Wisconsin and Armour Institute of Technolgy. In Fellowship from 1937 to 1941. Farmer from 1941 to 1947. Since 1950 has had his own practice. Over 100 executed projects, mostly in Wisconsin.

Geiger, John W.; Architect

Born in Fairbault, Minnesota, 1921.Attended University of Minnesota for five years studying architecture. Discharged from Army Air Force in 1946 as a Captian. In Fellowship from 1947 to 1954. Supervised construction of Zimmerman house, Manchester, New Hampshire, 1951–52. At Taliesin 1952–53. Supervised FLLW temporary exhibition pavilions at New York and Los Angeles 1953–54 and briefly Oboler "desert concrete" house. Private practice in Los Angeles 1955–64. Residential work including 1959 "Pacesetter" of *House Beautiful* with John Hill. In retail business, 1963–85. Retired; limited residential practice. Helped establish Taliesin Fellows as President.

Glickman, Mendel; Structural Engineer, Professor

Born Vitebsk, Russia, 1895; immigrated to U.S. 1905. Plant Engineer, International Harvester, Milwaukee, 1922–29; Chief American Engineer at tractor plant, Stalingrad, USSR, 1929–31. Part-time at Taliesin from 1932 to 1967, consulting engineer with FLLW and TAA. In 1949 Professor and chairman of architecture and engineering at the University of Oklahoma School of Architecture. Died in 1967.

Goodrich, Burton (Burt), Architect, AIA

Born Exeter, New Hampshire, 1911. Received B.S. in architecture at University of New Hampshire. In Fellowship from 1934 to 1942 and from 1944 to 1946. In private practice since 1950, Lake Oswego, Oregon.

Goss, Robert (Bob/Gunner)

To Taliesin from Cornell and Navy. In Fellowship from 1939 to 1941.

Green, Aaron; Architect, FAIA

Educated at Alabama State College, Chicago Academy of Fine Arts, and Cooper Union. In Fellowship from 1939 to 1943. Own San Francisco office since 1951. West Coast Rep and Associate Architect of FLLW and TAA from 1951 to 1972.

Guerrero, Pedro E. (Pete); Photographer

Born in Arizona, 1917. Attended Art Center School in Los Angeles from 1937 to 1940. In Fellowship from 1940 to 1941. Since 1946 architecture photography for *Architectural Forum, Architectural Record, House and Garden,* and others. Famous photos of FLLW work.

Harkness, John C. (Chip); Architect, FAIA, NCARB

Born New York City, 1916. Received B.S. and M.S. in architecture from Harvard University. In Fellowship 1940.

Henken, David T., and wife, Priscilla

In Fellowship from 1942 to 1943. Responsible for "Usonia," early co-op housing development in Pleasantville, New York, 1947. Built exhibition pavilion and house for "Sixty Years of Living Architecture" exhibition, NYC. Campus planner, Nassau College, Long Island, New York; campus planner Pratt Institute, Brooklyn, New York.

Hill, John DeKoven (Johnnie); Architect

Born Cleveland, Ohio, 1920. In Fellowship from 1937 to 1953 and from 1963 to date. Supervised construction and furnishing of Lowell Walter residence, Quasqueton, Iowa; Douglas Grant residence, Cedar Rapids, Iowa; Carroll Alsop residence, Oskaloosa, Iowa, and Jack Lamberson residence, Oskaloosa, Iowa. From 1953 to 1963, Architecture Editor, *House Beautiful;* later, Editorial Director. In 1963 returned to Taliesin to work with TAA. Now honorary chairman of Board of Directors, FLLW Foundation.

Howe, John H. (Jack), Architect
>Born Evanston, Illinois, 1913. In Fellowship from 1932 to 1964. Head draftsman with FLLW. With Aaron Green office, San Francisco, from 1964 to 1967. Private practice in Minneapolis, Minnesota, 1967. In 1966 invited to Japan to lecture at Nihon University. In 1975 named visiting professor at Nihon University, which published illustrated brochure of his work through 1975. Retired summer of 1992.

Koch, Hans; Craftsman + Free-thinker
>From New Jersey. In Fellowship 1935–36, 1940–42 and 1946–47. Died in 1947.

Lautner, John; Architect FAIA
>Born in Marquette, Michigan. Recieved B.A. in English, Northern Michigan University. In Fellowship from 1933 to 1939. Supervised construction of Sturges residence, Brentwood Heights, California, and Arch Oboler gate house and Eleanor's Retreat, Santa Monica Mountains, Malibu,California. Military construction in California during World War Two. Associated with Douglass Honold, Los Angeles, 1944–46. Private practice, mostly houses, since 1946. Work widely published in the United States, Europe, and Japan. Died 1994.

Lee, Charles Gordon; Architect
>Received B.S. in Architecture at University of Pennsylvania. In Fellowship 1941 to 1942 and 1947 to 1948. Worked on drawings for Pittsfield, Massachusetts, housing project and Civic Center projects for Pittsburgh, Pennsylvania. Private practice in Denver 1948–66. Died in 1966.

Liebhart, Fred; Architect FAIA
>Born in California, 1924. Student in planning at University of Denver. In Fellowship from 1948 to 1949. In private practice since 1952.

Lockhart, Kenneth Burton (Kenn); FCSI
>Born in Charles City, Iowa, 1916. Attended Minneapolis School of Art from 1935 to 1937and University of Iowa in 1937. In Fellowship 1939 to present. Since 1959, staff of FLLW Foundation, TAA, and FLLW School of Architecture. Died 1994.

Maiden, Rowan; Architect
>Born in Piedmont, California. In Fellowship from 1939 to 1941. Married Germaine ("Gerry") Schneider, summer 1940. Private practice in Big Sur area, California. Designed Nepenthe. Died early 1950s.

Masselink, Ben; Writer
>Born in Grand Rapids, Michigan, 1919. Attended DePauw University for three years. At Taliesin summers 1938 and 1939 and fall and winter 1940. In U.S.M.C from 1941 to 1945. From 1945 to 1960, tile setter's helper with spare-time writing for *Collier's, Saturday Evening Post, Playboy,* and others. Book of short stories and five novels published 1957–67 by Little Brown. Since 1960 writing for TV and movies.

Masselink, Eugene; Artist, Graphic Designer
>Born in Grand Rapids, Michigan, 1910. Received a B.A. in painting at Ohio State University. Studied with Hans Hoffman, UC Berkeley. In Fellowship from 1933 to 1962. Secretary to FLLW 1935–1959. Secretary to FLLW Foundation and member of board of directors, FLLW Foundation, until his death in 1992. Started Taliesin Press in 1941; designed and printed many publications from Taliesin. Did abstract works for many FLLW projects, including H. C. Price office, Price Tower; residences for H. C. Price Sr. and Jr. Also decorative panels for residences by other architects including C. Montooth and A. Parker.

Matthews, Peter; Architect, Professor, and Mary, his wife
>Born in Wanstead, Essex (East Saxon), 1921. Five years in RAF (learned to fly with USAF in

Alabama and Georgia, then became flying instructor at Yuma and Luke Field, Phoenix, Arizona, where he married Mary Phillips). In Fellowship from 1946 to 1948.

May, Robert Carroll (Bob); Architect
Born in Urbana, Ohio, 1914. Received a B.S.in architecture at University of Michigan. In Fellowship from 1939 to 1942. Ran his own office from 1948 to 1960 in Hartford, Connecticut, and joined with several offices from 1960 to 1970. Since 1971 has been living in Springfield, Pennsylvania, and conducting limited practice of architecture.

Meyer, Leonard E.; Architect Bureaucrat
Born in Madison, Wisconsin, 1920. In Fellowship from 1938 to 1940. Employed by various architecture firms in Washington, DC, area, 1949–63. Associate, Nicholas Satterlee & Associates, 1963–70. Since 1970, Office of Construction, Veterans Administration, Washington, DC, as hospital designer and value engineer.

Molny, Robin; Architect
Born 1928. Student at Carnegie Institute of Technology. In Fellowship from 1949 to c.1954. Supervised construction Maurice Greenberg residence, Dousman, Wisconsin. Worked in several offices in Chicago and Aspen. In private practice in Aspen.

Mosher, Robert Keeler (Bob); Architect
Born in Bay City, Michigan. In Fellowship from 1932 to 1942. Office of Strategic Services, 1942–45. Reconstruction work, Sante Fe Railroad. Architect U.S. Air Bases in Spain, late 50s; stayed on to establish practice in Marbella, Costa del Sol. Specialized in large villas. Died 1992.

Oliver, Kelly; Architect, AIA
Born in Denver, Colorado, 1926. At Taliesin from 1949 to 1956. Supervised construction of the John Gillin residence and of the Kalita Humphreys Theatre in Dallas, Texas. Partnership with David George, Dallas, 1959–62. TAA 1956–66; since 1966 manager of Colorado office FLLW Foundation, responsible for all projects in Rocky Mountains area. Also since 1966, in private practice in Denver.

Peters, Svetlana; Musician
Daughter of Olga Ivanovna Milan Lazovich and Vlademer Hinzenberg, who were married in 1916. Olga Ivanovna (Olgivanna) left Hinzenberg, probably in 1918, and became a member of Gurdjieff's Institute for the Harmonious Development of Man. When the group moved to Paris in 1922 Svetlana was sent to live with her uncle, Vladimir Lazovich, and his wife, Sophia. After Olgivanna's divorce from Hinzenberg and her marriage to FLLW, Svetlana was adopted by FLLW and came to live at Taliesin. Listed as a charter member of the Fellowship in 1932. For a few years she lived with the family of Margaret Jean Cree in Chicago and began the study of music. In 1935 she married William Wesley Peters, and since marriage was not approved by Mr. and Mrs. Wright, she and Wes left the Fellowship. They returned in 1937 and Svetlana began to play an important role in the musical life of the Fellowship. Two sons were born to this marriage, Brandoch in 1941, and Daniel in 1944. Daniel and Svetlana were killed in an automobile accident on September 30, 1946.

Peters, William Wesley; Architect, NCARB
Born in Terre Haute, Indiana, 1912. First member of Fellowship, June 1932. In 1935 married Svetlana Wright (see above). Was a leader in work of Fellowship. Did much of the engineering design of FLLW projects, sometimes assisted by Mendel Glickman. In 1959 became a leading member of the FLLW Foundation, TAA, and the FLLW School of Architecture. Died in 1991.

Pond, Robert W. (Bob); Architect
Born 1926. In Fellowship from 1950 to 1954. Supervised FLLW Turkel house and Lindholm filling station. Designing Architect for Indiana University, Bloomington. Retired 1993.

Rana, Mansinhji M.; Architect, F.I.I.A.
    Born in India, 1922. In Fellowship from 1947 to 1950. After Taliesin lectured in Europe on
    FLLW, then returned to India to teach at School of Architecture and to open his own office.
    Until retirement in 1980, was Chief Architect to the government of India. Work included India
    pavilions at New York World's Fair 1963 and Expo '67, Montreal, as well as Nehru's mau-
    soleum and gardens. New Dean of Suchant School of Art and Architecture, New Delhi, India.

Rattenbury, John; Architect, NCARB
    Born in Canada, 1929. In Fellowship from 1950 to date. Since 1959 staff member of FLLW
    Foundation; planner and architect with TAA; instructor in design and planning, FLLW School
    of Architecture.

Rattenbury, Cornelia "Kay" Davison
    See Davison, Cornelia "Kay" Schneider

Rebay, Roland von; Engineer, Architekt BDA
    Born in Germany, 1926. In Fellowship from 1948 to 1950. Received engineering degree from
    University of Munich in 1966. In private practice in rural Wessling, about 150 family homes.

Schweizer, Nils Mark; Architect
    Born in Maryland, 1925. Architecture student at University of Georgia and University of
    Zurich. In Fellowship from 1948 to 1949 and from 1950 to 1952. Went to Florida in 1950s to
    supervise FLLW construction at Florida Southern College. In private practice in Florida until
    his death.

Tafel, Edgar; Architect FAIA
    Born in New York City, 1912. In Fellowship from 1932 to 1941. While in Fellowship, supervised
    construction of Fallingwater, Johnson Wax administration building, houses for Lloyd Lewis,
    Bernard Schwarz, Charles Manson. During World War Two served in U.S. Air Force. Began pri-
    vate practice in NYC following war. Work included First Presbyterian Church House, NYC, and
    Fine Arts Building at State College, Genesco, NY. Author of *Apprentice to Genius,* 1979. Instru-
    mental in preserving 1912 Little House Living Room in Metropolitan Museum and Dining
    Room in Tafel's Allentown Art Museum. Member Taliesin Council, FLLW Foundation. Editor of
    "About Wright."

TenBrink, Howard; Contractor
    In Fellowship from 1941 to 1943. Came to Taliesin from Autoworkers Coop for which FLLW
    designed rammed-earth housing project in Detroit. Assigned to CO camp in Wellston, Michi-
    gan, during World War Two, from 1943 to 1946. After World War Two started construction busi-
    ness in Modesto, California. Retired.

Weston, Marcus; Architect
    Born in Spring Green, Wisconsin, 1915. Son of William Weston, carpenter who built much of
    Taliesin I, II, and III. In Fellowship from 1938 to 1942 and again in 1946. A CO in World War
    Two, sent to Federal Correctional Institution, Sandstone, Minnesota. Paroled to work in hospi-
    tal, Ann Arbor, Michigan. Work in private architectural offices, including William Kaeser, Madi-
    son, Wisconsin. Now retired and living near Spring Green.

Wright, Eric; Architect
    Born in Hollywood, 1928. Son of Lloyd Wright, grandson of FLLW. In Fellowship from 1948 to
    1956. After Taliesin worked in association with his father, 1956–78. Since 1978 has his own
    practice.

Sources

The source of this account will be largely my own memory, supplemented and freshened by some rather sketchy notes, poor substitutes for a diary, which I made from time to time. I now wish that I had kept a diary and had written at greater length instead of making these notes, which in some instances have ceased to have any meaning.

These notes, however, were made as reminders for letters, some rather lengthy, which I wrote to my parents and friends. I wrote my parents regularly, on a weekly basis, but whenever I went home for a visit I told my mother that this increasing collection of letters should be thrown away. Unfortunately my suggestion was eventually followed. When I started writing this account, after the death of both my parents, only a few of these letters were to be found. Fortunately, another apprentice's mother did save his letters. When Robert May learned that I was working on this account he volunteered to send me "thirty-one pages of notations extracted from contents of letters written by Robert Carroll May while at Taliesin." These notes cover the time between January 1940 and May 1942 when Bob left the Fellowship. They proved most helpful.

Luckily, several of my friends to whom I also wrote rather regularly, but at different intervals, did save my letters. These included Professor George M. Beal and his wife, Helen; Marcus Weston; Robert and Ann Pond; Roland v. Rebay; Howard TenBrink; and John Mitaraky.

The letters I wrote to the Beals are now in the archives of the Department of Special Collections in the Kenneth Spencer Research Library at the University of Kansas. With them are also letters to the Beals from Mr. and Mrs. Frank Lloyd Wright and apprentices with whom the Beals became acquainted in the summer of 1934, when they were at Taliesin as apprentices, and with whom they corresponded in the following years.

Marcus Weston kept many of the letters I wrote him during World War Two and following his departure from the Fellowship late in the summer of 1946. He returned these to me when he learned that I was working on this account. Ann Pond permitted me to make copies of most of the letters I wrote to her and her husband. This correspondence began in the summer of 1953 and continued until I left the Fellowship in 1955. Roland v. Rebay sent me a few of the letters I sent him between the spring of 1950, when he left the Fellowship, and 1952, when he returned to Germany. Howard TenBrink kept the letters I wrote him during World War Two when both of us were at camps for conscientious objectors. He sent these to me when our correspondence was resumed a few years ago. And John Mitaraky, a friend with whom I became acquainted while in CO camps during the war and with whom I corresponded after the war, sent me a few of the letters I wrote him.

All of these letters and copies of letters are now in my possession and will be deposited with the Department of Special Collections, Kenneth Spencer Research Library, University of Kansas, Lawrence, Kansas, following the publication of this book.

Appendix A

Sources of information with regard to buildings mentioned in the text.

Adelman, Albert, house, Fox Point, Wisconsin
Schemes 1 and 2, Futagawa, Yukio, editor and photographer, and Bruce Brooks Pfeiffer, text, *Frank Lloyd Wright Monograph 1942–1950* (7) A.D.A. EDITA Tokyo 1988, pp. 124–25. Photos of Scheme 3, p. 126.

Scheme 3, Wright, Frank Lloyd, "A Four-Color Portfolio of the Recent Work of the Dean of Contemporary Architects, with His Own Commentary on Each Building," *Arch For* XCIV (Ja 1951), pp. 86–89.

Anderton Court Shops
Futagawa, Yukio, editor and photographer, and Bruce Brooks Pfeiffer, text, *Frank Lloyd Wright Monograph 1951–1959* (8) A.D.A. EDITA, Tokyo 1988, p. 77.

Anthony, Howard, house, Benton Harbor, Michigan
Cottage for Maginel Wright Barney, Futagawa, Yukio, editor and photographer, and Bruce Brooks Pfieffer, text, *Frank Lloyd Wright Monograph 1942–1950* (7), p. 210.

House for Howard Anthony, *Frank Lloyd Wright Monograph 1942–1950* (7), pp. 250–52.

"Seven Lessons from Frank Lloyd Wright," *H & H* VI (N 1954), pp. 98–105 and cover.

Auldbrass, plantation, Yemasee, South Carolina
Wright, Frank Lloyd, "Frank Lloyd Wright," *Arch For* LXXXVIII (Ja 1948), pp. 95–96.

Beth Sholom Synagogue, Elkins Park, Pennsylvania
Futagawa, Yukio, editor and photographer, and Bruce Brooks Pfeiffer, text, *Frank Lloyd Wright Monograph 1951–1959* (8), pp. 152–62.

Cloverleaf Housing Project, Pittsfield, Massachusetts
Futagawa, Yukio, editor and photographer, and Bruce Brooks Pfeiffer, text, *Frank Lloyd Wright Monograph 1942–1950* (7), pp. 6–8.

Wegg Talbot, "F.L.L.W. versus the U.S.A.," *AIA Journal* LIII (Fe 1970), pp. 48–52.

Wright, Frank Lloyd, "Frank Lloyd Wright." *Arch For* LXXXVIII (Ja 1948), pp. 80–81.

Exhibition House, built as part of the "Sixty Years of Living Architecture" exhibition, New York, New York
"Frank Lloyd Wright Builds in the Middle of Manhattan, Shows How to Make a Small, Simple House Rich and Spacious." *H&H* IV (N 1953), pp. 119–21.

"Frank Lloyd Wright's Contribution to Your Daily Life." *House B* XCVIII (N 1958), pp. 264–69.

Exhibition Pavilion, built to house the "Sixty Years of Living Architecture" exhibition, New York, New York
    Futagawa, Yukio, editor and photographer, and Bruce Brooks Pfeiffer, text, *Frank Lloyd Wright Monograph 1951–1959* (8), p. 106.

Gillin, John, house, Dallas, Texas
    Futagawa, Yukio, editor and photographer, and Bruce Brooks Pfeiffer, text, *Frank Lloyd Wright Monograph 1942–1950* (7), pp. 322–25.

Grant, Douglas, house, Cedar Rapids, Iowa
    Futagawa, Yukio, editor and photographer, and Bruce Brooks Pfeiffer, text, *Frank Lloyd Wright Monograph 1942–1950* (7), pp. 108–9.

    Wright, Frank Lloyd, "Frank Lloyd Wright," *Arch For* LXXXVIII (Ja 1948), p. 72.

Guggenheim Museum
    "Frank Lloyd Wright's Masterwork," *Arch For* XCVI (Ap 1952), pp. 141–44.

    Futagawa, Yukio, editor and photographer, and Bruce Brooks Pfeiffer, text, *Frank Lloyd Wright Monograph 1942–1950* (7), pp. 37–43. Annex pp. 170–71.

    "The Modern Gallery; the World's Greatest Architect at 74 Designs the Boldest Building of His Career." *Arch For* LXXXIV (Ja 1946) pp. 81–88.

    Wright, Frank Lloyd, "Frank Lloyd Wright," *Arch For* LXXXVIII (Ja 1948), pp. 136–38.

Hartford, Huntington, house, Los Angeles, California
    Frank Lloyd Wright Monograph 1942–1950 (7), pp. 146–47.

Hartford, Huntington, Cottage Hotel Group, master plan
    Frank Lloyd Wright Monograph 1942–1950 (7), pp. 148–49.

Hartford, Huntington, Cottage Hotel Group Center
    Frank Lloyd Wright Monograph 1942–1950 (7), pp. 153–55.

Kalil, Dr. Toufic, house, Manchester, Vermont
    Frank Lloyd Wright Monograph 1951–1959 (8), pp. 182–83.

    Futagawa, Yukio, editor and photographer, houses by Frank Lloyd Wright 2, Tokyo A.D.A. Edita.

Keland, Willard, house, Racine, Wisconsin
    Frank Lloyd Wright Monograph 1951–1959 (8), pp. 126–27.

Ladies Home Journal, "Glass House"
    Frank Lloyd Wright Monograph 1942–1950 (7), p. 61 (see Lowell Walter house).

Loeb, Gerald M., "Pergola House," Redding, Connecticut
    Frank Lloyd Wright Monograph 1942–1950 (7), pp. 58–59.

    Wright, Frank Lloyd, "Frank Lloyd Wright," *Arch For* LXXXVIII (Ja 1948), pp. 93–94.

Morris, V.C., Gift Shop, San Francisco, California
"China and Gift Shop for V.C. Morris, San Francisco," *Arch For* XCII (Fe 1950), pp. 79–85 and cover.

Frank Lloyd Wright Monograph 1942–1950 (7), pp. 228–31.

Nelis, Henry J., house, Minneapolis, Minnesota
Frank Lloyd Wright Monograph 1942–1950 (7), pp. 260–63. (Plan shown is not plan of house as built, but plan before revision. Drawings of elevations are of the revised plan.)

"A New House by Frank Lloyd Wright Opens Up a New Way of Life on the Old Site," *H & H* IV (N 1953), pp. 122–27.

Pittsburgh Point Park Civic Center, Schemes #1 & #2. Pittsburgh, Pennsylvania
Frank Lloyd Wright Monograph 1942–1950 (7), Scheme #1, pp. 196–99; Scheme #2, 200–3.

Point View Residences (Apartment Tower for the Edgar J. Kaufmann Charitable Trust), Schemes #1 and #2
Frank Lloyd Wright Monograph 1951–1959 (8), Scheme #1, pp. 59–61; Scheme #2, pp. 102–3.

Price, Harold, Jr., house, Bartlesville, Oklahoma
Frank Lloyd Wright Monograph 1951–1959 (8), pp. 88–91.

"The Look of American Life at the Top Level," *House B* XCVIII (N 1956), pp. 258–65.

Price, Harold, Sr., house, Paradise Valley, Arizona
"Grandma House" for Harold Price, Sr., *Frank Lloyd Wright Monograph 1951–1959* (8), pp. 128–31.

"The Look of American Life at the Top Level," *House B* XCVIII (N 1956), pp. 258–65.

Price Tower, Bartlesville, Oklahoma.
Frank Lloyd Wright Monograph 1951–1959 (8), pp. 64–71.

"Frank Lloyd Wright's Concrete and Copper Skyscraper on the Prairie for the H.C. Price Co.," *Arch For* XCVIII (May 1953), pp. 98–105 and cover.

"The H.C. Price Tower," *Arch Record* CXIX (Fe 1956), pp. 153–60 and cover.

Wright, Frank Lloyd, "The Story of the Tower, the Tree that Escaped the Crowded Forest," New York: Horizon Press, 1956.

Rogers Lacy Hotel, Dallas, Texas
Frank Lloyd Wright Monograph 1942–1950 (7), pp. 134–37.

Wright, Frank Lloyd, "Frank Lloyd Wright," *Arch For* LXXXVIII (Ja 1948), pp. 121–26.

Sturges, George, house, Brentwood, California
"Frank Lloyd Wright: The Residence of Mr. and Mrs. George Sturges, Brentwood, Calif." *Arts and Arch* LVII (Ap 1940), pp. 14–15 and cover.

Wright, Frank Lloyd, "Frank Lloyd Wright," *Arch For* LXXXVIII (Ja 1948), p. 151.

Taliesin West, Scottsdale, Arizona
Wright, Frank Lloyd, "Frank Lloyd Wright," *Arch For* LXXXVIII (Ja 1948), pp. 81–87, 152–55.

Unitarian Church, Madison, Wisconsin
"First Unitarian Church, Madison, Wisconsin, Frank Lloyd Wright," *Arch For* XCVII (De 1952), pp. 85–92.

Frank Lloyd Wright Monograph 1942–1950 (7), pp. 172–75.

Wright, Frank Lloyd, "Frank Lloyd Wright," *Arch For* LXXXVIII (Ja 1948), pp. 118–19.

Walker, Mrs. Clinton, house, Carmel, California
Frank Lloyd Wright Monograph 1942–1950 (7), pp. 264–67.

"A Planning Lesson from Frank Lloyd Wright. How Big Can a Tiny House Be?" *H & H* V (Mr 1954), pp. 98–105.

Walter, Lowell, house, Quasqueton, Iowa
Frank Lloyd Wright, "A Four-Color Portfolio of the Recent Work of the Dean of Contemporary Architects, with His Own Commentary on Each Building," *Arch For* XCIV (Ja 1951), pp. 82–85.

Frank Lloyd Wright Monograph 1942–1950 (7), pp. 62–67.

Wright, Frank Lloyd, "Frank Lloyd Wright," *Arch For* LXXXCVIII (Ja 1948), p. 77.

Wright, David, house, Phoenix, Arizona
Frank Lloyd Wright Monograph 1942–1950 (7), pp. 286–91.

"Frank Lloyd Wright: This New Desert House for His Son Is a Magnificent Coil of Concrete Block," *H & H* III (Je 1953), pp. 99–107 and cover.

"A Modern Castle in the Air," *House B* XCVIII (No 1955), pp. 278–81.

Wright, Robert Llewellyn, house, Bethesda, Maryland
Frank Lloyd Wright Monograph 1951–1959 (8), pp. 85–87.

"The Man Who Liberated Architecture," *House B* XCVIII (No 1955), pp. 244–45.

"A Poetic Image Realized in Concrete Form," *House B* vol. 101 (Oc 1959), p. 302.

Y.M.C.A., Racine, Wisconsin
Frank Lloyd Wright Monograph 1942–1950 (7), pp. 270–72.

Index

NOTE: Mr. and Mrs. Wright have not been included in this index since their names appear on almost every page. This also true of "The Fellowship" and of Taliesin, and Taliesin West. These two principal residences were constantly in the process of expansion and renovation.